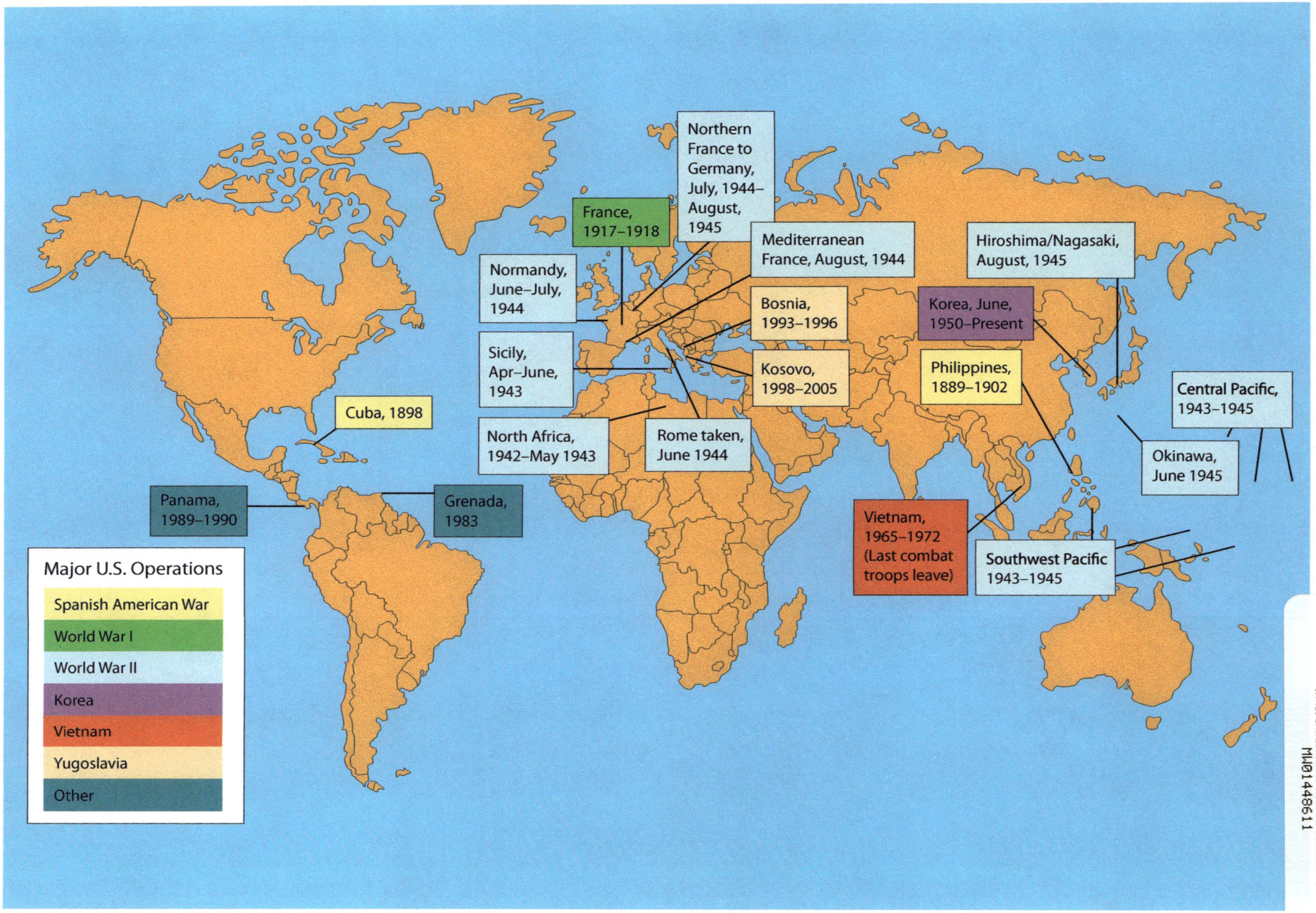

Modification of © Volina/Shutterstock.com, courtesy of Caitlin Curtis

Fifth Edition

Modern American
MILITARY HISTORY

Robert F. Ritchie IV
Herbert S. Pieper
Liberty University

Kendall Hunt
publishing company

Cover image © Shutterstock, Inc.

Kendall Hunt
publishing company

www.kendallhunt.com
Send all inquiries to:
4050 Westmark Drive
Dubuque, IA 52004-1840

Copyright © 2015 by Robert F. Ritchie IV
© 2016, 2017, 2019, 2021 by Robert F. Ritchie IV and Herbert S. Pieper

ISBN 978-1-7924-6825-4

Kendall Hunt Publishing Company has the exclusive rights to reproduce this work, to prepare derivative works from this work, to publicly distribute this work, to publicly perform this work and to publicly display this work.

All rights reserved. No part of this publication may be reproduced, stored in a retrieval system, or transmitted, in any form or by any means, electronic, mechanical, photocopying, recording, or otherwise, without the prior written permission of the copyright owner.

Published in the United States of America

Contents

Acknowledgments — v

A Note on Just War Theory — vii

Foundations of American Ways of Fighting — ix

I. The Foundations of an American Way of Fighting: Wars of the Colonies — 1

II. The Foundations of an American Way of Fighting: Wars of the Early United States — 25

III. The Spanish-American War — 61

IV. World War I — 75

V. Between the Wars — 89

VI. World War II: North Africa to Europe — 99

VII. World War II: The War in the Pacific — 117

VIII. The Korean War — 133

IX. Vietnam — 151

X.	Volunteer Forces, New Strategies, and Doctrine	171
XI.	The First Iraq War	179
XII.	9/11, Enduring Freedom, and the Second Iraq War	185
XIII.	Afghanistan	195
XIV.	The War Continues and Spreads	203
XV.	Cyber Warfare	207
XVI.	Hybrid Warfare and Potential Future Conflicts with China and Russia	213
	Glossary	237
	Bibliography	255
	About the Authors	261

Acknowledgments

As co-authors, we would like to take a moment to recognize those who made this book a reality. A very special thanks to Stephanie Wright for her work on editing this manuscript as well as the procurement of pictures. Noelle Henneman, your constant guidance and help as we marched through the publication process with Kendall Hunt was and is still invaluable. Finally, to Dr. Carey Roberts for your adjustment of schedule and powerful leadership, your provisions are dually noted by the both of us. Individually, Mr. Ritchie would like to thank Stephanie Megan Wright who went above and beyond the typical role of student-worker, therefore allowing adequate time to be spent on this work. Mr. Pieper would like to thank Herbert W. Pieper for not only his years of service as a Marine, but also for his role as father, and for the initial spark which the interest in the topics related to military history aflame. Judith Pieper; to the woman who taught her children and grandchildren to love history and country, your devotion to the education of your family equipped your grandson with the tools necessary to create this book. For these things, we as the authors are eternally grateful.

Telling the story of America's rise to military greatness is an honor. We are excited to offer enhancement in the areas of naval and technology as provided by Mr. Pieper, in order to offer a fuller picture of America's military history. Profiles in Christian servanthood is an idea that both of us have shared and cultivated together. It is our hope that this third edition provides readers with a greater understanding of the complexities that modern American military history are made of. Thank you again to those who have supported us in this endeavor.

A Note on Just War Theory

The act of war—armed conflict between two nations—has been a controversial topic for millennia, and rightly so. War means killing of the innocent. War cheapens human life. War leaves death in its wake. War makes brothers into enemies. But **is war ever justified?**

The first question one must ask is: **What is justice?**

Justice was the preeminent virtue identified by Plato. He wrote of its complexity and mystery: "The last of those qualities which make a state virtuous must be justice, if we only knew what that was. . . . I mean to say that in reality for a long time past **we have been talking of justice, and have failed to recognize her.**"[1] Plato defined justice essentially as self-governance.[2] For him, injustice was anything outside of self-governance, where evil itself originated.[3] Further, Plato routinely paired temperance, another virtue, with justice. Here, the seed of just war theory was planted.

Plato wrote in the *Republic*, "Now, **can we find justice without troubling ourselves about temperance?** I do not know how that can be accomplished."[4] Indeed, justice has never been seen in isolation. Justice—the idea that people receive what they deserve in accordance with their self-governance—must be tempered and given in appropriate proportion to the crime or the good deed, respectively.

From Plato's views of justice flowed the eventual idea of just war theory—the philosophy ordered around the question: **What is a just cause for war?**[5]

In the Western tradition, there are three ways to think about war: pacifism, holy war, and just war theory.[6] **Holy war**, engaged in by the likes of crusaders, implies that soldiers fight to protect the faith, achieve spiritual glory, and mold society in the shape of their religion.[7] While this idea comes from a place of religious intent, its followers often use the name of God in vain to accomplish their own ends. Holy war, in an effort for vindication, mistakenly imagines that mankind can speak on behalf of God Himself. **Pacifism** is the idea—particularly popular among Anabaptists, Quakers, Mennonites, and other Protestants—of a commitment to nonviolence and peace.[8] This view, while favored by many due to its lack of combat, is idyllic, and overlooks the moral obligation of the state to protect its interests and its people.[9] Pacifism, in an effort for peace, confuses moral action with nonconfrontational action. **Both theories, in their own way, forsake justice.**

Just war presents a middle ground which is intent on a "bent toward justice."[10] It combines the need for justice and tempers it with prudence, just as Plato had theorized. Throughout history, there have been three prevailing views of just war theory: the Augustinian, Westphalian, and

---

1. Plato, *The Republic*, trans., Benjamin Jowett (Internet Classics Archive, 2009), accessed November 12, 2018, http://classics.mit.edu/Plato/republic.html, Book IV.
2. Plato, *The Republic*.
3. Plato, *The Republic*.
4. Plato, *The Republic*.
5. Paul D. Miller, *Just War and Ordered Liberty* (Cambridge: Cambridge University Press, 2021), 5.
6. Eric D. Patterson, *Ending Wars Well: Order, Justice, and Conciliation in Contemporary Post-Conflict* (New Haven: Yale University Press, 2012), 21.
7. Patterson, *Ending Wars Well*, 24.
8. Patterson, *Ending Wars Well*, 25.
9. Patterson, *Ending Wars Well*, 26.
10. Patterson, *Ending Wars Well*, 27.

Contributed by Bess Blackburn. Copyright © Kendall Hunt Publishing.

Liberal traditions.[11] However, there are a few pervading points which remain common throughout each tradition: the commitment to questions of **jus ad bellum** and **jus in bello**. Jus ad bellum encapsulates the reasons as to why a nation should go to war. These include questions of just cause, comparative justice, legitimate authority, right intention, probability of success, proportionality, and last resort.[12] Jus in bello includes reasons as to how a nation should fight a war it is currently in. These include concerns like noncombatant immunity, proportionality, and right intention.[13]

The God of the Bible is no stranger to the concept of justice. In the Psalms, God is often accompanied by the theme of justice. In Psalm 89, God is described: "**Justice and judgement are the habitation of thy throne**: mercy and truth shall go before thy face."[14] Further, the idea of "just war" manifests itself in the wars of the Israelites. Israel is God's chosen people—a holy people" who are "above all the nations which are above the earth"—and the lands that they conquered were their inheritance from God Himself.[15] Many times, God commanded His people to take the land by force—leaving none alive.[16] This was a form of God's justice before He sent His Son. God is just, God is jealous, and make no mistake: His purposes will be, just as they were in the days of old, fulfilled. Unlike Holy War, the God of the Bible's commands were completely just because He is fully God, and He is wholly just.

However, God's justice has many forms—including not only open warfare, but the redemption of the world. Jeremiah writes of the coming Messiah, saying that "the days come, saith the LORD, that I will raise unto David a righteous Branch, and a King shall reign and prosper, and **shall execute judgment and justice in the earth**."[17] Justice is tied to the Messiah, to Jesus. It is **God's justice**—what we, as sinners, deserve for our sin—which is both poured out on the Messiah at the time of His crucifixion and death.[18] The Christian believes that—only through the work of Jesus Christ, through repentance of sin and by faith alone in Him as Savior—he or she is **justified by faith**.[19]

In Micah 6:8, the requirements of humankind are made clear: "**to walk justly**, and **to love mercy**, and **to walk humbly**" with God.[20] Just war theory thinkers are intent on keeping tempered justice at the center of war. While the questions of going to war and questions during the war itself will always be ethically challenging, **just war theory presents a framework with which to view war that aligns with a Biblical worldview**. In a sinful world, each government is morally obligated to defend its sovereignty and people in a rightly ordered, ethical manner.[21] Just war theory considers simultaneously the need to walk justly—to not forsake the moral obligation to protect—while also remembering to love mercy and walk humbly—to temper earthly justice so that it is not inordinate.

In sum: **Is war ever justified? Yes.** The idea of just war is to achieve peace in spite of the sinfulness of the earth. Just war theory helps us to answer complex questions of war by focusing on the centrality of justice—illuminated by God's Truth—in a dark world.

---

11. Miller, *Just War and Ordered Liberty*, 6–8. Essentially, the Augustinian Tradition is the application of medieval Christian political theory, which can be found in writers such as Augustine and Thomas Aquinas. The Westphalian Tradition was born in the early modern Enlightenment (after the Peace of Westphalia in 1648) and focused less on transcendental issues like natural law and more on pragmatic legal reasoning. The Liberal Tradition began to take precedence after World War II and attempts to rectify the shortcomings of Westphalian philosophy with an Augustinian approach that is "shorn" of its theological and teleological commitments.
12. Patterson, *Ending Wars Well*, 28.
13. Patterson, *Ending Wars Well*, 28.
14. Psalm 89:14, *King James Version*.
15. Joshua 1:1–4; Deuteronomy 14:2.
16. Joshua 10:19; 2 Samuel 5: 17–25.
17. Jeremiah 23:5.
18. Matthew 27:46.
19. Romans 3:28.
20. Micah 6:8.
21. Proverbs 31:8–9.

Foundations of American Ways of Fighting

Continual frontier conflicts from 1607 to 1890 contributed to the development of a unique American way of fighting (AWoF). Unlike today, continual frontier attacks would prevent Americans from forgetting the costly combat lessons they had previously learned. The colonist's occasional adversary, the American Indian, represented the epitome of an unconventional warrior. Native-American culture reflected a fierce individualism concurrent with an inability of the various tribes to unite. European settlers discerned divisions and exploited diplomatic opportunities within the fluidly changing political environments. A unique military institution emerged employing aggressive strategies and tactics.

Throughout the 17th and 18th centuries, an AWoF emerged that shaped strategies and tactics. A strategy designed to defeat a mobile and elusive foe eventually served to focus violence upon Indian "centers of gravity" of homes and food by attacking from different directions using **converging columns**. Tactical innovations represented a synchronicity of Indian fighting and European traditions. A forested frontier with vertical obstacles such as trees prevented the clean and neat use of linear warfare or "front lines." The use of skirmisher tactics involved using terrain for cover and concealment while lightly loaded fast-moving riflemen maneuvered like hunters attempting to encircle the enemy for the kill –all without close supervision. Incredibly efficient Native-American unconventional forces attacking unpredictably from any direction served to create an American military capable of decisive strategic objectives using both conventional and unconventional operations and able to utilize maneuver and firepower in tandem with Indian allies. Native-American culture reflected a fierce individualism. The inability of different tribes to unite created opportunities for settlers to discern diplomatic divisions and therein confront fluidly changing political environments. Unpredictable patterns of fighting within a forested frontier without obvious front lines also served to mold colonial institutions from ones of European derivation into new types of military instruments capable of a unique style of warfare. Aggressive strategies served to focus violence upon Indian "centers of gravity" of homes and food. Tactical innovations also represented a synchronicity of both Indian fighting and European traditions thereby creating what would become a winning world-class military machine.

The colonial **militia** provided the work force while the European emphasis on linear warfare would borrow from the Indians to create skirmisher or "skulking" (Indian-style fighting techniques or tactics). A European linear pattern of warfare proved inadequate against the vertical borders of trees in the eastern forests. Offensive maneuvering and encirclements using terrain and trees for cover and concealment worked best against an elusive foe. The colonists soon realized that in order to survive they must eliminate the enemy; thus strategy dictated winning the "war" through a need to defeat the elusive Indians by hitting them so they could not escape. Operations conducted to achieve these strategies resulted in battles using horrific **total war tactics** to burn the enemy out and to starve the Indians into submission by destroying their food supplies. The colonists called these terrible attacks "food fights." Strategy soon mirrored tactics through pincher type movements of forces attacking from different directions known as **converging columns**. Seizing the strategic initiative, colonists had developed a terrible means of destroying an elusive foe who had previously fought at a time of their own choosing and subsequently was able to escape over large areas. The duration of the colonial experience would see the employment of strategies using converging columns in tandem with food fights and the use of skulking tactics in an attempt to seize the strategic initiative from an elusive foe capable of amazing endurance, masterful ambushes and martial prowess.

The Native-American, unlike the European colonists, saw no glory in fixed combat and represented the most mobile, tough, light infantry possibly ever produced on the planet. A hunter-gatherer culture based on constant **movement** in an attempt to procure precious food supplies probably served as a catalyst to the creation of an aspect of the AWoF, placing a premium on rapid movements and even impatience lasting to the present day. The Colonial period would also see a growing martial or military tradition within the new European-American colonial culture that offered social and cultural reinforcements that honored military service. The colonies increasingly relied on and even eventually required the use of **indigenous peoples** or scouts to accompany militia expeditions. The colonial militia required the service of all ages from teenager to old age, and thereby created a rite of passage and created an early tradition of military service. Over time, the militia ranks increasingly filled up with pools of young male volunteers willing to cross state lines to earn land or money. By the 1750s, an American military tradition had established ways of fighting developed from the local level of society in close contact with the Indians, and methods of warfare percolated up to eventually affect strategies and larger-scaled operations.

By the time of the French and Indian War, a reliance upon and the eventual institutionalization of non-linear tactics would produce the rangers and begin the transformation of military units in America into laboratories of non-linear warfare. American infantry skirmisher techniques turned European theory into reality. The European soldier demonstrated robot-like obedience in submission to authority; essentially a part in a large sort of machine that stood in marked contrast to Americans who prized a self-regulated individual that used aggressively offensive, rapidly moving non-linear tactics of fire and maneuver, raised in a culture honoring the warrior. The French and Indian War had led to the permanent foundation of military units formally recognizing the fundamental differences between the machine-like soldier (European origin) and the more individualistic warrior (Native-American).

During the early 18th century, innovations in **firepower** marked the American military experience. The development of the rifle with unparalleled levels of accuracy would combine with the musket to form an unbeatable team. This integration of old and new rifle and musket represented another combination of methods of conventional and unconventional warfare, or those of European military traditions with that of a roughhewn American frontier culture. The implementation of new technologies with proven techniques—not just throwing out the old in favor of the new—would establish a precedent for the elegant integration of fires into the combined arms systems the U.S. military uses so artfully today. The American Revolution ultimately used the rifle-musket combination in tandem with profound leadership to produce victory and independence.

George Washington's vital leadership and choice of subordinates ultimately led to a winning mixture of European line warfare and colonial skirmisher tactics. Washington led and maintained a vital component of regular soldiers drilled in conventional warfare and capable of standing up to the British in toe-to-toe fighting. Meanwhile, partisans such as Francis "Swamp Fox" Marion, Henry Lee III, and other partisans honed unconventional and irregular techniques in the south using the Indian fighting methods developed over the centuries prior. Daniel Morgan and his riflemen represented an unconventional group, and when deployed in tandem with Nathaniel Greene's regulars, provided a lethal and winning combination in battles throughout the southern campaign that decimated the British army and would lead to eventual victory.

The formative years of the new nation continued to see militarily experienced leadership direct the nation politically, which was instrumental in the creation of a new Constitution and ultimately establishing a permanent national army into being. A **learning-army** is one placing a premium on integrating new concepts and technologies. The military continued to demonstrate adaptability and emphasized academics; a legacy of George Washington's 18th century leadership and perpetuated during the 19th century by Winfield Scott. Washington had overseen the creation of West Point and an army setting the example in terms of morality, cleanliness, and with disciplined ranks of soldiers capable of conventional line tactics and, perhaps most importantly, representing the virtues of the revolutionary ideals; neither a threat to the government nor the liberties of its citizens.

American naval traditions of excellence in technology remained on full display with innovative exhibits ranging from marines to submarines. Heroic battles at sea were combined with land warfare to create a winning combination projection of power sufficient to protect the infant nation, vulnerably blessed with enormous amounts of coastline. Through imagination and adaptability, a tradition of naval successes started with the amphibious transports of Washington's army while John Paul Jones audaciously raided offshore Great Britain. Naval contributions proved victorious on land by the Army to win the revolution, when aided by French sea power. After Yorktown, the Navy showed the new American flag off to its best advantage as it fought a quasi-war with France, confronted North African pirates, and even built metallic monsters capable of cudgeling one another during the civil war.

A new nation eventually used indigenous peoples or scouts to defeat inside and outside threats to the new Republic during the last decades of the 18th century. The new Constitution emerged ensuring a permanent military footing with a commander-in-chief. Eventual military victory in the old North West would break the Indian threat there while animosities with Britain on land and sea would result in the largely conventional war of 1812, and the largely unconventional war within a war against the southern tribes. A tradition of martial glory continued to place leaders such as General Andrew Jackson in positions of political authority, and the debate over the role the army played and the best means to deploy firepower reflected a dualistic balance of views inspired by rivaling militia and regular army leadership. Brimming with confidence after the Battle of New Orleans and armed with a nationalistic enthusiasm, Americans would continue to fight long unconventional wars that destroyed the last Native-American cultures east of the Mississippi River.

The war in Mexico achieved rapidly impatient assaults with combined operations and once again used converging attacks from land and sea. The dualism of militia and regular army views came to the forefront politically as America's incredibly successful and rapid military victory in Mexico resulted in an enormous amount of territorial expansion while expeditionary land grabs started California's eventual entry into the union. With the discovery of gold, Americans headed "out west" creating new frontier roles for the Army as settlers headed into Indian lands. The Army, while initially successful in attempts to protect southern tribes and frontiersmen, found its mission interrupted by the American Civil War.

The Civil War essentially reflected the use of large, mostly conventional armies often moving in converging columns and in communication with new technologies using conventional methods of linear warfare. Most battles resulted from their proximity to strategically important railroads and telegraph lines. Increased amounts of accurate firepower from muzzle-loaded rifles and seemingly unending Union artillery barrages decimated draftees who had replaced volunteer militias. On the civil war battlefield, commanders feverishly sought to extend linear formations while, often in frustration, attempted to either maneuver to the flank of their opponent or prevent the flanking of their force. Ultimately, a bloody war of attrition appears to have vindicated Winfield Scott's original Anaconda Plan, an attempt to squeeze the confederacy with naval power in tandem with peripheral land skirmishes. The civil war taught a never-to-be-forgotten lesson to the American military: the need to minimize casual-ties through offensive speed and maneuver. The appearance of huge union forces sweeping through the south on horseback during the civil war would presage future wars of armored columns impatiently sweeping across the world.

The Army won the American west after the Civil War with a combination of new technology and old. The Army in the 1870s remained smaller than the police department of New York City today, nevertheless the Army had to maintain the peace over a huge area of the American west.[22] Using a fixed fort system and constant patrols, the army eventually wore the Plains tribes down. Remembering and utilizing old proven methods, but building upon them with new ideas, the army officially created Indian Scouts, and utilized converging attacks and food fights during winter just as they had at Jamestown and New England so many centuries before. An innovative and learning-army continued to implement new technologies such as railroads, telegraphs, and breech loading rifles. A seemingly never-ending supply of immigrants arrived on those trains, armed and using barbed wire to cordon off their land. The range closed and marked an end to the Native-American way of life. By adapting the latest in firearms and using proven techniques developed from the nation's earliest days, the American military emerged onto the world's stage in fighting trim ready to take on its destiny of a premier global force.

Foundations Technologies

Tomahawk

A tomahawk, also known to the Powhatan tribe as a war club, represented the favorite hand-to-hand weapon of the Native Americans during the French and Indian War and the American Revolutionary War. These traditional Native American hatchet-style weapons often consisted of stone and wood and could be used for a variety of purposes. Tomahawks, when introduced to the Europeans, soon saw production in iron. Once made of iron, the tool purpose of the weapon grew even larger. The Native Americans' unconventionally asymmetric warfare made the tomahawks ideal for hand-to-hand combat, and its short-distance ability to be thrown made it vital to the success of their tactics. The tomahawk allowed the user to be mostly mobile, while still being deadly. This technology is a great example of the beginning of the American Ways of Fighting characterized by fast maneuver and rapid impatience.

Early tomahawks were usually made of a light wooden handle and a thin square blade. More often than not, they would have one thick spike protruding from one end of the blade. These spikes could be used as tools or weapons. As time went on, the tomahawk became steel in both blade and handle. The tomahawk has found employment as a tool and a weapon for American soldiers from the French and Indian Wars to the current conflicts in Iraq and Afghanistan.

Musket

The Brown Bess Musket, standard issue for British regulars, was a muzzle-loading, smoothbore musket. The Brown Bess presented one of the most commonly used weapons in the American Revolution on both sides of the war. A primary weapon of the British army, American Colonists who were often led by former British military men also used this weapon. The Brown Bess Musket fired a single shot .69-caliber ball, or a cluster style shot which fired multiple projectiles similar to that of a shotgun. This made the weapon versatile for many types of battles. Amazingly versatile, the largest drawback of this weapon proved to be range. The smooth barrel resulted in an inaccurate shot. This did not affect the British line and volley fight approach in open field, but became an issue in aseptic and frontier fighting.

There were two variations of the Brown Bess in the American Revolution: the Short Land Pattern and the Long Land Pattern. The long land pattern had a 46-inch barrel length and overall length of 62.5 inches, while weighing approximately 10.4 pounds. The short land pattern had a 42-inch barrel length, overall length of 58.5 inches, and weighed approximately 10.5 pounds. The Short Land was shorter, less bulky, and less heavy than the Long Land. Most American fighters implemented the Long Land Pattern due to a desire for increased accuracy which was of vital importance to the hunter.

---

22. Boot, 147.

Chapter I

THE FOUNDATIONS OF AN AMERICAN WAY OF FIGHTING: WARS OF THE COLONIES

An American soldier who volunteered to serve the country and wearing an arrowhead device of the Special Forces emerges somewhere around the world today, perhaps bearded and wearing a ball cap, separating him from the endless rows of well-disciplined and clean shaven uniformed soldiers on the other side of the forward operating base. Entering a helicopter bearing the name of a Native-American tribe, perhaps the Blackhawk, and departs into a combat operating base possibly named for another Native-American tribe, say the Apache, all while catching a glimpse of a Washington Redskins game on a TV in the corner as he dusts off his weapon with the name Colt engraved upon it. Supporting this soldier is firepower from tomahawk missiles fired from the navy and plans for an upcoming operation will most likely include diversions, feints, and elements of surprise and maneuver involving forces converging from different directions toward an attack objective. Our imaginary soldier represents the American military experience, a winning combination of old and new. Today's American military usually seems to lead the way in international efforts, but what is often ignored is the degree to which an American way of fighting emerged over a long series of wars that allowed the U.S. to become a mix of the preeminent conventional and unconventional military force that it is in the world today.

The story of how a unique military war machine first developed constitutes the foundations for the American military experience that began with encounters between Europeans and Indians over an expanding and often unforgiving frontier. A unique way of fighting necessary for survival emerged during a time in history that saw the blending of the individual warrior of the native-American culture with that of the conventional line tactics of the European soldier. The American military experience from Jamestown in 1607 up until the closing of the frontier during the 1890s consisted of the development of militias, volunteers, and a permanent regular force capable of adopting total warfare for survival in the conventional and unconventional arenas.

Historic interpreters demonstrating the firing process of matchlock muskets at Jamestown.

Source: Library of Congress

Colonists quickly understood the need for utilizing total warfare, an ability to discern the enemy's vital vulnerabilities while maintaining a conventional military force in the form of the militias. A continually volatile and fluid frontier created a blend of Native-American and European ways of fighting in dark forests, offering vertical borders without front lines. A need to differentiate Indian allies from foes in a politically fluid, rapidly changing environment would represent the germination of what today we call military intelligence. A series of global conflicts eventually institutionalized a military tradition of using precise firepower and individual maneuver. The frontier experience served to prevent military leaders from forgetting how to fight an unconventional enemy, avoiding complacency and falling back on the western tradition of the line. Intermittent wars against Seminoles, Blackhawks, and Sauk/Fox would prove a training ground for leadership in the Mexican War. The Civil War would create an enormous war machine capable of strategic maneuver on a scale previously unimagined and would lead to reforms that would maintain a huge conventional standing force capable of stepping out onto the world scene. Finally, the wars against the Native-Americans in the west would be the finishing school for an American way of fighting at the strategic level with maneuver and converging columns, and the institutionalization of indigenous peoples as guides or scouts. Finally, an ability to determine rapidly the use of total warfare through the determination of the enemy's vitals and an ability to win in a conventional or unconventional fight. The world now witnesses a type of Pax Americana held together on the increasingly narrow shoulders of a dedicated and patriotic American people providing the only military force capable of policing the entire globe.

The Medal of Honor

"For conspicuous gallantry and intrepidity at the risk of life above and beyond the call of duty...."[23] The Congressional Medal of Honor, the highest medal for valor that is awarded to members of the U.S. Armed Forces, is the rarest and most prestigious medal to be awarded for actions of extreme bravery. Since its establishment during the American Civil War, the Medal of Honor has been awarded to 3,508 soldiers, marines, sailors, airmen, and coast guardsmen.[24] Of these recipients, over half received the honor posthumously.[25] The actions that warranted the Medal of Honor are as varied as the recipients. From tearing down the fence impeding the Union's charge near Antietam Creek to sneaking the USS Barb into the thirty-foot deep Mamkwan Harbor and sinking six ships during World War II, these feats that warranted the Medal of Honor represent the most daring and courageous acts in American history.[26] Although it took several forms and faced opposition from many, the Medal of Honor has a long, rich history.

The Colonial Wars

The **Powhatan Wars** in Virginia saw Europeans who increasingly had to rely upon themselves in a new and frightening world. Assuaging Indian anger and frustration with their increasing arrivals, Pocahontas married John Rolfe, effectively ending the First Powhatan War fought from 1610 to 1614. By

---

23. Dwight J. Zimmerman, *Uncommon Valor: The Medal of Honor and the Warriors Who Earned It in Afghanistan and Iraq* (New York: St. Martin's Griffin, 2011), 77.
24. "Archive Statistics," The Congressional Medal of Honor Society, http://www.cmohs.org
25. "Archive Statistics," The Congressional Medal of Honor Society, http://www.cmohs.
26. The Boston Publishing Company ed., *The Medal of Honor A History Above and Beyond* (Boston, MA: Boston Publishing Company, 2014), 28–29.

1622, with the beginning of the Second Powhatan War after surprise attacks wiped out about a third of the settlers, the Indians had become frustrated and fearful of the increasing numbers of settlers threatening their livelihoods. Many of the settlers had poured into Virginia under the head right system, whereby sponsors received land for bringing immigrants across the ocean; now many cowered in fear. Desperate times produced desperate measures, and the emergence of the armed began. The distribution of firearms, from armories directly to the citizenry, started an American tradition of private gun ownership, and one that would be regretted by leaders of the colony about a half century later.[27] The initial use of "food fights" to hit the enemy's vital supplies and adjusting to wars of attrition focused on the Indian's food supplies, reflected the inability of the colonists to use European methods of fighting in the vertical borders of the forest. Unable to see or even find a foe who refused battle in the open—European style—forced the American military in its formative years to develop a second nature ability to attempt to win conflicts by seeking the vital point at which an enemy could be defeated, and in the process avoiding battle and casualties. By the Third Powhatan War in 1644, the high loss of colonists would begin to fight wars of elimination and marked the establishment of a segregated southern society as palisades and walls separated "Indian country" from the settlements on the Virginia Peninsula. Conflict in Virginia had created a vengeful armed citizenry developing the fierce independence of the individual away from centralized control. The colonists would see a means of fighting that reflected a merging of European and Indian methods, and the resulting synthesis would be truly American.

The Pequot War of New England in 1637 probably had some connection to the Indian wars in Virginia as the news of conflict spread rapidly through the frontier. Like the settlers in Virginia, the Puritans would initiate a total war of extermination upon the Pequot tribes. When the neighboring Narragansets refused to come to the aid of their beleaguered neighbors, the militia maneuvered so to encircle the Pequot settlement on the Mystic River, a combined unit of militiamen from Massachusetts, Rhode Island, and Connecticut had used Indian allies who had accompanied them. When the Puritans burned the settlement and killed those who tried to escape, the Indians saw the horrors of European warfare. Withdrawing in horror after the Pequot War, the Indians would increasingly rely upon torture and cruelty in isolated incidents as they sought a way to deal with the purveyors of this new and terrible way of warfare of flames directed at food and families.

Analysis

The inherent weakness of Native American culture and its disdain toward any measure of centralized control, or an ability to bring the tribes together, revealed itself. A hunter-gathering culture required expansive hunting grounds and the unending jealousy over undefined frontiers combined with disease and the eradication of huge populations contributed to the eventual weaknesses of the Indians militarily. A fluid, unwritten system of tribal alliances and wars created an environment made to order for colonists who learned to play off different sides and to use violence to "set an example" to the other tribes in the area.

Having discarded their pikes and armor, the American or Colonial militia began its adjustment; from a total reliance on conventional war as practiced in Europe to a new form of warfare entirely. European warfare had become increasingly ideological and religious in intensity with all sides seeing eternal ramifications for success and failure. Fresh from the largely religious wars of the thirty-year war to the wars in the Netherlands and Ireland, those of British ancestry who would command the American militia had few reservations about using this total warfare. In contrast to the colonists, the Indians believed the key to glory in warfare consisted of touching or landing a blow upon an opponent. In Indian cosmology, no heaven or paradise awaited a fallen warrior; in fact, to fall in warfare would likely condemn the warrior to an eternity of misery walking alone. Instead, to the Indians, the key to victory in warfare lay in remaining alive.

The European idea of holding and taking ground continued to ensure the line methods to hold ground and maximize firepower, a fruit of the Enlightenment would continue, but the lack of a front

---

27. Ferling, John. *Struggle for a Continent: The Wars of Early America.* Wiley-Blackwell: NY, 1992, 24.

in the forest and the vertical obstacles of the trees created the need to modify European tactics. An increased reliance upon encirclement and maneuver combined with the use of Indians to destroy Indians would continue to develop until 1675. The foundation of the colonial military was the militia.

Typical colonial militias consisted of universally conscripted youth required to attend drills from ages of 16 to 60 with only few exceptions for political and spiritual leadership. These drills, while somewhat amateurish by the high standards of our reserves today, involved community involvement with spectators, dancing, and the consumption of alcohol. The idea of service as part of the social-cultural hierarchy reinforced the importance of familiarity with weapons and each citizen acted under the requirement to own a musket. A rite of passage into manhood established and supported the use of the firearm and the mandatory service to the *community*. Other examples of local involvement with the military included the use of garrison fortresses or neighborhood blockhouses complete with loopholes for firing upon an attacking foe with cover provided by thick walls for protection designed to house families.[28] As noted above, during the Powhatan and Pequot wars, it was the American pattern of taking the first blow that seemed to justify retreating into the blockhouse and then subsequently emerging in patrols to punish the offenders. Only by using Indians, however, could the militia hope to be effective in their attempt to locate, encircle, and kill the enemy.

A firmly established American military tradition of using Indian allies and an individual reliance upon firepower and allies had congealed by the 1670s. By the time of **King Phillip's War** in New England in 1675, a Community provincial council actually required soldiers home in the event that Native-American allies or Indian Guides began or ceased fighting. In Virginia, the House of Burgesses issued a legal requirement for citizens to carry weapons whenever outside their homes.[29] Increasingly, the Indians now carried their own firearms and, as usual, the New England forces had remained closely attuned to the "foreign relations" of the tribes. Within the state militias, a gradual transition from compulsory service to the use of experienced volunteers in various types of wars, alternatively both conventional and unconventional in nature, honed a unique American military.

When it appeared the Narragansets and the Wampanoags would come together to unite, the Puritans felt they had to act. As the New Englanders had problems actually finding their new foes, it increasingly became necessary to discard all non-gunpowder weapons such as swords and pikes. Lightly dressed, using crawling formations, the colonists continued to break entirely from European style warfare. When the enemy finally had been closed within the Great Swamp Fight of December 1675, the English burned the Indians out as they had during the Pequot War of 1637. The Indian chief, known as King Phillip, was eventually captured due to betrayal by other Native-Americans. The colonists proceeded to act with the same hunter qualities of the butcher; by severing the chief's body and grotesquely displaying it in various locations, most noticeably his head that remained as a sort of open-air display for years afterward. The results on the colony showed a casualty rate of 1:35 residents exceeding losses for the U.S. in the Revolution, Civil War, and World War II![30] The employment of total warfare indeed remained high. With Total Warfare, using modified tactics and requiring Indian Guides, the making of a new type of military force had truly begun. Continuing the use of Indian auxiliaries, the colonials withstood repeated counterattacks and eventually won a war of attrition after breaking the enemy down through time, using weather and patrols to sap enemy morale.

By the time of **King William's War** in 1689, the Americans and Indians found themselves at the center of a series of global conflagrations. In what surely seemed to the colonials like a titanic struggle of Protestantism vs. Catholic, flashed anew with the aging French King and his ambitions to realign international relations to the end of a much-feared mega state.[31] In large measure, a perspective of intense global rivalries for power must have merged with the spiritual views of the colonists who saw a Papist scheme in supporting the Indians and probable designs for control in North

---

28. Leach, Douglas E. *Arms for Empire*. Macmillan: New York, 1973, 49.
29. Ferling, *Struggle for a Continent*, 51.
30. Ibid., 58.
31. Leach, *Arms for Empire*, 117.

America. The importance of Native-American allies would be demonstrated now on a larger or strategic scale. When the powerful five nations of the Iroquois (ranging from Maine to Pennsylvania) attacked the French, the Americans also discovered just how important natural borders, such as mountains and rivers, are to warfare. Natural borders and the lack thereof had already affected tactical views with encirclements, maneuver in the woods, and soon would become strategic in scope using converging columns. The area between the Great Lakes and the St. Johns River bordering the north of modern day Maine reveals a series of rivers generally flowing from north to south. The ability to travel on rivers, allows a minimum of friction of distance or cost and tended to favor invaders from the north, particularly in the pre-industrial age.

The Iroquois, or Indian allies of the colonials had attacked north in 1689, infuriating the French and their Huron allies. Devastating Lachine, a small city outside of Montreal, led to counterattacks by the French and their Indian allies—the Hurons—the dreaded enemy of the Iroquois and fierce competitor for furs around the Great Lakes. Continual reprisals by the French led by Louis de Buade, Comte de Frontenac, launched a type of war he called la petite guerre—today also known as guerilla war. Numerous ruthless frontier raids that eliminated entire villages and killed uncounted numbers of colonists at the cruel hands of the French allied Abenaki tribes during the 1690s essentially forced the development of a new strategy.

Attacking toward the capital of Quebec, Americans intuitively seemed to realize the importance of the St. Lawrence River as the key to controlling the Canadian American border. An attempt to drive into Canada from New York and New England simultaneously would attack in converging columns. While a naval effort against Port Royal would succeed, one on Quebec would fail. A long series of brutal frontier engagements would further stress colonial locals; some even think the combined pressures of an unsecure boundary and horrific expensive warfare may have even created the conditions for social hysteria such as occurred in the Salem witch trials.

A strategic modification of the local or tactical envelopment, this large scale or strategic attack into Canada reflected an early example of the ability of Americans to think bigger using the movements, food fights, and guides they had learned in the non-linear environments of the forests during previous wars. Grasping the significance of geography and the natural borders (and lack thereof) of the northern frontier, the fierce frontier fighting would continue into the next world war: Queen Anne's War.

The problems of European royal succession and the balance of power in Europe would lead again to war in North America in 1702 with **Queen Anne's War**. An all or nothing approach to warfare also seemed to emerge during Queen Anne's War as Americans once again marched up the Champlain Valley using a route previously attempted in the last war. The Indians now consisted of about ten percent of American forces, which again used converging columns. When the previously agreed support failed to arrive in time to take Quebec in 1711, it quickly became apparent that the British could not be counted upon.

Two major factors resulted from these latest two wars (King William and Queen Anne) for empire. The first would be the costs in terms of casualties and inflation, tempered with the painful memory of losses of ten percent of the population in New Hampshire killed or captured. Americans continued to build garrison houses on the frontiers with taxes raised to painful levels. Conditioned to see an enemy surrounding them, Americans would always seem to remain on a sort of war footing. A new American self-confidence had emerged in terms of self-sufficiency, particularly in light of New England successes in Nova Scotia.

In addition to a permanent militia, a military-industrial complex of sorts had also started that saw the continued existence of the militias in a new form. **Volunteers** consisted of younger, single males who would eagerly cross state lines to enter into conflicts and became a permanent part of the militia landscape. Perhaps a function of high unemployment, the volunteers proved eager and willing to serve across state lines for money. The beginnings of a truly permanent, interstate force built upon a tradition of individualism, supported by a frightened culture that honored the soldier, had met with a new propensity to view strategy as a reflection of the tactics of a frontier without front lines.

Violence around the south demonstrated the tri-dimensional struggle for North America waged between European powers, colonists, and Indians. The importance of maintaining an awareness of Indian relations and keeping a finger on the pulse of changing frontier, political landscapes, and Native-American alliances forced Americans in the formative years to think outside themselves. What must have seemed strangely confusing to British Americans with a traditional recognition of national borders after the Treaty of Westphalia nonetheless saw opportunities for growth on the southern frontier. As early as 1702, the attempt by South Carolinians to take St. Augustine, Florida had failed, but a long war involving various tribes would occupy each decade of the timeline for half a century. The South Carolinians fought the Tuscarora War in 1711 where large numbers of the Yamassee Indians served to account for victory against the Tuscarora. Eventually fleeing north to join the Iroquois, this left rival tribes courted by the French and Spanish in the southern frontier. The Creeks represented the largest of the Indian powers to the south of the Appalachian mountains in what is today Georgia and Alabama. The Choctaws allied with the French in Alabama and Mississippi. To the north of the Choctaws were the Chickasaws across Tennessee who had allied themselves with the English. Eventually, the Yamasees would turn on the South Carolinians, and here the amazing complexities of inter-tribal politics revealed itself on the southern frontier of the colonies.

Eventually by 1715-16, South Carolina allied with the Cherokees. Through diplomatic maneuvering, the South Carolinians employed the services of this huge tribe of Appalachian Indians ranging from North Georgia to southern Virginia and thereby created a second front against the Creeks. A pattern developed in this labyrinth of fighting and diplomacy with the interesting result of the Indians initially making great gains, but eventually the colonials still prevailed. High costs as always took a toll and worse, the cost in lives in the southern colonies exceeded even those of the New Englanders in King William's war.[32] The south continued to learn quickly as had the north, to identify potential allies and to use them against their Indian foes. To beat the Indian one must have an Indian ally.

By the eve of the **War of Jenkin's Ear** in 1739, a little known war between England and Spain and one with an even stranger name, the attempts by Georgians to attack St. Augustine met with the same failures encountered when the Charlestonians had attempted to attack earlier. South Carolina was still licking its wounds from the Stono Rebellion attempted to guard its valuable rice-growing coastal lowlands when the Spanish attacked St. Simon's island. Like weary boxers, the Spanish proved as unsuccessful in their attempts to expand into the English coastal areas as had South Carolina's earlier attempts at St. Augustine to the south.

As once again the world ignited into another global conflict, the War of Jenkin's Ear would morph into **King George's War**. The true disaster was the forced impressment of American colonials in a South American operation at Cartagena during the spring of 1741. British incompetence left Americans confused over whether to be bitter at the seeming ineptness of the British command, or to be angry at the humbling experience of treatment as second-class citizens. The Americans died like flies from disease and of the 3,600 troops in the American Regiment supported by volunteers from eleven colonies, only 600 came home alive.[33] The name of the sole competent commander, Vice-Admiral Edward Vernon, has as a legacy the name of Washington's home at Mount Vernon. Meanwhile, the war moved north.

Further estrangements between colonists and Great Britain occurred with another failure of the British to support a converging column assault into Canada reminiscent of failures in 1709 during Queen Anne's War. Even the single military victory in the expanded war now called King George's War waged from 1744 to 1748 failed! A successful siege of Louisburg on Cape Breton Island conducted by New Englanders represented the greatest victory by the English in the war. One can only imagine the hurt and anger after the treaty ending the war gave Louisburg back to the French! Were the British unable to see the strategic significance of this area so vital to New England? What was

---

32. Ferling, *Struggle for a Continent*, 58
33. Alison, Wm. T, Grey, Jeffery, and Valentine, Janet G. *American Military History 2nd Ed.* Pearson: Upper Saddle River, NJ, 2013, 29.

it about maneuvering that the British found so hard to understand? Americans surely questioned the competence of the British by this point. The failures by the British to support the 1746 invasion against Quebec and the Louisburg decision probably left Americans thinking that next time Louisburg would need to be taken, the British could have the job. In yet another global world war, it would cost the British an investment of 9,000 troops and 40 ships to reclose the same deal![34]

Analysis of Early Colonial Wars

The first colonists encountered a forested continent with few cleared areas capable of conducting open line warfare in the European style. Rules of warfare quickly went out the window as total warfare emerged. Later known as food fights, an Indian culture refusing fights to the death, raiding and seizing the initiative at times of their own choosing and then simply melting away, forced the colonists to destroy food stores and essentials of the Indians. The use of Indian guides by the 17th century had already become almost mandatory. The ability to discern the potential ally with an enemy required a clear understanding of cultural differences and a means to use them diplomatically. A dawning realization that perhaps the British lacked either the desire or even an ability to see an enemy's center of gravity planted a seed of doubt into the black and white worldview of the Americans. If the British could not adapt to the non-linear maneuver type of tactics used in a forest with fronts or on a strategic level with converging columns, what kind of ally would they make, and is this the role of the "good Indian or the bad?"

The French and Indian War

The continued refinement of an American Way of Fighting occurred as acculturation between Indians and settlers on the frontier saw the continuing importation of European technologies that Americans adapted to militarily. Starting at Jamestown, a need to understand the native-Americans continued to provide a sometimes-painful reminder of how to fight or relearn a type of warfare that essentially marked the emergence of an Army capable of fighting, both conventionally as soldiers, but also unconventionally as warriors. The basic stages of the French and Indian War can be broken down into three major stages.

Essentially the French and Indian War from 1754 to 1763 attempted to secure the Ohio Valley, and reseize Louisburg while simultaneously recapturing Fort Duquesne, and finally the British and Americans would be able to take Quebec and Montreal. The result saw Great Britain in possession of the North American continent and attempts to control the Indian problem with the Proclamation Line of 1763 would reflect the challenges of a greatly enlarged empire. The chief lesson from the French and Indian war is that an American Way of Fighting institutionalized into units, such as Rogers' Rangers, would mark the beginning of a force capable of challenging the British. The laboratory for the creation of an American military had begun at Jamestown and continued to the French and Indian War.

George Washington started a world war. As a young officer in the Virginia Regiment, George Washington obeyed the orders of Virginia's governor, a major stakeholder in the Ohio Company, by advancing north toward **Ft Duquesne**, modern day Pittsburg, on a June day in 1754. Using initiative, Washington's aggressive actions led to firing upon a French detail and subsequently saw Virginians prudently hurrying to build a fort they would call Fort Necessity. Attacked the next month by the French but with fearful losses, the French somewhat miraculously allowed the English colonists to leave safely and live to fight another day. Most remarkably is the extent to which the **Ohio Valley** had now become the center of gravity of the North American continent. Here the French feared seeing their colonial enterprise divided not only from east to west, but from their holdings on the lower Mississippi as well.

---

34. Peckham, Howard H. *The Colonial Wars 1689-1762*. University of Chicago: Chicago, IL, 1964, 119.

Revenge may have belonged to the British but such would not occur in the year 1755. Major General Edward **Braddock** selected by the Cumberland ministry in London to advance toward Ft. Duquesne, marched in a line of columns toward the important strategic site of modern day Pittsburgh located on the vital confluence of the Alleghany and Monongahela Rivers. While not nearly as rigid as many would indicate in future references, a single line nonetheless portended disaster when the advance party ran into an ambush. Densely crowded within a forest, retreating soldiers falling back under the onslaught could only collide into following troops with predictable confusion. While Braddock did not survive this encounter, Washington and his fellow officer Thomas Gage (who would later lead forces up Bunker [Breed's] Hill in 1775) did. Excited by a major defeat, the Indians shifted their allegiance toward the French while excited war parties of Native-Americans swept up and down the frontier. Even the vitally important Iroquois rapidly started to lose interest in supporting the British, leaning toward loyalty to the French instead.[35]

Subsequent British and colonial attacks north in 1756 fared little better than Braddock's attack. Governor Shirley, who took over as commander-in-chief after Braddock's death, attempted to attack Fort Niagara, but failed. Meanwhile, that September, William Johnson nearly destroyed at Lake George but contributed to the war effort with the use of skirmisher tactics and the use of line with tomahawks and muskets. This small success in an otherwise bleak year would convince the new Prime Minister that Americans represented good stock for investment.

A new Prime Minister named William **Pitt,** the "Great Commoner," replaced the Duke of Cumberland's government. Cumberland was known as the "butcher," so nicknamed for his cruel forays into Scotland. Pitt immediately started planning for the remediation of reverses administered by French generals such as the Marquis de Montcalm and his Indian allies; a modern Frontenac (see King Williams War above). Montcalm conveniently looked the other way when he allowed his Native auxiliaries to wipe out a surrendering American army, releasing further flames on the frontier. What was it about Pitt that enabled him to formulate a winning strategy in the New World? The answer is that he thought outside his own culture. Pitt made a decision to see the world war as just that—a world war—and one that included different cultures alien to his own. Forsaking the timeless mistake of fighting the last war—Pitt recognized this war in America was only a smaller part of war in India and Africa. The difference being the Americans had learned from the finest light infantry on Earth—the American Indian!

Reversing earlier disastrous policies of forcing conscripting colonials into British units, Pitt recognized, as did many of his subordinates, the fiercely individualistic culture of America. The militia system, representative of this egalitarian culture, had developed into an increasingly volunteer force. Washington demonstrated this in the Virginia Regiment, where two-thirds of the forces he led toward Fort Duquesne had volunteered. Most of the volunteers came from the Tidewater and Piedmont regions where land proved scarce. Under Pitt, a new strategy of acknowledging colonial grievances and the cultural and institutional distinctions between local militia units previously confused with colonial expeditionary units emerged. Taking into account colonial sensibilities had the effect of wisdom trickling down through the chain of command, thereby creating fertile ground for new ideas.[36]

The year 1758 would be a turning point for the British in North America as a combined force of Americans and British marched together towards Ft. Duquesne, near the same vital area in western Pennsylvania so eagerly sought for by both Washington and Braddock three years before. To the northeast, the capturing of Louisburg further improved British positions in North America as well. With the Indians always watching to see which of the encroaching European powers would most likely win the fight, a military-diplomatic triumph ensued as the British began to reverse earlier failures. The emergence of Rogers' Rangers represented the institutionalization of the lessons learned by the British, as they finally seemed to grasp the need to fight in America by using American meth-

---

35. Leach, Douglas E. *Arms for Empire*. Macmillan: New York, 1973, 359.
36. Alison, Wm. T, Grey, Jeffery, & Valentine, Janet G. *American Military History* 2nd Ed. Pearson: Upper Saddle River, NJ, 2013, 40.

ods. The Rangers proved to be a uniquely American invention and one that would prove important in 1759 as the British attempted to clear the frontier after their victories at Quebec and Montreal.[37]

A seemingly inevitable British victory still not guaranteed, the 1759 campaign up the Hudson Valley into the Lake Champlain region of New York by Lord Geoffrey Amherst would coincide with the advance up the St. Lawrence River to Quebec by General James Wolfe. Probably aided by Rangers, Wolfe would advance to the Plains of Abraham where he and Montcalm would proceed to kill each other in open, traditionally European line-style combat with the result being British victory in the New World. The British would remain in control of most of North America now with the need to maintain order amongst a host of frontier peoples.

A charismatic figure would emerge in the American Midwest named Pontiac in early 1763, just before the Peace of Paris would be signed ending the French and Indian War. Pontiac, an Ottawa chief would be one in a long line of tragic Indian leaders desperate to slow down the influx of settlers and the destruction of their cultures. In what appeared to be a mystical call to arms, a "Delaware Prophet" emerged calling upon the Indians to throw off their dependence upon the white man and the material trappings of this foreign culture. Pontiac seems to have exploited this message when he used it to gain support from the Huron, Ottawa, and Potawatomi tribes. **Pontiac's Rebellion** saw Pontiac's tribes attacking a series of strategically important forts on the lakes, whose growing strength included the Delaware, Shawnee, and Miami, together attempting to take Fort Detroit, failing when French aid did not appear. The British in turn attempted to send military support to the frontier. Further, despite attempts by the Queen's rangers, British attempts to replicate the successes of Rogers' Rangers, and to defend Forts throughout the Great Lakes, then shifted to attacks in Pennsylvania. By October, the wide spread frontier rebellion had ground down due to lack of French support and the ability of the British to crush resistance. With Pontiac went the last chance for the Indians to stop European immigrants from flowing into the areas west of the Appalachian Mountains. Later Indian leaders would emerge attempting to unite the various tribes in similarly mystical ways, but Pontiac probably represented the last try that even came close to accomplishing the task of saving a disappearing way of life. With British attempts to maintain a greatly enlarged global empire, London oversaw the drawing of a Proclamation line. Somewhat reminiscent of Bacon's Rebellion, this honest attempt to limit colonial freedoms to preserve the Indians as subjects while reducing frontier violence would prove to be a key factor in the American Revolution of 1775.[38]

Analysis of the French and Indian War

The French and Indian War saw an American Way of Fighting emerge from the interaction of immigration and the shared acculturation of the frontier between settlers and Native-Americans. The emergence of superior light infantry would prove instrumental in the winning of the latest world war discussed in this chapter, but certainly not the last.

The French and Indian War saw European Warfare merged with the tactics and style of fighting developed by the American colonists over the proceeding century and a half. Individuals spread out and moved from tree to tree, adjusting their tactics to the terrain known today as light infantry (foot soldiers). The first light infantry had emerged in theory in 1756 with the published memoirs of the French Marshall Maurice de Saxe. Saxe characteristically expressed a profound Enlightenment view of the 16th to 17th century period when great minds reflected on the lessons of antiquity and systematically sought scientific ideas to explain the world around them. Perhaps reflecting on the Roman legion's use of the lightly armed skirmishers or peltasts, Saxe wrote of the use of individuals firing rifles in waves of light infantry using natural terrain for protection in small groups. This observation was a half century ahead of its time, and before the French and Indian War! Saxe's observations are even more remarkable when one realizes such military views occurred simultaneous to the revolutionary use of conventional tactics. In Europe, Frederick the Great of Prussia astounded Europe with an ability

---

37. Leach, *Arms for Empire*, 476.
38. Utley, Robert M., & Washburn, Wilcomb E. *Indian Wars*. Houghton Mifflin: Boston, 1977, 102.

to move enormous amounts of troops in column and to move them diagonally, called the oblique. The ability to mass lacked the resilience of the less decentralized light infantry skirmishers.

America didn't invent the light infantry, but the emergence of the institution is a genuinely American innovation. The British according to Max Boot "had considerable experience of irregular warfare . . . in North America with Indians and rangers. Red coats certainly knew enough to break ranks and seek cover in battle when possible. . ."[39] While the Europeans had no doubt discovered earlier the skills of the German Jager (hunter) and those of the French Chasseur, it would, however, be in America where German immigrants would truly rediscover the secrets of antiquity and find the means of applying it to the reality of skirmisher tactics, creating a premier American light infantry armed with rifles. The true genesis of the infantry would not emerge from the automaton armies of individuals submissive to the state; rather it would emerge from where central control saw a balance with the rights of the individual on the frontier. The practical emergence of the rifleman in America fulfilled enlightenment theories, but also filled a need as ancient as war itself.

For all of military history there has been a dynamic or a conflict in attempting to defeat an enemy. To defeat a foe you must first find them and then defeat them with force. The challenge is to find them, which necessitates spreading forces out and the key to defeating them is to mass your forces together. For example, think of your hand. When you are feeling your way around in the dark, you depend on the fingers for touch. In the event you need to use force quickly, you must pull your hand together into a fist. The fist cannot cover as much area as effectively as the extended fingers, but it is more effective at destroying an enemy once found. To attempt to find an enemy or to maneuver with the fist would result in a type of "whack a mole," like the children's game at arcades where one finds themselves flailing away using force, but indiscriminately and with little effect. By adopting the technology brought to America by German immigrants, the Americans were on their way of adopting another aspect to the aforementioned American ways of fighting in a way that would create the potential for the ability to fight conventionally and unconventionally.

The Ancient Romans had used the formation or Legion in battle line but its true genius lay in the use of lightly armed peltasts and velites; generally youth lightly armed with javelins or darts who would wear the enemy down before retiring into the rear of the army formation. The Romans achieved a mighty empire in part due to this ability to enable skirmishers to slow an enemy down using the less regulated warrior-like hunter, throwing the spear and using terrain to its best advantage. The ancient Greeks and Romans also knew that an arrow, if properly fletched, would spin. This spin would provide not just stability in flight but also greater range. The American woodsmen represented the fast moving type of unregulated hunter who naturally used terrain and maneuver in an attempt to encircle the enemy. Now the frontier needed a weapon with longer range than a bow and arrow.

During the 18th century, German immigrants brought a long-range weapon that used the ancient concept of spin to America. The word *riffeln* is a German term used as a verb to describe to cut or groove. The German immigrants to America tended to settle initially into Pennsylvania, but by the 1750s the fruits of their labors, the rifle, would be widespread throughout the areas west of the tidewater in Virginia.[40] The primary difference between the Jager pieces used in Germany and this new rifle made in Pennsylvania was about a foot in length. The effect of this elongated barrel was to allow for greater accuracy and longer range of the ball or round fired. A higher velocity bullet enhanced this accuracy by possessing a flatter trajectory upon leaving the firearm, since it tended to move faster, therefore falling less in flight before hitting the target. The use of a patch in the barrel when loading the bullet created more muzzle velocity, and this in turn enabled bullets to travel with more speed and therefore could possess the same or even more stopping power with smaller bullets. Smaller bullets translated into more bullets and cost savings for poor frontiersmen. As Alexander Rose explains, a pound of lead would create in 75-caliber about eleven rounds (the name still used in the military for bullets—due to their use in muskets) while the reduction to a 50-caliber bullet would more than triple this quantity to thirty-six.[41] In addition to increased accuracy and the ability to carry more bullets, the

---

39. Boot, Max. *Invisible Armies*. WW Norton: New York, 2013, 63.
40. Rose, Alexander. *American Rifle: A Biography*. Random House: NY, 2009, 21
41. Rose, *American Rifle*, 20.

colonials again, according to Mr. Rose, hit with incredible accuracy with their rifles at 200 yards hitting ten for ten shots in the bullseye while the old reliable musket would only hit at a rate of four for ten. In large measure, this was indeed a function of powder measure too.

Powder flasks measured carefully the amount needed, and individual owners of weapons would upon receipt discharge their pieces against snow or sheets to see how much residue would remain from wasted powder. Each riflemen knew the amount of powder necessary to prevent waste and ensure a most efficient shot. A merging of scientific and intuitiveness had therefore combined to lead individual marksmen to be incredibly accurate shots, adjusting the powder to their individually crafted weapons. Similar to the example of the closed and open fist, the American frontier by the mid 1700s saw a combination of cultures and technology to answer the age-old military dilemma of balancing force with economy. Out of the French and Indian War would emerge military leaders that would seize the opportunity to develop acquired facts later to be creatively employed as ideas.

In the Americas during the 1758 approach toward Fort Duquesne or modern day Pittsburg, the march presented what essentially had amounted to an open-air laboratory for the development of infantry tactics. The conversations between officers serving under British Brigadier General John Forbes would result in a new and improved American Way of Fighting. Colonels George Washington with Henry Bouquet would forge a friendship based on mutual trust that would agree to utilize "scalping parties" of infantry that would keep an enemy off balance while certainly providing much-needed intelligence in such a fluid and concealed environment as the Americas presented. Washington explained that a preference for the European method of exhibiting authority, subordinated to the egalitarian or individualistic style of fighting for the Americas, and uniforms should follow this trend with an Indian style using hunting jackets, leggings, and moccasins.

Rogers' Rangers truly represented the institutionalization of an American Way of Fighting begun during the early days of the Colonial with the initial recognition by Europeans of the need for light infantry capable of acting independently of the line or regular army troops. According to the expert Max Boot, the emergence of Rogers' Rangers coincided with the discovery of light infantry. By the 1750s in Europe, the French had clearly recognized the impossibility of fighting a foe armed with skirmishers without being likewise in possession of these lightly armed foot soldiers.[42] These green-clad warriors led by Robert Rogers, who had grown up on the war-torn frontier of New Hampshire, developed a scientific study of the ruse, surprise, deception, and use of cover; the same modern military methods taught to the Rangers and Commandos of World War II.

The important point is America led the way in the merging of unconventional warfare tactics represented by the ability to fight on line against armies with unconventional tactics of the light infantry operating independently, due to the lessons learned on the frontier. Perhaps more important in American military history is how the American frontier simply would not allow participants to forget the same lessons Saxe had glimpsed, but laid largely forgotten in Europe. Human beings are always quick to forget the lessons of the past and armies are no different. The Europeans would learn during the French and Indian War many of the lessons of the frontier, but then just as quickly, tended to forget them. Meanwhile, Americans living on the frontier would not have the luxury of fighting since the frontier would continue to remind them of the need to use tactics the next time they became hungry or afraid.

By the time of the American Revolution, British light infantry consisted of tough, lean men capable of keeping up with a horse at four to five miles per hour, along with mighty Grenadiers, the largest and strongest troops designed for close combat and the role of the bayonet. The difference between British and American infantry by the time of the Revolution would be the rifle, held by a soldier acting in tandem with other individuals exercising the independent freedom of self-control typical of the warrior.

The American Revolution

The American Revolution found the British forced to adjust to a different type of fighting in North America and to understand the true nature of the social-cultural conflict they faced. Exposed to

---

42. Boot, Max. *Invisible Armies*. WW Norton: New York, 2013, 63.

unexpected and irregular violence at Lexington-Concord, the British mistakenly believed they faced a local rebellion, one that required isolation. Unable to hold in Boston, the middle colonies phase of the war similarly attempted to separate rebellious New England from the middle colonies in an effort to contain. Finally, British attempts to rally loyalists perpetuated the mistaken belief a sectional rebellion could be isolated by appealing to southern loyalists. By the last phase of the war, just as the British had adapted to an American Way of Fighting and an understanding of the intense individualism of American culture, time had run out for the imperial cause.

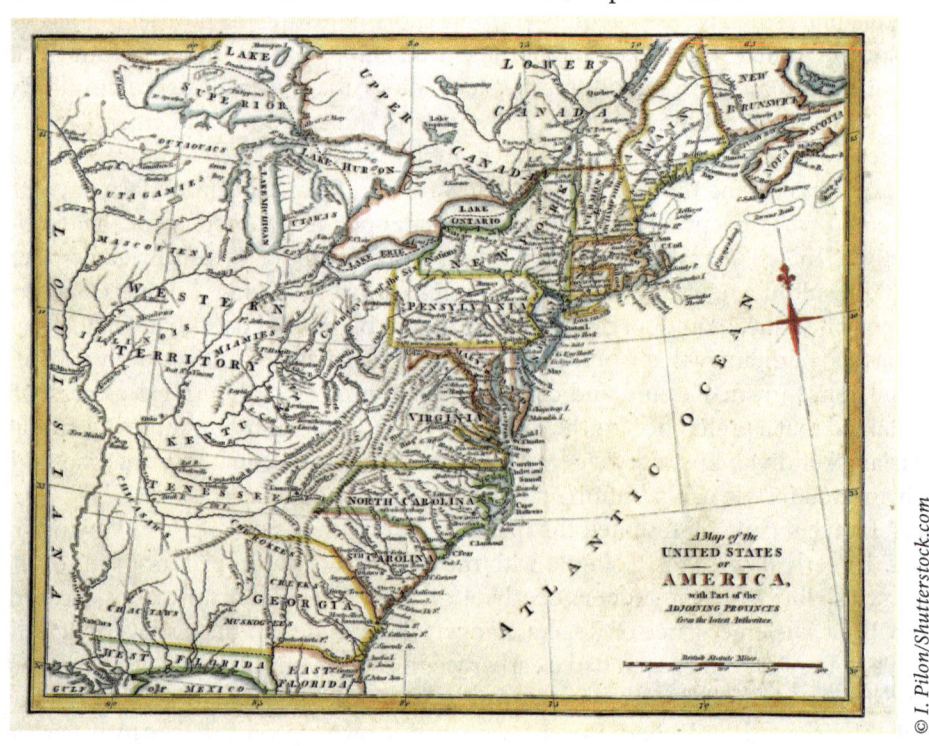

Early map of North America originally printed in 1795.

New England Phase

When the British commander in Boston, Major General Thomas Gage, received orders in Boston in April 1775 telling him to round up rebel leaders and supplies in the **Lexington-Concord** area, it probably seemed unlikely another world war would begin—this time in Massachusetts. Marching the ten or so miles in what probably constituted the worst kept secret of any operation in military history, Gage's subordinates marched to the town of Lexington where informants had reported caches of war materials existed. As the British marched up the road, the militia fell out and, after doing their traditional duty, were quickly called back into line. Nervously standing up to the recently arrived British, they were prepared to call it an easy day with honor defended when someone—somehow and somewhere—ordered British troops to open fire. In confusion, the militia quickly broke ranks and the British continued up the road to Concord to confiscate cannons and cannonballs, soon thereafter to lay in the bottom of a creek. Standing

The Battle of Lexington, April 1775.

guard over their pillaging comrades at nearby Concord Bridge, companies of British light infantry began to receive occasional fire. Pulling back and colliding into the remainder of the invading battalion's troops, just arrived from dumping the cannon into the creek, it appeared the entire countryside now seemed to be coming alive. With the fire increasing, and after brief tactical engagements that involved forming a line, firing, charging, and reforming back up, the lead British units fell back to Lexington and supposed safety behind the ranks of arriving reserves.

British soldiers caught their breath and within the hour, seeing duty accomplished, began to return back to the safety of Boston's battleships. The days marching back to Boston quickly, however, became a gauntlet of well-aimed fire, as the countryside seemed to be exploding with anger. These British light infantry men of endurance, able to keep up with horses on the march, or at least in theory, really represented little more than British attempts to copy American methods of combat. Trained to finish a fight with a bayonet assault, the British soon found themselves utterly worn from continual formalized assaults against patriotic citizens now increasingly furious with the redcoats. When the British at last stumbled back into Boston Harbor under the mercifully protective fires of the battleships in the harbor, they had indeed started a war by their simple march on Lexington-Concord.[43]

The British would have been fine staying permanently in Boston Harbor if the Americans had not been so obviously digging in with new recruits to the north of the city at **Bunker Hill**; although really Breed's hill, 400 yards or so distant, the name still stuck. The British eventually launched frontal assaults up the slopes in two waves and met with last-second aimed rifle fire two different times. Eventually, through force of inertia and with the Patriots out of ammunition, the British took the hill. Never again would Generals Gage and William Howe ever force a frontal assault against Americans. The American rifleman and the American Way of Fighting combining conventional and unconventional frontier-Indian fighting had emerged.

Dorchester Heights overlooking Boston Harbor next saw cannon dragged by oxen under watchful patriot leadership from Fort Ticonderoga in upstate New York. Now overlooking the British fleet and out of range of gun elevations, the British began to contemplate abandoning Boston Harbor as the Second Continental Congress, having met to discuss Lexington-Concord, and authorized the raising of an army under a General or Commander-in-Chief George Washington. With the abandonment of Boston, the British began to implement what they thought would be a military strategy capable of isolating the rebellion, thereby containing those hot heads up there in New England and opted to move to the comforts of New York, where they expected a more enthusiastic reception from loyalists.

George Washington by Rembrandt Peale c. 1850.

Middle Colonies Phase

On July 4, 1776 within hours of the Declaration of Independence being signed, 130 warships carrying 30,000 British troops arrived in New York City.[44] Eschewing frontal assaults as Washington hoped, instead of another attempt such as on Breed's Hill, the British engaged Washington in a series of battles and maneuvers generally reinforcing the prevailing notion of an easy victory in the works.

---

43. Perret, Geoffrey. *A Country Made By War*. Random House: New York, 1989, 10.
44. Alison, Wm. T, Grey, Jeffery, & Valentine, Janet G. *American Military History 2nd Ed*. Pearson: Upper Saddle River, NJ, 2013, 52.

Valiant efforts by American soldiers demonstrating the amazing resourcefulness and a spirit of endurance to the cause of freedom enabled Washington to safely retreat from Brooklyn across the East River into Manhattan. Wiped aside, the Army fled the thirty-mile march to White Plains. Avoiding a leashed dog appeared to be the role Washington preferred when he abandoned White Plains barely staying out of British reach as the Continentals fled across New Jersey. Desperate for a victory, an opportunity came when Washington used his army's unique resourcefulness and attacked across the Delaware River into Trenton on Christmas 1776. Subsequent victory at Princeton in January enabled the Army to seek winter quarters in Morristown, NJ. Meanwhile, the half-century long obsession with taking Canada was in full swing.

Washington crossing the Delaware.

To the far North the previous winter, Benedict Arnold, wounded and bleeding in the snows of Canada (again) failed in a converging column assault (also again) on both Montreal and Quebec. Montreal fell, but Quebec would not. Driven out by the British, the Americans now had to relearn the lessons of attacking Canada that winter of 1775-1776 in yet another future war. Meanwhile, the British under Sir Guy Carleton, just as obsessed with fighting the last war, attempted to advance down the New York highway south from Canada to Lake Champlain. Again, American innovativeness saved the day, building a fleet from scratch in a naval race that saw the Americans win. Losing the Battle of Valcour Island did not matter; Carleton's delay forced him to return to Canada to await the next year's campaign. Frittering away valuable time, Howe's inability to crush Washington and New Jersey and Arnold's terrific leadership in New York had saved the patriot cause for another year!

Benedict Arnold, 1741-1801

The next strategic attempt to pacify the interior of the United States would come in **1777** when Sir Henry Clinton was to march up the Hudson River Valley and meet with General John Burgoyne who would be approaching from the north through Lake Champlain. Attempting to advance through forested areas, Americans cut down trees forming abatis or roadblocks to slow the advance. An incident well publicized by the media of the day included the murder and mutilation of a young woman by Iroquois allies of the British. American frontiersmen poured upon the British and a combination of incredible marksmanship and skill in selecting terrain by Generals Gates and Benedict Arnold, now known as an "American Hannibal" saw continued victories at Freeman's Farm near Bemis Heights, key terrain the British failed to reconnaissance, and the all-important eventual retreat by Burgoyne into **Saratoga**. The French, still licking their wounds from the last war, took note of this American victory. American forces also succeeded in ripping apart the six nations of the Iroquois by convincing the Oneida and Tus-

The Real American Rifleman, 1780

14 Modern American Military History

carora to aid the American cause. Indian ambivalence to the British cause also prevented a link-up from the west through the Mohawk Valley. The year 1777 also proved an exciting year as the British efforts in Pennsylvania continued.

Possibly attempting to protect Philadelphia the previous year with attacks at Princeton and Trenton, Washington seemed to continue to see the role of his Continental or regular army soldiers as a sort of force-in-being. Believing Philadelphia to be the key to maintaining morale and with a Continental Congress meeting on the move, Washington waited throughout the spring for the British to make their moves.

General Sir Henry Clinton replaced Howe as Commander of the British Army, boarded his troops aboard ship in New York and disappeared over the horizon. While Washington marched all over the mid-Atlantic desperately attempting to anticipate where the sea-sick Red coats would stumble ashore, the British ended up landing at Head of Elk about sixty miles south of Philadelphia a month later,[45] only about ten miles closer to the city than they had been when they loaded up! Such dithering had in large part helped to keep the Patriot cause alive, but time was running out for both sides when Clinton's troops began to march toward Philadelphia. Hitting Clinton at Brandywine Creek in September of 1777, the British advantage showed when the British assaulted the Continental's flanks in a decisive defeat. Still, the army reformed in good order still alive to fight another day. Attacking at Germantown, Washington's plan appears overly complex with four columns attacking from different directions—converging columns or Indian fighting on a huge scale! After a miserable winter of 1777-1778 at **Valley Forge**, Pennsylvania, those winter soldiers who stuck it out would continue to be the strengthened backbone that would draw the various colonies together. Drilled by a charismatic Prussian Frederick Wilhelm Von Steuben, Washington's army was achieving a level of conventional fighting ability; one able to win at Saratoga and to draw the attention of the French.

At Monmouth, New Jersey, Washington's well-honed conventional soldiers now wearing blue attacked the British rear as Clinton now had opted to return to the comforts of New York. Monmouth saw a seesaw battle, the longest of the war and one demonstrating the Americans could exchange blows and hold their own. This last pitched battle in the northern theater of the war proved the American cause would last, and a conventional force could achieve victory if properly supported with sea power. Meanwhile, to the south, a true demonstration of an American Way of Fighting emerged.[46]

Valley Forge, 1777. General Washington and Lafayette visiting the suffering part of the Army.

Baron von Steuben drilling Washington's army at Valley Forge.

Southern Phase

Imagining the rebellion existed primarily in New England, and unable to motivate the loyalists of the mid-Atlantic cities to emerge from the safety of their fleets, the war planners in London now convinced

---

45. Alison, *American Military*, 36.
46. Alison, *American Military*, 49.

themselves the southerners surely had a measure of sanity. After all, an aristocracy dwelt in the south and in appearance seemed quite similar to the Lords who governed over England. Clinton landed in Savannah, Georgia in December of 1778 and, in what appeared to be an easy victory, determined a move on Charleston should occur. Remarkably, a yearlong delay in commencing the attack seemed to reinforce American views that a measure of insecurity existed in the strange British chain of command where a lower ranking knight (Clinton) now had command over a Lord in the form of Charles Cornwallis. The delay in attacking Charleston, America's largest southern city, allowed the Americans led by Benjamin Lincoln to form a huge army he had promptly pulled into Charleston after failing to liberate Savannah. Soon bottled up and smashed to pieces by British artillery, Lincoln surrendered in May of 1780 in one of the greatest disasters of American military history.[47]

In one of the psychological mistakes of the war, a British cavalry commander named Banastre Tarleton intercepted and murdered in cold blood Continental soldiers approaching Charleston. This incident at **Waxhaws**, SC went far in polarizing southerners toward support of both the British and the Patriot causes, but mostly the Patriots. Sending General Gates south and going over the head of George Washington, some of the best troops in the American Army began to head south. Making a stand against a British southern strategy of attempting to reach out to those loyalists in the surrounding plantations, Lord Cornwallis fought Gates at the **Battle of Camden** in August of 1780. Yet another disaster for the Patriot cause, Gates had foolishly placed his militia on the flanks where advancing British cavalry isolated them and the British light infantry flanked them. Camden represented one of the worst losses for the Americans during the entire war. Cornwallis, now encouraged, moved into North Carolina and into a hornet's nest.

At **King's Mountain** on October 1780, a bold young British officer attacked with many of the 20,000 loyalists the British had recruited in the south. Attacking up steep terrain against an American foe using cover and concealment—Indian style—the British impaled themselves on deadly firepower. The Americans hung loyalists, many of whom had committed fierce crimes, to set an example to the other loyalists in the south. The message seemed apparently received and went far to slowing a burgeoning civil war in the south between people loyal to Britain and those committed to the cause of independence. Next, Washington sent to the south his acting quartermaster Nathaniel Greene. Greene had Steuben now as well as Daniel Morgan from Virginia. With these talented subordinates, he divided his forces against the numerically superior British.

Chasing after Morgan's men by January of 1781, Tarleton attacked in an area near the North Carolina and South Carolina border called the **Cowpens**. With his back against the river not far from King's Mountain, Morgan faced the dully-unimaginative frontal assaults of Tarleton. The genius of Morgan was his understanding of the differing capabilities of his regular line soldiers, the continentals and the militia. Placing the militia out front of the regulars where they could get off a couple well-aimed rifle shots, the militia would fall back behind the musketeers, holding the firm blue line—the continentals. By preserving his sharpshooting militia in reserve, Morgan was able to counterattack the British hitting them on both flanks. The subsequent battle, though a small affair in the larger scheme of things, nevertheless would lure the now outnumbered Cornwallis to attack the Americans where recruits and troops flooded in from Virginia and the north.

At the Battle of **Guilford Courthouse**, the British found themselves desperate for supplies and needing either to retreat to the coast or having to fight their way out. The aggressive Cornwallis chose the fight and masterfully defeated the Americans, but in the process won a pyrrhic victory. Desperate for supplies after suffering 25% losses, Cornwallis headed for the port city of Wilmington. Greene obliged by heading his patriot army south to fight at Hobkirk Hill, suffering yet another loss, but actually increasingly winning in what had become a war of attrition in the south with time working against the British. The British retreating from Hobkirk Hill again had achieved a costly victory, and found themselves retreating to Charleston as Cornwallis fell back on Wilmington. Partisan unconventional-warfare had blossomed in South Carolina and a "hearts and minds" type of campaign had tipped the scales against the British. Greene's last engagement of the war came at Eu-

---

47. Ibid., 54.

taw Springs, where his starved troops attacked the British who yet again won another victory with catastrophic losses of about half of their troops to Greene's one quarter. As Geoffrey Perret says in his masterful narrative, "The British had no desire to beat Greene again. Winning by losing, Greene simply charged too high a price."[48]

By the spring of 1781, French naval support and a new U.S. naval tradition well underway (see analysis below) would leave Sir Clinton rubbing his hands in New York, afraid to leave vulnerable supply lines to American privateers. While Clinton sat in place with Washington watching him for three years, Cornwallis moved toward Yorktown. As Cornwallis pursued Lafayette through Virginia, Admiral deGrasse with 29 warships left the Caribbean. The Marquis de Lafayette now instructed to hold Cornwallis while Washington finally decided it was time to leave New York. An amazing foot march and an even more amazing series of successes saw Lafayette and Washington together surround the British who had sought the secure deep-water port off **Yorktown, VA**. After a series of entrenchments, attacks, and constant mortaring, unable to be resupplied by the British navy after the defeat of the Battle of the Capes during September of 1781, Cornwallis finally capitulated surrendering his 8,000 men to Washington's combined French-American forces of about 16,000 on October 19, 1781. The war had ended at last.

The result of the American Revolution was 25,000 Americans dead and this war would remain the longest ever fought until Vietnam. A little less than one percent of the colonial population died in the war compared with over 1.6 percent in the Civil war. When one takes into account the population of America at this time of about 2.5 million, one begins to see the levels of sacrifice made by the American people for their independence.[49] The key to remember is the relatively low population of the colonies. As with all wars, the problem of what to do with a large post-war army and the typically American attempts to disband it quickly would cause problems, as would the usual economic downturns resulting from the end of armed conflict. Perhaps no one could have stood for the principles of the American Revolution as George Washington had.

The taking of Yorktown.

The surrender of Cornwallis at Yorktown, 1781.

Analysis

The American Revolution represented two contenders racing to understand the most effective means of fighting in North America. America learned the quickest. The ability to innovate tactically, merging European and Indian-style fighting combined with an ability to keep the Indians largely neutral and to use partisan to reinforce population loyalty to the patriot cause, ensured victory. A man of many shortcomings, the indomitable George Washington had kept a regular army together while eventually recognizing the irregular nature of American Ways of Fighting. Conversely, the British failed to gather Indian support and to understand the limitations of a loyalist and mostly

---

48. Alison, *American Military*, 60.
49. Boot, Max. *Invisible Armies*. WW. Norton: NY, 2003, 77.

coastal people in affecting their cause. The British effort illustrates the recipe for defeat by projecting their own values into America, and by failing to understand that rebellion had swept the nation, not just New England. Convincing themselves of the certainty of their success, the British either could not, or refused, to understand the nature of American culture. Americans limited by their own experiences certainly made mistakes too. Leadership and innovations would win the Revolution and reflected a changed and bifurcated culture of settlements and frontiers epitomized by the American Ways of Fighting that had emerged.

George Washington is often referred to as the "indispensable man." From the hindsight of history, it is hard not to agree. A man with many shortcomings, he often appeared to be somewhat limited in imagination. When it came to leadership, this aristocrat had no peer in his ability to embody the virtues of the American Revolution. According to the great Geoffrey Perret, who so much of this work is indebted to, George Washington never admitted to a mistake. He never appeared to have an intimate friend, and he certainly had more than his share of personal ambitions.[50] Sometimes obsessed with how he would appear to others, he tended to project a perceived gallantry upon the enemy.[51] Nevertheless, Washington inspired an incredible loyalty and his endurance seemed at times super-human. Just about the time he seemed to be finished off, he returned to the fight with a blow staggering his opponent. In addition to endurance, Washington's lack of creativity and simple focus made him a man who others felt could be trusted and understood. Incredibly loyal subordinates included Alexander Hamilton and many others who recognized the limitations of the man's military talents, but would follow him anywhere.

During the American Revolution, the Continental Congress authorized fourteen gold and silver medals to be awarded.[52] Following European traditions, these medals were only for officers, with men such as George Washington, Horatio Gates, and Harry Lee being awarded the medals. Washington broke this tradition when he created the Medal of Military Merit, referred to as the Badge of Military Merit, on August 7, 1782.[53] This badge was the first military award in U.S. history, as well as the first award that an enlisted soldier could receive.[54] As a result of many of the records being lost, the specific criteria for the Badge of Military Merit is not known. Only three enlisted soldiers were awarded the Badge of Military Merit. After the Revolutionary War and by the War of 1812, the medal was forgotten because it was authorized by Washington and not by Congress. Therefore, it was more of a personal award rather than a national award. Chief of Staff General Douglas MacArthur on February 22, 1932, re-established the Badge of Military Merit as the Purple Heart presented to those wounded or killed in combat.[55]

© OneSmallSquare/Shutterstock.com

Demanding the army be neat, clean, physically fit, and one pure of vice, the American army alternatively wearing green for militia and blue for the continentals, remained intact under a man who George III reputedly said would be the greatest man who ever lived—were he to actually return power to the state. A modern Cincinnatus on the Roman model, George Washington embodied the American ideal

---

50. Boot, *Invisible Armies*, 44.
51. Middlekauff, Robert. *The Glorious Cause*. Oxford: London, 1982, 353.
52. The Boston Publishing Company ed., *The Medal of Honor*, 28–29.
53. Zimmerman, *Uncommon Valor*, 49.
54. Zimmerman, *Uncommon Valor*, 49.
55. "Commentary on Badge of Military Merit," The American Revolution, http://link.galegroup.com/apps/doc/EJ2153000357/UHIC?u=vic

that exists in our army to this day. Nevertheless, it was his trust of commanders on the spot and an ability to delegate that separated him from a Napoleon. Obsessed with New York and guarding Clinton like a caged tiger staring in a mirror, Washington remained transfixed and unable to break through British sea power or formidable defenses. While Washington waited for three years to fight Clinton and Howe, some of the true victories of the war developed while he and his faithful army stood watch.

Naval innovations also occurred at an institutional level leaving a legacy of unsurpassed American sea power traditions that continue to this day. Some of the key decisions made by the Second Continental Congress resulted in thirteen frigates commissioned initially. Eventually more than ninety vessels would put to sea launched by both the states and the Continental Congress, and while never enough to contend for control of the oceans, they had a decided effect in forcing the British to stay along the coasts where sea power remained supreme.[56] Amazing sea battles such as John Paul Jones leading the Bon Homme Richard (42 guns) vs. the Serapis (50 guns) in April of 1778 and the subsequent surrender of the British ship to American boarding parties while the outgunned American vessel sank, stirred youthful classroom imaginations for generations. The later September 1779 engagement in the Irish Sea was where **John Paul Jones** frightened British citizens on the coast in a psychological operation on turning many against a war who probably didn't even know an American War even existed. Jones' North Sea forays no doubt effected the debates in Parliament as to whether the war should continue.[57] Arguably, the naval forces could be determined to have been the most innovative of the services during this period.

John Paul Jones

The British had used marines since King William's War, but these had been Royal or British Marines. American Marines did not become a recognized force until the Continental Congress created the Continental Navy in August of 1776. Shortly thereafter it was recognized that soldiers of the sea would need to be aboard American naval vessels. An armed invasion of New Providence Island in the Bahamas saw marines and sailors launched to shore in a raid to procure war supplies in their first amphibious operation. Performing admirably, during the summer of 1776 the Continental Marines continued recruiting efforts in Philadelphia at the famous Tun Tavern where Marines recruited the previous year. Escaping Philadelphia when the British first arrived, the Marines joined with the Army and Brigadier General Cadwaladar's brigade of Pennsylvania militia where the marines certainly saw action with the brigade at Princeton.[58] Additional naval initiatives of this time included the beginning of submarine warfare and an amazing transport service.

War often sees many innovations in military history, but none so dramatic as David Bushnell's invention before the war of gunpowder capable of underwater detonation. The year before at Lexington-Concord, Bushnell had developed a submarine capable of exploding a submarine mine. This amazing inventor then proceeded to design and build the *Turtle*, a one-man craft designed to deliver a mine into an enemy warship's hull. Receiving Washington's permission, the first attempt to place mines under British warships proved unsuccessful, but a demonstration of what the future of naval warfare could become continued Yankee ingenuity.

Other demonstrations of American creativity and initiative existed with the 12th Continental Regiment, also known as the Marblehead Regiment, and often referred to by historians as Glover's

---

56. Perret, *A Country*, 60.
57. Martin, James K., & Lender, Mark E. *A Respectable Army: The Military Origins of the Republic, 1763-1789.* Harlan Davidson: Arlington Heights, IL, 1982, 143.
58. Millet, Alan R., & Maslowski, Peter. *For the Common Defense.* Free Press: NY, 1994, 14.

amphibians. These men, former Massachusetts sailors, formed the regiment serving as soldiers. Thinking outside of the box, these men operated barges and small boats. Dramatically saving the American army when Washington desperately needed to get across the East River to escape the British, the usefulness of this unique unit continued. When fortunes seemed to be at the lowest toward the end of that month, these men had the ability to adjust to the needs of the army to ensure its survival. According to Lynn Montross, the amphibians deserved the credit for the Trenton and Princeton victories.[59] Repeatedly we will see Americans throughout history epitomize the strength of freedom with an ability to improvise and use the initiative creatively. The Marblehead men certainly embodied the American army's history of innovation and "thinking outside the box."

Whether the American successes at unconventional warfare simply represented imagination or arose from a necessity dictated by geography remains open to debate. Either way, Americans had gradually started fighting a war that ultimately took advantage of the huge area the British attempted to control and the American use of limited time to best advantage eventually wore the British war effort down. Time favored the Americans, but it would remain necessary to keep a conventional force in the field. Nowhere did this operational brilliance of trading space for time achieve the level of results it did as much as in the southern campaign. Likewise, the successful ability to control the Indians on the frontier would be instrumental in winning the war.

Just as the patriot cause required excellence in the creation of a Continental Army or an American naval prowess or the use of French assets at sea, the Americans to win the war had needed unconventional forces or partisans. Defeating the British also required success at winning the "hearts and minds" of the southern people or the British attempts to contain the enthusiasm of the loyalists. Like the Americans in the later years of the Vietnam War, the fact that Americans could eventually use force and terror in combination with conventional forces ultimately served to tip the scales to the side of the patriots in the War for Independence.

The mix of conventional and unconventional forces won the American Revolution. While Washington, with the help of Steuben, could create a permanent standing army of the line, the Continentals; the contributions of partisan leadership remained key also. The Continentals could give what Max Boot calls the "one-two punch," with the irregulars weakening the army of occupation until a conventional force could administer the coup de grace. This method of fighting—later dubbed "hybrid warfare" by 21st century strategists—has usually been the surest road to success for an insurgency."[60] How did American successes contrast with those of British attempts to woo an uncertain population?

Cruelty learned in the long frontier wars proved itself a determining factor in gaining loyalty to the patriot cause. Ultimately and especially in the south where frontier Indian wars had just recently begun to smolder down, the control by men such as Thomas Sumter, **Francis "Swamp Fox" Marion**, and Andrew Pickens since 1775 obviously demonstrated to the wavering colonists who would still be around when the British left. Leading harassment actions against Cornwallis' Army also served to foil attempts by the British to gain loyal followers.

Francis Marion's **partisan** operations had a lack of headquarters and few formalized supply efforts. The inability of the British to determine any real center-of-gravity to destroy the American operation resulted in frustrated British attempts to destroy these operations. The partisan

Marion's brigade crossing the Pedee River, SC 1778, on their way to attack the British force under Tarleton.

Source: Library of Congress

---

59. Montross, Lynn. *War through the Ages*. Harper & Row: NY, 1960, 426.
60. Boot, *Invisible Armies*, 78.

bands stayed on the move avoiding sedentary occupations for extended periods. When the "Swamp Foxes" headquarters in the Pee Dee River region at Snow's Island finally was overrun by the British, the partisans simply moved on to another location. Not only did the British appear incompetent in destroying the partisans, they ran out of valuable time as Americans skillfully used propaganda to wear down British patience and public opinion back home in their failed attempt to convince the Americans of their "staying power."

In contrast to the successes of the American partisans, the British had, nonetheless, adapted to the frontier tactics of the Americans and dressed in green loyalists who operated behind the lines as well. An example would be the Queen's Loyal Virginia Regiment that by 1777 had been renamed the Simcoe's Rangers. These Americans attempted to capture weapons and turn the public to the British side by demonstrating they could travel throughout the countryside. One incident involving Simcoe's Rangers is illustrative. In 1781 while Cornwallis pursued Lafayette through Virginia, he detailed the Rangers to raid into Point of Fork, Virginia, and sent Banastre Tarleton's cavalry to Charlottesville. The Rangers succeeded in finding weapons evacuated from Richmond but could find nothing but hostility in the surrounding countryside. Tarleton's legion meanwhile had been proceeded only minutes before by a local citizen of Paul Revere type fame, Jack Jouett.

Jack had heard of the Legion's plans to raid Monticello and the British plans to capture the author of the Declaration of Independence, thereby scoring a publicity coup. Both the use of Simcoe's Rangers and Jouett's ride demonstrated the use and failures of British rangers attempting to use stealth to convince the countryside of Britain's permanency and intentions. British ranger actions merely served to demonstrate unpopularity of the British cause and revealed an inability to maintain secrecy, not much different from that at Lexington-Concord six years before, when local militias had known of the redcoats approach![61]

Much of the eventual credit for the successful hybrid of unconventional and conventional tactics used in the southern campaign lay with George Washington. Never interested in working with the Indians, Washington had not forgotten the lessons he had learned in the French and Indian War. Drawn into the formality of conventional struggle—always a weakness for the wealthy leader removed from the front lines, he nonetheless recognized that partisans alone could not win the war. Washington would proceed to order Nathaniel Greene south, where it seems Greene wisely also recognized the inherent limitations of partisans and began to engage in the brilliant use of trading space for time using General Harry "Light Horse" Lee's cavalry.[62] In other words, by delegating authority to trusted subordinates, Washington, who had never really understood the use of cavalry and had perhaps even forgotten many of the lessons of the frontier, allowed others to exploit and develop a recipe for victory.

To win a partisan war, one simply must be able to understand the culture. The British could not understand the Americans well enough to determine they had a different view of freedom. While partisans used ruthless tactics in the south to remind the wavering loyalists they would still be around when the British had left, the English could not convince enough loyalists of the worth in laying down their lives. As the noted author Max Boot has said, British forces were harsh enough to alienate the Americans, but not terrifying enough to bring them to heel.[63] The parallels with the Viet Cong in Vietnam are again eerie.[64] The British strategy in the south had attempted to secure a perceived higher population of loyal subjects but the partisan efforts proved to be their undoing. Interestingly it would be Nathaniel Greene's ancestor Wallace Green who as Commandant of the Marine Corps would unsuccessfully attempt to create similar partisan efforts to win the "hearts and minds" of the Vietnamese (see CAC/CAP in the Vietnam War chapter) in opposition to big army conventional warfare proponents such as William Westmoreland. Forgetting the military lessons of the past can be expensive and deadly!

More than a century and a half of the development of an American Way of Fighting had emerged. Steuben and Washington together represented the standardized fighting both practiced

---

61. Simcoe, John. *A History of the Operations of a Partisan Corps Called the Queen's Rangers*. Bartlett & Welford: New York, 1844, 212.
62. Boot, *Invisible Armies*, 74.
63. Boot, *Invisible Armies*, 78.
64. Martin, *A Respectable Army*, 15.

and perfected on the European continent reflecting the power of massed formations and firepower. Washington, like most western leaders throughout history, naturally preferred this conventional line fighting so characteristic of the enlightenment, while Daniel Morgan reflected the independent skirmisher and the American ability to merge the new with the old.

Daniel Morgan held shooting trials to determine who could join his unit and would have the privilege and benefits of being a rifleman. Joining a rifle company required a high level of proficiency, but the benefits of better treatment attracted many prospective recruits. The **riflemen** of Morgan's unit tended to reflect the "little army" mentality we see today. Wearing civilian type clothes, the riflemen even faced less tasking and reveled in their statuses of elites described in hyperbole and receiving extra pay.[65] Washington quickly discovered the problems with elites when he had to put down potential mutinies. Morgan's regiment of rifles teamed up with the forces of General Horatio Gates at Freeman's Farm. The geographic distinctions of this team are interesting. Most men from the wealthier and cleared east preferred muskets, with their shorter range but deadly in mass, while most frontiersmen from the western parts of the states preferred rifles. Working together these two weapons systems proved lethal while the rifles could shoot from bushes and trees, targeting British officers and Tories or loyalists. Like the partisans above, the riflemen could not win a battle by themselves; to take ground required the mass fire of the muskets and the soldiers who could stand their ground.

The cruel punishment reaped upon captured American riflemen reflected British frustration with these violators of established rules in warfare. An example of the treatment most captured riflemen received is demonstrated at the Battle of Long Island where Americans bayonetted to trees showed the contempt held by their captors and frustration at an inability to defeat them.[66] The riflemen went into battle recognizing the cost of his elite status.

In his book, *American Rifle*, Alexander Rose reflects on American society and the idea that an obedient culture ruled by the best tended to reflect the view of those who believed soldiers armed with a bayonet represented the true measure of a just society. Naturally led by the best, these soldiers would demonstrate complete obedience; in short, they would receive imposed discipline. Alexander Hamilton voiced an opinion reflecting the view of the musket-type school of thought that, without officers, frontiersmen were ". . . too independent to be useful."[67] Hamilton considered soldiers "essentially animals...trained to attack," and in fact, viewed soldiers as ". . . the nearer the soldier approach to machines perhaps the better."[68] This Hamiltonian view of the courageous and honorable fighter closing with the enemy held to a long cherished western tradition stretching back to the Ancient Greeks who portrayed the noble Greeks as fighting with hand-held weapons whereas the more sinister and cowardly relied on bows and arrows. The Jeffersonian view tended to prefer the riflemen.

Thomas Jefferson believed that the rifleman personified the individual craftsman in war. Here, the discipline exhibited by the fighting man existed unimpeded; rather a property of self-discipline. Followers of the Jeffersonian school included Charles Lee and Horatio Gates who argued for "People's War of National Liberation." Such a modern type of view believed that fighting according to European methods and form, simply would create another essentially "royalist" social hierarchy.[69] While according to Mr. Rose, Jefferson was convinced American success should be attributed to aimed fire, an opposite view seemed to be held by Federalists who favored the massed volley fire of muskets. Voicing an opinion of these "big army" proponents, Charles Lee, an early advocate of unconventional fighting, apparently had a rather low opinion of Alexander Hamilton, who Lee referred to as a "son of a ____."[70] Such diverse views reflected the nature of not just soldiers, but society and the emerging politics of the Republic in general. Fortunately, for the American patriot cause, George Washington oversaw the adoption of both philosophies, thereby ensuring victory!

---

65. Rose, Alexander. *American Rifle*. Random House: New York, 2008, 45.
66. Rose, *American Rifle*, 59.
67. Ibid., 60.
68. Ibid., 60.
69. Rose, *American Rifle*, 61.
70. Ibid., 62.

The end of the American Revolution left a nation tenuously held together. The Army, under the leadership of George Washington, represented the glue that built the United States. Investments in an army would create a large standing force. Though initially unsuccessful in defending the old northwest, the Army would eventually crush the Indians attempt to build a confederacy. Eventually frontier fighting would lead to the War of 1812. The War of 1812 reflected a conventional effort that allowed Andrew Jackson to emerge first as an Indian fighter, and then as a hero at the Battle of New Orleans. With the end of the War, nationalism emerged and the army went back to the old business of fighting native peoples and eventually secured all areas east of the Mississippi River.

General Andrew Jackson

Key Terms:

Powhatan Wars
Pequot War
King Phillip's War
King William's War
Queen Anne's War
War of Jenkin's Ear
King George's War
Volunteers
George Washington
Fort Duquesne
Ohio Valley

Braddock
Pitt
Pontiac's Rebellion
New England Phase
Lexington-Concord
Bunker Hill
Middle Colonies Phase
1777
Saratoga
Valley Forge
Southern Phase

Waxhaws
Battle of Camden
King's Mountain
Cowpens
Guilford Courthouse
Yorktown, Virginia
John Paul Jones
Turtle
Partisans
Francis Marion
Riflemen

Chapter II
THE FOUNDATIONS OF AN AMERICAN WAY OF FIGHTING: WARS OF THE EARLY UNITED STATES

The Need for a Standing Army

Victory at Yorktown in 1781 and the subsequent Peace of Paris of 1783 may have achieved a win on the battlefield, but few believed the Revolution could truly succeed. Where else had a Republic earned its freedom and persevered to keep it? Even the Romans had ceased being a republic and an empire under the authority of a strong man, so failure seemed inevitable. The historical distrust of a military establishment is revealed in a quote from the period, ". . . however necessary it may be, [it] is always dangerous to the liberties of the people . . . Standing armies in time of peace are inconsistent with the principles of republican government.[71] The smart money said Washington would eventually have to be a dictator and smarter people around Washington with opposing views of military roles agreed. Several forces, but none greater than George Washington, served to ensure a permanent standing army and eventually preserved the Republic.

The soldiers themselves at the end of the war presented a problem. As in all wars, what do you do with huge numbers of armed soldiers, mostly men, who face a changed society and often times an economy numbed by peace? At the end of the American Revolution George Washington successfully stood down the **Newburgh Conspiracy**. A group of influential soldiers had united in their demands for the Continental Congress to promise war payments before being disbanded, thereby threatening the authority of the New Republic. Historical sensibilities seemed to dictate an old fear of standing armies as threats to liberty. The conspiracy seems today to only be a minor episode, however, it took the power of George Washington to demand the requisite loyalty of the soldiers necessary to put this episode to rest. Washington's contributions did not stop with merely the Army, it continued into the new government.

Military considerations factored into the creation of the Constitution. The new government of the post-Revolutionary period saw limitations spelled out by the Articles of Confederation. When a war veteran named Daniel Shays led a mob protesting taxation policy in Massachusetts and marched on Springfield in Massachusetts in 1785, the Massachusetts state militia dispatched the mob but only after some considerable effort. When George Washington heard of the rebellion and considered the limitations placed on the Confederation Congress' efforts to quell it, Washington felt the time had apparently come to amend the Articles and to create a more powerful government—one capable of defending itself from the Indians and their British allies in the Northwest; perhaps

---
71. Schweikart, Larry, & Allen, Michael. *A Patriot's History of the United States*. Penguin: New York, 2004, 32.

even the Spanish to the South. When George Washington went to a party everyone wanted to be there, so when he decided to attend the Second meeting of the Constitutional convention in 1776 at Philadelphia—everyone who was anyone turned out!

The new Constitution addressed the dual military concerns of those who favored a strong central government and a regular standing army, with those who felt the rights of the states needed to be paramount and favored the state's militia. The first Article of the Constitution ensured the power to declare war to be the prerogative of the legislature, and the executive in Article 2 would be the Commander-In-Chief, obviously a not-so-subtle nod of the head to the great George Washington whose influence had made the Constitution a possibility. Furthermore, Article 2 additionally described the need for a well-regulated militia and reflected the somewhat divided political opinion on the proper seat of military power within the nation. Still, the creation of a Constitution with established roles for the military and the executive branch represented a transition to peace that ensured the Republic would survive.

The debate over the nature and tactics of a disciplined army consisting of regular soldiers, one fighting in line with muskets and bayonets overseen by disciplinarians versus the view that liberties called for the militia-style force of independent Indian fighting frontiersmen armed with rifles and using skirmishers tactics, constituted a political divide that continued until the fall of 1790. Little Turtle emerged as a charismatic leader of the Miami, Shawnee, Potawatomi, and Chippewa tribes. Native American support by British soldiers who had annoyingly remained in the old Northwest frontier, served to convince American leaders of the need for a standing regular army. It would nevertheless take a few militia defeats before a regular army finally emerged.

Initiating a role that would provide the U.S. Army a frontier mission for the next 102 years, the first attempt by an American army to police the frontier and attempt to prevent the bloodshed of innocents failed miserably. Josiah **Harmar**, a continental army veteran obviously well past his prime represented the authority of the new U.S. government when he led a punitive expedition into the frontier. Leading frontiersmen, not soldiers, Harmar divided his forces and entered unfamiliar territory with no guides or indigenous peoples to lead him. Once again, the importance of the study of military history is revealed with the failure to use Indian Scouts. An unnecessarily costly lesson of the penalties exacted for forgetting the lessons of the past and the cost of relearning them. Little Turtle lured the expeditionary troops into a valley by burning buildings and pretending to be withdrawing. When the American troops pursued, they walked into an ambush and then fled without any semblance of unit integrity, leaving behind 183 troops.[72] Little Turtle magnanimously allowed Harmar to leave with his remaining troops who, when safely back east, of course promptly declared victory. This did not fool President Washington, however.[73] The defeat of the expedition eventually resulted in the doubling of the size of the army.

Another attempt in August 1791 to cow the Native Americans in the old Northwest saw a repeated defeat of a militia by Indians on the frontier. Ordering up the Kentucky militia to serve in a punitive expedition, a repeated failure to use native scouts or indigenous peoples as skirmishers faced certain defeat.[74] In an attempt to hold high ground on the Wabash River, **St. Clair**'s force eventually faced encirclement, forced to break their way out with tremendous losses.[75] Amid gory scenes of bloodshed, two-thirds of the force faced annihilation or capture—the greatest Native American victory in terms of numbers ever achieved against the Army.[76] At last Congress decided a regular army needed to be created.

The **Legion of the United States** created in 1792, represented the real birth of a U.S. Army to be a permanent standing force of 1,800 troops, 4 regiments of infantry, and a corps of artillery and engineers.[77] The idea behind the legion beckoned back to the ancient world, imitating that most

---

72. Perret, Geoffrey. *A Country Made By War*. Random House: NY, 1989, 84.
73. Utley, Robert M., & Washburn, Wilcomb E. *Indian Wars*. American Heritage: New York, 1977, 113.
74. Perret, *A Country*, 84.
75. Utley & Washburn, *Indian Wars*, 114.
76. Perret, *A Country*, 84.
77. Alison, Wm. T, Grey, Jeffery, & Valentine, Janet G. *American Military History 2nd Ed.* Pearson: Upper Saddle River, NJ, 2013, 72.

successful of Republics—Rome. The idea behind the legion consisted of a vision of a large force coming together on the battlefield, each subordinate unit organically composed of a small independent formation. Within the independent force would be all necessary fire support and cavalry capabilities—a mini-army. The Legion represented a realistic compromise between Republican fears of insufficient security and a realistic recognition of lean congressional resources.

The **Militia Act of 1792** only created a vast "paper army" according to Geoffrey Perret. In actuality, it represented timeless state prerogatives and continued to require all males from 18 to 45 to serve as members of the militia if they were free men. This pleased the Jeffersonians who remained distrustful of the abuses of line commanders. The Militia Act essentially left it to the states to maintain their own armies as they determined necessary. Washington's advice to use a central government approach to bases, depots and coordinating with the states was met with a cold shoulder.[78] Armed with a Legion of regular line soldiers, Congress expected Washington to leave the militia alone. In desperation and needing a win, the new Army went forth to avenge Harmar and St. Clair.

"Mad Anthony" Wayne, who advanced like a frontier prophet into the woods of the Old Northwest, briefly stopped to bury the remains of St. Clair's expedition the year before. Effectively utilizing a cavalry screen, at the site of a break in the woods created by a tornado called **Fallen Timbers**, Indians attacked from all sides. The innate aggressiveness and perhaps a touch of vengeance from the disasters of previous years propelled the volunteer cavalry forward as it attacked the frightened Indians. The regulars demonstrated iron discipline; stood and fired in formation. Breaking into retreat with the Americans on their heels toward their British allies located at Fort Miami, the Indians soon found themselves abandoned by the British who feared an incident with the Americans.[79] Fallen Timbers ensured over a decade of peace on the frontier of the old Northwest.

With the **Treaty of Grenville** agreed to in 1795, Indians ceded half of Ohio and part of Indiana. The Indians fell into lethargy after British abandonment. One Indian did not honor the Treaty of Grenville, however: a handsome young man named Tecumseh, who had earlier participated in St. Clair's massacre.[80] After 1796 support also began to slide with the loss of its popular commander. With no permanent administrative framework to guide the army, it had somewhat become a

General "Mad Anthony" Wayne

Wayne's defeat of the Indians.

---

78. Clark, J.P. *Preparing for War*. Harvard University Press: Cambridge, MA, 2017, 12
79. Perret, *A Country*, 86.
80. Perret, *A Country*, 104.

personality cult following a specific example of leadership, thereby threatening the existence of the Legion as an institution.[81]

The creation of West Point in 1794 represented a major development in the struggle between the Federalists, who advocated a strong central government and a standing military, and those Jeffersonians who tended to favor state rights. A familiar pattern in American political history of a candidate's views changing once elected continued when Thomas Jefferson became President in 1801. Initially teaching mathematics to Artillerists and Engineers at **West Point**, New York, the permanency of the academy received formal establishment with the Peace Establishment Act of 1802. The supporters of Jefferson, or Republicans could rally behind a "civilizing" influence of academia in the distrusted army. Teaching engineering skills—the highest form of practical science for the times; and artillery, the highest form of firepower—an interesting compromise resulted.[82] The army continued to be a foundation stone for American institutions including academics.

West Point, 1820s

Source: Library of Congress

> Early in American history, many leaders were hesitant to have an award system. Having recently gained independence from England, the founding fathers objected to hereditary honors and titles.[83] As a result of this objection, individual awards for meritorious actions were rare. Before the Medal of Honor, an American soldier could be recognized for bravery by either official praises or by brevets. Official praise involved receiving a letter with the thanks of Congress; a brevet, in contrast, is a temporary promotion. The recipient of a brevet could be addressed by his new rank and could wear the corresponding insignia. However, he would not receive the pay of the new rank.[84] In any case, brevets and official letters of praise proved to be inadequate to recognize the feats of bravery shown by soldiers and sailors during the Civil War.

During the formative years of the Republic, the Navy continued to advance technologically. In 1798, the Congress established a Navy Department and shortly thereafter created the United States Marine Corps for fighting from the tops of the ships. Serious naval building programs to include twenty-four warships would supplement six frigates already commissioned. Brimming with adolescent confidence, the young American nation took offense after the XYZ affair saw American emissaries subjected to bribes by the French government; itself somewhat miffed with the Americans since the agreement with Britain known as Jay's Treaty appeared to give a shot in the arm to Anglo-American relationships. Late 1800 saw an undeclared war between France and the U.S. called the **Quasi-War with France**, consisting of actions at sea. Ending obligations to France from the American Revolution, the technology and seamanship of America's Navy had established it as a future force of vast potential.

February of 1799 saw the ***U.S.S. Constellation*** squared off against the French warship *L'Insurgente*. After numerous broadsides, the superiority of American gunnery began to show. Surrendering to the Americans, the French had lost seventy crew compared to only five of the Americans. A year later the *Constellation* again faced off against a larger French warship and, despite over four hours of

---

81. Clark, *Preparing for War*, 12.
82. Perret, *A Country*, 101.
83. Zimmerman, *Uncommon Valor*, 48.
84. Zimmerman, *Uncommon Valor*, 50.

bludgeoning fury, the Americans still drew in close to board the French ship when suddenly the mast fell. Unable to bag the goods, the United States Navy had proven itself and cut its teeth on the long naval traditions of the European powers.[85]

Despite cost overruns, military crises such as the Quasi War continued to teach the young nation the importance of maintaining an army as well. The legacy of this two-year long war included the permanent establishment of the staff organization of the Army supply, administration, medical, and the inspectorate components in 1799.[86] The need for cannons and powder resulted in the creation of foundries to make the guns and armories to store and maintain them, the largest placed at Harper's Ferry, Virginia. The Quasi War saw an American military establishment on land and sea with a measure of permanency and the respect due to a young nation emerged while the taking of bribes ceased.[87]

U.S.S. Constellation

When an ambitious pasha Yusuf Karamanli demanded the generally pacifistic Jefferson to give him a ship like his competition the Dey of Algiers had, he found a young nation ready to fight for its honor in the Tripolitan War of 1801–1805. Choosing naval action over appeasement, early embarrassing attempts to negotiate the coastline resulted in a grounded U.S. ship quickly taken hostage. Subsequent attempts by U.S. sailors demonstrated audacity and gave more experience to a future team of naval leadership. A sort of Pearl Harbor type excitement at the prospect of an American ship being taken had led to audacious naval-versus-fort gunnery duels and daring raids—everyone a U.S. success! The development of the Navy continued in the "real world" school of waves and cannons, far from the impassioned start and stop emotions of the young Republic. Even the young Marine Corps got in on the act when Lieutenant Presley O'Bannon and his seven marines protected the Dey of Algiers; and to this day, every marine officer proudly wears a Mameluke patterned sword in commemoration of this event.[88] Now not only Europeans respected the U.S. Navy, but pirates of North Africa had received proper instruction, taught to respect the U.S. as well.

The **Chesapeake & Leopard Affair** on June 22, 1807 saw a U.S. vessel barely clearing United States coastal waters, suddenly fired upon by a British ship before it had even cleared for action. This naval action in itself would not result in war, but like the later Lusitania sinking in 1915, itself a major cause of America's entry into World War I, unprovoked aggression by the British against a U.S. vessel served to further convince "War hawks," or congressional representatives from the newly carved western states, to eventually demand war.

Jefferson in these early days of the republic had to be content with a vigorous protest to the British Government for redress. The Orders in Council system had resulted in a system of legal codes designed to help Britain in the Napoleonic Wars against France. The legal codes eventually expanded in interpretation to allow for the boarding by British naval Captains onto the vessels of any nation trading with France. Exuberant commanders eagerly anticipating additional prize money in the field often exceeded their authorities. The Chesapeake and Leopard Affair occurred during Jefferson's last year in office in 1808. Even though Jefferson continued to prefer the militia to the regular military establishment, actions such as Tripoli and the Chesapeake affair went far to change his views towards the needs of a large standing army. President Jefferson eventually oversaw a three-fold increase in the size of the Army.[89] Still, the death grip France and Britain had on each other would continue to create a deadly atmosphere that would eventually draw America into war.

---

85. Alison, *American Military*, 81.
86. Clark, *Preparing for War*, 13.
87. Ibid., 91.
88. Ibid., 93.
89. Clark, *Preparing for War*, 14.

The War of 1812

Many historians refer to the **War of 1812** as the second war for independence. This somewhat complicated and often bungled war combined with a smattering of dramatic American victories brings to mind an accidental victory, and perhaps even one the U.S. achieved despite itself. The result would be a moral victory and emergent nationalism, but the long war occurred over four different theaters of war; first, the old Northwest (to be differentiated from the Oregon territory) area of Michigan, Ohio and Upper Canada. Second, the Central theater of Upper New York and the Lakes where Winfield Scott would emerge, and then third, the Chesapeake area. A final victory in the southern city of New Orleans saw the emergence of the leadership of Andrew Jackson, a notorious Indian fighter. Besides the British, the Indian menace brought America to war again. As the bellicosity of the Indians increased, the European powers yet again seemed bent on humiliating the Americans at sea while American foreign policy seemed inept and impotent to respond.

Initial attempts by Jefferson to halt all business with the British and French in the form of an Embargo had achieved little other than to put the U.S. into a serious economic downturn. Years later the birth of American industry under this protective move would vindicate the **Embargo**, but all Americans knew in 1807 consisted of economic pain. Further attempts at economic abstinence in 1809 at the end of the Jeffersonian presidency resulted in a new attempt at coercing trade and tagged with the unfortunately named **Non-Intercourse Act.** The Act forbade trade with either the British or French but allowed the president to end the Boycott at his pleasure when such offending nations decided to stop impressing American sailors and other obnoxious actions. Essentially the Embargo had said we would not deal with anyone except on our own terms, and now the Act offered to be friends with whoever would stop picking on us. The upshot of this economic and diplomatic maneuvering drew America closer to France when the wily Napoleon offered to stop picking on us. Forced to agree with France, America inadvertently joined a contemporary death-struggle with Great Britain. The British had established **Orders in Councils**, essentially a system of blockades designed to prevent any trade with France; to enforce a naval blockade fiercely confronted any nation whose shipping even appeared to be involved in dealing with the French. British treatment of American shipping and the impressment of sailors combined to remind Americans of the Chesapeake and Leopard affair, heightened frontiersmen fears of the British and their Indian allies ambitions in the old Northwest. The occasional Indian raid had continued to remind Americans of their threatening presence. A decade after the battle of Fallen Timbers, the British had armed the Indians again in the old Northwest and still occupied forts hanging like a sword of Damocles, dangling menacingly over the newly cleared lands west of the Appalachians.

By 1811 the handsome and charismatic Tecumseh had ventured into Creek territory in the deep south on a remarkable six month journey attempting to unite the tribes in a last ditch effort to restore a way of life to the lands east of the Mississippi River region. Tecumseh, handsome veteran of St. Clair's massacre and of the Battle of Fallen Timbers, collaborated with his equally ugly brother, Tenskwatawa. The ugly brother had preached a seemingly timeless message reflecting a revivalist type message repackaged. The latest attempt to reunify the Indians followed the view of Handsome Lake as well as that of Pontiac generations before. The general outline of the message that would continue to emerge into the 1890s reflected a vision of turning away from the White Man's liquor and abstaining from the corrupting influences of materialism. An important component in any attempt by Native-Americans to resist encroaching culture required an attempt at achieving unification across the tribes, one capable of defeating the adversary.[90] The message went mostly unheard by those people already on the government's dole, but Tecumseh's vision received an excited audience in the young men who tended to see the ugly brother as the one with the more powerful message; attack now! [91]

The tribes began to gather at a place called Tippecanoe River in northern Indiana at Prophet's Town. Both the British and the Americans had begun to lose control as Indians, infuriated by unfair

---

90. Perret, Geoffrey. *A Country Made By War*. Random House: NY, 1989, 104.
91. Borneman, Walter R. *1812*. Harper Collins: NY, 2004, 31.

land deal shams, and white frontiersmen determined to have those lands as unscrupulous agents, offered alcohol and weapons, stirring up a volatile situation bound to explode. William Henry Harrison, the future president, soon led troops of regulars and militia into the vicinity of Prophet's Town where Indians struck on November 7, 1811. The troops held until the Indians ran out of ammunition and subsequently marched into Prophet's Town burning and destroying the hopes of the Native-Americans in the leadership of Tenskwatawa. As tribes continued to rise along the frontier, it appeared the gathering at Tippecanoe had achieved little more than to make the Indians angrier and served only to unify them. Subsequent attempts to increase the size of the army back east faced vigorous opposition from New England, who had since long-forgotten their frontier days. Madison confronted Congress with a request for a declaration of war based on issues of impressment, British actions at sea, and the actions of the Indians in large measure also supported by the British.

James Madison, the smallest man ever to be President, represented a type of aristocratic brilliance befitting the heir of the Jeffersonian experience. This diminutively sized, but brilliant theoretician made a somewhat comical figure with his sword nearly touching the ground. Taking the U.S. to war, the initial couple of years had few victories and many defeats, but leadership emerged from the battlefields reflected the scholarly and civilized style of fighting inherent in the line and musket volleys with the individualistic style of Indian fighting. These two capabilities would eventually merge, producing an eventual moral victory in the War of 1812 over Britain and the Indians. In the conventional fighting early on in the war, the theater of concern seemed to be the old Northwest area. A series of disasters would ensue tempered with a naval victory on Lake Erie.

Governor William Hull marched on Detroit July 1812 and managed to seize defeat from the jaws of victory when he suffered a nervous breakdown; a victim of psychological operations that threatened terror. Hull suffered a nervous breakdown as British forces led by General Isaac Brock and Tecumseh bumbled into an American double envelopment and had just wandered into the gun range of loaded cannons on the fort. On the verge of winning, Hull's surrender oversaw the greatest surrender of troops and supplies between the American Revolution and Bataan in World War II.[92]

James Madison, President of the United States

Source: Library of Congress

General William H. Harrison next ordered his Army of the old Northwest into the wilderness to crush the Indians, Harrison ignored President Madison's instructions to take Detroit back. Harrison's equally ambitious and somewhat incompetent subordinate, James Winchester, a man greatly despised by his own troops and eager to make a name for himself, drove his cavalry screening force far out to come to the aid of an American force attacking a Canadian at Frenchtown on the Raisin River. When counterattacked, Winchester was captured and ordered his men to surrender also. For three days unmentionable atrocities occurred known as the **Raisin River Massacre** as Indians spread captive American blood on the snow. The American hold on the old Northwest now hung by a thread. The successes of the Battle of Fallen Timbers vanished, now erased.[93]

Further organizational failures by the militia occurred at Queenston Heights where one of the richest men in New York, Stephen van Rensselaer, sent a diversionary attack with 30,000 militia, 2,000 regulars, and eighty boats to Ft. George, about seven miles from the heights. With the mission to pin down and divert British forces, the plan for a second assault would finish the enemy off. Political considerations prevented the attack and though the heights successfully saw seizure by Captain

---

92. Perret, *A Country*, 109.
93. Ibid., 112.

John E. Wool, reinforcements would not cross due to legal considerations of crossing the national border and besides, Rensselaer's boatmen did not want to take them.[94] As the bridgehead saw systematic destruction and was slowly wiped out, even sorrier events would yet occur. Major General Henry Dearborn seemed to agree with the British General Sir George Prevost that perhaps they should together, give peace a chance. Neither men budged to fight the other. A subsequent attempt to enter Canada was done by Dearborn, the old veteran of the Revolutionary War who appeared to have morphed into something slightly more gentle, hence the nickname Granny. Dearborn's attempts resulted in equally pathetic results when the Militia once again refused to cross into Canada. Another attempt to cross the Niagara saw Rensselaer's new replacement, Alexander Smyth, twice fail to cross the Niagara and his army disbanded.[95] The year 1812 did not represent much in the way of American victories it seemed, nor would the militia receive laurels of war that year. It would be up to America's fighting navy to improve fortunes.

The Battle of Lake Erie revealed a Navy full of fighting fury and motivated by actions at sea, where the *Chesapeake* vs. the *Shannon* saw further laurels heaped on the U.S. Navy. On a Spring Day in 1813, a bright spot in a war of darkness emerged when the *Shannon* poured a deadly fire into the *Chesapeake* the moment the American vessel came into range. The Americans, both ill trained and unfamiliar even with one another, nevertheless fought fiercely against a veteran British crew fresh from the Napoleonic Wars. The U.S. Navy never forgot the uttered words of a dying American Captain James Lawrence, "Don't give up the ship. Fight her till she sinks." American sailors and marines together fought in fierce hand-to-hand combat until forced below decks. Marines up in the upper decks stayed at their stations in spite of the desperate situation until all lay dead or wounded. A small group of seamen and marines at bay on the forecastle put up a desperate fight against the enemy who eventually closed in and slew them to the last man.[96] The *Chesapeake* may have been captured, but it never surrendered.

Perry's victory on Lake Erie, fought September 10, 1813.

The next area in the war centered on the central area of the border of the U.S. and Canada. The fighting around the lakes represented an American race against the British to build a fleet. The Battle for Lake Erie represented another victory in the rapidly growing traditions of naval excellence. By September, Oliver Hazard Perry had established dominance on the Lake after building a green ship navy, in what amounted to a naval arms race on the banks and engaging the British at close range. Aggressively attacking, the huge blue flag flew over the flagship *Lawrence*, named for the now famous captain killed in the encounter with the *Shannon*, and displayed the words, **"Don't Give up the Ship."** With a couple weeks advantage in training, the American fleet decided who would control the Lakes. Both the British and Indians were desperate for supplies on one side, and the Americans were in equally bad shape on the other.

Oliver Hazard Perry, U.S.N.

---

94. Perret, *A Country*, 110.
95. Ibid., 111.
96. Metcalf, Clyde H. *A History of the United States Marine Corps.* Putnam: New York, 1939, 61.

The *Lawrence* bore the brunt of the battle when the British placed all of their fire upon her for two terrible hours as decks ran sticky with blood and guts. Fighting three ships at once, the *Lawrence* finally abandoned when the five surviving sailors, including Perry, took to a lifeboat where they paddled to the *U.S.S. Niagara*, firing double shots which finished off the three British ships the *Lawrence* had fought to a halt. Perry sat among the wreckage and inscribed the words: We have met the enemy and they are ours . . ."[97]

The British, forced to abandon Ft. Detroit by the loss of Lake Erie, now saw Americans invading Canada, ferried across the water by Perry's ships. At the **Battle of the Thames** on October 5, 1813, the Kentucky Cavalrymen riding hard through forests and demonstrating the skill of American woodsmen on horseback, smashed through the British lines situated about 300 yards from the American lines. With cries of "remember the Raisin!" screamed, the Americans whipped into a frenzy, conducting themselves with the same recklessness as had their adversaries on the Raisin. Atrocities committed made Tecumseh's body virtually unrecognizable. The brave Indian leader had determined to stand and fight rather than to flee, and he had paid the price. With his death went Anglo-Indian ambitions in the old Northwest. The War, meanwhile, continued to the east in the Central theater of Operations.

Battle of the Thames, respectfully dedicated to Andrew Jackson Esq., President of the United States.

Source: Library of Congress

The previous spring of 1813 had seen major raids conducted, when in April General Henry Dearborn had attacked York near Toronto, Canada, but was met with disaster. The British in response attacked at Sackett's Harbor in May, where they met General Jacob Brown. Brown represented a newer breed of officer more professional and nationalistic in outlook and with a view that would go far to redeeming the conduct of militia and political officers who had thus far often produced less than excellent results. The increased reliance on new regular regiments to expand the country's land forces and the fruits of professionalism dropping from West Point had begun to create a professional force capable of victory.[98] Defeating several determined attacks, the Americans continued to meet with mixed results with back and forth battles in the upper New York Area and the eventual mismanagement of the deplorable Major General James Wilkinson, whose corruptness exceeded only his incompetency. Wilkinson's inability to work in tandem with his subordinate Major General Wade Hampton resulted in a failed attack on Montreal—something apparently destined to happen in every colonial and U.S. military endeavor up until the 18th century—resulted in American defeats at Chateauguay and Chrysler's Farm in New York and Canada. A soldier who had served under Wilkinson emerged, however, in the tradition of George Washington.

Like Washington, **Winfield Scott** believed primarily in conventional operations. As we shall see in the Seminole Wars, like Washington, irregular warfare and the patience of the frontier fight held little to enthuse Scott. A scholar and one who would

Winfield Scott, Lieutenant General of the U.S. Army

© Everett Collection/Shutterstock.com

---

97. Perret, *A Country*, 120.
98. Clark, Richard, & Knake, Robert K. *Cyber Warfare*. Harper Collins: New York, 2010, 67.

set the example for generations of soldier-scholars, Winfield Scott would represent what Geoffrey Perret called, "the Scott tradition" for any soldier exhibiting bookishness.[99] While Brown held back the British at Sackett's harbor, Scott studied. Winfield Scott's brilliance would influence generations of military leadership up until the Civil War and he would represent a figure of military strength and competence. Winfield Scott is one of the most important forgotten figures of early American military history.

By 1814, the war began to turn a bit in favor of the Americans. The Battles of Chippewa and Lundy's Lane would see an American army well-drilled and holding its own conventionally, but by summer's end the British would find not much had changed since the Revolution, America still occupied a lot of space and Americans had remained just as stubborn. The Battle of Chippewa represented a tie, but Scott's well-disciplined troops now had more than held their own. Standing toe to toe and exchanging volleys with the British, an impeccably executed bayonet charge closed the deal. Fighting at **Lundy's Lane** with only 1,000 troops to the British 1,800, Scott attacked boldly and fought into the dark. According to one source, veterans of earlier battles and the Napoleonic Wars claimed this was the fiercest fight ever witnessed to date.[100] While the numbers revealed a tie, the British lost about thirty percent and the Americans forty, but as is often the case, numbers do not tell the whole story.[101] Americans had gained confidence in themselves and their leadership. It is important to recall the British remained a global superpower at this time and in the process of defeating the legendary Napoleon, had found themselves held to check by the Americans. Morale is an ever-important aspect of warfare!

The British went on the offensive in August of 1814 and attacked toward Fort Erie. During a heavy rain downpour, the attacking British forces actually breached the fortified walls of Ft. Erie, but as they turned cannon toward the occupants inside the fort, a spark from the muzzle blast of the cannon fell through the flooring into a stockpile of gunpowder, blowing the British forces away. Nine hundred casualties out of 2,500 attackers proved more costly than even Lundy's Lane. This third campaign for the Niagara region resulted in yet another failure, while the American militia received laudatory complements from General Brown who continued to develop subordinate leaders as he had Winfield Scott.[102] The final attack of the central region would fall at Lake Champlain in New York.

The British had defeated Napoleon and with his exile to Elba, over 8,000 troops prepared to attack in America. The basic British idea consisted of a plan to attack the United States from the north, somewhat reminiscent of Burgoyne in the Revolution, while the British navy and assigned troops hit strategic points on the seaboard to the south around the Chesapeake Bay.[103]

By September 1814, while the battle for Erie still raged, British General Sir George Prevost slowly advanced south toward Plattsburg, New York, while another naval arms race similar to that of Lake Erie again saw British and Americans desperately building fleets on different sides of the lake. The Americans won again. American troops had previously left Plattsburg to go to Niagara and the few militia and regulars who occupied it would rigorously defend the lightly defended fort. Prevost, suddenly becoming cautious, proceeded to pull rank on his junior naval Captain George Downie, ordering him to attack the American fleet sitting in the bay adjacent to Plattsburg facing the open water of Lake Champlain. While Prevost's troops waited situated on high ground across the river staring at the American forces, American shipbuilders had performed miracles. The Brown Brothers, Adam and Noah, had replicated what they had done for Perry on Lake Erie, except in even less time. Master Commandant Thomas Macdonough placed his green wood fleet brilliantly using geography and his knowledge of seamanship. By placing his small fleet just inside the mouth of the bay at Plattsburg in line, Macdonough had ensured that any north wind necessary to bring the British fleet to attack him

---

99. Perret, *A Country*, 123.
100. Allison, Wm. T, Grey, Jeffery, & Valentine, Janet G. *American Military History 2nd Ed*. Pearson: Upper Saddle River, NJ, 2013, 107.
101. Perret, *A Country*, 124.
102. Borneman, *1812*, 197.
103. Allison, *American Military*, 108.

would necessitate the bows of their advancing ships to face his line of broadsides.[104] However, dramatically Macdonough used initiative and imagination to achieve maximum firepower. At the crucial moment of the battle, he had arranged for the ship *Saratoga* to spin 180 degrees around using winches and anchor chains, in time to give the final deathblow of the naval battle, achieving an American victory.[105] American ingenuity had defeated the second blow of the one-two punch planned for the British in America for 1814, but what had happened on the coast earlier?

The late summer of 1814 would find Admiral Alexander Cochrane and British General Robert Ross both working in tandem, hoping to cash in on the rich prizes and notoriety they would obtain from attacking the rich American coastal cities and the national capital. Instead, an empty campaign would result in growing American confidence reflected throughout the south and the emergence of an unconventional warrior.

On August 24, 1814, the British fleet and soldiers crossed the Potomac River landing in Maryland where they fought the first engagement of their march on Washington D.C. Landing at Bladensburg, MD, Ross immediately brushed off the militia and fired scary, but ineffective, rockets at the Americans. Lined up in subsequent lines of defense, the Americans, in what started as an orderly retreat by an American regular army, began. As the troops arrived in the subsequent lines, things grew complicated and eventually confusion ensued and resulted in panic. The third and final line of American marines and sailors stood and fired devastating grapeshot into the faces of the leading British light infantry troops, causing numerous casualties.[106] With shouts of "board them," the American marines and sailors provided the only notable resistance that day. So fast did American troops run that few American prisoners saw capture in these "Bladensburg Races."[107] Madison went onto the battlefield looking probably a bit ridiculous with his borrowed dueling pistols at his waist. The Father of the Constitution found it convenient to retreat expeditiously, along with the rest of his government attendants, when British rockets began landing.[108]

Marching into Washington the British commanders quickly realized that no one remained to surrender the city. A complete evacuation to include the seat of government left an empty city. Attempts to hit the American "center of gravity" with a knockout blow had failed just as it had during the American Revolution it seems. The lesson here is the limits of military force. Great damage to world public opinion resulted by burning libraries and public buildings; Ross's decision appeared to be barbarous practices, or what today would be called bad optics. Perhaps even more important, it seems from this point on Americans had started to fight more fiercely throughout the American theaters of war, or maybe just out of anger and shame for the burning of the nation's capital.

At Baltimore, attempts to use bomb ships by Admiral Cochrane to flatten Baltimore failed when the British had to keep them out of range of Fort McHenry. The bombs bursting in air found immortality when Francis Scott Key, observing the bombardment from a prison ship, put the words to music creating the National Anthem. American militia had stood firm at Baltimore, killing Ross at the Battle of High Point as the growing courage of the troops revealed itself in severe numbers of British casualties. The morale of the war had seemed to change, eventually forcing Cochrane to withdraw his ships from the Chesapeake Bay where

Francis Scott Key (1779-1843) awakes on September 14, 1814, to see the American flag still waving over Fort McHenry. "Defense of Fort M'Henry"

---

104. Borneman, *1812*, 206.
105. Perret, *A Country*, 127.
106. Millett, Allan R. *Semper Fidelis*. Macmillan: New York, 1980, 49.
107. Perret, *A Country*, 125.
108. Perret, *A Country*, 125.

he then sailed to Jamaica and attempted to force a series of ports from the Americans in Pensacola and Mobile Bay. Each time Cochrane attempted to come ashore, militia led by Andrew Jackson would defeat him.

Andrew Jackson emerged as an important military leader during the Southern Phase of the War of 1812. This fascinating character represented the militia ideal. Andrew Jackson fought the Creeks and, with relentless ruthlessness, destroyed them. Jackson's reputation emerged onto the stage of national attention at the Battle of New Orleans, and together with Jackson's participation in the First Seminole War, he would emerge as a true national hero on his way to the White House.

President James Madison balanced his desire for America to expand into Spanish Florida, as part of a secret Congressional plan designed to support Spanish uprisings in Florida with a Presidential desire to appear above board well within the limits of international law. When the War against Britain in the War of 1812 started, this pretense at non-interference dropped amid attacks on Amelia Island by private adventurers. Though the hopes of eventual popular uprisings that would bring Florida into the union failed, Andrew Jackson's victories against the Creeks would ultimately set the path for the eventual integration of Florida into the United States with the Adams-Onis Treaty of 1819.

The Creek Wars represented a sad continuation of the seemingly constant Indian Wars and reflected a war within a war fought in the American south during the War of 1812. Tecumseh had visited Creeks back in 1811 and had lobbied hard for them to join his confederation. By 1813, civil war had broken out between the Upper and Lower Creek Indian tribes when a massacre led to the deaths of 500 men, women, and children at Ft. Mims, about thirty-five miles north of Mobile, Alabama. Spanish officials took advantage of the situation by offering to arm the militant Red Stick Warriors (Creeks).[109] The federal government chose to intervene. By November of 1813, eager volunteers from Tennessee, Georgia, and Mississippi joined with Madison's federal troops as the Americans and their Cherokee and Choctaw allies attacked in converging columns from three directions, with the primary attack coming from Tennessee. Andrew Jackson led the way.

Andrew Jackson destroyed the Creeks through time-proven methods of Indian fighting and by pure will. Engaged in tough fights until March of 1814, Jackson methodically built a series of bases on the Tennessee River. As he moved slowly south, forces under General John Coffee attacked the Creeks at Tallasahatchee on November third. Using an advantage in numbers and supplies, the troops under John Coffee attacked. Davy Crockett, who would become famous from his frontier exploits, said of the battle later, "We shot them down like dogs."[110] As a lack of supplies saw militia starting to melt away, Jackson, still half-dead from previous dueling injuries, doggedly kept on. Fighting a slow war of attrition soon presented an overwhelming victory as Jackson's forces approached Horseshoe Bend.

The **Battle of Horseshoe Bend** on March 27, 1814 represented the end of the Red Stick warriors and a catastrophic defeat for the Creek Nation. Jackson used a double envelopment to destroy his foes. General John Coffee's Tennessee cavalry attacked across the Tallapoosa River while Jackson's men frontally assaulted the fort placed on the bend in the river. Jackson's troops killed over 1,000 Creeks in a crushing victory. When Red Eagle approached Andrew Jackson to surrender, the sick and weak Jackson magnanimously allowed the Chief to walk from the lines unencumbered.[111]

So desperate had the Indians become, they reportedly were "picking up the grains of corn scattered from the mouths of the horses."[112] The Treaty of Fort Jackson resulted in the United States acquiring more than 20 million acres of land. Jackson had crushed the Indians, who received little of the expected help from the British and Spanish they believed forthcoming. Jackson had moved too fast, it seems. Some of the Chieftains instead fled to Florida, where the Spanish governor had earlier congratulated them after the massacre at Ft. Mims.[113] Many of these same Indians would fight in the Seminole Wars. Meanwhile, Jackson received a promotion to Major General of Regulars and

---

109. Borneman, *1812*, 144.
110. Perret, *A Country*, 128.
111. Utley, Robert M., & Washburn, Wilcomb E. *Indian Wars*. American Heritage: New York, 1977, 129.
112. Ibid., 129.
113. Perret, *A Country*, 129.

assumed command of the U.S. southern forces headquartered in New Orleans, where he waited for the expected blow from the British.[114]

The Americans repulsed British attempts to take Mobile Bay in Sept 1814 when land-based artillery and disciplined regulars held their own against attempts by Royal Marines to storm ashore. Jackson, with characteristic energy, seized the initiative by attacking Pensacola. Once again, charging with Coffee's Tennessee cavalry and 4,000 troops that attacked from the east after making a diversionary feint to the west of the city. As the Americans entered the city, the British had sailed safely away.[115] The real fight would be at New Orleans, the strategic prize on the Mississippi River, and would see Andrew Jackson emerge into the national limelight.

The emergence of Andrew Jackson resulted from an overwhelming military victory against the British at **New Orleans** early in 1815. The Battle for New Orleans began when Lieutenant General Sir Edward Packenham arrived fresh with experienced troops; this hero of the battle of Salamanca in the Napoleonic wars would dig his own grave as well as for many of his troops in New Orleans. Jackson had earlier gambled New Orleans would be the target for the British and he quickly took advantage of the natural defenses of the area. Militia, free blacks, and even pirates had joined forces, expecting pardons for earlier depredations while Jackson declared martial law the last month of 1814. Boldness and initiative combined with 6,000 troops would ensure an overwhelming military victory over the British, who landed about 14,000 total forces.

General Andrew Jackson on horseback commanding U.S. troops in the Battle of New Orleans, January 8, 1815.

The Royal Navy wiped aside opposition at Lake Borgne. On the 22nd, an advance force probed within seven miles of New Orleans hit when Jackson again seized the initiative in a night attack, stalling the British advances, giving him more time to prepare defenses. By brilliantly using both natural and fabricated obstacles, Jackson won the battle before it started. With the Mississippi River on one flank and a swamp on the other connected by a canal, he covered fire from three defensive lines, throwing up everything but the kitchen sink. Cotton bales had been hauled in and piled up to compensate for the high water table and wet soil.

On New Year's Day 1815, an ineffective artillery duel accomplishing little to help Packenham took place in preparation for the great battle. A week later on January 8, 1815, the British General ordered the attack. Signaling for the assault to begin with a rocket, British troops assaulted the five-foot tall mud wall known as Line Jackson. As the Red Coats leaned forward after daybreak and into a wall of deadly lead, virtual suicide resulted. Jackson's four ranks of riflemen laid down a burst of aimed fire every fifteen seconds. Overwhelming firepower as well as flanking fire from a gunship on the Mississippi stopped the assault dead in its tracks. The British commander had overthought in his planning when he assigned troops to lay down fascines, bundles of sticks to help them negotiate the anticipated physical obstacles. Complex plans under fire quickly turned into confusion. Turning the wrong way in the deadly slaughter house, the 93rd Highlanders of the British Army charged and paid the price when a naval thirty-two-pounder loaded with triple shot fired into their exposed left flank, knocking ranks of men down like bowling pins. In little over half an hour the British lost 300 killed and 1,200 wounded in comparison to Jackson's mere thirteen dead and thirty-nine wounded.[116] One spectator described the silent battlefield as a sea of red because of the scattered red coats laying side by side.[117] The

---

114. Allison, *American Military*, 112.
115. Ibid., 113.
116. Allison, *American Military*, 114.
117. Borneman, *1812*, 290.

overwhelming American victory at New Orleans ignited nationalistic passions and went far to preventing the sectional breakup that had been threatened with the Hartford Convention.

The New Orlean's victory would ensure provisions of the **Treaty of Ghent** dictating (again) that British forces would finally leave America. The War continued even as it had ended. The British hit at Mobile on February 8, 1815. The British had signed earlier treaties such as the Treaty of Paris in 1783 and had not left the old Northwest. If the Battle of New Orleans had gone the British way, who was to say they would have ever left?

Seminole and Blackhawk Wars

Winfield Scott developed a professional standing army painfully reduced by a Congress still suspicious of a standing military. Scott toured Europe to study their militaries and demonstrated an autodidactic willingness to embrace education as an auto. One of the few setbacks this greatest of forgotten leaders in American military history ever faced would be an instructive reminder of the American propensity toward quick efficient actions, something war seldom ever is. **The Seminole Wars** would be a proving ground for the young nation buoyed with confidence after the War of 1812 and would represent a continuation of the winning tradition of combining militia and line in tandem with the need to fight unconventional war. The First Seminole War in December 1817 served to temper nationalistic zeal while serving as a sober reminder of the present dangers on the borders of the nation. Secretary of War John Calhoun ordered Andrew Jackson south where he promptly attacked Pensacola.

First Seminole War 1817-1818

The Seminoles represented a name given to an amalgam of Creek Indians and freed slaves who had interbred with various other native-peoples. After the War of 1812 and the treaty of Ghent, by the summer of 1816, Brigadier General Edmund P. Gaines dispatched forces from southwest Georgia to the Apalachicola River where American gunboats tore apart the fort occupied by runaway slaves. A series of raids ensuing would cause Gaines to send troops into Northern Georgia just across the border from Florida, demanding the turnover of fugitives. When received, Gaines ordered reprisal burnings of the Indian villages; the resultant movement of Native-Americans fleeing south into the Floridian swamps presaged the beginning of attacks starting the First Seminole War. Jackson, sent to Florida on a mission to punish the Seminoles, exceeded his instructions when, after burning food stores and destroying villages, he proceeded to take Florida from the Spanish after attacking Pensacola. Jackson promptly installed a provisional government and paved the way to American expansion through the **Adams-Onis Treaty of 1819**. Andrew Jackson, now front and center on the national spotlight for his apparently decisive victories in New Orleans and now Florida, would emerge as a symbol of American nationalism. Meanwhile Florida would go on as a frontier through two more wars.

Second Seminole War 1836-1842

The Second Seminole War of 1836-1842 reflected a national removal policy sweeping through America. Friendly Seminoles feared Osceola who gained a following after dramatically driving a knife into the government offer to send them south for recompense. Seminoles cut off and killed two companies of U.S. soldiers in Dade's Massacre in December of 1835. Appointed by President Andrew Jackson in January 1836, Winfield Scott blundered about for months attempting to use conventional forces and converging columns to defeat what essentially represented a counterinsurgency. The Seminoles attacked in small bands, disappearing as fast as they appeared. In disgust at the inconclusiveness, Jackson sent America's premier soldier, Winfield Scott, to Alabama to oversee a minor Creek uprising. Seizing the strategic initiative, the Seminoles attacked Gaines at Tampa in fierce fighting, but then chose not to attack when Scott's replacement, Thomas Jesup, offered fixed battle hoping for a victory. Eventually Jesup seized various leaders including Osceola, under a flag of truce in October of 1837, when a different type of Indian fighter had emerged: Zachary Taylor.

In contrast to Scott, known as "old fuss and feathers," in part due to his preoccupation with details and military smartness, Zachary Taylor represented a sort of Grant-type figure, plainly and tenaciously single minded in his approach to war. Taylor won a major victory at the Battle of Lake Okeechobee, but later discarded the notion of the type of conventional fight Scott had found so attractive. Taylor decided victory would only result from the time-honored method of exerting pressure on Seminole food stores, as stated in earlier advice given by the ultimate Indian fighter Jackson.[118] By maintaining constant patrols, the Indians had been unable to plant crops. Relentless pursuit, dangerous patrols, and an emphasis on the food fight would be the type of warfare that reflected an American success throughout the panorama of the entire Indian military experience, and the no-frills leadership of a somewhat singularly determined and patient officer like Taylor would continue to point the way for future successes in the American West.

Eventually replacing Taylor in April 1839, Major General Alexander Macomb, a burner, saw the intensity and cruelty of the fighting increased by the time General Walker K. Armistead introduced the use of bloodhounds. Water and disease took their tolls until August 1841, when Colonel William J. Worth took command. Combining the total warfare efforts of his predecessors into a combined arms force of naval and army patrols, he eventually starved the Seminole peoples into submission by attacking their foodstuffs and means of support. Food fights sadly continued to be an effective means for defeating the Indians, just as it had since the beginning.

Black Hawk War

The Black Hawk War represented the final sad chapter in the destruction of Native-American culture east of the Mississippi River. On a spring day in 1832, Black Hawk lead the Sauk and Fox peoples across the Mississippi and into Illinois in an attempt to return to their traditional lands, the governor of the state attempted to stop what he characterized as an "invasion." When 300 militiamen attempted to confront the Indians at a fight known later as "Stillman's Run," the Illinois men ended up running in cowardly fashion from the approximately 40 warriors in the confused fighting. The panic of the militia, though obviously not a victory tended, to whip up more anti-Indian feelings throughout the state. Swelling roles of volunteer and regulars under Winfield Scott would see a relentless pursuit of the beleaguered Indians. In the aftermath and excitement of their victory at Stillman's Run, further massacres observed by Abraham Lincoln would shape anti-native sentiments for generations. Eventually retreating back to the Mississippi river and into Wisconsin, the now whittled down forces of Black Hawk faced defeats at Wisconsin Heights and at the Battle of Bad Axe on 2 August 1832. Trapped on the banks of the Mississippi, Black Hawk escaped as the majority of his followers perished. Captured by 25 August, Black Hawk surrendered and gave up large parts of Iowa, representing the end of the Indian Wars in the Old Northwest.

Analysis

Scott's leadership represents the natural order and conformity inherently at risk in an egalitarian society. The Indian frontier served to remind Americans how they must fight a war with no fronts. One of Scott's few defeats, the Seminole Wars reveal how impatience defeated this brilliant general with a profound preference for set piece line battles. Scott disregarded Jackson's advice to relentlessly pursue the enemy; seeking out, finding their homes, and forcing them to defend them. Scott further received advice to follow a type of "food fight" strategy by hitting the Indians where it would hurt, a winning formula since colonial days. Scott voiced later how he rejected unconventional warfare for fear it would ". . . [fix] upon him the character of a partisan officer, whereas it was his ambition to conduct sieges and command in open fields, serried lines, and columns."[119] Furthermore, Scott did not follow his own requirements to minimize supplies, carrying an excellent collection of wine

---

118. Clark, J.P. *Preparing for War.* Harvard University Press: Cambridge, MA, 2017, 44.
119. Clark, *Preparing for War*, 42.

into the field with him. Lacking in ruthlessness and determined not to violate his own moral code, Scott, while a brilliant leader who would oversee the intellectual growth of the army, simply could not bring himself to engage in the type of total warfare necessary to win in Florida.[120]

Scott later even faced an inquiry on his conduct launched by the furious President Jackson who believed another relief of Scott by Jesup, this time in Alabama, had demonstrated incompetency. This diverging view of warfare between conventional and the more expedient and unconventional against the Indians would eventually subside and Scott would continue in a brilliant military career. Conventional excellence in Mexico followed service under President Van Buren during the Cherokee removal of 1838. The emergent Gaines-Scott rivalry essentially reflected the homespun pride of the militia traditions and the embodied American Spirit personified by Andrew Jackson in contrast to the European elitist ideal that Scott represented. Out of this diversity in views would emerge another victorious general and president—Zachary Taylor.

The War with Mexico

The war with Mexico consisted of a short conflict characterized by American boldness, aggressiveness, a need to be attacked first, and a political contest between the President and an Army balanced in forces between militia and professionals. An impulse to move west, described by historians as Manifest Destiny, consisted of the natural societal seeking vertical or natural borders ultimately in the form of the Pacific Ocean. A large part of this movement west consisted of Southerners, who moved to Texas and into a collision with the values of a Mexican Revolution; a centrally controlled government under Santa Ana and the sensibilities of the United States.

1845 Map of the Texas Republic, United States, Mexico, and Central America.

James K. Polk, a Tennessean mostly forgotten today, both idolized Jackson and supported the militia concept. Distrustful of the professional military, his paranoia heightened with the realization that virtually all his generals had Whig Party sympathies. This most partisan Democratic leader, President Polk would work himself to an early grave in an attempt to fulfill all of his campaign promises within a single term

---
120. Ibid., 44.

and no one knew better than he the risks of creating military heroes. A loyal disciple to the great Andrew Jackson, Polk's dedication to party politics would be plagued by the threatening emergence of another "man of the people," either Zachary Taylor or the scholarly and aristocratic Winfield Scott.

Zachary Taylor, beloved by the militias and regulars alike, presaged the humble appearances that would mark American leaders like Ulysses Grant. John S. D. Eisenhower in the book *So Far From God* tells the story of a conversation Taylor had with one of his men somewhat humorously, illustrative of the nature of the General and his ability to produce no frills results:

Zachary Taylor (1784-1850)

> *A certain lieutenant who prided himself on belonging to one of the first of the State of Virginia went up to headquarters to obtain a glimpse of the general. Seeing an old man cleaning a sword in a bower, the officer went in and addressed the bronze-faced old gentleman hard at work in his shirtsleeves: "I say, old fell', can you tell me where I can see General Taylor?" The old "fell" without rising replied, "Wull, stranger, that is the old hoss's tent," pointing to the headquarters. "Lieutenant, if you please," said the F.F. V. "And by the way, my old trump, whose sword is that you are cleaning?" "Wull, Colonel," replied the old man, "I don't see there is any harm in telling you, seeing's you're an officer. This sword belongs to the general himself." The lieutenant took off his sword and said, "My good man, I would like to have you clean my sword, and I shall come tomorrow to see the general and then I will give you the dollar." The lieutenant was on hand the next day, and seeing his old friend of the day before standing under an awning conversing with some officers, he beckoned to him to come over. The old gentleman came out, bringing the lieutenant's sword. The lieutenant was profuse in his thanks and, giving the old man a poke in the ribs, said, "Come, old fatty, show me General Taylor and the dollar is yours." The "old fatty" drew himself up and said, "Lieutenant! I am General Taylor" — he turned slowly around—"and I will take that dollar!" The next day the general had the lieutenant introduced in due form.*[121]

Throughout American history, there has been a dualistic cultural notion that the "bad guy," often seen in a black hat, shoots first but somehow the good guy (white hat) responds and, in righteous vindication, ultimately wins the fight. This means of fighting war proved true in Mexico, at Fort Sumter, Pearl Harbor, and even on 9/11. During the war with Mexico, the first blow would fall at the **Battle of San Jacinto.** Texans rose up and fought in righteous indignation after hearing the news of Mexican atrocities (black hats) at the Alamo and later the Goliad River. On 21 April 1836, Texans (white hats) zealously ambushed at the Mexican Army conducting a siesta. Mexico granted Texas independence and agreed to a border of the Rio Grande River. A decade of Mexican civil war then transpired and questions of borders arose again. Polk, following Andrew Jackson's advice, sent Zachary Taylor south. Taylor's demeanor was one of plainness, simplicity, and stubborn tenaciousness like the volunteers who adoringly mobbed toward him willing to join the looming fight against Mexico. On April 4, 1846, Mexico declared war—attacking Taylor's encamped troops on the north side of the Rio Grande, killing sixteen. The "bad guys" had drawn first! Now the "good guys" would respond, or at least that is how history has tended to tell the tale. The truth more accurately is the American Army, utilizing both conventional and unconventional initiatives, destroyed one of the finest armies ever created.

On May 13, 1846, Congress, in response to the President's request for war, extended the militia's term of service from three to six months and called for 50,000 volunteers to serve for twelve

---

121. Eisenhower, John S.D. *So Far from God*. Doubleday: New York, 1989, 36.

months, or the duration of the war at the President's discretion.[122] The navy used steam ships for the first time at war to blockade the coasts of Mexico, preventing foreign resupplies in what came to be a tediously boring but important aspect of the war.[123] Meanwhile, American troops, like avenging angels, moved south.

At **Palo Alto,** outnumbered three to one, Taylor admonished his men that "their main dependence must be in the bayonet.[124] It would be the American artillery progenitors of a long tradition of West Point emphasis and excellence, however, that showed its skill when it outgunned the Mexicans. The "Flying artillery" mobile, horse pulled and firing grape shot made perfect for close range fighting, filled the gaps in the American lines as infantry formed squares against attacking Mexican cavalry. Napoleonic Warfare was at its finest; pennants, brass glittering, colored uniforms, and precision movements all. Halting only to let the smoke clear, the Mexicans attacked in columns made to order for the "bowling ball" of the artillery, which quickly destroyed them through overwhelming firepower, tossing men aside as if bowling pins. The Mexicans faced total shock at the outcome of Palo Alto, certainly not to be the last adversaries of America to do so. The Mexican commanders in briefing their troops had greatly underestimated the United States; thinking sectionalism and the military weakness of these pale people to the north would result in their rapid battlefield destruction.[125] Morale was always important in war and on full display as the army advanced to Buena Vista.

Mexican-American War, Battle of Palo Alto, May 8, 1846.

Taylor pursued the Mexican army south, seemingly on pure aggression—no strategy, just driving forward while the American Navy let Santa Ana return. The wily Mexican leader was welcomed as a savior, now apparently forgiven by those who had previously fought him for power. The Americans, in a particular nuance of diplomatic underhandedness, had let this "Napoleon of the West" (as he called himself) back into the country as it would later transport Emilio Aguinaldo during the Philippines war a half century later. The wisdom of knowing the adversary learned in the Indian Wars apparently had atrophied. At Monterrey, good fortune favored the bold.

A diversion on the city of **Monterrey** on September 20, 1846 turned into a full frontal assault that worked! Avoiding a fierce black castle to the north of the Mexican city, Taylor sent his best officer, Captain William. J. Worth on a reconnaissance-in-force to hook around the city and avoided the dark northern castle standing like a monolith standing guard to the north of the city. A magnificent assault by Mexican lancers started the opening moves for an American advance on the city. Repulsed with skirmisher tactics, the Americans boldly assaulted up the heights of Federacion Hill, turning the sole Mexican artillery piece there and firing with remarkable targeting on enemy positions to the east of the same hill mass. With a single shot knocking out an enemy gun on Fort Soldado, the road to the city now lay open.[126] Taylor allowed the Mexicans to depart when the Americans surrendered the city. Polk furiously told Taylor to stay put—better to keep a popular general from getting too big for his britches! Taylor followed his own logic instead and attacked again at Saltillo. Reconnaissance by the Texas Rangers revealed to Taylor Santa Anna's army nearby. With Santa Anna in pursuit, the Americans pulled up to a ranch about six miles from Saltillo at a system of natural defiles in the earth called Buena Vista.

Buena Vista represented a virtual who's who of America's Civil War history. Many young officers and future political leaders would cut their teeth into the "glory" of combat under Taylor during the

---

122. Millet, Allan R., & Maslowski, Peter. *For the Common Defense.* Free Press: NY, 1994, 149.
123. Ibid., 150.
124. Ibid., 145.
125. Millet, *Common Defense,* 146.
126. Eisenhower, *So Far,* 133.

fight. Hurriedly forming into a giant V-shaped formation, apparently the volunteers did not have the drill experience of an army capable of forming a line. Fortunately, the Americans had surreptitiously created a fire pocket capable of dealing out murderous flanking fires. Firepower annihilated the approaching Mexican army. Mississippi riflemen extinguished the lights of brightly colored Mexican cavalry from long range, but it would be the fierceness and valor of the hand-to hand combat in short range that Henry Clay would remember as he fell wounded beside his Kentucky troops. Cool under fire, Zachary Taylor instructed Braxton Bragg of future western theater Civil War fame to double shot his guns "and give 'em hell!" The first salvo of artillery staggered the Mexican line, while the second and third lines slowly fell back from the onslaught.[127] The Mexican Army continually attacked repeatedly and narrowly achieved defeat each time. In one harrowing battle, Jefferson Davis, the future President of the Confederacy, demonstrated manly martial qualities by leading lancers and men with bowie knives hacking into the Mexican infantry. Buena Vista would be the turning point of the war from which Mexico would remain on the defensive for the rest of the time. Taylor's war now ended and he waited to take Polk's place as President in the White House.

Meanwhile, back home the opposition Whig Party denounced "Mr. Polk's War," but wisely played to patriotism by supporting it. Better to support the binding and intoxicating drink of Manifest Destiny. The destiny of Americans to see their nation expand to the Pacific received help from military expeditions.

When Fremont planted the American flag in the Northwest of Oregon and Northern California back in 1845, he determined to return, and did with a third expedition west. Lawlessness and a lack of control served to pull the Army to the coast as well as appealed to America's yearning to continue moving west called Manifest Destiny. Rapidly placing a star for Texas on a flag with a bear, Fremont raised the flag of California up over San Francisco, really without any legal authority.[128] While to the south Admiral Stockton sent armed sailors ashore to post further claims. Kearny headed west, gained the loyalty of New Mexicans and protection from marauding Kiowa and Commanches, then sent forces into Utah to protect the Mormons while a task force of mounted volunteers headed south to link up with Taylor's army under Alexander W. Doniphan. Immortalized in military history by super human accomplishments, the expeditions of so few soldiers had added so much land to the United States so quickly as to boggle the imagination.

The real battle for **California** rested on the aggressiveness of Brigadier General Stephen W. Kearney, who by example kept armed cavalry in the saddle, and the victory against the Mexican forces of Andres Pico represented one of endurance. Crossing deserts, thirsty, starving, and enduring incredible hardships, Kearney stayed on the offensive using old frontier tricks of masking weakness with boldness. Kearney's efforts to keep the dragoons going paid off when he approached Southern California. The Navy, under Admiral Robert F. Stockton, arrived about forty miles distance southeast of present day Los Angeles. Meanwhile, Kearny and less than a couple hundred mounted dragoons defeated the forces of Andres Pico at the battle of San Gabriel, and the Battle of Mesa ended, winning the fight for California when Los Angeles surrendered on January 10, 1847.[129]

Winfield Scott seemed to presage George Marshall in a future century. With intense loyalty, the scholarship of Scott and the enthusiasm of the young men around him, many of whom would become Civil War leaders, led to the largest and most

Landing of the American forces under General Scott at Vera Cruz, March 9, 1847.

Source: Library of Congress

---

127. Bauer, K. Jack. *The Mexican War 1846–1848*. MacMillan: New York, 1974, 216.
128. Perret, Geoffrey. *A Country Made By War*. Random House: NY, 1989, 159.
129. Eisenhower, *So Far*, 229.

successful amphibious assault before World War II at **Veracruz**. On March 9, 1947 sailors rowed boats full of troops and supplies ashore. Protected with covering gunfire from a "mosquito fleet" stationed off the beaches and outside of grapeshot ranges from Mexican artillery, the landing truly was America's first D-day. Historical records later released on the eve of the Spanish American war a half century later revealed a level of planning unparalleled. Intricate plans of combat loading ensured armed men with rations would be taken from troop transports to smaller naval vessels and then to surf boats neatly stacked by size within each other. In short, successive steps of transport were designed to take advantage of the increasing shallowness of the waters against an armed enemy.[130] Taylor had done his job too. Santa Anna's army shattered from Buena Vista had to quell a revolt in Mexico City, further contributing to American successes. Coming ashore unharmed, the Americans faced a stone fortress overlooking the beach. Naval gunfire neutered the threat.

Moving inland, the five-month campaign to take Mexico City was a masterpiece of maneuver. Avoiding battle whenever possible, the lessons of Lundy's lane showed in Scott's attempts to prevent injuring Mexican pride or causing them to ignite in anger the way the British had in America in 1812. Awaiting Scott's army on the road was Santa Anna at **Cerro Gordo**. Sending Robert E. Lee, an engineer, to blaze a trail to the rear of the Mexicans, Scott then had his artillery hoist the cannons up a thin and dangerous trail to the Mexican rear. On April 18, the Mexicans panicked and the victorious confident American army drove on to Mexico City healthily resupplied from Veracruz.

Scott's 14,000-man Army faced Santa Anna's, surrounding Mexico City with 30,000.[131] Eschewing frontal assaults continued to execute brilliant maneuvers. Losing control of his exited soldiers, advancing to **Churubusco,** Scott with little room to maneuver and through fighting hand-to-hand finally succeeded on the third try to take the bridgehead. A sixteen-day armistice allowed the Mexicans to rebuild their defenses. Attacking on September 8th toward Molino del Rey (King's Mill) winning an extremely costly victory as the army, almost out of energy, reached Chapultepec castle. Continual artillery caused the fortress to fall and finally executing street fighting as a division, Scott marched down the causeway into the city. American artillery fired from a church belfry down into the surrounding plazas and streets. Aggressiveness and U.S. firepower convinced Santa Anna he must surrender the city.

Mexican-American War, the storming of Chapultepec, September 13, 1847.

Historians have long held up Scott's victory at Mexico City as one of the perfect occupant. While no doubt exaggerated, timely actions against bandits early on saw large fines parceled out to the alcaldes or the mayoral magistrates of the offending areas. Scott reached into the politician's pockets and found it worked wonders, as did humane treatment.[132] In fact, so efficiently did Scott employ local officials to deal with Mexican matters and military commissions to handle those of Americans and their interests, that a serious movement to incorporate the movement into the United States or even to offer the control of the nation to Scott emerged.[133]

Somewhat ironically, not only had President Polk fulfilled his campaign promises of "manifest destiny," he had also created his own replacement with a hero, Zachary Taylor; he created another success story in General Winfield Scott, who would later run for President himself. An attempt to receive a surrender probably contributed in large measure to Polk's failing health. Ignoring orders from Polk as Taylor had done at Buena Vista, at Mexico City Trist accepted a peace treaty totally ne-

---

130. Henry, Robert Self. *The Story of the Mexican War*. Da Capo: New York, 1989.
131. Perret, *A Country*, 135.
132. Bauer, *The Mexican War*, 269.
133. Ibid., 327.

gotiating on his own authority that the Senate would subsequently approve. The short length of the war contributed to unity, since sectionalism and an anti-war party did not have time to mobilize.[134]

California would be the scene of the discovery of gold within less than a month of the **Treaty of Guadalupe-Hidalgo.** The strange condition whereby a conqueror bought land from a subdued opponent, the Mexicans sold the United States the western lands for fifteen million dollars as well as claims for the land of California, New Mexico, and other parts of the American west. The Wilmot Proviso proposed to prohibit the introduction of slavery into the newly acquired territories in Mexico. The issue of slavery would ignite sectional differences, ultimately leading to Civil War.

Analysis

All wars help to spread new cultures. According to Geoffrey Perret, the terms entering the American lexicon included cigarettes, moustaches, and chewing gum. Meanwhile the use of steamboats for transport, telegraphs to communicate, and anesthetics for pain relief saw their advent in the Mexican War. More important in the context of the balance of conventional wars and unconventional wars and the American Ways of Fighting, the item of most importance perhaps would be the arrival of the war correspondent.[135]

The creation of West Point and a third generation of professionalism had ensured a disciplined amalgam of professional skilled engineers and artillerymen with an experienced corps of officers prepared to lead an expanding army of volunteers. General Winfield Scott and the brilliance of his lieutenants continued to examine scientifically the most efficient use of the line or regular army. Like Washington, who never quite grasped the use of militias but hired people around him who did, likewise Winfield Scott did his part to continue the long tradition of conventional military excellence and leadership.

The militia had also proven itself yet again. In an age of endless wars and global empires, it's easy to criticize the undisciplined rabble of the militia and volunteers, but to do so is to miss the point. America is not Europe and the nation is an empire today because of the energy and vibrant determination of free peoples so vividly demonstrated in the breathtaking victories of Mexico. Freedom loving Americans fighting in line as soldiers and more independently as aggressive skirmishers or warriors proved to be a winning combination in Mexico. In the years leading up to the Civil War, the Native Americans of the western plains would serve to remind Americans just what it means to be American and another long painful reminder that Americans can't win with a European-type army of aristocratic officers and machine-like dull-minded obedient automatons or soldiers.

The Civil War

Winfield Scott's Anaconda Plan depended on grinding the south down in a long patient encounter. Years ahead of his time, the great general had anticipated what victory would require. An American propensity toward rapid impatience would delay the workings of the Anaconda plan. By the time the winning strategy of using the coastlines, naval and technical superiority of the north, and the utilization of geography prevailed, the war had ground on for four long years. Ultimately, the key to success for the north would be control of the Mississippi River and the securement of Mobile Bay. A naval blockade and the grinding away of Union

The United States at the outbreak of the Civil War in 1861.

---

134. McCaffrey, James M. *Army of Manifest Destiny*. New York University Press: NY, 1992, 206.
135. Perret, *A Country*, 168.

troop strength in the upper south and on the coasts would destroy the Confederate States of America. Still, it is always easier to plan than to produce.

America essentially divided over the slavery issue after California entered the Union. A state's rights effort to protect property or to hold people in bondage conflicted with a militant nationalism and religious reform spreading throughout the north. First shots fired by Confederates at Charleston prevented the *Star of the West,* a Union ship, from resupply of the Union garrison outside the harbor. Lincoln proceeded to call up the militia for ninety days. The Confederates had quickly created a government and a Constitution in Montgomery, Alabama, and chosen the Mexican War veteran Jefferson Davis as President. Davis, wounded at Buena Vista, represented the martial romance of the south. Ft. Sumter would represent, in cowboy movie fashion, yet another classic "bad guy;" draws first, exciting northern passions and mobilizing Union volunteers' passions like avenging angels in righteous anger.

The Battle of First Manassas fought in July **1861** essentially proved the war would not be short. Like Winfield Scott, who used maneuver to best advantage in Mexico, General Irvin McDowell attempted to turn Beauregard's left. Confusion ensued in the Yankee ranks after Confederate troops dressed in blue fired on Union artillery; Confederates who had earlier been pushed off the hill attempted to attack again while fresh reinforcements poured in from nearby railroads. Virtually all Civil War Battles had a railroad line nearby or in some measure entered into the calculus of the excuse to fight. The result was a ruined picnic lunch for many of the Washingtonians who had come to see the battle as the Union army fled north. On July 4th, in response to Lincoln's request, Congress upped the ante by giving him more troops to the tune of half a million volunteers for three years.

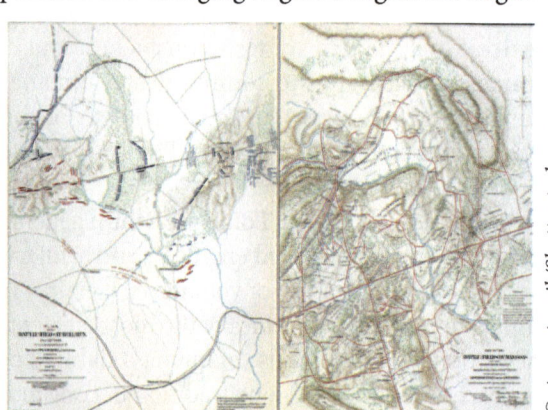

Maps of the battlefields of Manassas, July 21, 1861.

© steve estvanik/Shutterstock.com

> The Civil War did not begin well for the Union. The first two years from 1861–62 marked the low point for both the Union army and navy. Although the navy was the first to have the Medal of Honor established, the concept originated with the army. Assistant Adjutant General Lt. Colonel Edward Townsend first proposed a Medal of Honor.[136] In addition to serving as the assistant adjutant general, Lt. Colonel Townsend was the chief of staff for General Winfield Scott. Townsend suggested the Medal of Honor to General Scott shortly after the First Battle of Bull Run in July 1861, but the general soundly rejected the idea because it "smacked of British frippery and was wholly inappropriate to the republican principles laid by the founding fathers."[137]

The year **1862** saw simultaneous Union invasions in both the eastern and western theaters. While Lee rejected Scott's request to take over the Union's efforts, success would ultimately be the ruin of McClellan. A foreshadow of General Douglas MacArthur in both personality and career, McClellan had always been a brilliant young prodigy bound for great things. In historical hindsight, his campaigns in far western Virginia may have actually ensured a northern victory when he secured the Ohio River Valley—the strategic center of the U.S. since the French and Indian War. Indeed, no one questioned the competence of General McClellan as he marched with methodical slowness on Richmond. Indeed, by 24 May Union balloons could see the city. While McDowell's col-

---

136. Zimmerman, *Uncommon Valor,* 51.
137. Zimmerman, *Uncommon Valor,* 51–52.

umns headed south via the Shenandoah Valley, Confederate General J.E. Johnston hit McClellan in a series of swamp fights known as the Seven Days Battles. McClellan ended up retreating back to the James River saved by his artillery and the fiercely prodigious use of firepower that would mark American military forces ever since.

Minor peripheral actions (for those not there at least) occurred in March at Pea Ridge in Missouri, while the same month saw the Sante Fe Trail in the New Mexico territory secured as southern forces deflected back to Texas.

In the Western Theater Forts, Donaldson and Henry ensured the loss of Kentucky and most of Tennessee to the Confederates from February to April of 1862. "Unconditional Surrender," Grant emerged with the capture of Kentucky, and the Confederacy faced a terrific strategic loss with this fall. Further attempts to keep Grant from advancing failed. Not a cautious general like McClellan, he achieved victory without orders, letting his results speak for themselves—and Lincoln listened.

Grant's victories would continue throughout 1862 and into 1863 when he took the vital rail junctions at Corinth in northern Mississippi, and from there to the terrible fighting in April at Shiloh, Tennessee. A basic tie turned into a morale win in the North where the public hailed it as a victory. Confederate attempts to retake Corinth and Kentucky would fail at Perrysville about the same time as the Battle of Antietam in the east. A brilliant use of artillery at Perrysville, Kentucky allowed General Don C. Buell to stay on the defensive while Braxton Bragg murdered his army in frontal assaults against the high ground.[138] A turnstile of commanders came and went while U.S. Grant lingered in exile in the west. By December of 1862, Confederate forces faced yet another sound defeat at Murfreesboro outside of Nashville in Tennessee.

In the Eastern Theater from April to July, as the Union Army had approached Richmond cautiously (see above) and at the conclusion of the Seven Days Battles, General Robert E. Lee quickly moved north, adjacent to the previous year's fighting at the vital rail junction in Northern Virginia. The Battle of Second Manassas saw Lee's Army of Northern Virginia moved so deftly and with remarkable speed as to flank the newest member of the Union high command, Major General John Pope's army, before he could respond. Replaced by Lincoln and more egotistical than ever, General McClellan, despite having received a lost set of battle orders, still could not move decisively enough to destroy Lee's Army, which he allowed to escape after a horrendously bloody series of disastrous engagements delivered piecemeal throughout the day on September 17, 1862. Lincoln wisely took the opportunity to issue the Emancipation Proclamation, offering the southern states still "in rebellion" to return to the Union with their slaves. Knowing they would not, Lincoln still had achieved a moral victory over Constitutional law and set in motion the war machine bound for victory at Appomattox.

General George McClellan.

General Ulysses S. Grant (1822-1885).

---

138. Perret, Geoffrey. *A Country Made By War*. Random House: NY, 1989, 238.

Although General Scott rejected the idea, Secretary of the Navy Gideon Welles approved of it. The morale of the navy was especially low due to the high number of officers who resigned their commissions to fight for the Confederacy. Gideon Welles was able to get support in Congress through men like Senator James W. Grimes from Iowa, chairman of the Committee on Naval Affairs. On December 9, 1861, Congress proposed Public Resolution 82 creating the Navy Medal of Honor.[139] The bill passed in both houses and was signed into law by President Abraham Lincoln on December 21, 1861.[140] The Army Medal of Honor would not be created until General Winfield Scott retired as commanding general of the U.S. Army, and Secretary of War Edwin Stanton advocated for its creation. Senator Henry Wilson proposed a bill authorizing the creation of a Medal of Honor for the army, and President Lincoln signed the bill into law on July 12, 1862.[141]

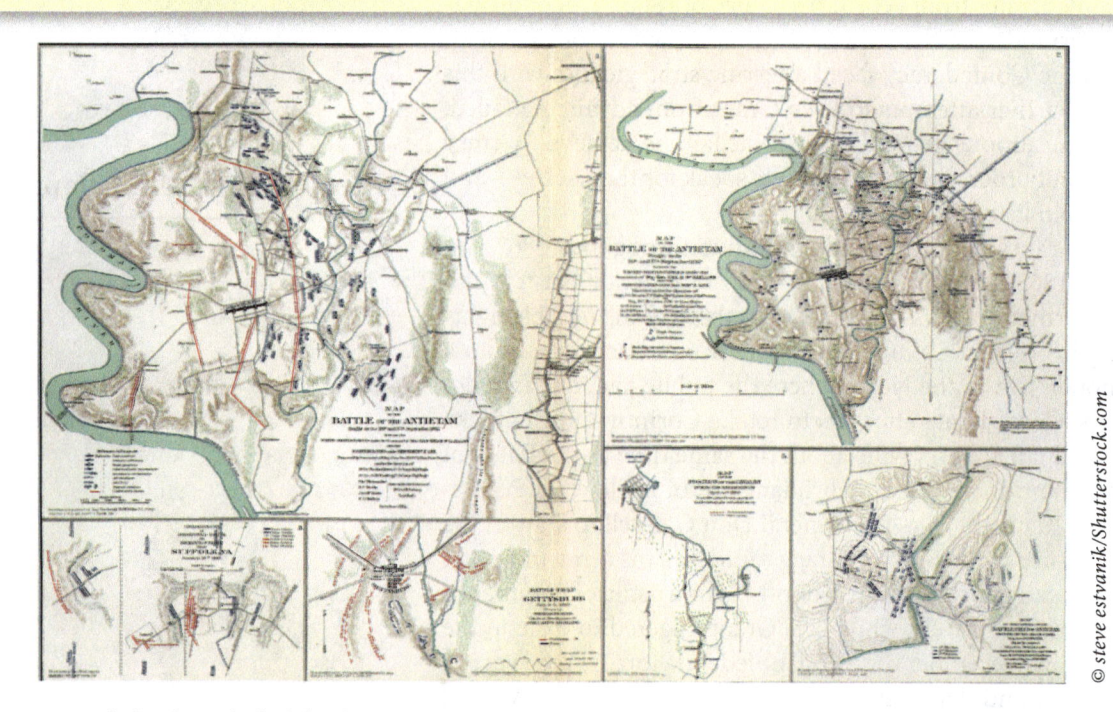

Maps of the battlefield of Antietam, 1862.

In the meantime, gloom continued to emanate from the Union Command. The popular McClellan, relieved yet again, would proceed to pursue his dreams in an attempt to become president with the Democratic nomination in 1864. Meanwhile at Fredericksburg, Virginia in December 1862, General Ambrose Burnside launched six frontal assaults with over 12,000 casualties and appearing almost mad, he about drove his army nuts on an infamous mud march to nowhere in an attempt to pursue Lee. Lincoln, seeking another general, hired General George Meade.

The year **1863** would prove to be the high water mark for Confederate ambitions. The Mississippi River had been a hard nut to crack. Attempts to do so had achieved much, but the little remaining proved paramount. In 1862, Admiral Farragut had come up the river past New Orleans, and then Port Hudson only ninety miles away fell the next month. By July 4,

Admiral David Farragut of the U.S. Navy.

---

139. The Boston Publishing Company ed., *The Medal of Honor*, 13.
140. The Boston Publishing Company ed., *The Medal of Honor*, 13.
141. The Boston Publishing Company ed., *The Medal of Honor*, 14.

1863 after a long siege ended, Confederate hopes to control the Mississippi by the victorious and tenacious General U.S. Grant would have the full attention in the White House as the South began the slow defensive war bound to lead to defeat.

Other hard fought battles in the Eastern Theater included Chattanooga and Chickamauga. Chattanooga, another major rail intersection, eventually surrendered the city by September 9. General James Longstreet arrived from Virginia and reinforced General Braxton Bragg's army of 66,000 men. At Chickamauga, five miles southeast of Chattanooga in dark Georgia forests, the Union army fell back behind log walls. The Confederates poured through a Union gap, but the units under George H. Thomas' corps held their ground. As deadly a battle as Antietam, two equally difficult and disliked commanders, Bragg, who would lose the services of Longstreet (who in disgust had packed up and headed east) and Rosecrans would be shortly relieved.[142] At Lookout Mountain on November 24, 1863 Grant's troops attacked, regaining not just the high ground, but also the morale needed for a drive on Atlanta!

Back east at Chancellorsville, VA, Lincoln's newest prima donna in charge named General Joseph Hooker, failed to use artillery effectively and instead allowed Lee to slip by his flank in a manner reminiscent of Lee putting the slip on Pope the year before on his way to Antietam. By 1863, attempts to take the war north and, in partial desperation, Lee's Confederate Army collided at Gettysburg. Union cavalry wisely chose high ground and ultimately Union troops occupied a series of fishhook shaped high ground, Lee's army would impale itself against northern steel. Attempts to take the southern hill known as Little Round Top saw the Union valiantly hold, while the next day Lee faced frustrating delays in his command as General J.E.B. Stuart and James Longstreet had difficulty providing either intelligence or results. In partial frustration, Lee ordered a frontal assault against the Union center, similar to one he had experienced in the Mexican War where, as a younger officer, he witnessed Winfield Scott's desperate assault at Churubusco. The wounded army of Northern Virginia limped south as changes to the Army of the Potomac continued.

The Battle of Gettysburg. View from the summit of Little Round Top at 7:30 P.M. July 3, 1863.

---

142. Perret, *A Country*, 227.

> Like the Badge of Military Merit, the Navy and Army Medals of Honor were only intended for enlisted personnel. They were also only meant to be temporary medals awarded for actions during the Civil War. However, in March 1863 Congress made the award permanent, and army officers were eligible. However, navy officers would not be eligible to receive the Medal of Honor until March 3, 1915.[143] The first Medal of Honor was awarded to Private Jacob Parrott on March 25, 1863.[144] As an example of early awards, his citation reads, "One of the 19 of 22 men [. . .] who, penetrated nearly 200 miles south into enemy territory and captured a railroad train at Big Shanty, Ga., in an attempt to destroy the bridges and tracks between Chattanooga and Atlanta."[145] As the bloody Civil War continued, the military would submit hundreds of soldiers' acts of gallantry for Congress to recognize.

By **1864** Lincoln had wearied of Meade's inaction after Gettysburg the previous summer, and with less and less patience for the slowness of his subordinates decided to bring Grant east. The contrast of Robert E. Lee and Ulysses S. Grant has made for endless historical comparisons due to the times they each represented. The son of "Light Horse" Harry Lee, Robert's father passed on to his son an appetite for a lost aristocratic ardor and the association with military glories. Having faced a year in debtor's prison and a failed plantation owner, the disciplined intense son surely equated the military past of his father with glory and perhaps even redemption. Grant, on the other hand, had failed at everything he had ever done, hated West Point, and avoided military parades and uniforms. Repulsed by the sight of blood, this son of a shopkeeper nearly became the town drunk and saw war eventually through the eyes of a very modern and practical war manager.

Contrasts aside, Grant moved south and with him, a blue juggernaut leaving a trail of desolation and bloody cart ruts as men groaning filled what seemed a never-ending train of ambulances headed north for burial and amputation. Recognizing the unending wealth of firepower Grant's army now possessed, Lee chose areas of dense woodlands forcing the armies to fight in smaller units as he continued to fall back under the unrelenting pressure of this hero of Vicksburg.

June 2, position near Cold Harbor.

Source: Library of Congress

Grant cut Sheridan loose in columns of four on horseback spreading for thirteen miles, attacked and destroyed Confederate cavalry in what would presage the army's relentless armored columns to be deployed in Europe eighty years later during World War II. The geography of rivers forced delays on Grant as well as continued to funnel the Union army to the Southeast away from the defenses of Richmond. The "butcher" Grant, as painful and vengeful wails cried for justice through the north while fatality lists nailed to walls grew longer, continued with a coldly fixated

---

143. Zimmerman, Uncommon Valor, 53.
144. "Recipient Detail- Parrot, Jacob," The Congressional Medal of Honor, https://www.cmohs.org
145. "Recipient Detail- Parrot, Jacob," The Congressional Medal of Honor, https://www.cmohs.org

gaze to relentlessly push across the rivers of Virginia until he hit a very hot Cold Harbor in May of 1864. Located about 20 miles to the northeast of Richmond, 7,000 men in blue ceased to live within about twenty minutes. The Army, and perhaps even Grant, never recovered from psychological effects of the assault at Cold Harbor. What could be called "Cold Harbor syndrome," according to Geoffrey Perret, had revealed itself where disembarking armies like Butler's Army of the James outside of Richmond immediately dug in without attacking. Troops seen writing their names on paper attached to their backs saw the need for dog tags as certain death had become too real. Detached troops from Grant's army likewise had lost its willingness to die at Petersburg. Commanders like Meade may have reinforced this syndrome when he attacked with a frontal assault, the only part of the confederate trenches truly heavily armed.[146] General Phil Sheridan was sent to the valley of Virginia where Confederate James Early held him to a slow burn of destruction, meanwhile a siege mentality increasingly set in around Richmond.

Burial party on battlefield of Cold Harbor.

A brief expedition up the Red River to the north of Texas was an attempt to keep the French out of the war. No more Saratogas! However, the real action in the east occurred at Atlanta. The largest southern city's fall began when Sherman, during June of 1864 at Kennesaw Mountain, attempted a Cold Harbor type of assault that left 3,000 blue-coated Yankees permanently laid down on the battlefield.[147] Sherman ignored Lincoln's orders, and out flanked and out raced John Bell Hood to Atlanta in a style that would have made Zachary Taylor proud. By September 2, 1864, Hood Abandoned Atlanta sealing Lincoln's re-election, saving an increasingly depressed north running short on patience and facing draft riots in New York City.

Lieutenant General W. T. Sherman and staff.

By November and into December of the year 1864, the battles of Franklin and Nashville saw last gasp attempts by the Confederacy to save the west when Hood advanced against General George H. Thomas, one of the greatest and least known northern commanders who stood his ground in Tennessee. Thomas broke out of prepared trenches, ignoring repeatedly the orders of the President and all those others looking over his shoulder, and instead only went after the confederates when they had totally eviscerated themselves against his lines. The brilliantly executed subsequent pursuit represented the only battle of annihilation in the

General George H. Thomas.

146. Perret, *A Country*, 245.
147. Perret, *A Country*, 247.

entire Civil War. Hood's army virtually disappeared never to be seen again.[148] Ignoring seniors far back in the rear began to be contagious as Sherman, also tired of the occupation of Atlanta, finally ignored his orders; instead marching toward Savannah and then through the Carolinas.

Richmond would finally fall in **1865** but the war still had a few terrible weeks left. The March 25th attempts by the Confederate army to break out of the defenses from Petersburg, VA to the south of the capital city of Richmond had failed. Sheridan, sent west to flank Lee from breaking out, sent his dragoon army where it overwhelmed Confederate forces at Five Forks. By April 2nd Lee had abandoned Petersburg for Amelia, hoping to be resupplied. Finding Union depredations had made foodstuffs and supplies destroyed and unavailable, Lee headed west, and as the Appomattox River narrowed, so did his chances of making it to the railroad at Lynchburg. Hopes to head south to meet up with General J.E. Johnston down in North Carolina failed when New Jersey cavalry cut off the approach on the old Stage Road a few miles south of the town of Appomattox.

The Confederacy surrendered at Appomattox where now sitting in a glass case at the Confederate museum in Appomattox, VA is the jewel-encrusted sword, the symbol of the dead confederacy's last hopes. Lee offered his sword to Grant, who in typical Christian fashion refused it and offered forgiveness by allowing the Confederate soldiers to keep their horses and even personal weapons, kindly offering them food in an act of magnanimity to shape American views toward the vanquished in future wars, even up until the present. As auction cries for souvenirs echoed from the McLean house, the sight of the surrender, the Generals parted ways and a new era of American expansion remained under way, that even the terrible and mysterious assassination of the President less than a week later could not undo.

Civil War naval innovations included the use of Confederate commerce raiders aboard ships, the most successful of which was the *Alabama*, commanded by Captain Raphael Semmes. Southern commerce raiders often waited at Cuba to intercept California gold bound for New York, watching steamship timetables. Real damage done in particular to the whaling industry occurred, where 1/10 of all whalers sank at the hands of Confederate raiders. A need to innovate in large measure served to lead to the use of a new substance: petroleum.[149]

Civil War Union soldiers in trenches before the Battle of Petersburg, Virginia, June 9, 1864.

Appomattox Court House, VA.

Battle of Hampton Roads, "The first battle between 'iron' ships of war."

---

148. Perret, *A Country*, 248.
149. Perret, *A Country*, 235.

52 Modern American Military History

The Civil War also saw the first naval engagements between ironclad ships. After four hours of a slug-match in March of 1862, wood-piercing rounds from the *Merrimac* bounced off the *Monitor's* superstructure while the *Merrimac's* sloping tops ricocheted the shots from the *Monitor*. A short fight, but one loaded with long-term ramifications for the navy, the day of the sailing ship would be numbered. Southern blockade-runners contributed 80% of the south's needs while Union steamboats could supply almost two corps for three days. It took advancing armies in most cases to stop the flow of life saving materials.[150]

By April of the same year, Flag Officer David G. Farragut takes New Orleans thereby splitting the south virtually off from the trans-Mississippi West. Vicksburg, falling in July 1864, would completely divide the Confederacy from its source of leather and beef to the west.

While Charleston, South Carolina represented a rich port that remained safe nearly until the end of the war, by August of 1864 Farragut had entered Mobile Bay, and by year's end Admiral David D. Porter took the last available port at Wilmington, North Carolina. By January, Fort Fisher fell to Porter in tandem with powerful land forces. With Charleston's final capitulation, Galveston, Texas remained the Confederacy's only port to the outside world. Winfield Scott's Anaconda Strategy, while slow, finally crushed the south into submission when used in tandem with huge, aggressive and highly mobile land forces.

Battle of Mobile Bay.

Analysis

Firepower proved irresistible to the Union Army. Federal guns rarely stopped once the firing started, while ammo-starved Confederate guns held back awaiting the inevitable infantry assaults.[151] Artillery found its role in supporting dug-in infantry awaiting attack.[152]

Small arms represented enormous firepower as well. The Rifle Musket represented a hybrid weapon of sorts, designed to take advantage of rifling and the cylindroconoidal bullet, while increased muzzle velocity under constraints of the technology of the day, required it to be a muzzleloader. Colt's interchangeable parts, offered exponentially increased firepower and increased production forced costs down. Soldiers clamored for the breechloaders; and in fact, Abolitionist John Brown even armed his insurrectionists with them.[153]

The Spencer Carbine proved so revolutionary that the inability of soldiers to get one in their hands created so hot an anger politically that President Lincoln would eventually remove the head of Ordnance before the first Spencer Carbines, rifles that could be loaded from the breech or rear, enabling the shooter to fire from a covered position and not standing, became available.[154] Perhaps even more revolutionary than the single shot carbine was the metallic cartridge, saving time over the laborious muzzleloader.

The Carbine by war's end had essentially saved the role of cavalry, creating seas of fast moving dragoons under Sherman and Sheridan, using converging columns and presaging the armored columns that would converge across Europe in World War II.

Union soldier with Spencer Carbine and revolver.

150. Ibid., 234.
151. Ibid., 237.
152. Ibid., 239.
153. Rose, Alexander. *American Rifle*. Random House: New York, 2008, 116.
154. Ibid., 147.

Frontier Constabulary: The Plains Wars

United States policy before the Civil War had been one of Indian removal. The War with Mexico, and the subsequent discovery of gold in California would initially see settlers moving fast through Indian country. The Civil War and the Homestead Act of 1862 would create situations that would inflame relations varying from the Sand Creek Massacre of 1864 to the Little Big Horn in 1876. The years from 1879 to the 1920s, the U.S. had two goals: first detribalization, and the second the destruction of Indian culture.[155]

The Army would use the western plains as a finishing school for the modern military experience by balancing the desires of social elites to focus only on the western traditions of line warfare with the recognition of limitations of conventional force. American institutional memory needed to be reminded of how to fight an enemy while using the natural environment to best effect and keeping the tribes separated and from unifying. Like the Steppe warriors of Asia, the Native-Americans of the west rode with lightning speed, raiding and breaking off the fight when things did not go their way.

The Army had a tough job of trying to enforce polices it did not necessarily approve of. The rough fighting, hard drinking, and charging full-speed-ahead Army that finished off the Confederacy chaffed under pontificating humanitarians; hated greedy frontiersmen stayed frustrated with government corruption and incompetence, as evidenced by broken treaties, and saw the Indians as savages who committed terrible atrocities. Between a virtual rock and a hard place, the Army as professionals respected their Indian foes and their warrior culture, yet served a nation "back east" where alternative views of destroying the Indian culture and talk of assimilation swirled about. Some of the more romantic visions of the noble savage reflected the idealism of man's proper place in the world of nature. Eventually, failures and the increased movement of people on the railroads shaped a coherent policy. The ultimate strategy to achieve frontier peace would rely on placing the Native Americans onto reservations.[156]

Army marksmanship had declined dramatically. The use of heavy shot during the Civil War created a situation where the ranges required for accurate shooting so perfected during the early years of the colonies and republic had allowed shooting skills to atrophy in the face of overwhelming firepower in the hands of hastily trained militia volunteers. Unlike the early Indian wars, where ambushes and accuracy of shot with pre-planned targets ruled, the West saw American marksmanship decline precipitously. Choosing out centers of gravity in an effort to pin the enemy down, the Army and Indians had largely lost their ability to shoot straight.

Before the Civil War, migrants moving to California for gold resulted in pioneers moving quickly through "Indian Country" across Wyoming and Montana, putting whites into contact with the Sioux, Cheyenne, and Arapaho tribes to the north, and to the south Commanche and Kiowa. In the southern plains, the Army had the unenviable task of standing guard between the southern plains tribes and the hated Texas Rangers. Covering amazing distances and trying to defend the rights of Indians and settlers, it is a miracle that a small army forced to patrol such a large area of the American west could do what it did at all.[157]

Between the Mexican and Civil Wars, an attempted strategy consisted of a series of imposing forts or a **fixed post system.** The system revealed the degree to which Kiowas and Commanches had visited greater devastation on the Texan and Mexican frontiers in ever-greater numbers since the Mexican War. A fragile U.S. hold also remained on the Santa Fe Trail. Meanwhile further north, Sioux and Cheyennes still simmered in anger at past injustices and defeats. The tribes continued to fail to act in concert and never would unite, thereby limiting their effectiveness, but regardless, settlements west in the 1850s had been slowed down on the frontier.[158]

The possible deterioration of unconventional warfare skills as well as the beginning of building forts tended to create a belief within the mind of the Native-American brave of the feebleness of the

---

155. Weeks, Philip. *Farewell, My Nation.* Harlan Davidson: Arlington Hts., IL, 1990, 233.
156. Millet, Allan R., & Maslowski, Peter. *For the Common Defense.* Free Press: NY, 1994, 252.
157. Utley, Robert M. *Frontiersmen in Blue.* Macmillan: New York, 1967, 58.
158. Ibid., 141.

white man.[159] Outbreaks of violence during the 1850s saw circles of violence as the Sioux responded in kind to the rash behavior of a junior lieutenant who burst into their lands, demanding to know who had killed a Mormon settler's buffalo. Subsequent affronts in 1855 by "Butcher" General William S. Harney intimidated them with converging columns of unexpected infantry and cavalry. In fear, the Indians scattered in a helpless rout as the soldiers cut them down mercilessly with both shot and sabers.[160] Such stupid and immoral actions by the army would continue the cycles of violence for a generation to come, interrupted by the Civil War.

Invariably when natives of the upper plains became involved in a fight, so did those of the south. The Kiowa and Commanche, whose depredations on settlements were worse than their northern neighbors, faced their first defeat when, in the autumn of 1858, Major Earl Van Dorn followed up on the devastation rendered earlier that spring by the Texas Rangers, and the formation of about 350 soldiers under Van Dorn resulted in close quarters fighting where fifty-six warriors laid dead. The next spring Van Dorn continued until the Battle of Crooked Creek where he annihilated a Comanche band trapped in a ravine. The Texans and Mexicans still feared the Kiowa and Commanche and a growing pattern of alternating north-south cyclical frontier violence that would continue until after the Civil War.

By the 1860s, the Army had built a series of forts known as the fixed-post system and prevailed over roving summer columns. The army learned to single out particular tribes for reprisals in responding to aggressions. Fixed-posts allowed resupply and a defensive-offensive blend that wore the Indians down.[161] Maintaining steady war on a peacetime budget, all while protecting aggressive settlers who wanted preemptive war and the moral rights of the Indians while recognizing the fast and easy victory of total warfare, with an American debate as to the humanness of Indians.[162]

In January 1861, the Army confronted Cochise of the Chiricahua as the Warm Springs tribes of Apaches turned from warring on Mexicans to fighting the U.S. Army. A series of escalating hostage situations occurred with 2nd Lieutenant George N. Bascom. The lack of professionalism in soldiers "banished out west" while the Civil War raged did little to solve the problem of cyclical frontier violence. This second incident by an Army officer leading to violence leads to questions of the quality of officers posted in the West as a whole new series of escalations had started anew.[163]

In the year 1862, Santee Sioux led one of the surprisingly few uprisings that occurred during the Civil War. Starting with frustration at limited hunting grounds, a dare by a brave returning from a bad hunting trip soon spun out of control, when finally after a terrible week in August 1862, over 800 whites lay dead. Cries for retribution during September saw the governor of Minnesota calling up the militia and using the massive firepower available to wipe out thousands of braves until finally the largest mass execution in history occurred. The beginning of an eight yearlong plains war had ignited.[164] As always, when one tribe became angry, tension tended to spread, and this time towards the south.

One of the worst frontier episodes in America's history occurred in 1864 when a 3rd Colorado Cavalry volunteer regiment anticipated the end of their enlistments. Desirous of a final opportunity at achieving a measure of fame, the troops participated in a meeting on 28 September with Black Kettle, chief of the Cheyenne. The tribe believed they could leave and did so a bit confused, unaware of a state of war. Colonel John W. Chivington hated all Indians and apparently anybody who did not. Later in November Chivington authorized an attack against a camp located at Sand Creek in a broad barren valley. Peacefully settled and flying an American flag, only one brave stood up to the onslaught of unexpected soldiers. The bluecoats proceeded to murder any native-Americans who fled the frightening scene. An approving public cheered body parts displayed on the stage in Denver and subsequently paraded through the streets. The understandable effect of one hundred scalps certainly caused fury to break out on the plains anew.[165]

---

159. Utley, Robert M., & Washburn, Wilcomb E. *Indian Wars*. American Heritage: New York, 1977, 172.
160. Ibid, 186.
161. Utley, *Frontiersmen*, 345.
162. Ibid, 176.
163. Ibid., 176.
164. Ibid., 204.
165. Utley, *Indian Wars*, 207.

The army, by 1865, saw two important and related precedents emerge. **Winter campaigns** made Indians vulnerable to exposure and eventually broke their morale. The time-proven winning combination of **food fights** and total war steadily together with fierce continental climate and cold eventually demoralized and undermined the will to resist.[166] With the arrival of the railroads, armed combat veterans building and protecting them, and each foot of track laid, a small portion of the Indian way of life died.

In 1866, the Fetterman Massacre in Wyoming demonstrated the price of killing soldiers. The fort's chief scout at Fort Phil Kearny had warned Captain Fetterman, "Your men who fought down South are crazy! They don't know anything about fighting Indians," the Captain replied with laughter. Captain William J. Fetterman had openly bragged about how his 80 men could beat the Indians.[167] Chief Red Cloud and his lieutenant Crazy Horse had earlier destroyed soldiers on the Bozeman Trail. In December, confident Civil War veteran Union soldiers found fighting Indians to be very different from confederates. Troops armed with a mixture of muzzle-loading Springfield rifles capable of single shot only, and Spencer Carbines, breech-loaded single shots with metallic cartridges, went out after their enemy. Captain Fetterman chased after a decoy by Crazy Horse and rode into an ambush that wiped out his command. A later close examination of the gruesomely mutilated corpses revealed very few bullet wounds. According to the fort surgeon only six men had actually died from bullet wounds.[168] Apparently, shooting skills on both sides had definitely declined.

Subsequent fights during the first two days of August in 1867 introduced the Indians to the cost of killing soldiers. Armed with newly arrived breech-loading rifles, the Army taught the Indians that it did not pay to attack those who wore blue. Initial concerns and skepticism of the soldiers towards their standard issue weapons had revealed the men before missions taking off their boots so they could tie their laces around the triggers in the event they needed to kill themselves to prevent capture.[169] The new weapons, however, increased soldiers' confidence. The increased volume of fire, if not accuracy, contributed to Red Cloud's surrender at the treaties of Ft. Laramie in 1867, and by 1868, Sitting Bull stood as the chief of future Sioux resistance.

The 1868 Grant Peace policy tended to paternalistically treat the Indians like children. General Phil Sheridan, after the failure of the peace in 1868, vowed to wipe out the continual Indian problems with one long winter campaign. Bringing Lt. Col. George A. Custer out west cut short a sentence Custer had been serving for leaving his post without authorization to see his beloved wife. Max Boot compares Custer to Banastre Tarleton and Robert Rogers of Rogers' Rangers fame, in that he brought down problems on himself and his men through his aggressiveness and perhaps lack of foresight. Custer had finished dead last in his West Point Class of 1861, but proved conspicuously gallant in the Civil War.[170] The plan consisted of using the now typically American converging columns and went directly after the Native American winter camps, sending Custer into the Washita Valley to further destroy. Winter tactics worked well with the Kiowa, Commanche, and Arapaho gathering at Ft. Sill for winter rations promised to those willingly accepting peace.[171]

The Indians, during the time of Sitting Bulls' leadership, discussed excitedly how the Hunkpapa leader had a vision of victory during a sun dance of "many soldiers falling into our camp."[172] The Sioux and Cheyenne had never before, nor would ever again be as united, confident, or well led; nor as angry.[173] Failing to understand the concept of mining rights, the Sioux did understand the desecration of their sacred Black Hills. When scattered Sioux ordered to reservations failed to go, the army went into war mode. The Army moved in using the traditional converging columns, with Maj. Gen. Alfred H. Terry coming from the east, while Brig. Gen. John Gibbon would come from the west. The great Indian fighter George Crook would advance from the south and attempt to throw out prospectors.

---

166. Utley, *Frontiersmen*, 346.
167. Rose, Alexander. *American Rifle*. Random House: New York, 2008, 159.
168. Ibid., 160.
169. Ibid., 161.
170. Boot, Max. *Invisible Armies*. WW. Norton: NY, 2003, 142.
171. Utley, *Indian Wars*, 225.
172. Utley, *Frontiersmen*, 264.
173. Utley, *Frontiersmen*, 262.

Crook felt he needed reinforcements, halted and barely survived in large measure due to the help he received from Crow and Shoshone allies.[174] Going to ground after Crazy Horse with more than 2,000 braves had fought him hard, one of the three converging columns had halted.

Meanwhile, Custer and the 7th Cavalry arrived ahead of Terry's main body and found the Indians by the Little Bighorn River. Custer had planned on waiting for Terry when he feared native scouts had spotted his presence. In typically aggressive fashion, he divided his command and attacked immediately.[175] Marcus Reno with only 180 troops hit the village from the south while Capt. Frederick Benteen and 160 troops went off following retreating braves. Custer took the rest of the command and struck the center of the village without a reconnaissance. Reno earned the title of coward when he grounded his men and kept them safe after fighting for ten minutes in a dismounted skirmisher line.[176] Thousands of Indians swarmed cross the Little Bighorn in response to the arrival of the troops. Troopers fought while single-shot Springfield Carbines jammed. According to Geoffrey Perret, some men in pairs put their Model 1872 Army Colts Peacemakers to each other's heads and on the count of three saved each other from certain tortuous death.[177]

The Battle of Little Bighorn.

Source: Library of Congress

By late afternoon Benteen had returned and rejoined Reno. Together they held off the Indians until Terry appeared. Terry possessing feared mountain howitzers frightened them off. Terry and Crook in response to the massacre started a relentless winter campaign, which failed to catch the Sioux who themselves broke off into separate groups. Eventually crushing Cheyenne camps, the demoralized Cheyenne came over to the U.S. while the Sioux later followed suit coming in from the cold, having seen the writing on the wall.[178]

When Custer and his men found themselves surrounded by Crazy Horse, proof of the decline in American shooting skills emerged. Firing single-shot Springfield Carbines, the forces under Custer, overwhelmed by the Indians, experienced numerous cases of jamming of their Springfield rifles, and the apparent inability of the troops to be able to fire accurately would account for controversies after the war regarding whether the need for more firepower would actually be the answer to the problem of marksmanship. The irony of the decline of shooting skills contrasted with the American frontier experience that demanded accuracy in long range shooting skills. Despite the fame of buffalo hunters who could pick off the individual animals one at a time from a distance sufficient for sound signatures to not alarm the herds, the Indians had themselves become so dependent on close in shooting during the hunt they had long ceased using sights on weapons. Instead, they would rush in quickly in massive numbers such as happened to Custer.[179] The Army had apparently deteriorated in its firearms practice as well, mirroring the poor shooting of the Indians.

On the American centennial of the U.S. in 1876, a furious public demanded action. Blue coats flooded into the west and the Sioux hunted relentlessly. Continual campaigning by Crook and Nelson Miles continued to wear angry Indians down. Obliterated by firepower at the Battle of Wolf Mountain in 1877, Lakota Sioux and Northern Cheyenne surrendered to Crook upon advice of Crook's system of emissaries and informants, or **Indian Scouts**. Chief Crazy Horse died in a scuffle by his own knife in mysterious circumstances. Sitting Bull would ultimately surrender in 1881 to American authorities, worn down by hostility from Canadian tribes and informed upon constantly

---

174. Utley, *Indian Wars*, 239.
175. Perret, Geoffrey. *A Country Made By War*. Random House: NY, 1989, 269.
176. Utley, *Indian Wars*, 243.
177. Perret, *A Country*, 269.
178. Ibid., 270.
179. Rose, *American Rifle*, 166.

by scouts friendly to the U.S. Army.[180] After a series of strange encounters with various Wild West shows and meeting with Annie Oakley, Sitting Bull would return home. When a social hysteria known as the Ghost Dance began, fears of another uprising by authorities led to an attempt to take Sitting Bull prisoner by police, which erupted into a shootout. With Sitting Bull's death ended three centuries of virtual non-stop wars serving to mold and create a great Army.[181]

The last great Indian fighter was Nelson Miles. By 1877, Miles, like Crook, believed in the benefits of Indian allies and he made extensive use of them. The Cheyenne and Sioux, supposedly prisoners, in actuality served as scouts helping to identify camps in often-decisive ways. A spy system of which little record is left also tormented discord amongst the hostiles and kept Miles informed of their temper and intentions. Steadily a Northern Plains defense system would continue to be constructed limiting movements and finally the **railroads** caused people to flood in, overwhelming the hunting grounds and culture.[182]

General Neslon Miles.

Source: Library of Congress

Miles would be the last of the Commanding Generals of the Army molded on the plains of the American West. Sherman, Sheridan, and Nelson Miles would leave a lasting mark on the Army. By the time the frontier closed, the skills learned by the Army in pacifying the finest light infantry on Earth would teach it to go on to the Philippines, where it would continue the pattern of manifest destiny, and ultimately, empire.

After years of debate and controversy, the United States had a medal to recognize the individual actions of bravery by soldiers, but it led to some unfortunate, unforeseen consequences. Not only was the Medal of Honor the single medal recognizing bravery, but the criterion to qualify for the award was vague. The original criteria for the Medal of Honor was, "gallantry in action, and other soldier-like qualities, during the present insurrection."[183] These vague criteria led to the Medal of Honor being awarded for many unheroic reasons during and after the Civil War. For example, all 864 members of the 27th Maine Regiment were awarded the Medal of Honor for simply reenlisting.[184] Unfortunately, this is not the only example of the Medal of Honor being awarded casually. Many veterans of the Civil War nominated themselves for the Medal of Honor for fraudulent acts of bravery. For example, Lt. Colonel Asa Gardner nominated himself, stating, "I request, I be allowed one as a souvenir of memorable times past."[185] He would receive the Medal of Honor. From 1891–97 over 500 Medals of Honor were awarded for acts of gallantry from the Civil War.[186] As the number of recipients of the Medal of Honor for the Civil War reached 2,445,[187] the Medal of Honor was in danger of losing its prestige and honor. Many recipients who had truly performed acts of extreme courage and bravery, risking their lives in the process, resented how easily Congress and the president authorized the Medal of Honor. The military administration began to address this problem as early as 1878.[188] Review boards, commissioned by the War Department, began to make standards for the awarding of the Medal of Honor.

---

180. Utley, *Indian Wars*, 266.
181. Boot, *Invisible Armies*, 152.
182. Utley, *Frontiersmen*, 291.
183. Zimmerman, *Uncommon Valor*, 53.
184. The Boston Publishing Company, ed., *Above and Beyond: A History of the Medal of Honor From the Civil War to Vietnam* (Boston, MA: The Boston Publishing Company, 1985), 33.
185. Zimmerman, *Uncommon Valor*, 58.
186. Zimmerman, *Uncommon Valor*, 58.
187. Zimmerman, *Uncommon Valor*, 54.
188. Zimmerman, *Uncommon Valor*, 59.

Analysis

The stoicism of the Plains Indians and the feathers they wore showed the values placed on striking their foe. The game was survival, but in terms of endurance and fighting ability, the Native-Americans exhibited a more aggressive and tougher disposition than the typical U.S. Army soldier; probably a function of the hunting culture producing those warriors. Still, it would be the inability to detach from that culture of individualism and formula for glory utilizing individual courage and fighting skills could not defeat a centrally controlled, mission focused U.S. Army.[189] The Railroads teeming populations pushing West determined to destroy the buffalo, the basis of the cultures. The 1874 Regular Army in size was 27,000 officers and men; smaller than the police department in New York City today.[190] The Army continued to hone an ability to conduct relentless patrols, relying on the institutionalization of Indian guides and scouts, and conducting winter campaigns against food supplies, continued to build on the same operational successes it had since Jamestown.

During the decades after the Civil War, and leading up to World War I, several commissioned review boards established clearer criteria for the Medal of Honor. As a result, the Medal of Honor would regain its preeminence as the most prestigious award for valor. The first consequential review board, commissioned by Secretary of War Russell A. Alger in 1897, established a method to determine if one should be awarded the Medal of Honor.[191] Not until April 1916 would a commissioned review board address the issue of fraudulent awardees of the medal. President Woodrow Wilson authorized the standards for the Medal of Honor to be reviewed. The review board was led by Lt. General Nelson A. Miles, a Medal of Honor recipient himself. For the next several months, all recipients were reviewed according to the new standards. During this time period, the criteria "for conspicuous gallantry or intrepidity at the risk of life, above and beyond the call of duty" was created.[192] By the time the review board ended in February 1917, they had rescinded 911 Medals of Honor.[193] This event became known as the "Purge of 1917."[194]

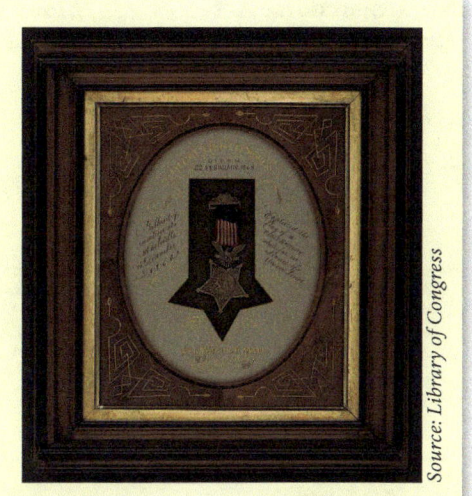

Civil War Medal of Honor for Private Wilbur F. Moore of Co. C, 117th Illinois Infantry Regiment.

Source: Library of Congress

---

189. McGinnis, Anthony R. "When Courage was not enough: Plains Indians at war with the U.S. Army," *The Journal of Military History*. 76, no. 2 (Apr 2012): 455.
190. Boot, *Invisible Armies*, 147.
191. The Boston Publishing Company ed., *The Medal of Honor*, 94.
192. The Boston Publishing Company ed., *The Medal of Honor*, 94.
193. The Boston Publishing Company ed., *The Medal of Honor*, 95.
194. Zimmerman, *Uncommon Valor*, 69.

Key Terms:

- Newburgh Conspiracy
- Harmar
- St. Clair
- The Legion of the United States
- The Militia Act of 1792
- Fallen Timbers
- Treaty of Grenville
- West Point
- Quasi-War with France
- *U.S.S. Constellation*
- Chesapeake & Leopard Affair
- War of 1812
- Embargo
- Non-Intercourse Act
- Orders in Council
- Raisin River Massacre
- "Don't Give up the Ship"
- Battle of the Thames
- Winfield Scott
- Lundy's Lane
- Battle of Horseshoe Bend
- New Orleans
- Treaty of Ghent
- Seminole Wars
- Adams-Onis Treaty of 1819
- The Blackhawk War
- Battle of San Jacinto
- Palo Alto
- Monterrey
- Buena Vista
- California
- Veracruz
- Cerro Gordo
- Churubusco
- Treaty of Guadalupe-Hidalgo
- 1861
- 1862
- 1863
- 1864
- 1865
- Fixed Post System
- Railroads
- Winter Campaigns
- Indian Scouts
- Food Fights

Chapter III

THE SPANISH-AMERICAN WAR

Matthew 8:8-9 "For I also am a man under authority, having soldiers under me. And I say to this one, 'Go,' and he goes, and to another, 'Come,' and he comes, and to my servant, 'Do this,' and he does it." When Jesus heard it, He marveled, and said to those who followed, "Assuredly, I say to you, I have not found such great faith, not even in Israel." NKJV

Check out an animated map of the events of the Spanish-American War at this link: https://www.khpcontent.com/

1898

25 Jan	The *USS Maine* arrives in Havana harbor
15 Feb	Explosion on the *USS Maine*
29 March	President McKinley delivers ultimatum to the Spanish requiring Cuban independence
25 Apr	Congress declares a state of war with Spain
1 May	Battle of Manilla Bay Philippines
29 May	American "Flying Squadron" arrives off the coast to blockade Santiago Cuba
12 June	Emilio Aguinaldo declares Philippine independence
1 July	US forces seize El Caney and hills overlooking Santiago harbor (Kettle and San Juan)
3 July	Naval Battle of Santiago
28 July	Ponce Puerto Rico surrenders to US troops
29 July	US troops begin ground offensive from Manila Bay to Cavite Philippines
13 Aug	Spanish surrender Manilla to US forces
10 Dec	Peace of Paris; Spain relinquishes Guam and Puerto Rico to the United States

1899

4 Feb	War begins in the Philippines between the United States and Filipino insurgents
13 Nov	Aguinaldo announces a guerilla war

1900

2 Jan	First Panay campaign
5 May	Gen. Arthur MacArthur replaces Gen. Elwell S. Otis as CG and mil. Gov.
15 Apr	US troops attacked in Samar
6 Nov	President William McKinley reelected
22 Dec	MacArthur differentiates scouts from constabulary

1901

12 Feb	MacArthur announces an end to resistance in central Luzon
23 Mar	Funston captures Aguinaldo
28 Sept	Balangiga Massacre on Samar
31 Oct– 10 Nov	Reprisals for Balangiga massacre
28 Dec	Waller begins Samar March

1902

31 Jan	Senate hearings regarding war crimes in Samar begin
4 July	President Teddy Roosevelt announces an end to the war in the Philippines

Go to www.khpcontent.com to watch a video introduction for this chapter.

Cuba and Puerto Rico

The Spanish-American War represented a major deviation from previous armed conflicts. Up until this point, a nation that was essentially isolationist with a government built upon the framework of a constitutional republic turned into an empire. The change would be slow and unintentional, most likely unexpected, but America would step away from a securely contiguous state bound by oceans and with this war would never again be the same. For the purposes of this study, it is important to understand the framework of this largely unknown war and to see the beginning of patterns that would reoccur in subsequent military struggles.

The **American Ways of Fighting (AWoF)** described in this book are the national strengths and weaknesses as reflected in the military endeavors of the modern, or post-Civil War, experience. What is often a strength, however, can be exploited by an enemy as a weakness. The first of these various ways of warfare (AWoF) described and used throughout this book is **speed** and **maneuverability**. The tendency of Americans to move rapidly is a probable result of our frenetic frontier experience and the nearly simultaneous explosive growth of American cities at a time in history when technology and globalization continually made the world a smaller and faster place. The influx of immigrants into busy port cities during the transition of sail and steam technologies and the westward movement—continuing up until the Vietnam War—may in part explain why the US military represents the best aspects of a "fast break" type of team. Virtually unbeatable on the battlefield in the rapid give and take of combat, an ability to move quickly and decisively is also the American military's greatest weakness. Like many of the AWoF described in this book, the ways of American warfare represent both strengths and weaknesses.

The result of a rapidly efficient military is that it has trouble with slow and drawn out conflicts. This is not just a problem unique to the military, but an American problem as well. Americans become **rapidly impatient**. A long-term perspective is quickly being replaced by a technologically dependent short-term view as evidenced by a shortage of savings and planning. Likewise it is no surprise that the American military conducts itself best in a fast tempo environment and simultaneously is challenged by a long drawn out fight. This is precisely what the United States confronted in the Spanish-American War.

As an outgrowth of the Second Great Awakening, during which highly-educated northern women led a religious revival that demanded the wiping out of perceived evil conduct, the U.S., led by and eager to oblige media, rushed into war. This began the dawning of the age of political progressivism which focused on rectifying the wrongs of the world. This zealous attitude reemerged within a generation of the post-Civil War reconstruction. The villains in this new conflict would not be slave-holding Southerners this time, but rather the Spanish who had attempted to put down colonial revolts in nearby Cuba. Using methods that American surrogates repeated half a century later in Vietnam, the Spanish attempted to subdue a population using the new technologies of barbed wire and block houses. Unfortunately, this seemingly barbaric attempt to separate **insurgents** from the population met with disastrous results in a tropical environment. Americans—one of the most literate societies on Earth—eagerly consumed the **Yellow Press**' lurid and sinister portrayal of Spanish motives. The role of the media in the Spanish-American war proved a harbinger of the power in bringing Americans into war and, in some future cases, out of it. Before long, an anguished President William McKinley, haunted by his own memories of the Civil War, would be confronting war fever—the American propensity to go into action quickly.

The U.S. government ordered the **USS Maine** to visit Cuba in January of 1898 as a result of publicized operations by a vindictive Spanish government against the Cuban people. An explosion in the boiler room of the ship in February turned America's wrath on the Spanish in Cuba. A paper leaked around the same time insulting President McKinley and further angered the American people. The

Spanish apologized for the whole mess, but the American people, raised in a proud revolutionary tradition, had sided increasingly with the Cuban people. *The Yellow Press*, led by men such as Randolph Hurst and Joseph Pulitzer, who were competing for the sale of newspapers, fed a literate public hunger for events—the more salacious the better! American business had much at stake in Cuba as well.

A later American investigation of the explosion determined a submarine type of mine to have been the culprit for the explosion of the *USS Maine* in Havana harbor. The inquiry soon after the incident discounted the Spanish claim that no geyser of water had been spotted, nor had any other indication of the kind existed. A proposed Act of War went before the American Congress.

Perhaps in retrospect, the most amazing aspect of the Spanish-American War was the ability of the U.S. army to attempt to transform nearly overnight from a frontier force attempting to enforce a reservation system to one projecting force across the Straits of Florida and into the Caribbean. Loading out of Tampa, Florida, railroads were supposedly backed up as far as South Carolina as supplies of every type arrived for shipping. The army itself, following the declaration of war declared by Congress, sought to take Santiago Bay, the site of the explosion.

Only recently vindicated by naval investigations, the American propensity for speed and emotion brought the nation into a true war fever. Young men fought for the chance to fight as their father's had in the Civil War. Songs were sung and the ladies turned out in fine apparel to greet this opportunity for the heroic. This great time for all epitomized war fever, and Americans excitedly saw this demonstration of the unification of the Northern and Southern states as a Crusade-type adventure to fight evil abroad just as the evil of slavery had been eradicated at home. For all of its mobilization and speed, however, the army still moved too slowly for the media and a public baying for action.

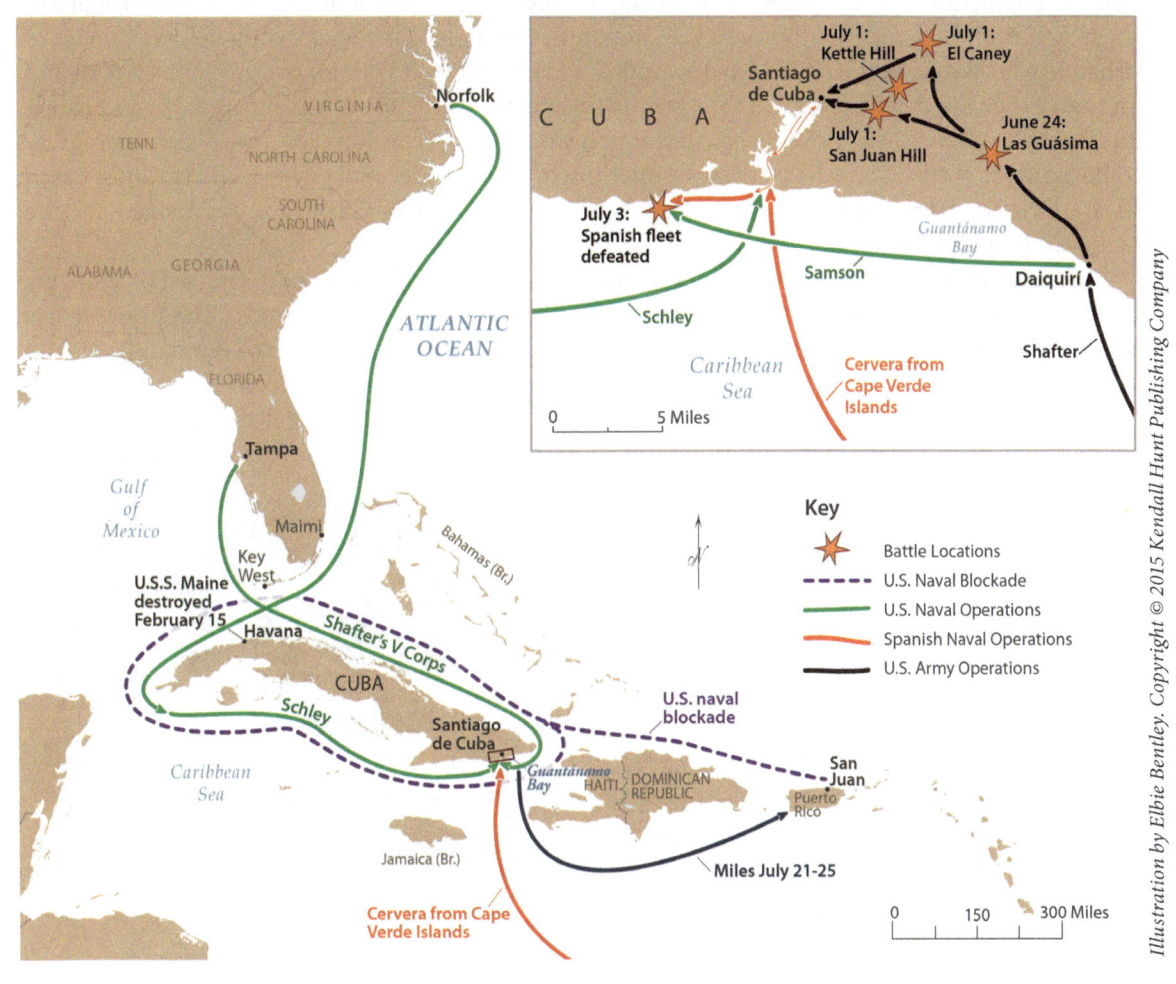

Figure 3.1 Spanish-American War—The Caribbean Theater

The American army in those days carried a new generation of weapon: the **Krag-Jorgenson** five shot rifle. This smokeless, powdered repeater represented a major technological change from the musket of a generation before as had breech-loading artillery, the more advanced being the French-produced Hotchkiss with a range of 3,500 yards firing a relatively small 1.56 inch shell, but clouding the battlefield and still not firing smokeless powder. Unable to match the Spanish 75 mm cannons, Hotchkiss returned with a three-inch upgrade, which usually still fired in a generally direct fire mode. Supporting artillery at the San Juan heights would indeed be silenced by Spanish counter-battery fires. The infantry, wearing a version of the familiar American cowboy type hat, went into battle without indirect fire support and instead relied more often on direct fire from the first American machine gun—the Gatling gun.

Major General William R. Shafter moved with great deliberation under the summer heat for good reason when he led the assault on Santiago. Mocked in the media, this older and somewhat corpulent individual faced the true realities of the impending invasion. Initially landing at Daiquiri, Cuba, under the direct supervision of the V Corps (note: Corps are always marked with Roman numerals), the operational leader during the landing and the 2nd Division commander, Major General Henry W. Lawton demonstrated his own mastery of logistics. The amphibious assault is one of the most complex **operations** for planners. Despite some initially amateurish attempts at landing, such as forcing horses to swim ashore for want of landing craft, successful combined arms planning resulted in a bloodless seizure of the beachhead under the cover of naval gunfire. Meanwhile, the U.S. Marines snatched up Guantanamo Bay, about forty miles east of Santiago Bay, and liked it so much they have kept it until the present day.

Advancing slowly towards the San Juan heights and facing a potential **enfilade** fire from Cubans in the town of El Caney, Shafter ordered Lawton to initiate a somewhat overly complex series of urban firefights to take the city.[195] Lawton appeared again to fight with an overly complex plan, but after an expensive day-long attack, threatening fires halted as the town was secured. Many historians feel that in retrospect a simple holding action would have been sufficient, but the vulnerability to flanking or enfilade attacks is always something a commander must consider. Having secured El Caney, the army then moved on to its ultimate objective—Santiago, overlooked by the commanding heights.

The final assault by American infantry on San Juan Hill, a couple of miles to the east of Santiago, employed light artillery and Gatling guns (known as coffee grinders to the troops). The failure to use indirect fire weapons was a terrible mistake on the part of the U.S. command. No commander should ever deploy forces without using all possible supporting arms. Nevertheless, boldness ruled the day as the thin blue lines attacked in the semblance of a **frontal assault**, simultaneously up both adjacent Kettle and San Juan Hills. Avoiding protection from enemy fire, or **cover**, and in clear sight of the enemy with no **concealment**, the attack went on. Fortunately for the Americans, the Spanish had placed their forces on the top of the hill where they were essentially "skylined," and they had abandoned **defilade** fortifications so that direct fire **artillery** weapons fired from 600 to 800 yards wreaked havoc upon them. A wise defensive commander should always use the military crest and never the actual crest of the hill, preventing troops from being observed or skylined by the enemy. The earth is your primary means of cover and must always be used for protection when possible.

---

195. David F. Trask, *The War with Spain in 1898* (New York: Macmillan, 1981), 246.

General "Fighting-Joe" Wheeler, the only former Confederate General to lead U.S. troops after the War, embodied the spirit of aggression that was typical of U.S. forces when he slipped and said he wanted to attack "the Yankees—dammit, I mean the Spaniards." Shafter consistently had to hold this bold commander back, but the American propensity to keep moving won the day and ultimately led to success on the Santiago heights of San Juan and Kettle Hills! Utilizing a traditional American strength had other positive unintended consequences, too.

The African American or black troops from the **cavalry**, in a still largely segregated military, contributed mightily to the successful hill attacks. One must wonder if the genesis of much of the future changes in the military's, and ultimately the nation's, attitudes towards segregation did not begin here as well. A future president, Teddy Roosevelt, added to his claim for fame and demonstrated his military prowess. Perhaps one of the most important aspects of this battle involved the use of black troops from the 9th Cavalry (not spelled Calvary where Jesus died) and the 10th Cavalry "Buffalo Soldiers." The African-American troops performed valiantly, and with few exceptions these troops gained the affections of their commanders; in particular a future army leader John J. Pershing who said, "We officers of the 10th Cavalry could have taken our black heroes in our arms. They had again fought their way into our affections, as they here had fought their way into the hearts of the American people."[196] Meanwhile the white officers of the 10th Cavalry had some of the highest casualty rates of the war. Leaders must always command the respect of their soldiers, and this respect must be earned through a demonstration of resolve. By sacrificing alongside their men, many future leaders saw the merits of an integrated military in Cuba. In October 1901, the first President to officially entertain a black guest would be former trooper Teddy Roosevelt, "who had served alongside the 'buffalo soldiers.'"

With the heights of San Juan Hill now taken by the attacking **infantry**, and with the Spanish fleet retreating ignominiously from the harbor, the first major phase of the Spanish-American war concluded with a treaty. With the Spanish fleet gone from Santiago Bay, further operations in the Caribbean would bear witness to the effective use of **converging columns** in Puerto Rico under the leadership of Major General Nelson A. Miles. During July of 1898, in the waning days of the Spanish-American War, Miles proclaimed the Americans as liberators, not conquerors, and proceeded to use his troops in columns of approach from different areas. American troops found themselves mostly welcomed by the Puerto Ricans. This decision by Miles to spread troops out in the face of uncertain resistance reflected the impact of the Indian Wars the U.S. Army had been engaged in for the last century on the expanding frontier. Learning to live off the land and covering huge expanses by relying on individual initiative, the use of converging columns represented another AWoF and one uniquely American. Attacking an enemy through converging columns requires great synchronicity, but offers the opportunity to take large areas. This technique most likely emerged during the Indian Wars where large areas had to be policed with few troops. Deploying forces over distances requires an element of non-supervision and is a function of developed leadership. The ability to act decisively and entrust subordinates is in the best tradition of the American military and represents a major reason the deployment of land forces has been a mostly American affair in the last half century. Sadly, the treaty signed on August 12, 1898 with Spain did not end American involvement in the war but instead would only serve as the beginning of a much larger series of wars over the next century with as yet no signs of slowing down.

A major casualty in the occupation of Santiago was the usual army afflictions of drunkenness and disease. Accosting a police officer, Lawton, the drunk logistician of Daiquiri fame, received a stern admonition from President McKinley and had to take an oath to avoid alcohol to maintain his position in the army.[197] This popular commander reflected a serious moral problem facing all

---

196. Ibid, 247.
197. Spencer Tucker, ed., *The Encyclopedia of the Spanish-American and Philippine American Wars* (Santa Barbara: ABC-CLIO, 2009), 330.

U.S. troops confronted with the boredom of occupation duties. Disease also swept through the ranks, in particular yellow fever and typhoid; dysentery and other tropical diseases became commonplace. Adding to the problem, the medical services greatly underestimated the amount of disease that would be encountered. A process of quarantining troops returning to the United States in large measure reflected the public's fears of the high-disease rate experienced by the army.[198] While only 379 soldiers were killed, more than 5,000 died from disease during the war. Proper prior planning in the area of logistics at times has revealed an American propensity to act first and then to plan second. **Logistics**, the study of supply and maintenance, may not be exciting but it is absolutely vital to mission accomplishment. Without question, the war fever of America had required these men to do their duties, and the result would be an empowered and confident young world power now permanently on the world scene.[199]

The Philippines

One of the important things to remember about warfare is that a war rarely ends with the expected consequences. In fact, one could argue persuasively that wars never end; they simply continue on in a different form and in different areas. Both arguments could be said for the Philippines. The U.S. Army is most of all a learning army. Many in our society today, including this writer, would not enjoy academic opportunities if not for the excellent schooling provided by the military services. The U.S. Army would as an institution learn a vital lesson in the Philippines in a new type of war for the Americans referred to as "unconventional" or "guerilla."

Courtesy of The U.S. National Archives

The American entry into the Philippines arguably arrived on the desks of Washington, D.C. quite unexpectedly. Evidence exists showing the real focus of the Spanish-American War from the standpoint of the United States remained on the island of Cuba. Unforeseen consequences always occur in warfare. Due to a centuries-old history of Spanish colonization, the Philippines would become an American responsibility for years to come. Initially the American fleet arrived for the purpose of destroying the Spanish ships in Manila Bay, and, as we have seen in recent wars, the U.S. found itself increasingly embroiled in attempting to "win the peace."

On May 1, 1898, smartly attired in white, Admiral George Dewey gave the initial command to open fire on the Spanish fleet. The U.S. Navy and its superiority proved instrumental in the Philippines War. Geography, as always, played a major role, but as an institution the army had not benefited from the intellectual and technological advances of the navy. A long-time favorite of the Democrats and progressives, the navy enjoyed both strong budgets and technical efficiency. Enjoying political favor, and with the philosophical leadership provided by Admiral Alfred T. Mahan, the navy stood ready to serve. The United States had developed a first-class navy just in time to help win a far-flung war by exploiting the vulnerability of an enemy that needed desperately to control the communications, supply, and sea routes between more than 7,000 islands of the Philippine Archipelago. The army, on the other hand, had to do a lot of learning in the mud.

Armies in the United States tend to be viewed more as a threat by non-conservatives, and the American Army had continued the pattern of being somewhat neglected. Relegated to a frontier

---

198. Ibid, 393. 4 Ibid, 393.
199. Geoffrey Perret, *A Country Made by War* (New York: Random House, 1989), 290.

status in the years since the Civil War, the army had been kept small. A learning army it remained, and the volunteers who quickly filled the ranks would nevertheless learn by trial and error how to win a non-conventional war led by mostly exemplary officers who had cut their teeth throughout the Indian Wars.

Before America entered the Philippines, Emilio **Aguinaldo** had established a reputation as a revolutionary leader by seeking Spanish reforms. In exile in Hong Kong, Aguinaldo had been contacted by the Americans and mysteriously returned to the Philippines. Aguinaldo later claimed a deal had been struck for an independent Philippine nation. Returned to power in May of 1898, American forces had also landed on July 25 and thus began what Brian McAllister Linn describes as a "curious triangular contest" between the Americans, Spanish, and the Filipino revolutionaries led by Aguinaldo.[200]

During the First Battle of Manila, fought in August of 1898, a tragic and comic display occurred whereby the Spanish and Americans together agreed to pretend to engage in combat. The plan's intent served to enable the Spanish to retreat with honor. Unfortunately, no one bothered to tell all of the troops on the line. After a brief firefight, an eventual Spanish retreat left the Americans and Philipinos uneasily watching each other over gunsights, complicating Major General Wesley Merritt's attempts to keep the revolutionaries from occupying Manila, the capital of the Philippines. With the Spanish now leaving, the American army settled into the long, slow occupation—the type that bores and doesn't bring out the best in American troops. Drunkenness and misbehavior soon abounded, in large part because of bad attitudes. Many of the troops had signed up to fight for Cuba's freedom, not the Philippines'. These "**volunteers**," euphemistically designated in a similarly political manner later applied to the term "advisors," represented a major political and legal challenge. The Constitution simply did not allow for the use of the militia outside of the United States. Bypassing this legal nicety then and now represents a major weakness for the American armed forces and works against American public support abroad, at times historically speaking. Consistent with the Ways of War and the love of speed, the American people seemed to quickly lose interest in empire building. This explains the consistent pressure on American army leaders to be imaginative and creative.

Major General Ewell S. Otis did not lack for bravery. Demonstrating courage on Little Round Top during the battle of Gettysburg, this hero from the Civil War, like Aguinaldo and possibly George Washington, had a propensity to do things by the book. Otis' style reflected rigid timetables and "by the numbers" operations. Perhaps his background as a lawyer had trained Otis to see the world through the rational, ordered type of eyes so admired and sought after in military men from yesterday to the present. Otis's efficiency, moreover, had initially proved itself when American troops deployed to the Philippines arrived more quickly and efficiently, particularly in comparison to their counterparts in Cuba. Efficient and methodical were traits destined to reward any future leader, nevertheless these same strengths also limited Otis's warfighting ability when he ascended to a command position. Otis's personality sadly prevented him from effectively earning the loyalty of either subordinates or the media.[201] While Otis organized his unhappy volunteers who were mostly contemptuous of what they perceived as their rigid regular army leaders, Aguinaldo also succumbed to the temptation to form a Western-style fighting force.

The Second Battle of Manila in February of 1899 occurred when a firefight broke out and immediately began spreading along the American lines. Fearing a major attack from Aguinaldo's rebels, the Americans conducted a brilliantly simple and aggressive assault under naval and artillery fires to secure the city of Manila and to drive out resistance. The enemy generally just slipped away and the war entered a longer phase similar to the Indian Wars of the old West that pitted Americans against a tough determined enemy that could survive off of meager supplies while working within a muddy, rain-soaked and generally harsh environment the enemy knew very well.

---

200. Ibid., 23.
201. Brian McAllister Linn, *The Philippine War* (Lawrence, KS: University Press of Kansas, 2000), xx.

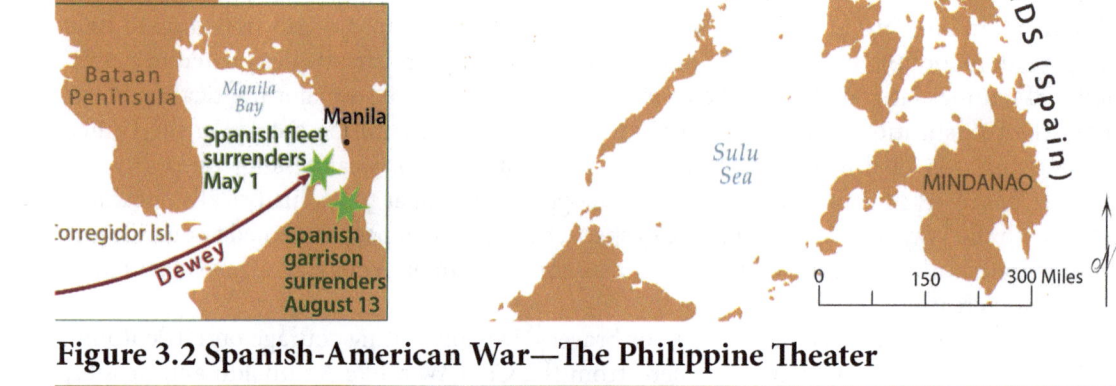

Figure 3.2 Spanish-American War—The Philippine Theater

The war in the Philippines would continue on for years. General Otis continued to use converging columns (AWoF) but increasingly he adhered to rigid timetables and predictable road marches. Ensuring the trains "ran on time," Otis demonstrated a paradox in military leadership. Seeking order and efficiency is the avocation of the military officer, and in particular the staff officer—more on these in the next chapter—but one must never forget that the use of military history is an art. As an art, it is extremely subjective, or human. Humans at their core are unpredictable and irrational. The quest for luxury or change is one such example of this human propensity. To properly conduct forces in an operational sense requires the commander's employment of his unit's strengths while capitalizing on the enemy's weaknesses. Rigidity is the real enemy! The fighter must attempt to see the fight through the enemy's eyes; in other words, being sensitive to the surroundings, culture, economy, and social strengths and vulnerabilities of the opposition. Instead of focusing a critical eye on the enemy, General Otis myopically saw the battlefield through American eyes.

Commanders arriving too late or too early at their destinations received punishment from Otis. The end result of patrols methodically launched into the countryside and the failure of Otis to accompany forces into the field resulted in a frightening propensity to see the situation as presented to him. Pandering and obsequious underlings helped prepare rosy reports to send to Washington, D.C. replete with powerful numbers that supported the view of the army's success and only requesting roughly 40,000 soldiers for the fight. The apparently now sober Major General Henry **Lawton** knew better and reached out to political connections to achieve a "surge" of soldiers: around a hundred thousand men. Lawton said he wanted to ". . . hunt down Aguinaldo the way he had hunted down Geronimo."[202] Ironically, this great American soldier would be shot in the field through the lungs by a Filipino soldier named Geronimo.[203]

Another lesson for the reader here is that the **chain of command** works two ways. What has made the American military a premier fighting force is its inherent ability and willingness to listen to both superiors and subordinates. If the leader does not listen to the advice of those under his/her command, one must expect the voices of subordinates to be heard somewhere else. One mustn't ever solely act on the advice of subordinates, but listening is always a must! So, as Otis sat studying his timetables with a magnifying glass measure of specificity, Major General Lawton and Lieutenant General Arthur MacArthur employed an effective counter-insurgency.

Recognizing the perspectives of the adversary, Lawton and MacArthur used a "**carrot and stick**" approach to pacifying the Philippines. As open-minded thinkers able to "think outside the box," Lawton and MacArthur demonstrated the operational art. They used their nation's total assets and strengths against the enemies' weaknesses. Executing unpredictable and violent attacks when necessary and using the speed of cavalry, Lawton and MacArthur allowed Americans to use the speed they so appreciated. Men ordered to patrol went out again and again, learning the countryside, the people, and the culture like the back of their hands. Pressure maintained on enemy hold-outs who refused American offers of assistance included forms of torture such as "water boarding," while enormous sums of money were handed out to those who ceased resisting—similar to the recent American war in Afghanistan. Aguinaldo and their troops continued to see their bases of support eroded with Americans building hospitals and roads. Otis's departure from the Philippines and MacArthur's subsequent command saw the reward of audacity and the use of the "carrot and stick" to wear the opposition down.

Through individual bravery and imagination as well as **learning and innovation**, the AWoF also revealed itself in the actions of Medal of Honor recipient Major Frederick Funston who single-handedly captured Aguinaldo. Ordered to proceed with this secret mission, the normally taciturn MacArthur, when approving the plan said, "Funston, this is a desperate undertaking. I fear that I shall never see you again."[204] Pretending to be a prisoner, Funston employed another successful way of war (AWoF) by using disgruntled former rebels. These indigenous peoples, many of whom came from the Macabebe community, represented the fruits of treating any people with dignity and compassion while simultaneously using force to prove resolve. The **Macabebe scouts** followed an earlier

Colonel Frederick Funston

". . . crossed the river on a raft and by his skill and daring enabled the general commanding to carry the enemy's entrenched position on the north bank of the river and to drive him with great loss from the important strategic position of Calumpit."

(At Rio Grande de la Pampanga, Luzon, Philippine Islands, 27 April 1899)

excerpt from Congressional Medal of Honor citation

From Overland Monthly, Vol. 48, No. 4, (October 1906), p. 257

---

202. H. W. Crocker III, *Don't Tread on Me* (New York: Crown Forum, 2006), 247.
203. Ibid.
204. Ibid, 249.

development in the Indian Wars that served as the successful model for the use of indigenous peoples and also showed the aspiring commander the importance of studying and understanding the enemy's culture and perspective. The Macabebes had originally been native to Mexico, but had been brought to the Philippines and remained outside the charm of Aguinaldo. Funston had native soldiers escort him, tied up, to Aguinaldo's secret headquarters where Funston proceeded to give up the ruse and captured the rebel leader.

It would be nice to be able to say the war ended here. The Revolutionaries hoped that the isolationist candidate for president in 1900, William J. Bryan, would be a "peace candidate who would grant the Philippines their independence." This hope of the enemy represented a predecessor of sorts of the "peace movement"—a reoccurring symptom of the same American war-weariness that had haunted Lincoln during the Civil War and would later visit presidents in Vietnam, Iraq, and Afghanistan. The war instead began to settle into a frustrating period, and it is at this time that Lawton was killed by a sniper during efforts designed to win over the population. A battle of nerves began with the race against time as the army attempted to subdue the archipelago while war weariness set in at home. Sincerely desirous of avoiding the trappings of empire, the "liberal" Republicans wanted to turn back to what they saw as a constitutional republic true to the values of the American Revolution. With McKinley's reelection hopes of peace for the insurrectos dashed, but the media nevertheless began to turn against the War.

One particularly terrible atrocity occurred on the island of Samar where forty-eight Americans were killed and hacked to death at breakfast. Headlines would reveal that their bodies had been desecrated. The "worst disaster since the Little Big Horn" worked its way into American reader's minds as the long war of nation-building continued.[205] The Army received more bad publicity, and the war effort ground on as Senate hearings and subsequent unfortunate comparisons to the Boer War revealed the U.S. Army had used similar tactics in the Philippines to those used by the Spanish in Cuba and by British forces in South Africa with barbed wire and blockhouses. Abuses both real and imagined now amplified concerns by a curiously bored public. An indignant media—the same that had whipped up war fever over such conduct in Cuba—now turned increasingly against the army. The aftermath of the Samar campaign demonstrated an important fact to future American commanders and leaders: the AWoF are absolutely dependent on a rapid conclusion to fighting. If not, war-weariness will likely begin to sap the strength of the military as morale sinks and soldiers begin to ask themselves, "Why are we fighting?"

In their first major war outside the contiguous United States, the American people became increasingly alarmed by what seemed an endless war in the Philippines. President Theodore Roosevelt, taking over as Commander-in-Chief after McKinley's assassination, declared the war over on July 4, 1902. This "mission accomplished" betrayed a longer war to come, similar to what American forces would experience in Iraq over a century later. As Luzon, the larger island to the north, became secure, it seemed the adversary simply moved to another island to the south. The U.S. Navy continued to take its toll on the insurrectos, however. Eventually in Muslim Mindanao, General James J. "Black Jack" Pershing achieved victory in placating the fierce Moro warriors through combinations of demonstrations of strength and by modeling dignity and an understanding of traditional authorities and courtesy. Burying jihadists with pigs but rewarding cooperation with development, the carrot and stick anticipated the "Anbar Awakening" in Iraq in 2006. The development of Pershing's leadership would prove instrumental to the development of a global fighting force. Like George Washington, Pershing's dignified and serious approach to leadership within the army would reinforce a tradition of clean precision and stoic bearing—grooming future leaders such as the great George C. Marshall, the eventual architect of the American Army during World War II.

---

205. Ibid., 249.

A highly divisive war, the Philippines quickly became a forgotten endeavor, except for the men who served. Virtually every army unit rotated in and out of the islands, as did every officer in the army. The war in the Philippines served as a catalyst for a frontier army to become an efficient expeditionary force and a weapon serving the constitution abroad in the next century. Another AWoF is the use of a **preponderance of firepower**; therefore, perhaps most importantly, the realization that innovative weapons such as smoke-less powders, bolt action rifles, and the popular .45 caliber Colt automatic pistol in themselves proved simply insufficient to win a "small war." To win the non-conventional war it was necessary to create fear in the hearts of the enemy, but it also required the personal touch as well. Utilizing combat patrols of indeterminate length and schedule, harsh methods, and a growing awareness of the culture through the **use of indigenous peoples** created a favorable atmosphere for victory and reflected the AWoF.

The United States, though remaining in the Philippines for years to come, had in many ways established a strong kinship with the Filipino peoples. Another result of the Spanish-American War in general would be numerous reforms mentioned in the next chapter. Perhaps most importantly, the unintended consequences of the war would lead to a collision between the Americans and the Japanese in World War II. Over 4,000 Americans died in the Philippine Insurrection. According to Geoffrey Perret, "The casualty figures revealed the kind of struggle it had been. More men fell in ones and twos, murdered in back alleys, in flyblown village bars, and in the arms of smiling girls, than fell in open combat." The Philippines war would reemerge in army consciousness much later, and it surely will again![206]

Technology of the Spanish-American War

The American Military has never been the largest fighting force in the world. Up until the Spanish-American War, it was a little brother next to its European counterparts. What made the American Military unique was its ability to develop new technology that fit modern military doctrines and tactics that were being developed in the 19th and 20th centuries. For European armed forces, their proverbial glass was full, so they needed to get rid of certain tactics to accommodate new technologies. As the United States entered the scene with an empty glass, they were able to adopt and adapt the best of the modern doctrines and tactics to fit the AWoF. Technology has had a large impact on the AWoF that developed in the modern area. The inventions, innovations, and mechanical processes have had an impact on all areas of the AWoF including speed, firepower, native intelligences, and the highly innovative military fighting tactics.

What is imperative to note is that America did not have a definitive answer to any military issue. What made American military technology so great was the ability to learn from past failures instead of giving up and starting over. The United States would create committees or assign researchers and innovators to look into issues that the army, navy, or air force would have in order to improve their fighting capability. This would be accomplished mainly through innovation and occasionally through new inventions. As each war is studied, be sure to pay close attention to the technology being used. Notice that when it fails, the United States fixes its past weakness and improves on its strengths. This theme can be seen throughout the study of Modern American Military History.

The Spanish-American War had some major advancements in military technologies. These technologies played a very important role in naval and land battles. American's advanced weapons were the major reasons for the defeat of the Spanish.

---

206. Perret, *Country*, 297.

In 1890, the United States launched its first modern, armored navy warship. These warships were designed to be fast, heavily armed, and were equipped with 18-inch armor. This new steam-powered naval ship now compared to their European counterpart. There was worldwide doubt as to the seaworthiness, power, and range of these warships. The Spanish-American War was the national stage America needed to prove the worthiness of its new warship.[207]

The Spanish had weapons with very limited range. Due to America's advancements in technology, they had a larger range, giving a clear advantage. One of the newest weapons was the Gatling gun. The Gatling gun was one of the earliest versions of the modern machine gun. The advantage of this weapon was that it had a larger kill radius and was easy to operate. The sheer ease of operation allowed for more men to use this weapon without previous training on the battlefield.

Another advancement in technology was the Hotchkiss Mountain gun. The portability of the Hotchkiss Mountain gun was its major advancement. The Americans were able to react faster to attacks than the Spanish. The Hotchkiss gun had two different size barrels: the 1.65-inch and the 3-inch. The army could accurately fire up to 2,000 yards at 43 rounds per minute. This technology was instrumental in the Spanish-American War and was the first generation of the artillery and machines that the American Military would use in the many wars to come. The focus of future technological advancements was to make them more powerful, mobile, and accurate.

Besides technological advances in weaponry, medicine was another advancement. Unlike the weapons' technology that was created during the Spanish-American War, medical advancement was necessary because of the amount of mass deaths due to the new diseases encountered on the battlefield. In the Spanish-American War, there was a 7:1 ratio of soldiers who died of diseases as opposed to actual warfare on the battlefield. Typhoid was the main killer. Virginia resident Walter Reed and his team were assigned to investigate typhoid. The result of the investigation was that flies were the major carriers, followed by human contact from human carriers. Reed told the military that sanitary measures were the best way to limit the spread of the disease. A few years later, a vaccination was created. The vaccination targeted the bacilli, which largely eliminated the threat of typhoid. This was important because it allowed American troops to become more mobile by their ability to operate on foreign, tropical soils without the threat of diseases.[208]

Key Terms:

American Ways of Fighting	***USS Maine***	**Insurgents**
Speed	**Krag-Jorgenson**	**Operations**
Use of indigenous peoples	**Enfilade**	**Logistics**
Rapidly impatient	**Frontal assault**	**Aguinaldo**
Preponderance of firepower	**Cover**	**Volunteers**
Learning and adaptable/innovative	**Concealment**	**Lawton**
	Defilade	**Chain of Command**
Maneuverability	**Artillery**	**Carrot and stick**
Converging columns	**Cavalry**	**Macabebe scouts**
Yellow Press	**Infantry**	

---

207. Barton C. Hacker, *American Military Technology: The Life Story of a Technology* (Baltimore: The Johns Hopkins University Press, 2007), 53.
208. Hacker, *American Military Technology*, 54.

Thought Questions:

Which of the AWoF described in this chapter did the army demonstrate in its liberation of Cuba and occupation of the Philippines?

How did the occupation of Iraq under Generals Abazaid and Casey mirror or differ from the planning of General Otis in the Philippines?

In what ways did Lawton and MacArthur's request for more troops parallel the surge in Iraq in 2005–06?

Chapter IV

WORLD WAR I

Matthew 24: 7-8 "For nation will rise against nation, and kingdom against kingdom. And there will be famines, pestilences, and earthquakes in various places. All these things are the beginning of sorrows." NKJV

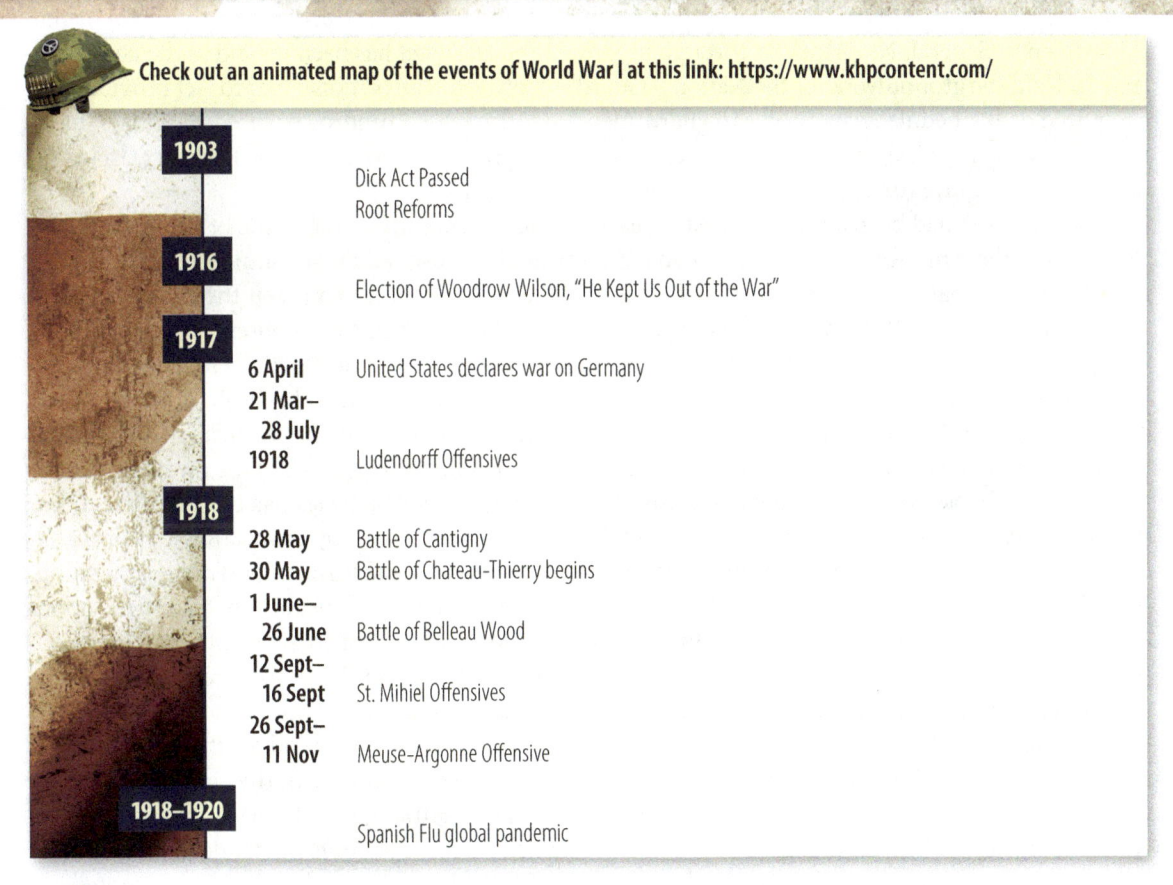

Check out an animated map of the events of World War I at this link: https://www.khpcontent.com/

1903	Dick Act Passed Root Reforms
1916	Election of Woodrow Wilson, "He Kept Us Out of the War"
1917	
6 April	United States declares war on Germany
21 Mar–28 July 1918	Ludendorff Offensives
1918	
28 May	Battle of Cantigny
30 May	Battle of Chateau-Thierry begins
1 June–26 June	Battle of Belleau Wood
12 Sept–16 Sept	St. Mihiel Offensives
26 Sept–11 Nov	Meuse-Argonne Offensive
1918–1920	Spanish Flu global pandemic

Go to www.khpcontent.com to watch a video introduction for this chapter.

The First World War is sadly one of the more forgotten aspects of American military history today. Nestled between the American Civil War and World War II, this war consisted of a complexly huge scale of operations and ended abruptly. One must remember the first large-scale foreign war America ever fought and the arrival of doughboys hastily thrown just in time into a confusing series of fights. The brutal and terrible nature of the Great War, both gigantic in scope and terrible in its consequences, with fighting on a scale throughout the globe at a level never seen by mankind, marked the beginning of the end of the European empires and the rise of an American century. Many serious Christian thinkers even suggest this horrific struggle represented one of the initial birth pangs indicative of the end times. This murderous fruit of the Industrial Revolution would kill with a deadly assembly-line efficiency, leaving a generation of war widows and shattered families. Mercifully the United States had experienced changes that enabled it to play a part in the war, but at the same time had the good fortune to stay out of World War I until the very end. Few people know the story of this war and the many personalities that emerged. Even fewer know the conduct and consequently horrible results, instead relying on a cheerful memory of the past to continue justification for war to achieve either idealistic or political ends. Hopefully the student of this chapter will never experience anything similar to this war, but the ability to learn from the mistakes and successes of the past is always profitable and never more so than for the one expected to forge their craft in the military.

One of the lessons of the Spanish-American War consisted of the realization that something simply must be done with the National Guard. Too rich in manpower to ignore, the citizen-soldier tradition had existed as long as the nation. To overcome legal challenges and to ensure a fighting reserve existed for future missions, the nation turned to the Dick Act. The **Dick Act** of 1903 provided for the training and funding of National Guard units to enable them to achieve levels of training commensurate with the regular U.S. Army. Additionally, the Dick Act would codify the circumstances in which the Guard could be federalized. Still controversial at the time of passage, the act was ruled unconstitutional by the U.S. Attorney General. Nevertheless, through precedent the Dick Act has been upheld as the law of the land and laid the groundwork for the National Guard Act of 1916. The National Guard Act provided for a required drill schedule recognizable to guardsmen today. Increased funding ensured National Guard capabilities and training existed then and continues to the present. Shortly after the Dick Act, an inspiration from the grave further improved America's fighting capability.

Emory Upton had been a thinker most of his army career. As early as the Battle of Spotsylvania in 1864 during the American Civil War, he had experimented with squad tactics similar to those developed by the Germans later in World War I. This brilliant military mind had seen the use of modern artillery in the Franco-Prussian War where he had been sent by the army as an observer. Nevertheless, this genius grew increasingly frustrated by what he perceived to be the quintessential American propensity to go to war unprepared. Suffering from depression and severe headaches, this brilliant young mind died from a self-inflicted gunshot to the head. Published shortly after his death, a former friend released Upton's manuscript entitled *The Military Policy of the United States*. Perhaps one of the most important aspects of the book would be military reforms of the regular army. His thesis has been a bedrock for debate concerning military preparedness (or the lack thereof) ever since by advocating a strong and expandable regular army as the centerpiece of an American defense establishment; no more depending on militias and volunteers. Instead a ready reserve would stand trained and ready to be mobilized upon command. Compared to the great naval thinker, Alfred T. Mahan (see last chapter), who had overseen the improvements of the navy, Upton is today considered to be Mahan's military counterpart.

The **Root Reforms** of 1903 saw the creation of America's General Staff and a system of professional education. West Point had existed for nearly a century, but a General Staff would require more specific education for senior officers specializing in various branches of the complex modern military. The War College and a series of service schools specializing in artillery and signal corps would soon follow. The high degree of specialty reflected in these schools portended the need for greater planning before future wars could be fought. An increasingly complex world represented by telephones, railroads, and motor cars required increasing technical knowledge of the craft of war.

The **General Staff** tasked with war planning started a tradition that has continued to the present. It is so important for the military to receive officers knowledgeable in history, geography, and other cultures—not just to fight, but to plan the fights of the future. As a winning football coach once taught the writer, "Football games are won on the practice field." For similar reasons, it is a sacred duty for the aspiring commander to understand the need for and importance of staff work. Napoleon once said, "An army moves on its stomach" (by the way, Napoleon said so many things one often wonders how he found time to fight). Remember, it is too easy to draw a blue arrow on a map. The challenge is logistics: to supply, train, and plan these operations—this is why you must attack your subjects in school with total devotion and diligence. Speaking of Napoleon, he deserves credit for the current organization of the American military into various corps; each corps in turn consisted of divisions and the division represented America's first line of defense in World War I.

The division at the time was called the "**square division**," and it reflected the American desire to take ground. With two divisions up and two behind, organizers believed a force could be moved more quickly. The American divisions received numerical designations, 1–25 for regular, 26–42 for National Guard (half of which would be draftees in WWI), and numbers 43 and up would be for the draftees and a smattering of regulars.

So how well did all of these reforms work? World War I ultimately saw a victorious American Army claim it had saved Paris from the Germans. Obscenely overstated, one cannot imagine how a spirit of confidence could not come from World War I. The Americans entered at the very end; just in time to participate in and arguably assure an Allied victory. Many Americans at the time could not understand why we entered the war.

Progressivism, defined here as the desire to reform government and to make it more responsive to the people, exhibited expansive tendencies that had led to the Spanish-American War. The American people watched with collective eyebrows raised as the Germans conducted unlimited submarine warfare in a war of oceanography against its island-enemy Great Britain. Increasingly the world seemed to be becoming smaller, what geographers today call globalization. The Americans had found their economy and culture inextricably intertwined with those of the Allied Powers: Great Britain, France, and Japan. An unfortunate series of blunders carefully publicized to the Americans by the British who controlled the trans-Atlantic cable saw the Germans promising through the **Zimmerman Telegram** to restore to Mexico the land it lost to the United States in the War with Mexico in the last century, if the Mexicans would help the Germans. Coming on the heels of the Punitive expedition, this caused an uproar.

The **Punitive expedition** saw American troops pursuing Pancho Villa, whose men had raided and killed U.S. citizens and military personnel. Crossing back into the Mexican border, the most noteworthy aspect of the expedition to catch Villa (which failed, by the way) was the use of aircraft and motor cars—the rapidity Americans loved was embodied in new technology. Leading this convoy was **John J. Pershing**, the former commander of black troops, hence the nick-name "Black Jack." Pershing's success in the expedition (or lack thereof) gave him publicity, allowing him to replace the hero of the Philippines, Frederick Funston, upon Funston's unexpected death as the head of the army. The stoic and ramrod-straight, silent Pershing would be a powerful figure who would embody the explosive growth and power of the American military forces for the remaining century.

General of the Armies John J. Pershing

General Pershing embodied the fruits of the Holy Spirit of both self-control and patience. Pershing set the standard for leadership throughout the modern American military history experience by his stoic and dedicated demeanor and bearing. The leadership trait of endurance would mark his successful career. Pershing cut his teeth as an army officer fighting the Apaches and he would eventually hold a position of command with the 10th Cavalry–originally "Buffalo Soldier" regiments. As one who had experienced the true diversity of the American military experience, his dour and stiff demeanor earned him the nick-name "Black Jack." Pershing's ability to work with different people served him well in the Philippines where he earned the respect of Muslim

> Moro leaders on the island of Mindanao. He used force as a last resort when improvements to infrastructures and displays of technology failed. Finishing the war as a Captain in the regulars, Pershing suffered the heartbreak of losing his wife and three daughters in a house fire in their California home. Enduring this tragedy, Pershing would by 1916 lead the punitive expedition into Mexico for the purpose of capturing Pancho Villa. Utilizing the new technologies of the motorcar, machine gun, aircraft, and modern communications techniques, Pershing received valuable exposure to the possibilities of supporting arms on the modern maneuver battlefield. When Frederick Funston unexpectedly died, Pershing went from Captain to General under the guidance of President Theodore Roosevelt. Roosevelt had himself escaped the confines of a political elite by serving in the Army and knew of Pershing's reputation in the assault on San Juan Hill, where Pershing had received the Silver Star. Pershing, like Roosevelt, would use the lessons of his military career, displaying the Army value of selfless service by developing a young George C. Marshall in World War I. Often criticized for his reliance on simple frontal assaults, the critics forget that the American Army had essentially transformed from a frontier police force swimming ashore in Cuba to, within a generation, sending millions to save France in World War I. One of Pershing's first acts in France involved visiting Napoleon's tomb and when offered Napoleon's sword, Pershing—instead of accepting it—bowed and kissed it as if to send the clear message of American humility, demonstrating the understanding of enormous French sacrifices compared to the American Army still unbloodied and unproven. Pershing's unselfish nature and humble habit of developing juniors would create a chain of Army leadership that would follow for the next half century.
>
> Enduring hardship and sacrifice, General Pershing's examples of self-control and stoic professionalism would be rewarded with the rank of General of the Armies, the highest rank attainable in the U.S. Army. More importantly, General Pershing served as a mentor and example to George C. Marshall. Through his selfless service and patience, Pershing in large measure would set the standard for American leadership in the decades to come.[209]

The First World War is often portrayed as a static bloodbath whereby the Europeans simply had bled themselves dry in an era of great technological change. Millions did die for reasons difficult to understand today. A long era of aristocratic order gave way to weakened empires eventually to be replaced on the world scene by the Americans as a premier world power. These large, seemingly always singing, fresh-faced young men, so blessed to stay out of the war until the last years, arrived at a key moment to turn the tide. Later, somewhat incorrectly but understandably, bragging they had saved Paris from the Germans, the Americans would receive a valuable jolt of self-confidence from World War I, in many ways leading to a permanent fighting force ready to expand—the sort Emory Upton could only have dreamed of. The story of how America entered this war is of interest to us.

Of the many inventions on the battlefield, the ship may ultimately have brought America into World War I; more specifically, the undersea ship or submarine. Essentially landlocked, the Allies, able to block the North Sea and Scapa Flow to prevent Germany from controlling the high seas after the Battle of Jutland in 1915, forced the Germans to turn to the use of submarines for total or **unrestricted submarine warfare**. German policy to authorize attacks upon neutral and belligerent shipping in all-out warfare in the war zone represented the key aspect of unrestricted submarine warfare instrumental to bringing the United States into the First World War. According to Harvey

---

209. Geoffrey Perret, *A Country Made by War* (New York: Random House, 1989), 315.

A. DeWeerd, the decision to build fleets of surface vessels by the Germans during both wars represented a mistake of historical proportions. Submarines would be the key naval warships emerging from both world wars, but with most pre-war funding going into surface vessels.[210]

Sweeping across the Great European Plains, the aircraft aided French forces in anticipating where the Germans were. The motor car brought the French troops to the front at record time. This intertwining of geography and technology is essentially what World War I seemed to be about from a grand strategic stand point. Terrible murder grounds such as the Somme and Verdun would see the exhausted nations of Germany and Britain staggering to stay in the fight, while their home populations grew hungry and more anxious.

The American president Woodrow Wilson was a complex personality. All politicians love power, and his ego demanded no less than any other. The last academic to serve as a president, Wilson, before becoming governor of New Jersey, had grown up in Virginia. Less suspicious of navies than armies, this man showed great interest in the traditional American demand for freedom of the seas. When the Germans began unrestricted submarine warfare, it became impossible for Wilson to ignore the demands of business and humanity by refusing to arm merchant ships or grant loans to the Allies. Generally a pacifist—Wilson had threatened to fire the General Staff for creating war plans—Wilson nonetheless went along with an obscure Democratic Party operative who had coined the slogan, **"he kept us out of the war."** This statement reveals the collective relief the American people felt at being relegated to the sidelines during the war. Nonetheless, a remarkably short time after achieving reelection, Wilson agreed to enter war. Wilson's cabinet represented men who seemed more likely to lead church revivals or anti-alcohol meetings than warriors. The isolationist and passionately Christian Secretary of State William J. Bryan eventually resigned in disgust, but one must ask oneself why the president, who had chosen a pacifist-like "efficiency expert," the diminutive Newton Baker, would take the nation to war? Small enough to blow away in a bad storm, this thin, nearly blind little man would surprisingly represent the best aspects of military civil relations with the General of the Armies of the United States: John J. "Black Jack" Pershing. On April 2, 1917 President Wilson went before a joint session of Congress to ask for a **declaration of war**. Watertight legally, with a public decidedly against a German victory in the War, and a chain-of-command in place with a clear mission for victory, the Americans entered the Great War.

The three dimensional battlefield of World War I had seen many developments. Americans had begun to lead the way in weapons' development. From Gatling to Browning, automatic weapons development had followed the inventors Maxim to Britain and Hotchkiss to France. American firepower seemed to be everywhere; from flying overhead in aircrafts, to inside the new invention of the tank, a mobile armored platform designed for the purpose of destroying the machine-gun nest. The rate of fire of 400–500 rounds a minute at ranges of 4,000 yards would explain the carnage of this war, witnessing the deaths of over 500 men in the opening minutes. In addition to the submarine and machine gun, the use of the deadly but fickle poisonous gas floating over the hundreds of miles of trenches greeted the American doughboys. No one is really sure why the name doughboy stuck or even what it meant. Some think it came from the Punitive Expedition to capture Pancho Villa where the men, covered by white desert dust, appeared to be dough-like. Regardless, Pershing encountered forces exhausted, but still innovative, when his Americans arrived.

At odds with the American propensity for firepower and maneuver, the Europeans had worked in trench warfare for years and looked pitifully at the new Americans with their big ideas. The use of **phase lines** familiar to commanders today, such as the Fire Support Coordination Line and the Forward Edge of the Battle Area, marked lateral limits for units on maps, making firepower accuracy and coordination easier. Limited by the use of the telephone and its easily cut wires, initial artillery bombardments, or barrages, might last days. Hopelessly attempting to destroy barbed wire innovations, including the M106 fuse that was designed to explode on contact, still provided insufficient support for troops to cross the moon-like landscapes of the battlefield; often only to arrive exhausted and

---

210. Harvey A. DeWeerd, *President Wilson Fights His War* (New York: Macmillan, 1968), 18.

without ammunition. Because of the vulnerabilities of field communications, which included relying on large telephones, runners, and pigeons, reserve forces would usually arrive too slowly to reinforce breakthroughs. The rail system used by the defense enhanced the advantage of **interior lines**, thereby enabling resupply of men, ammunition, and supplies generally favoring the defenders. In short, the advantage went to the Germans by 1917.

By the time the Americans arrived in 1917, the Ludendorff Offensive was building steam to unleash lessons learned by the German army. Utilizing light troops armed with automatic rifles (not machine guns—much lighter) and explosive charges, usually one behind the other in a staggered column-type formation and moving quickly like an "Indian run," these intelligent "storm troopers" would bypass enemy machine guns instead of frontally assaulting them. Using the reverse slopes of hills on the military crest (about a meter off the hill top), the advancing army would provide an automatic base of fire for the leapfrogging squads by basically firing overhead of the attackers and covering the advances. These "**shock-troop tactics**," along with shorter artillery fires, sometimes lasted only for a few minutes and were often fired to throw off the enemy as to the actual intended direction of the forth-coming attack. These tactics also used the mortar, which some military authorities claim to have been what really rescued the ability of infantry to remain the "queen of battle" in World War I. Unfortunately for the Germans, their earlier experiences with Allied tanks had convinced them the weapons proved to be unreliable. The Allies found they could themselves reduce expenditures of artillery because of the tanks with the direct fire capabilities their cannons provided. Regardless, fighting with what today might be roughly called assault weapons, these high-volume-firing, shorter weapons often would be fired from the hip as invading forces would rush to secure trench lines. German innovation almost brought success, and, had it not been for the new kids in town, probably would have worked.

Eschewing these expensively earned European trench fighting-techniques, the American pride in marksmanship and the bayonet as embodied in the M1903 Springfield rifle, continued to demand the Americans not be fed piecemeal into the breach of battle as the French and British commanders seemed to demand. When confronted by Ferdinand Foch who asked if "he were willing to lose the war?" rather than allow U.S. forces to submit to European leadership, Pershing calmly replied, "Yes, I am willing to take the risk."[211] The only reason Pershing could do this is because the Declaration of War President Wilson had received allowed him as Commander-in-Chief to delegate his authority to the Secretary of War, Newton Baker. The Secretary of War in turn supported Pershing entirely and this gave the Americans their chance to fight as Americans and to show what they could do.

American military leadership in the last century has understood the need for education. Some would say the army and military today are, as argued earlier, the premier educational establishments; taking relatively unmotivated men and women and educating them, propelling them to greater positions of responsibility in the nation—in many ways more effectively than the so-called educational system funded to do this job. Pershing believed it took a year to create a soldier. The Chief of Staff of the army, Peyton March, probably better reflected reality when he said six months. Nevertheless, the time to train an entire division to fight as a team remained about a year.[212] According to Geoffrey Perret, from whom much of this volume derives, General March had been given full authority over the various bureaus of the army and represented the fulfillment of the planning and coordinating role the Root Reforms and Emory Upton had sought.[213] Here lay the rub: the progressives in America

---

211. David Woodworth, *The American Army and the First World War* (London: Cambridge, 2014), 214.
212. Perret, *Country*, 317.
213. Ibid, 319.

had organized the vast material potential of the United States and turned it into a fighting machine effectively able to negotiate a peace involving the first attempt at an IGO (intergovernmental organization), namely the League of Nations. In retrospect, America's great purpose seemed to be to enable a one-world government to be created, which would in a different form over a generation later oversee the protection of the creation of the state of Israel.

For all of the advances in industrial production, the use of capital by the United States under men such as Bernard Baruch, the War Industries Board (WIB—note the beginning of "alphabet soup" for organizational designations) and their teams of "four minute men," quick to give speeches supporting the government and the need to invest in the war efforts, the American troops still remained without heavy weapons when they went into the fight. Terrifically blessed with small arms such as the Colt .45 automatic pistol and eventually the BAR, the American Army Division screamed out for 700 tons of supplies and food a day, placing a premium on ports for resupply—a harbinger of World War II.[214] As for manpower—where were all of these men needed for the war to come from?

The **Selective Service** created local boards for the purpose of obtaining soldiers. These local boards had the effect of pulling Americans in behind the war effort, and for their time, proved an ideal way for the army to escape blame for conscription. Not working so well in a later war, in World War I the Selective Service created what amounted to a first-class operation; with about half drafted and half turned down, the army became one of the more selective institutions in America indeed.[215] The growth of various government agencies and the involvement of government in the military and industry represents a progressive achievement and one that has continued to the present.

Winning the Battle of the Atlantic and using the convoy system whereby merchant vessels sailed together like herds of browsing animals wary of a lion, these ships quickly hurried to the center of the Atlantic where German subs could not reach them. Increasingly protected by torpedo submarine destroyers, as in World War II, much of the American industry would funnel its production to go into this battle of the Atlantic. Securing the Atlantic represented America's ability to send the much needed troops into Europe.

Virtually all of the tanks, artillery, and aircraft the American Army fought with in France resulted from foreign production. Aside from small arms, the Americans went into battle wearing British-type helmets and supported by European manufactured supporting arms. The primary contribution of America in World War I consisted of crossing the Atlantic with sufficient manpower and hard-charging infantry to be tossed into the meat grinder in time to possibly save France.

The **Ludendorff Offensive** literally knocked on the doors of Paris. Railguns capable of firing up to 70 miles and taking about three minutes to hit their targets spewed their deadly projectiles. As a preview of the rocket attacks used in World War II, it seemed the Germans would win the war. The British and French after 1916 had little left and the last spring offensive of 1917 had seen French divisions evaporated when 200,000 casualties left men planning mutinies.[216] Now in the spring of 1918, a large bulge in the lines—or salient as it is called in military speak—had created a situation ripe for the picking. Pershing ordered the American forces on May 28 into the fight at Cantigny. Here American morale received a firm boost when the elite shock-troops of Oskar Von Hutier's (the creator of the aforementioned storm trooper tactics) 18th Army saw themselves thrown on their backs—American style. No more men cowering in trenches here. The naïve but bold Americans under the Big Red One patch, the 1st Division, had arrived. From May 30 to June 17, the 3rd Division would enter Chateau-Thierry, hold, then counter-attack. U.S. Marines attacked into the forest at Belleau Wood and shocked the Germans with their marksmanship abilities, hitting German targets at unheard ranges of up to 800 yards. These fourth and fifth German offensives eventually ground down German hopes for victory. Losing over 5,000 men, and with a thousand killed in almost three weeks of fighting, the motivation of these combatants further turned German morale

---

214. Ibid, 323.
215. Ibid, 316.
216. Ibid, 320.

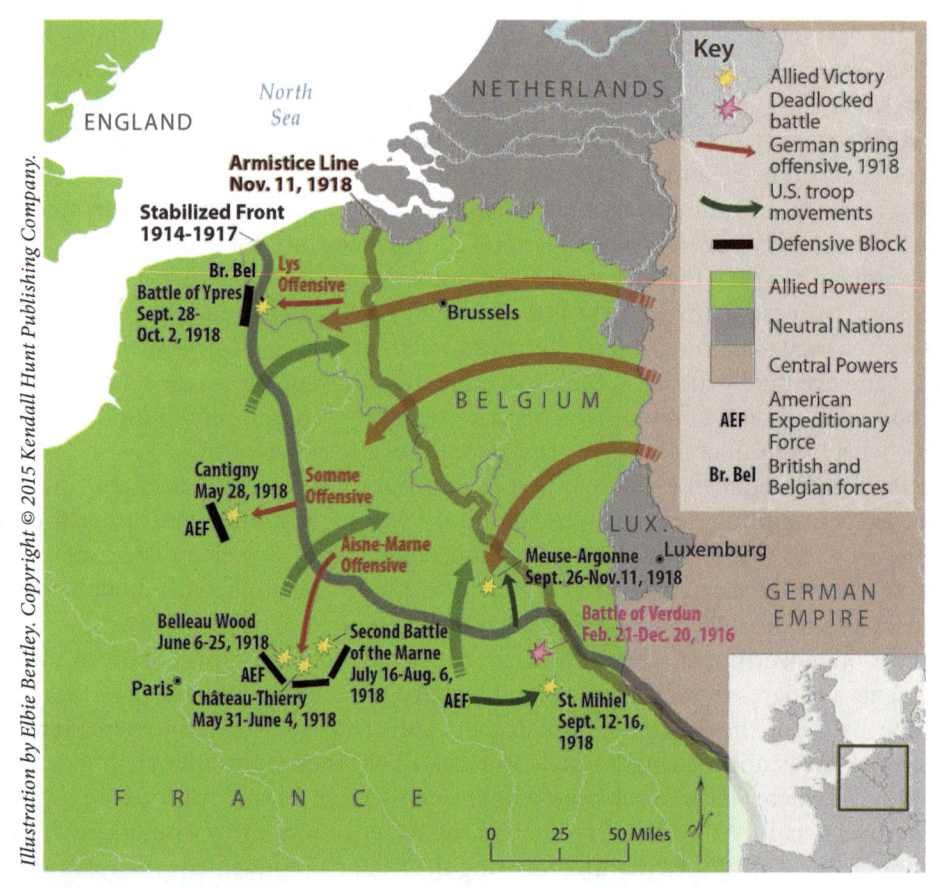

Figure 4.1 WWI

like prize fighters in the last round seeing a fresh opponent. After the Americans took Belleau Wood and held at Cantigny, Chateau-Thierry and Soissons, the tide had turned for the American-French-British alliance!

Events started to move quickly with the ending of the Ludendorff Offensive and the Allied advances. With the Amiens Offensive of August 8, German officers funneled troops into the line, often at gunpoint. Increasing numbers of Germans wanted the war to end and, at this crucial moment of poor morale on the German side, American troops participated in the St. Mihiel Salient Offensives of September 12–16. American military leadership continued to demonstrate both boldness and dedication. Marine General John A. Lejeune actually led the American 2nd Division at Mont Blanc, marking a historic event whereby a marine officer commanded army troops. During the first week of October, as a German Corporal named Adolf Hitler lay blinded by British chlorine gas, American-led Allies continued to advance.

Still not allowing the Germans to catch their breaths, the Allies quickly exploited this gift of the gods—more American manpower arriving daily! Sensing the Germans had reached the cracking point, with information from prisoners revealing desperation on the part of the Germans, the Allies counterattacked.

Pershing, ever the thinker, had chosen the Meuse-Argonne area as a place where he could demonstrate the AWoF—maneuver and firepower used aggressively in the open. The battles of the Meuse-Argonne Offensive would consist of three basic phases whereby subsequent lines of hills would be taken. The battlefield consisted of an enormous valley, flanked on the sides by the forest on the American left and the Meuse River on the right. The fighting seemed to be a confused affair with grenades, small arms, and the bayonet being used in a confused melee where junior troops often rose to the occasion; where records are sparse, the faces of courage emerged.

Many know of the exploits of the brave Christian pacifist Alvin York. The man who was dedicated against the use of alcohol and whose modesty prohibited him from allowing his fame to be used for commercial purposes, had single-handedly captured more than 130 Germans after killing 25 and taking out 35 machine gun emplacements.[217] Captain Frank Williams, another example of courage, used a Western style quick-draw approach. This former sheriff, according to H.W. Crocker III, killed four of the five Germans who held an American soldier captive. Finally, from Mr. Crocker again, we see a soldier who, when he ran out of ammunition, attacked machine guns with a pick axe.[218] No wonder the ferocity of the American attack forced back the Germans, who saw the Americans just keep coming no matter how many seemed to die. What did future leaders do during this brawl?

Examples of courage can extend to the realm of morale, too. **Douglas MacArthur**, who was such an important figure in 20th century military history and was the son of the General MacArthur described in the last chapter, famously exhorted Lt. Col George Patton not to worry when the shelling came too close: "You never hear the one that gets you." Demonstrably brave during the First World War, both of these future leaders would emerge from the Meuse-Argonne, as would the ultimate architect of the Second World War—the great **George C. Marshall**. After listening to his division commander unfairly receive a berating from General Pershing, Major Marshall reached out and grabbed the General's arm as he turned to leave. Exhibiting unbelievable moral courage in confronting the stern, dour General Pershing, Marshall demonstrated his knowledge of

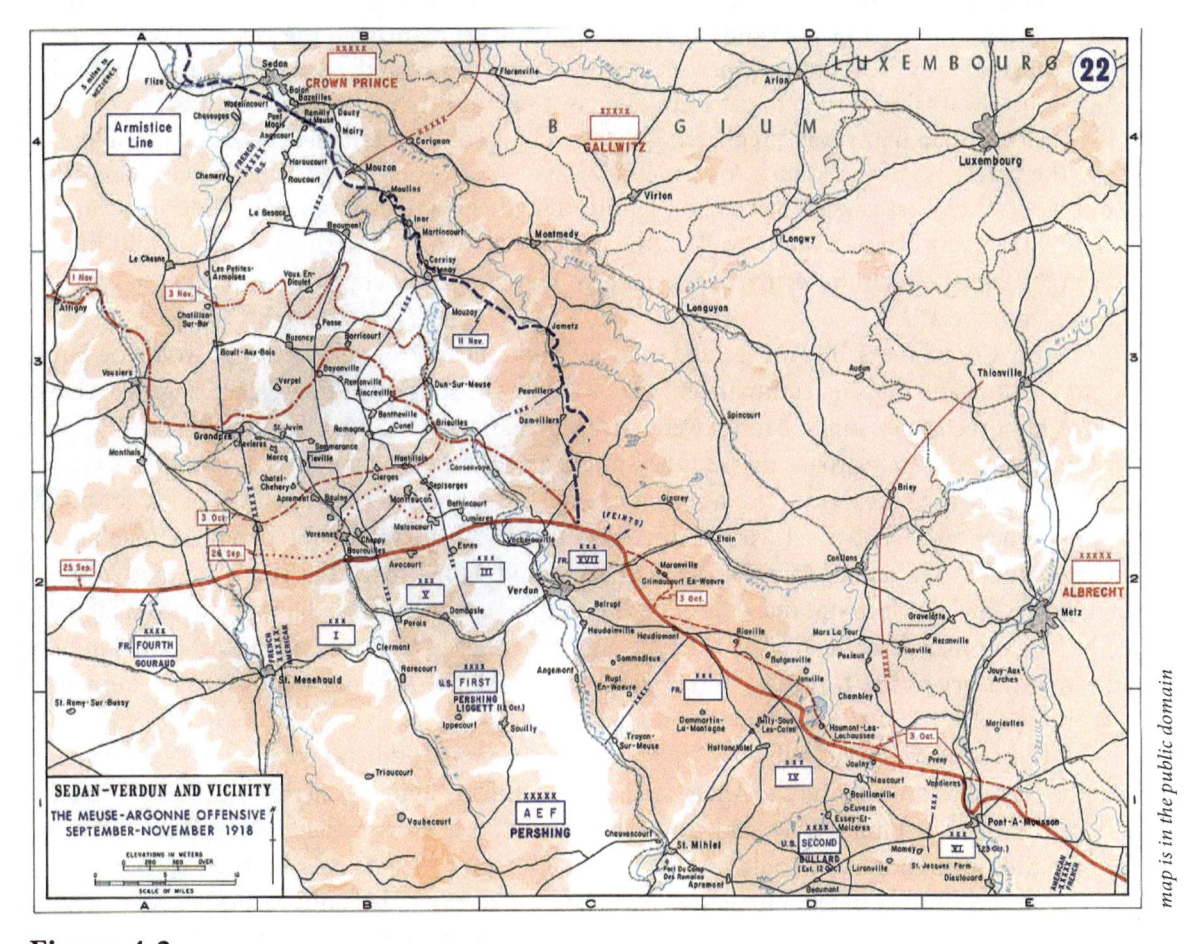

Figure 4.2

---

217. Crocker, *Don't Tread*, 264.
218. Ibid.

World War I 83

Corporal Alvin York

After his platoon had suffered heavy casualties and three other noncommissioned officers had become casualties, Cpl. York assumed command. Fearlessly leading seven men, he charged a machine gun nest, which was pouring deadly and incessant fire upon his platoon with great daring. In this heroic feat the machine gun nest was taken, together with four officers and 128 men and several guns.

(Near Chatel-Chehery, France, 8 October 1918)

excerpt from Congressional Medal of Honor citation

Courtesy of the United States Army

the situation to a degree exceeding those of his superiors. Pershing would not forget Marshall and would discuss events with him throughout the war. Meanwhile Marshall's friends consoled him for what would surely mark the end of his career. Nevertheless, Pershing was so taken by Marshall and his obvious abilities, the General continued to rely on the younger officer to keep the muddy roads organized for motor transport and supply, pushing the army through the great last offensive of the war. Marshall would eventually emerge to lead the army between the wars and through World War II, but he always found time to get counsel from General Pershing throughout his career, seeking his advice and, in many ways, replicating the leadership of the stern and dedicated old soldier.[219]

The fierceness of the Meuse-Argonne Offensive with its objective to cut the German rail line to Metz can be best gauged by General Hunter Liggitt who referred to the Wilderness campaign during the Civil War as a mere "walk in the park" in comparison to the fighting. Liggitt may have been the fattest man in the army; he is reputed to have taken his chef with him into the 1st Army in contrast to the 2nd.

Army Commander Bullard seemed to be lean and mean; fresh green troops would be pumped into the lines and division commanders were fired on the spot when they lacked aggressiveness.

A hundred square miles of forest were on the left flank and the heights of the Meuse River on the right. The crisscrossing roads marked the limited objectives throughout the fighting. The Germans had skillfully used the terrain to place concrete pill boxes and interlocking fields of fire for machine guns. When possible, barbed wire attempted to funnel advancing infantry into the machine gun-beaten zones. The names Montfalcon, Romagne, and Cunel mark the advances that Americans supported by French troops made through this desperate-to-the-finish hammering combat. A slug-fest fought on an individual level, the type Americans excel at, leaves the historian grasping only fleeting images of the fierceness and courage of the Meuse-Argonne—the last real campaign of World War I.

Overhead flew Colonel William "Billy" Mitchell, Captain Eddie Rickenbacker (the premier Ace of the First World War), and the American air forces mostly flying French aircrafts. Dividing themselves between reconnaissance and **close-air support**, it is here in the fierce and confused melee of the Meuse-Argonne one could justifiably argue the great debate over how the proper use of air power began. Torn between interdiction and close-air-support, this hotly contested issue continues today. At Meuse-Argonne, hitting the enemy's attempts at resupply, fuel, and logistic depots seemed a much more intelligent use of airpower to the great flier, who failed to see valuable and extremely

---

219. Thomas Ricks, *The Generals* (New York: Penguin, 2012), 24.

time-sensitive air assets as mere flying artillery; the expensive addition to the ground firepower already available. This hot topic, particularly sensitive to commanders on the ground, would continue to rear its head throughout air force history in the years ahead. To the man fighting on the ground, the use of air was obvious: to provide fire to aid in the maneuver and seizing of the objective. To the flier, **interdiction**, or the knock-out Clausewitzian-type blow directed at the center-of-gravity, would be the ultimate fulfillment of air power's potential.

On the eleventh hour of the eleventh day of the eleventh month in 1918, the German's agreed to an armistice. The idea that President Wilson's **14 Points** would allow the Germans to keep the ground they had taken, their army, and their dignity surely seemed to the Germans to be like the type of peace the Americans would have authorized Grant to allow at Appomattox. Later persuaded by the British and French at Versailles towards a more punitive stance, Wilson would agree to much harsher terms and reparation payments on a nation ravaged by disease and poverty at the end of the World War. The seeds to a greater conflict sown at Versailles left a very unsettled feeling that, in fact, this war would have to be refought. In future wars, however, there was a new kid in town. Busting with confidence and secure behind the oceans, the Americans began a celebration some believe continued throughout the 1920s.

Influenza may have been the most terrible result of the First World War. While it's almost hard to believe the flu did not exist a century ago, the first pandemic of this type swept through the weakened and tired populations of Europe and followed the soldiers home with grim results. Initially labeled the Spanish Flu, it is thought the disease actually originated in Ft. Leavenworth, Kansas and was brought to Europe by the Americans. In one day alone in Berlin, 1,700 people would die from the flu. In India it is thought six million may have perished. This pandemic virtually killed more people than the war itself with estimates of between 20 and 40 million people dead. This is the worst recorded pandemic in human history and seemed to be spread by the war.

World War I cannot be overstated in its significance for the world. The end of European dominance had arrived and the Americans would begin a century of projecting force abroad on a huge scale. With over seventeen million deaths worldwide, the American losses of just over 53,400 seemed small, but, to put this in perspective, it marked only a little over a half year of actual fighting—with numbers exceeding those of the Vietnam War. Americans indeed had been blessed to stay out of this war almost completely, the causes of which remain almost totally misunderstood to this day.

World War I represented the beginning of the Medal of Honor receiving more widespread recognition, with recipients such as Sergeant Alvin York, who singlehandedly killed twenty-five Germans and captured 132 more in the span of three hours on October 8, 1918[220]. World War I, considered by some historians to be the first modern war, also introduced new spheres of fighting, including aerial warfare. The first aviator to be awarded the Medal of Honor was 2nd Lt. Frank Luke of the 27th Aerial Pursuit Squadron.[221] Luke was awarded the Medal of Honor for his proficiency in destroying the 200-foot *Drachen* observation balloons, the most dangerous enemy aircraft to attack. Before he was killed in action on September 29, 1918, Lt. Luke destroyed fourteen balloons and five aircraft; he was awarded the Medal of Honor posthumously in December 1919.[222] For actions during World War I, 127 Medals of Honor were awarded.[223]

---

220. The Boston Publishing Company ed., *The Medal of Honor*, 125.
221. Norman S. Hall, *The Balloon Buster: Frank Luke of Arizona* (New York: Arno Press, 1928), 94.
222. Hall, *The Balloon Buster: Frank Luke of Arizona*, 94.
223. "Archive Statistics," The Congressional Medal of Honor Society, https://www.cmohs.org

Technology of World War I

World War I (WWI) and its technological advances are centered around one word: industrialization. Industrialization is the process by which the American culture and military transforms into a manufacturing society of goods and services. Industrialization takes individual labor and replaces it with mechanized, mass production through assembly lines. From this industrial innovation the United States created a great steel industry. Steel then became the backbone for the majority of technological advancements during WWI.

The first innovation that steel contributed to was making stronger and longer barrels for artillery. The main impact of this new artillery on the battlefield was in its ability to conduct long-range attacks with less structural flaws. Prior to this, cannon barrels would often experience implosions. The second major innovation was shielding. Steel shielding was used on tanks, aircraft, and naval vessels, making them more durable in battle. The new shielding also allowed for a newly designed artillery shell. Poison gasses such as mustard gas could now be stored and fired out of artillery and larger shells. The final, major improvement that steel offered to American technology was the recoil mechanism in machine guns. Steel recoil mechanisms last longer, giving the machine guns of WWI a longer life and a faster rate of fire compared to the Gatling gun of the Spanish American War. With mass production in assembly lines, machine guns were the largest cause of fatalities at the beginning of the war. This mass destruction was due to the fact that one machine gun replaced the firepower of 80 soldiers. New tactics soon began to form as a result of the monumental impact steel had on military technology. The major innovation that resulted from these new technologies was long-range tactics.

Inspired by the creation of aircrafts and tanks, long-range tactics was a unique creation in World War I. Aircrafts and tanks created a three-dimensional battlefield and changed the terrain options for warfare. During World War I, the location of battle focused on ease of mobility. This means that troops, cavalry, and artillery were not moved into terrain that men and horses could not easily access. The downside of long-range tactics was that commanding officers lost specific control of battles. Previously, commanders such as George Washington, Robert E. Lee, and Ulysses S. Grant could actually see the battle in front of them, and therefore control it. With long-range tactics, that was no longer possible. In WWI, a general could control miles of terrain and thousands of soldiers, but because of the lack of fast communication many new tactics and technologies were stalled and essentially futile.

The development of speed and mobility through the air, land, and sea would be a stepping stone in the technologies of firepower and mobility to win future wars. Following are military technologies that were developed in WWI. Most, if not all, were advanced and used in a greater capacity during World War II.

Flamethrowers could be vehicle-mounted, as on a tank, or man-portable. The man-portable flamethrower consisted of two elements: a backpack and a gun. The backpack element typically consisted of two or three cylinders. These cylinders would be filled with a flammable gas and a flammable liquid. The gun would have a trigger that would ignite the two flammable materials with an electrically heated coil. In World War I, the flamethrowers were extremely limited in range and would be very cumbersome due to the weight. They were highly effective in close proximity trench warfare. In areas of larger distances, however, the flamethrower was a limited weapon due to the weight.

Tanks were the finest examples of the AWoF in WWI. The idea of speed, firepower, and new tactics came together as one. It was so innovative that, in September 1917, the Commander in Chief of the American Expeditionary Forces requested that 600 heavy and 1,200 light tanks be produced in the United States. The first tank design was the Renault FT, also known as the FT-17. This was made to be more mobile and faster than its European heavy tank counterparts. Equipped with a machine gun, these were great anti-personnel machines. However, this tank had a poor performance on the battlefield. The body style lacked protection and the ability to cross a number of trenches while its condensed size led to cramped quarters and small ammo supplies. The important thing about tanks is that they replaced horse cavalry for the most part, but did not change the tactics of cavalry. Tanks, like their predecessor the horse cavalry, could not hold against ground troops without the support of ground troops.

Submarine naval vehicles were not a new concept in the U.S. military. Submarines were used in the Civil War to protect wooden ships from ironclads. The WWI R and S class submarine changed naval battles. They were equipped with Mark 10 torpedoes and had the ability to travel 5,000 miles (8,000 km) at 10 knots (5.1 m/s). The submarine became more mobile and gained the ability to do more serious damage with its fire power. This changed the tactics of naval warfare by creating battlefields both above and below the water.

Aircraft played a pivotal role in WWI. Early forms of aircraft were unarmed reconnaissance aircraft. This provided information on troop movements or enemy locations. As WWI became more about defense, trenches became the main battlefield; meaning that troops experienced very little movement. Because of this, aircraft became the superior weapon. Armed with personal weapons, mainly machine guns, aircraft took on the role of fighter planes. In 1917, accuracy of air fire increased with the invention of the .30-06 tracer round. As the war went on, more forms of aircraft were developed. Scouts, fighters, bombers, and ground attack aircraft all became early models of aircraft that would be instrumental in the wars to come.

The M1911 pistol is a semi-automatic pistol that uses a .45 caliber bullet. At the start of WWI, the M1911 pistol had become the regulation firearm for the U.S. Army. By the time the war was over, nearly two million M1911 pistols were made and sold to the government. The most famous story of the M1911 is the tale of Sergeant York. On October 8, 1918 in the Argonne Forest of France, Alvin York assumed command after his platoon suffered heavy casualties. He fearlessly led seven men, and charged a German machine-gun nest, which had caused the deadly fire resulting in the mass deaths of his platoon. In his heroic feat, York, with his trusty M1911, took the German machine-gun nest along with four German officers and 128 German soldiers.[224]

Key Terms:

Dick Act

Root Reforms

General Staff

Square Division

Progressivism

Pershing, J.J.

Zimmerman Telegram

Punitive Expedition

Unrestricted submarine warfare

"He Kept Us Out of the War"

Declaration of War

Phase lines

Shock-troop Tactics

Selective Service

Interior Lines

Ludendorff Offensive

Douglas MacArthur

George C. Marshall

Close-Air support

Interdiction

14 Points

Influenza

---

224. Chris Kyle, *American Gun: A History of the U.S. in Ten Firearms* (New York: HarperCollins Publishers, 2013), 145.

Thought Questions:

Some people think the First World War never really ended and the Second World War basically represented a continuum of the war. Do you believe this? If so, why? If not, then why not?

What tactical and technical innovations did the Americans present in World War I and how did these reflect what have been characterized in this book as AWoF?

What leaders emerged from the previous chapter and how would these leaders in turn develop subordinates for future conflicts?

Chapter V

BETWEEN THE WARS

Psalm 46:9 "He makes wars cease to the end of the earth; He breaks the bow and cuts the spear in two: He burns the chariot in the fire." NKJV

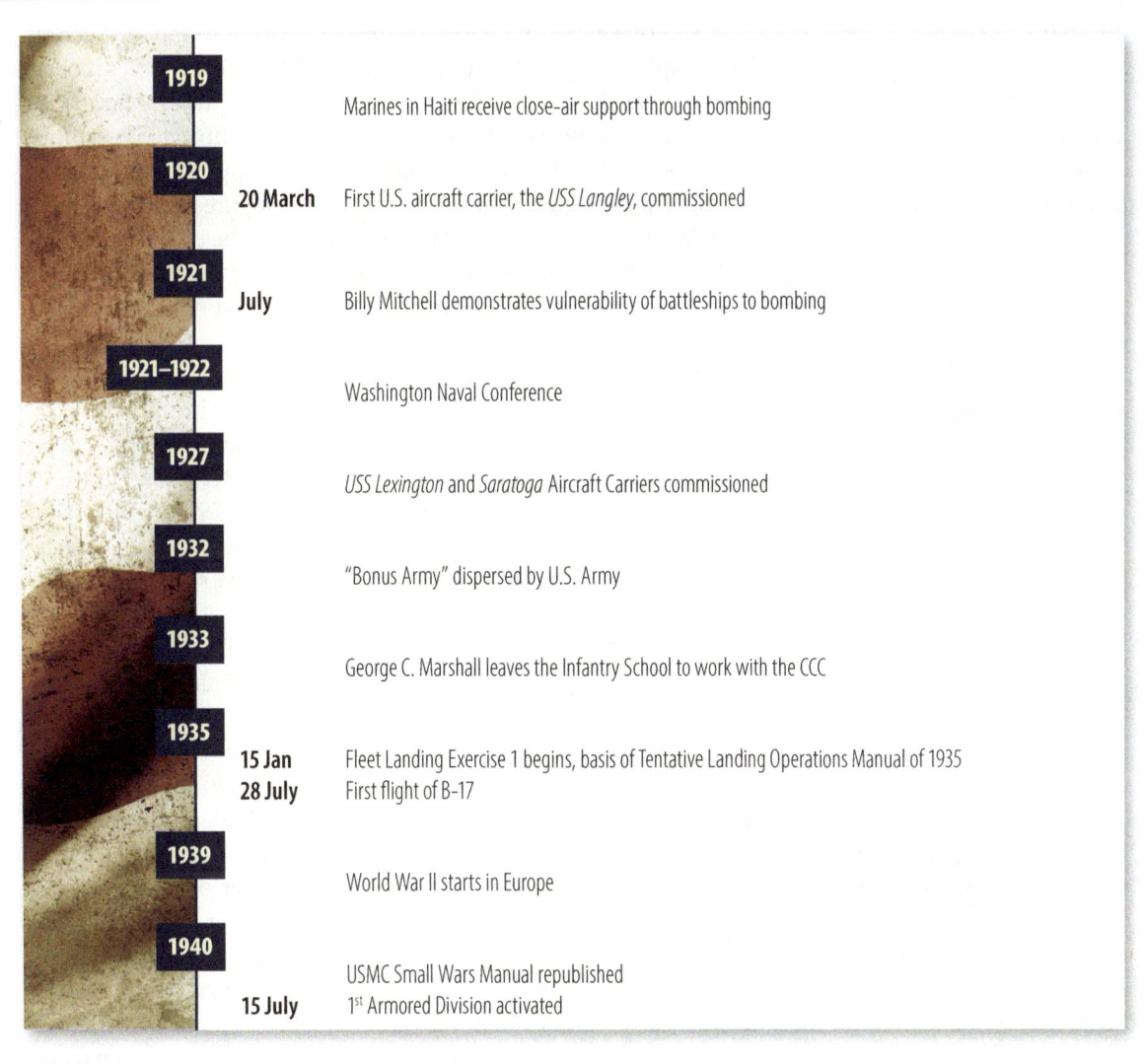

Year	Date	Event
1919		Marines in Haiti receive close-air support through bombing
1920	20 March	First U.S. aircraft carrier, the *USS Langley*, commissioned
1921	July	Billy Mitchell demonstrates vulnerability of battleships to bombing
1921–1922		Washington Naval Conference
1927		*USS Lexington* and *Saratoga* Aircraft Carriers commissioned
1932		"Bonus Army" dispersed by U.S. Army
1933		George C. Marshall leaves the Infantry School to work with the CCC
1935	15 Jan	Fleet Landing Exercise 1 begins, basis of Tentative Landing Operations Manual of 1935
	28 July	First flight of B-17
1939		World War II starts in Europe
1940		USMC Small Wars Manual republished
	15 July	1st Armored Division activated

Go to www.khpcontent.com to watch a video introduction for this chapter.

This chapter is a bit briefer than some of the others, but this is not to say it isn't as important! In the third chapter we discussed the need to fight with a long reach (artillery), maneuver (cavalry), and the ability to take a blow (infantry-engineers). We discussed the need to maneuver for the purpose of flanking the enemy in order to catch the opponent in a crossfire and to maximize power. The Western way of warfare tends to use linear and Euclidean patterns, maximizing this firepower. As you also know, **American Ways of Fighting** seem to favor high-speed, rapid maneuver and maximum firepower. The use of defilade, or covered positions, can minimize risk from the enemy while enfilade fires can devastate them. During the Philippines War we saw how the use of indigenous peoples, or scouts, proved invaluable. Rapidly maneuvering, aggression, and a preponderance of firepower combined with effective knowledge of the enemy's position through the use of indigenous people or scouts characterize how Americans tend to achieve success on the battlefield.

Another view of institutions such as the army and navy is called an **organismic approach**. Through this perspective the student sees an army, for example, as a being or body consisting of various parts functioning as a whole. For example, the ability to gather intelligence gives the commander "eyes" on the battlefield. The ability to move or maneuver the "legs" and so on. Utilizing this approach, the ability to adapt must be the institution's "memory." It is your duty as a student of this discipline or subject to glean what lessons you can from history or themes relating to the interaction of technology, strategy, tactics, and geography. Languages and cultures must be studied with an open mind in an attempt to determine inherent weaknesses and strengths. Exploiting these weaknesses and avoiding the strengths represents a sound approach towards operational planning. The ability of the various branches of the military to adopt technological changes and to apply these developments to their maximum potential while simultaneously developing and employing sound strategic planning and tactics would certainly help ensure victory in World War II. Often the contributions of servicemen between wars are ignored in the history books, but once again, "the game is won on the practice field." The unrecognized peace time veterans in military history have achieved the defeat of fascism and communism in the last century. So what did they come up with?

Every branch developed its own unique skills seemingly in preparation for World War II. In addition to learning the latest technology and anticipating the future, each service branch pursued institutional developments that utilized lessons from the past. Most would be remembered, but in future wars some of these lessons would be forgotten too. The Navy developed aircraft carriers and carrier air; the Air Force pursued bomber theory, while the Army ensured everyone could ride across the battlefield. Finally, the Marines developed various **counter-insurgency** warfare principles and the planning aspects of the unique amphibious assault. How did these various platforms, systems, and operational approaches occur?

America's Navy has always been our first line of defense. With two oceans and the Gulf of Mexico essentially surrounding the United States on three sides, it is no wonder naval forces in America are the best in the world. Numbering about nine carrier groups today, divided pretty much between the Atlantic and Pacific Oceans, our Navy also has about an equal number of large, decked amphibious ships (small carriers designed for amphibious assault) in the world currently on duty at any one time. This ability to project force over the 70% of the earth's surface covered by water is a function of naval developments between the wars.

When Samuel P. Langley flew his first aircraft off the deck of a house boat in the Potomac River, crashing about the same time as the Wright brothers' famous flight, he probably had little inclination to ponder the importance of these ships for the future. Nor would he or the people working diligently at the **Washington Naval Conference** of 1921 to 1922 have considered their attempts to limit the production of battleships, in what represented essentially an attempt at limiting strategic weapons likely to have foreseen the end of these massive giants as the premier fighting ships of the navy beginning within a generation. In fact, the great naval innovator and visionary Admiral William S. Sims claimed in 1920, "the Battleship is dead." Imagine the reaction of naval history students who had seen the battleship as the premier naval fighting platform throughout history. From the stand point of naval history, and the maximizing of firepower from the Age of Sail to Steam by using a linear approach, the idea of developing this rickety air arm and vulnerably fragile platform simply must have been seen as madness to many observers. However, shortly following the Washington Naval Conference, the Navy began investing directly in aircraft.[225]

Nevertheless, the aircraft carrier as described by Geoffrey Perret is a strange mixture of a weapon system. Incredibly powerful, with an incredible ability to launch force over huge distances, it is nonetheless a very vulnerable platform itself. With little more than an inch of deck steel covering bombs and fuel, these gigantic ships require much protection. Shuttling across the ocean's surface, small tenders bring fuel and remove items constantly while a ring of steel protects these "mother ships." The Navy, between World War I and World War II, experimented with rings or **circular formations** whereby the carrier, surrounded by frigates and destroyers—under the water by submarines and in the air with circling aircraft—became the base for any movement or pivot. If the carrier moved to the port (left) then so did the other vessels around it, providing defenses-in-depth.

The Air Force would remain a part of the Army and be designated as a service until 1926, a corps from 1926 to 1941, and finally an army air force until 1947. Advocating the use of paratroopers as early as World War I, Billy Mitchell proved to be an officer of iron-will and solid integrity. Grasping a vision of the potential for airpower, he participated in many high-profile attempts at using bombing to demonstrate the superior capability and potential of the air attack. Eventually, Mitchell would face the court martial for his outspokenness on subjects ranging from the poor defenses in Hawaii to the lack of safety in air travel. Nevertheless, by the 1930s, the Army Air Corps absolutely believed that bomber theorists prophesied correctly that, when used in tandem with ground forces, bombers need not be restricted to the messy strafing of trenches in the close-air support role described in the previous chapter, or merely protecting air space over the front lines, such as had been the case in World War I. Bombers could also be used to hit the enemy behind the lines, forcing him to withdraw war materials and guns from the front. Interdiction—hitting the enemy's means of production and vitals far behind the lines—remained the focus for the Air Force. The only concern by the 1930s was that no such bomber yet existed.

The **B-17** proved to be the solution. It possessed four engines and was believed capable of outrunning any pursuit aircraft (note the P, for pursuit, designation on early aircraft—for example, the P-40 Tomahawk) with speed and high altitude capabilities. The first truly hydraulically operated aircraft, this strategic four-engine bomber could secure the vastness of the Pacific for pre-war planners as a key piece on the chessboard of war.

The General Staff's War Plans Division had numerous color-coded plans to fill contingencies in every theater of the world. The Orange Plan would present a challenge to the emerging power of Japan. With troops still in the Pacific, the United States felt duty-bound to protect these colonial-type possessions and the U.S. troops located there. Across the Pacific during the 1930s, various groups of military were deployed under the euphemistic name of "**defense battalions**."[226] As they sat on lonely spits of sand in the huge Pacific Ocean with little more than gooney birds for company,

---

225. Perret, *Country*, 343.
226. Note the use of "volunteers" to skirt constitutional difficulties in the Spanish-American War would also see the periodic introduction of other euphemisms such as "advisors" in Korea and Vietnam or "peacekeepers" throughout the 1990s.

at times the troops surely must have wondered what they defended. Nevertheless, an American pattern seen on the banks of the Nueces River in Mexico or Fort Sumter, South Carolina prevailed here—that of the "speed bump." Believing just enough troops would mark a limit of American control, the troops in themselves did not constitute enough of a force to hold the line alone. In typical cavalry-to-the-rescue fashion, the idea existed that the Philippines would hold out from a Japanese attack while American forces, headed up with B-17s, would come to the rescue, so to speak. The air proved a fine medium for projecting force, but what about all of those islands across the Pacific?

The U.S. Marines always seemed in danger of losing their jobs. With Presidents McKinley and Teddy Roosevelt, and even at times with the Roosevelt administration, the Marines felt as if their collective heads remained near the chopping block of political leadership. The techniques utilized in Cuba during the Spanish-American War burned as a vision for developing doctrine for **amphibious warfare**. The imagination of the various American military institutions reinforce this author's contention that there are recognizable ways of warfare in the American military history tradition, one of which is innovation. Using the generous patriotism and brilliance of Andrew Higgins, future Marine General Victor Krulak realized the potential of these landing crafts, or **Higgins boats**, especially in light of current war plans. Higgins, who demonstrated a terrific ability to design and build watercraft, apparently was not much of a business man, having faced bankruptcy on occasion. The successful fulfillment of prototypes to Marine Corps specifications produced some of the most successful transport vessels ever used in war. In fact, Eisenhower would claim these boats were crucial to victory during the Second World War. Potential budget cuts and even institutional destruction may have been why the Marines demonstrated such innovations.

The Marines' mission in the Caribbean did not end with the Spanish-American War. The Marines pioneered innovation in terms of institutional mission and combined arms development throughout the post-World War I years and into the 1920s. Serving essentially as a colonial constabulary, or police force, the Marines actually commissioned sergeants as officers and developed leaders in low-intensity conflict. Commonly called **unconventional,** or guerilla warfare, this type of warfare has existed since the ancient world and essentially marks various levels of violence: from banditry or police work to the large scale use of militias or part-time soldiers. Americans have repeatedly fought these low-intensity or unconventional wars, but it seems the memory of them has been greatly overshadowed by conventional wars. As a student of military history, it is your duty to remember the hard-earned lessons often paid for in blood by earlier service members. You have a supreme responsibility to remember and record these lessons so we can quickly refer to them in the years ahead. John J. Tierney Jr. has said, "This means that much of American political culture is strategically 'ahistorical,' . . . leaving much of our reason frozen in a conceptual time warp. That is to say, nearly everything remains unique . . . or entirely new."[227] What secrets lay behind this ancient form of asymmetrical warfare—discovered in the Caribbean and by virtue of forgetfulness, so painfully ignored in Vietnam and relearned in Iraq—and why did the Marines remember the lessons?

The Marines as an institution have traditionally allowed for individual initiative, a historically American strength, and encouraged small-unit leaders to exercise authority. Due to ever present threats of extinction and unbelievably tight budgets (moneys are still controlled in large measure by the Navy) the Marines have forced leadership down to the lowest levels, as has the U.S. Army. Constantly patrolling, such as the army had done in the Philippines, the Marines learned their areas and the people therein by studying nuances of manners and culture. The Marine Corps learned during their sunny stay to utilize the full spectrum of warfare from policing unconventionally to battling with conventional tactics. The Marines earned the trust of indigenous peoples and quickly learned to use the aforementioned "carrot and stick" to placate areas by improving infrastructure and cementing personal relationships, while being ready to use the point of a gun to enforce the laws. In other words, the Marines capitalized on what the Army had learned in the Philippines. Operating from the Dominican Republic to Nicaragua, the Marines codified their experiences

---

227. John J. Tierney Jr., *Chasing Ghosts* (Washington DC: Potomac Books, 2007), 5.

in everything; from guarding railroads to establishing government services into the **Small Wars Manual**. This seminal work laid the eventual foundation for strategic debate in Vietnam and Iraq.

The last major innovation pioneered by the Marines in the Caribbean emphasized close-air support. As mentioned previously, the Air Force tended to favor using the scarce and time-sensitive resource of airpower for interdiction purposes. Nonetheless, the Marines practiced with bags of flour, dropping them from aircraft approaching targets at various glide angles. Apparently the Germans, who sent observers, left quite impressed and started Germany on a course of emphasizing close-air support over strategy with powerful ramifications for the future. By May of 1927 Marine Air provided support to forces attacking the Sandinista Rebels in Nicaragua. Many weapons later to be used in World War II saw their first employment between the wars fought in the Caribbean. Unfortunately many of the lessons learned regarding **unconventional warfare** against an armed insurgency would be forgotten.[228]

General Douglas MacArthur did something totally out of character when he stood his ground in the White House arguing with the President of the United States over the army's budget. Douglas MacArthur had waxed eloquently and in melodramatic fashion, saying the President would essentially be responsible for the future deaths of American soldiers. With seven Silver Star medals for bravery, this controversial general risked his career as he had his life. Vomiting on the steps of the White House out of nervousness may not seem very courageous, but MacArthur had done the right thing, putting the future of the Army ahead of his own ambitions. MacArthur, like King David in the Holy Bible, served bravely, but stumbled at the end. Perhaps one of the most colorful and central figures of American military history in the 20th century, MacArthur, without question, possessed moral courage and integrity. However, controversy always seemed to swirl about him. As a retired field marshal in the Philippines, where he had studied his father's earlier service, he received a gift worth millions of U.S. dollars in terms of today's values. One prefers instead to think of the humility and integrity of a John M. Browning or Hiram Maxim, both of whom refused to make money off their government designs of weapons. Later, shaking off the advice of his assistant Dwight D. Eisenhower, MacArthur used excessive force against American veterans when the "**Bonus Army**" descended into Depression-era Washington, D.C. The veterans were attempting to receive compensation for services in World War I. It was MacArthur's bright, young, chain-smoking assistant Eisenhower—who worked 16-hour days and would be one of the few non-World War I combat veteran soldiers—who would rise to heights of leadership, continuing the tradition of Pershing.

George C. Marshall remained the great planner of the U.S. Army. As you recall from a previous chapter, this brilliant young man had caught the eye of Pershing in World War I, and in turn would keep his eye on Eisenhower. It is said nothing in World War II happened without Marshall's knowledge or approval. The great George C. Marshall immediately set to work at the end of the First World War at the Infantry School at Fort Benning, compiling what he believed to be the lessons of World War I. Innovative and possessing, with a flair for genius when it came to simplifying the most complex problems, Marshall developed the army both tactically and technically. When one considers that the U.S. Army hovered near the 40th position in terms of size among the world armies—smaller perhaps than even Romania's—the ability to expand in classic Uptonian fashion is breathtaking. The expandable military is a function of the **triangular division**. Simply resting on threes from a military tradition as old as Napoleon, the ability to place a three-squad platoon within a three-platoon company symbolizes the army's ability to simplify quickly—a virtue in the confusing environment of the battlefield. The three companies would in turn constitute a battalion. This triangular division at a fighting weight of 15,000 compared more favorably to the more bloated and less flexible 25,000 of the previous "square division" and allowed an amazing ability to adapt to terrain.[229]

---

228. http://www.defensemedianetwork.com/stories/naval-aviation-centennial-the-marines-pioneer-air-support-in-central-america/
229. Richard W. Stewart, general ed., *American Military History Vol. II* (Washington DC: Center of Military History, 2009), 68.

General of the Army George C. Marshall Jr.

Courtesy of U.S. Signal Corps., U.S. Farm Security Administration/Office of War Information. Overseas Picture Division. Washington Division; 1944

Often seated in front of a portrait of General John J. Pershing that was suspended behind his desk, George Marshall never forgot his mentor and would continue to seek his advice to the end of the great general's life. George Marshall never forgot the stern bearing and non-political nature of his old boss. A straight shooter, the leadership trait of "knowledge" best described Marshall, and the Army value of Integrity can easily be seen throughout his career. George Marshall spent his time profitably after the First World War developing tactical problems and scenarios as the commandant in charge of instruction at the Infantry school at Fort Benning, Georgia. Complementing the lessons learned from World War I with new weapons, and thinking big in terms of production numbers of aircraft and weapons platforms, Marshall's contributions to the development of weapons, tactics, training, and personnel went far towards winning the Second World War and establishing future army leadership for generations to come. Marshall would be the mechanic that would get the American war machine running throughout World War II. No general would emerge without Marshall's approval. Famous for promoting and firing, Marshall continued an American tradition of expecting results and rewarding leadership. The "organizer of victory" oversaw the development of numerous future generals to include Omar Bradley and Matthew B. Ridgway.[230] In addition to knowledge, Marshall's integrity was on full display when he refused the opportunity to lead the greatest amphibious assault of World War II. Instead, he trusted the former major who, like himself, had been plucked from relative obscurity to general rank, Dwight D. Eisenhower. Throughout the titanic struggle of World War II, Marshall remained as the Chief of Staff of the Army in Washington D.C., recognizing his position there could not be adequately filled in time and essentially giving the glory to Ike.[231] Marshall's knowledge and integrity would be relied upon for Presidents to come, where he would continue to serve as Secretary of State after a wonderful career of service in the U.S. Army.

The triangular division also gave birth to the **holding attack**. Relying on a base of fire from automatic weapons, the base unit provided cover while the other unit or units attacked the position from the flank either individually or in tandem. If the leader decided to maintain a reserve unit, the triangular structure allowed for this as well. This tactical innovation would be improved upon throughout the Second World War, but the bedrock for victory lay in the Army's use of the triangular division and its employment in a holding attack. Now all that was needed was speed and leadership.

The seeds of future army leaders in World War II rested with its youth. The ability to develop peacetime leadership remains essential. During the Depression, Civilian Conservation Corps Camps, or **CCC Camps**, continued to be utilized by the Army for the purposes of maintaining a

---

230. Stephen R. Taaffe, *Marshall and His Generals* (Lawrence KS: University Press of Kansas, 2011), 323.
231. Geoffrey Perret, *There's a War to be Won* (New York: Random House, 1991), 18.

peacetime army, while serving in one of the numerous alphabet soup programs designed to help people through the Depression. Building bridges and planting forests under the meticulous supervision of veteran officers and enlisted leadership, young men—many from the city—received their first experiences of working in the field, living in tents, obeying orders, and fixing broken-down machines; all skills eventually needed on the battlefields of World War II.

The American Army created the world's first true mobile division with the **Armored Division**. Tipped with a spearhead of tanks, personnel could ride into combat safely aboard personnel carriers in the quintessential American mode—riding hard and fast as in the Indian Wars on the frontier. Unlike the much vaunted German blitzkrieg, every American soldier rode and fought from four-wheel-drive platforms, ensuring a mechanized force capable of crossing even difficult terrain. The Armored Division to this writer augers a premier (if somewhat unrecognized by historians) fighting force organized along the lines of the triangular division utilizing the holding attack. To ensure proper employment of these innovations, a codified doctrine known as Field Service Regulations FM 100-5 was created. Furthermore, FM 100-5 stated, "An objective may sometimes be obtained through maneuver alone."[232] In other words, by focusing on American military strengths, or the AWoF, the army leadership ensured future forces would operate as the lessons of history had dictated. Long gone were the days of the deadly frontal assault. Instead, a permanent record for how forces would be used entered the institutional consciousness of the Army. All of the military branches reflected the best characteristics of the AWoF—resiliency and innovation. America's Army is a learning army, gleaning and codifying lessons from the past and storing these lessons into its collective memory; diligently developing these themes for application to potential threats under a firm tradition of educator-leaders who would arrive prepared to fight the world's latest challenge to life and freedom—Fascism.

Technology between the Wars

After WWI, most of the world was in an economic slump except for the United States. This allowed the United States to enter into an arms race that was perpetuated by the cult of violence that WWI had unleashed. The interwar years were largely dedicated to research and development. The focus of the research was on fixing the failures of the new military tactics and technologies that had developed in WWI. The three main areas of concern that arose from WWI were long distance communication, aircraft, and the Navy. Following are a few technological advancements that were created to solve these issues. Though most of these were invented during the interwar period, most were not field tested or implemented until WWII.

Radio

When World War I started, the radio was still in the developmental and field testing stage. The Army radio equipment was very primitive due to the very short range of transmission and the overwhelming amount of atmospheric interference. Because of the poor performance of the radio during World War I, most radio transmissions were less reliable than wired telephones or telegraphs. However, radios did find a permanent home with the Navy at sea. The Navy radio stations had a higher-powered signal than those of the Army on the front lines. With a better performance at sea, the Navy was able to relay timely wartime news to its vessels across the oceans. The final dispatch of the war was from the U.S. Navy press announcing an armistice on November 11, 1918, via radio transmission.

By late 1941, when the United States entered World War II, the radio had vastly improved its technology from the primitive equipment available in WWI. The main improvement was the vacuum tube that allowed for bulky and heavy radios to become smaller in size. This resulted in lighter

---

232. Walter E. Kretchik, *U.S. Army Doctrine* (Lawrence: University Press of Kansas, 2011), 144.

weight, portable, battery-operated transistor radios that were encased in metal. This transformed the radio from a naval technology to an Army and Air Force field technology during World War II. Beyond handheld use by U.S. soldiers in the field, radios were now an integral part of every major technology of the U.S. military—including but not limited to airplanes, submarines, and tanks.

All the major problems were fixed between the wars for radio including transmissions, ability to travel greater distances, and reliability. These factors made radio a staple of the war effort, thus creating a unified communication network for the military forces that allowed for speed and firepower to coordinate at a much higher level.

Once transmission was at a functional level, security of the transmission became the next technological challenge. U.S. Marines solved the problem by employing Navajo Indians in their radio transmissions. Navajo is one of the most complex of all languages and became a reliable code for American military forces during World War II. The Navajo code project began with just 30 code talkers. These 30 men developed a virtually undecipherable code based in their native language. An example of the code was "Moustache Smeller," which was the code name for Adolf Hitler during the war.

Aircraft

Planes in WWI were all biplanes, meaning they had two sets of wings: one over the other. This was needed to create the proper structure needed for flight at the time. In the interwar period, technology in military aircraft rapidly evolved. Most aircraft had become monoplanes due to the new advancements in construction. The new body style of aircraft included new, sleek aluminum airframes with supercharged piston engines, which would eventually be replaced by jet engines.[233] The most popular U.S. innovations in aircraft were the P-51, and long-range bombers such as the B-17 (also known as the Flying Fortress) as well as the famous B-29.[234] By World War II, military aircraft included bombers, fighters, reconnaissance airplanes, cargo transports, gliders, blimps, and even jets. These new technologies and innovations also created faster aircraft. In WWI, aircraft engines were approximately 80-120 HP. After the interwar period they had advanced to approximately 750 HP-1800 HP.

Naval Advancements

The focus between the wars for the Navy was on seaborne assaults, especially after the failure of Gallipoli in WWI. This failure led to the redesign of seaborne assaults for the U.S. Navy, which led to new technology.

The first was the use of aircraft to decisively reshape war at sea. During the interwar period, the United States made substantial progress on the aircraft carrier. In 1922, the United States launched its first experimental aircraft carrier named the *USS Langley*. By 1927, the United States had two large aircraft carriers: the *USS Lexington* and the *USS Saratoga*. They were 888 feet long, 106 feet wide, weighed 33,000 tons, and each had a crew of approximately 1900 men. Besides their size, the ships were the fastest capital ships on the seas with a 180,000 HP engine that could reach speeds of 33 knots.

The second was the creation of the Landing Craft Vehicle and Personnel (LCVP) as well as the Landing Craft Mechanized (LCM). Designed in 1926, this sea craft was created for the bayou waters, meaning it excelled in shallow areas. It had a protected propeller engine as well as a flat bow with a retractable bow ramp. This made it easy for the craft to beach, unload, and refloat back to the sea quickly and effectively.[235]

---

233. Hacker, *American Military Technology*, 82.
234. Hacker, *American Military Technology*, 100.
235. Hacker, *American Military Technology*, 88

Key Terms:

- AWoF (American Ways of Fighting)
- Organismic Approach
- Counter-Insurgency
- Washington Naval Conference
- Circular Formations
- B-17
- Defense battalions
- Amphibious warfare
- Higgins Boats
- Unconventional Warfare
- Small-Wars Manual
- "Bonus Army"
- Triangular Division
- Holding-Attack
- CCC Camps
- Armored Division

Thought Questions:

What AWoF can be detected in the innovations and developments before World War II?

What innovations by military service which occurred during the period between the First and Second World Wars can you name?

Chapter VI
WORLD WAR II: NORTH AFRICA TO EUROPE

Psalm 33: 16-18 "No king is saved by the multitude of an army; A mighty man is not delivered by great strength. A horse is a vain hope for safety; Neither shall it deliver any by its great strength. Behold, the eye of the Lord is on those who fear him, On those who hope in His mercy, To deliver their soul from death, And to keep them alive in famine." NKJV

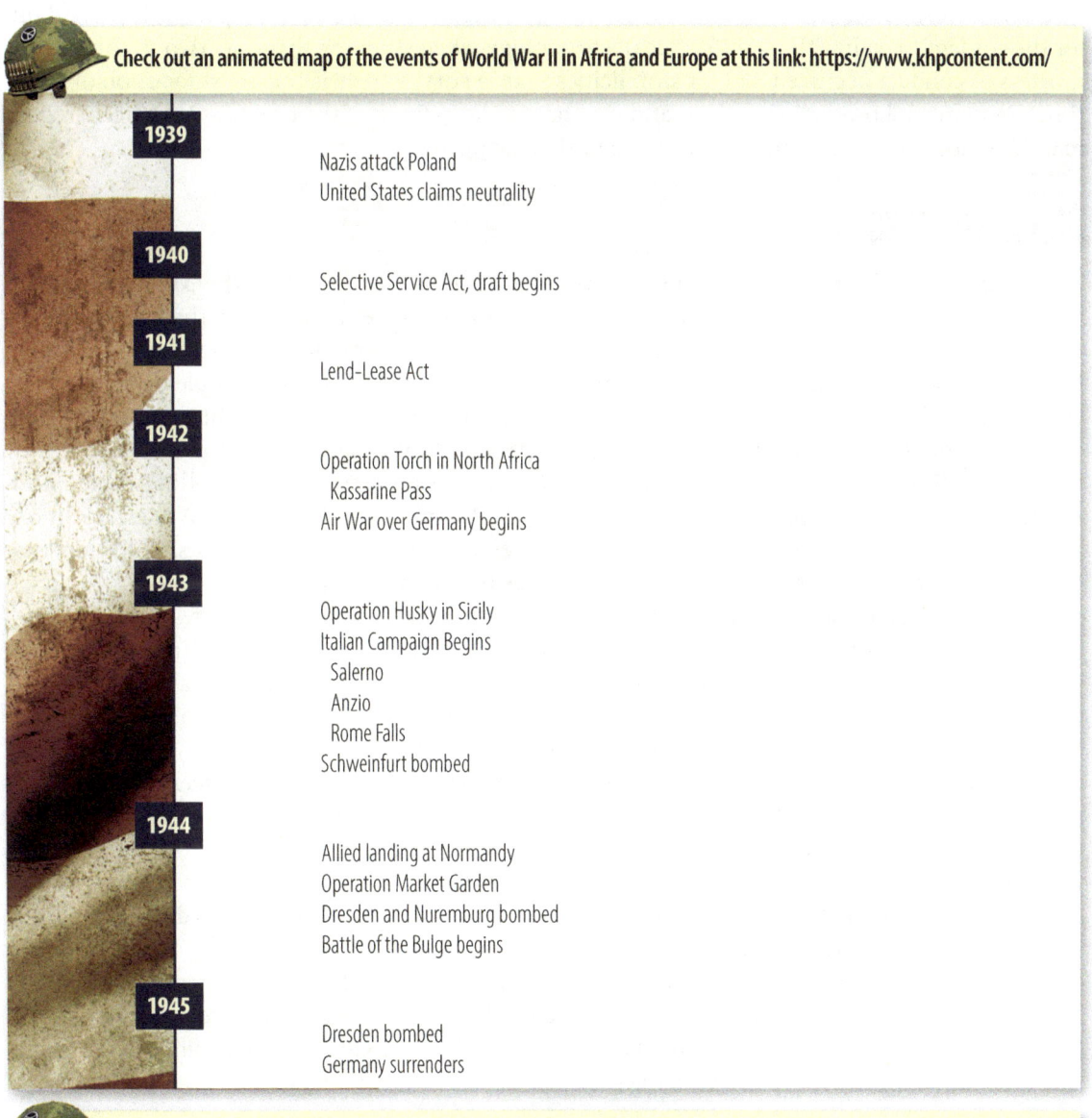

Check out an animated map of the events of World War II in Africa and Europe at this link: https://www.khpcontent.com/

1939
Nazis attack Poland
United States claims neutrality

1940
Selective Service Act, draft begins

1941
Lend-Lease Act

1942
Operation Torch in North Africa
  Kassarine Pass
Air War over Germany begins

1943
Operation Husky in Sicily
Italian Campaign Begins
  Salerno
  Anzio
  Rome Falls
Schweinfurt bombed

1944
Allied landing at Normandy
Operation Market Garden
Dresden and Nuremburg bombed
Battle of the Bulge begins

1945
Dresden bombed
Germany surrenders

Go to www.khpcontent.com to watch a video introduction for this chapter.

Many people have referred to World War II as the "good war." Books on the subject fly off the shelves in bookstores, and sales of videos and publications regarding the war are always high. It is the contention of this book that the explanation lay in a declaration of war, the support of the American people, and a series of visible operational successes resulting from the use of American strengths (AWoF). These successes did not come easily, but a goal clearly articulated, understood, and supported by the American people is the ticket for success in the use of military force. World War II saw the accomplishment of a mission, unlike the many wars that followed.

Like World War I, World War II represented the involvement of every climate and continent on Earth. Americans responded to the attack at Pearl Harbor, Hawaii and the subsequent German declaration of war on the United States by balancing American hatred for the Japanese with the need to fight a "**Germany first**" strategy. This balancing of needs saw Americans secure the Atlantic to land in North Africa and cross the Mediterranean, attacking the Germans from the south in Sicily and Italy while preparation planning continued for the greatest amphibious assault in history—D-Day in Normandy, France. The drive across Germany occurred simultaneously to the isolation of the Japanese military fortress of Rabaul in the Southwest Pacific and the two pronged assault across the Central Pacific and through New Guinea to the Philippines. A costly marine act would be followed on Okinawa and the dropping of the atomic bombs on Japan. It is important for the student to realize the significance of chronology when studying this war. Two simultaneous theaters of conduct occurred, but for simplicity's sake, a survey such as this must focus on one at a time. Remember, however, your dates and use these to keep track of the events as they occurred in real time, not within the artificial construct of this narrative.

Japan Attacks

Oil started World War II. This should not really surprise the student since the Middle East had been drawn along the lines of colonial possessions, in many cases simply over the availability of this greasy resource. No understanding of grand strategy can overlook the value of resources to a state, and this need changes with technology over time. The Japanese are a people densely populated (roughly half the population of the United States) in an area the size of California, with much of the land being unlivable. The one thing the Japanese do not have is oil or access to mineral resources. With the rise of industry and a *zaibatsu* elite of industrialists controlling capital and steeped in an ancient *bushido* code, the first of the East Asian nations to embrace Western technology and to avoid the yoke of colonialism, the Japanese, needed an empire. Why should they not follow the Western powers in obtaining the resources they desperately needed?

The Dutch East Indies (Indonesia today), in particular the Sultanate of Brunei, gestured provocatively. Oil-rich, the sun-dappled shores of the Southeast Asian islands beckoned. First would come Manchuria, however. The "Pittsburgh" of the East, Manchuria offered coal and iron along with other vital war minerals. Taking this area and invading China, the Japanese proceeded to obtain what later became described as "victory disease," a sort of manifest destiny where it seemed they could not lose, and Asia, at least, appeared destined to become their protectorate. Only one thing seemed to stand in the way of this empire spreading from Hokkaido to India, and that was the United States.

Stubbornly clinging to the Philippines and determined to place an embargo on the Japanese while drawing a line on the beaches of the oil-rich East Indies, the American's use of an embargo after the fall of Vietnam threatened to shut down the militarized state of Japan. This decision to draw a line changed the debate in Japan between the army bogged down in China and the navy ready to launch. Admiral Isoroku Yamamoto argued persuasively before the Naval General Staff how an attack by a combined fleet could give a year to consolidate the much-needed resources of South East Asia. Tasked with this attack would be Commander Minoru Genda who would face the problem of creating torpedoes capable of being dropped into the shallow lagoon housing the American naval fleet in the Pacific. The attack occurred unexpectedly on a Sunday morning when the aircraft carriers had fortuitously left the harbor, many of them bound for the Atlantic and throughout the Pacific.[236]

On Sunday morning, December 7, 1941, the first wave of Japanese bombers and fighters—189 total—dropped their loads and strafed, dropping their modified torpedoes with one foot of water to spare. A second wave of 170 torpedo/bombers followed 20 minutes later.[237] The American battleships waited like sitting ducks as torpedoes crisscrossed the harbor and bombs dropped from above. Despite the frantic efforts of intelligence agencies to determine the intent of the Japanese, coordination between services represented a harbinger of the need for joint operations in years to come. As Geoffrey Perret notes, the real problem for the Japanese at Pearl Harbor is they took their eyes off the ball. The purpose of the mission was to defeat the American Pacific Fleet for the purposes of securing oil, but oil lines crisscrossed the Hawaiian Islands. Had an enterprising bomber hit one of these oil wells, it is possible the Japanese could have secured their objectives; as it was, they only faced an enraged America.[238]

Meanwhile the Japanese continued to attack various U.S. holdings throughout the Pacific. A heroic stand occurred at Wake Island where a marine defense battalion sank four Japanese cruisers and destroyers, damaging eight more and shooting down waves of aircraft, killing a thousand Japanese. The inability of the Japanese to conduct efficient amphibious operations quickly became apparent. Almost at the same time as they hit Pearl Harbor, the Japanese landed in the Philippines where air attacks had effectively neutralized American aircraft. The tendency of General Douglas MacArthur to be caught unawares stands in marked contrast with his famous ability to bounce back. Unfortunately, the Japanese could land on Luzon, the large northern island in the Philippines, in numbers too large to repulse. However, the Americans, under General Jonathan M. Wainright, fought a brilliant series of **fighting withdrawals** during May of 1942, falling back on subsequent prepared divisions for the purposes of delaying Japanese advance across the Bataan Peninsula. Eventually, holed up in the vast tunnel complexes of the island of **Corregidor** in Manila Harbor, Eisenhower (Ike) received George C. Marshall's notice when he worked incredibly long hours attempting to bring relief to the besieged garrison. MacArthur received orders to escape by PT boat with his family and subsequently received the Medal of Honor as the President attempted to encourage a fearful and angry nation.

Despite a declaration of war granted by Congress—always a prerequisite for military victory—President Franklin Roosevelt (FDR) recognized the danger that German technology presented. Germany had declared war on us as we precariously stepped into the Jet Age; expatriates had warned Washington how German scientists neared a new and deadly technology. Balancing the war fever of the American people with the strategic imperative, a Germany-first war started. This would change because of the need for the production of vital war craft such as the Higgins boat (mentioned in the last chapter). The first step to getting to Germany would require securing the Atlantic, as in World War I.

North Africa

At the Arcadia Conference held between December of 1941 and January 1942, the Allied powers of the UK, Russia, and the United States agreed that Germany must be tackled first. America would first fight the Nazi war machine by landing in North Africa. With characteristic impatience, the Americans desperately wanted to attack the Germans directly, but the British staff officers presented a better case for an indirect road to Berlin. In light of the failures of raids at Dieppe and the

---

236. Perret, *Country*, 360.
237. Ibid., 362.
238. Ibid., 364.

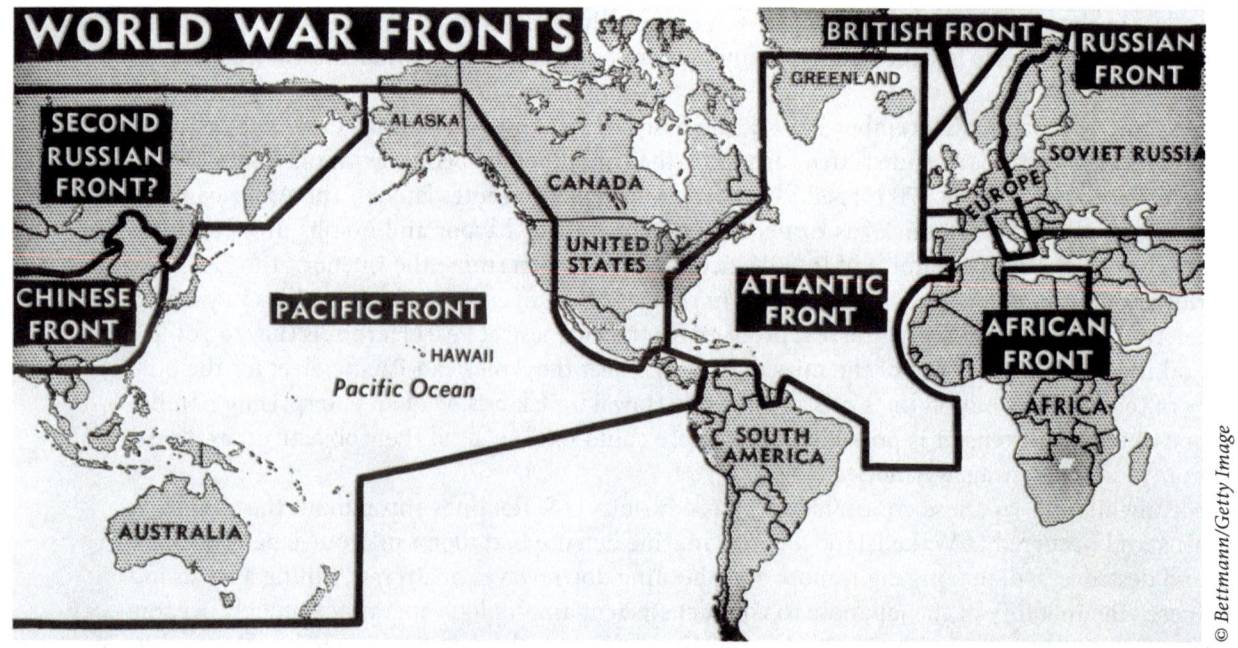

Figure 6.1 Compare these World War Fronts to Unified Combat Command at present.

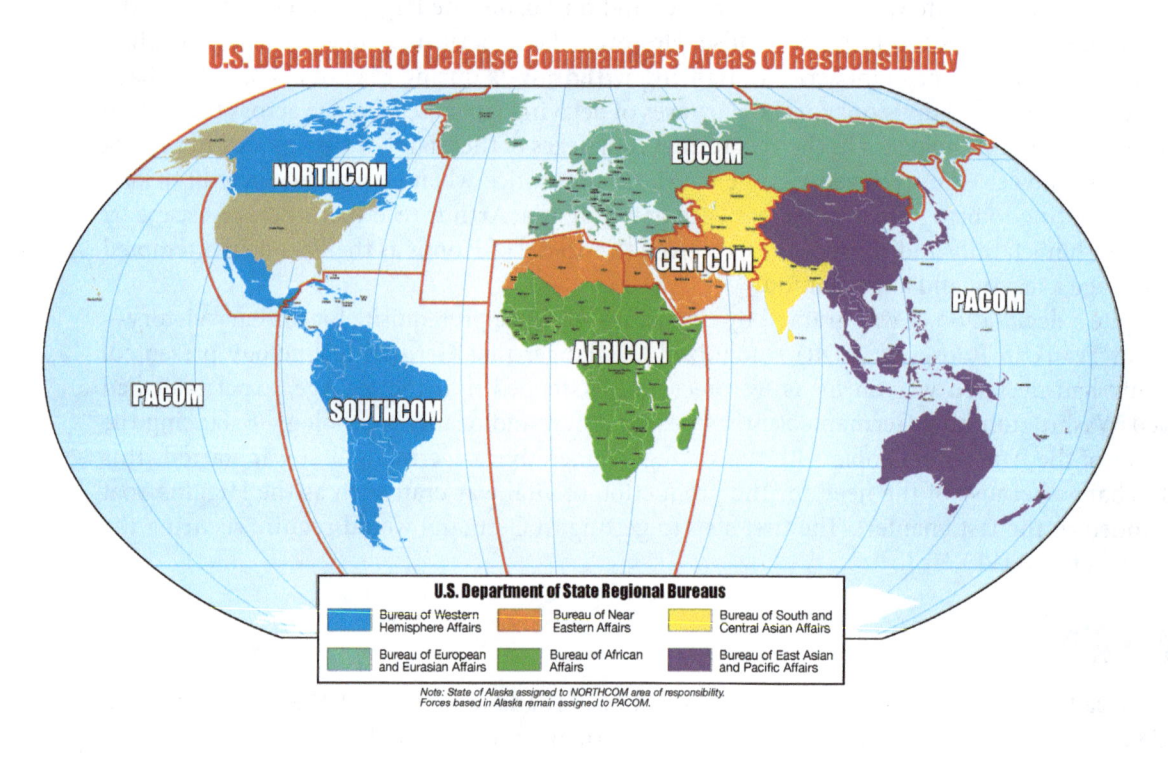

Figure 6.2

102 Modern American Military History

need for the American Army to gain some experience, in hindsight this probably represented the best action. Before troops could land in North Africa, a war of high-technology would be necessary to secure the Atlantic Ocean for transport shipping.

As in the First World War, the Germans decided submarine warfare represented the best hopes of the German Navy. After the sinking of the German ship *Bismarck*, the "Happy Time" for German submarines represented the sinking of over five hundred ships in six months since the Arcadia Conference. Ambitious German submarine captains had their fill of fat targets, even sinking ships off the coast of Virginia Beach, Virginia within the sight of vacationers.[239] The American Navy would play a vital role in taking back the Atlantic from these bothersome submarines through three advances: codes, radar, and new weapons.

The discovery of the German codes used at sea and the subsequent cracking of the codes came at the hands of the seizing of the Enigma machine by the Allies. The Germans had earlier cracked the British codes, but just as American code specialists had figured out the German code named Hydra, it changed to **Triton**. The security of the Triton code and the German ability to understand Allied communications gave them a distinct advantage. Development of radar detectors and electric torpedoes, which left no wake, enabled the Germans throughout 1942 to get a glimpse of victory. Hunting in "wolf packs," the German submarines ruled the waves during the summer of 1942. Sinking over five hundred tons of shipping a month, even the resource-rich Americans appeared doomed.[240] As has happened so often in American military history, blessings arrived just in time.

Triton was finally cracked in February 1943. At about the same time a new type of radar appeared that was not picked up by detectors and that allowed searching aircraft to follow submarine signatures, at the last second flipping on search lights before delivering fatal blows. Armed with new **Hedgehog** type depth-charges with contact fuses, the broken hulls of submarines began to litter the ocean's floor. By May of 1943, the Second Battle of the Atlantic had been won and now Americans could project force abroad.

Tunisia offered a stepping-off point into southern Europe where the Nazi beast could be stabbed in its vulnerable underbelly. The problem was getting there. Much of North Africa had been colonized by the French. The French had wisely been left to manage their colonial empire under the Vichy government overseen by the Germans. The huge expanse of North Africa worked perfectly into the AWoF of covering large pieces of ground in rapid fashion. The use of converging columns started with mixed results.

In Casablanca in French Morocco on November 8, 1942, the armored forces of the innovative General George Patton had over 300 miles to travel just to meet up with the central landing force at Oran. Patton had pioneered the use of FM radio and close-air support to allow rapid movements. Little resistance in Oran enabled the two to link up, but eventually leaving the cover of friendly aircraft and facing ship to shore gun duels, the Eastern task force landing at Algiers had a much tougher time of it. Combining forces to take the eventual objective of **Bizerte** in Tunisia, the Americans seemed on the way to success. Being squeezed between an American advance from the west and the British from the east, the Germans seemed about to be cracked. Instead Rommel seized the initiative against the plodding Americans with their huge cathedral type tanks. Lessons on the battlefield proved painful for the unbloodied and inexperienced to learn as always.

Faking withdrawal at Faid in central Tunisia on February 14, 1943, the Germans ambushed Americans with the dreaded German 88 gun—a high velocity cannon soon to be used in the anti-aircraft role. The Germans capitalized on their airpower advantage by hitting the Americans at Sibi bou-Zid; they obliterated the 168th Infantry Regt—an Iowa unit. As panzers (German tanks) surrounded the troops, pathetic examples of riflemen charged against armor. Columns

---

239. Ibid., 380.
240. Ibid., 384.

of American prisoners stretched east as far as the eye could see as the Germans took advantage of their lead by laying another blow, all while American leadership stayed safely in the rear hidden in underground bunkers.[241]

The American disaster at **Kassarine Pass** can be over-stated. Any army conducting a new form of warfare simply must be expected to make mistakes. Remember, there is never any shame in making mistakes—the shame should come from either being unable or unwilling to learn from the mistake. America is a learning army, and, though decisively beaten at Kassarine Pass, the army did not flee the battlefield. The Germans hit the Americans where they had deployed the weakest and were more thinly placed. The American left fell, pierced by a force of 90 panzers in a spearhead, including the formidable but overly complex tiger tank. On the right, tank destroyers' high velocity flat trajectory guns did not leapfrog back, but began to break. M-3 tanks (General Lee's) burrowed in, but, due to their heights, made easy targets, while Germans hit with airlifted artillery, light tanks, and infantry delivered from southern Italy. The failure of intelligence to tell the Americans where the Germans would hit was only part of the reason for the overall failure, and the hundreds of American tanks from the First Armored Division left burning on the road. With 3,000 killed and 4,000 prisoners in the hands of the Germans, it would be left to new American leadership to glean lessons.[242]

The U.S. failed to spread out anti-aircraft assets into the Western-style of neat linear fighting and instead segregated these assets to one part of the battlefield at Kassarine. American vehicles reflected a dependency on rapidity as it appeared the vehicles remained road-bound because of the mud from heavy winter rains. The good news was, although broken on the battlefield, the army did not break and run. Some units underwent small scale panic, but the army as a whole conducted itself courageously. A 28-year old army major named William Westmoreland commanded an artillery battalion and fought boldly over depressed gun barrels firing at point blank range without retreating. American leadership changed also. Noting General Mark Clark's unwillingness to take over the job of the American forces because he viewed it as a demotion, George Marshall opted to give the job to George Patton.

Worried about appearing old in a young army, Patton had driven his troops mercilessly across the deserts of California while training them to fight in North Africa. Developing combined arms around the armored mission, Patton would turn the army into a fighting force of unbelievable discipline and speed in the years ahead. But first, Bizerte. Meanwhile Ike's abilities were questioned despite relieving the field commander, and Marshall ordered General Omar Bradley to be a troubleshooter for the bruised army. Bradley had spent half of his career as an instructor and had an academic's mind when it came to leadership. George Marshall had dropped hints at the Casablanca Conference that perhaps Ike could use some help. Broke but not broken, the American Army would continue under solid and new leadership to stab its way to Bizerte, Tunisia.

With its long airfield, Bizerte again illustrated the tactical imperative of World War II. If oil controlled strategy, airpower had to control the air over the modern battlefield. Most army planning, therefore, had air support as a mandatory ingredient in any attack. As the British 8th Army hit from the east, the Americans advanced upon Tunisia with Rommel leaving and the end nearing for the Nazis in North Africa. The British, continuing to dominate strategic thinking, believed the key to destroying Nazi Germany rested in an indirect approach. Incidentally, the British Empire retained hopes of holding on to the Suez Canal and their colonial holdings in the Mediterranean. Taking the airfield of Bizerte, Tunisia would surely protect the Mediterranean, since anything floating can be sunk. The Americans had taken a blow and continued moving while learning and fighting. The 238,000 German prisoners taken in Tunisia would exceed those of Stalingrad three months prior, and North Africa promised a tough fight ahead. Not a first

---

241. Rick Atkinson, *An Army at Dawn: The War in North Africa, 1942–1943* (New York: Holt, 2007), 357.
242. Perret, *Country*, 387.

Manassas, Ia Drang, or Mazar i-Sharif in Afghanistan where overconfidence resulted from early victories, North Africa prepared the army for the long grinding and deadly task of winning the war still ahead.[243]

Sicily

Operation Husky was the name for the invasion of Sicily. By the fall of 1943 when this operation was undertaken, American forces still sought to isolate Rabaul in the Pacific, and the Central Pacific drive by the marines/navy team still prepared for Tarawa. The key to understanding the two different theaters lay with shipping. The availability of landing craft enabled Americans to project force across the roughly one hundred miles of Mediterranean Sea to this volcano-dominated island that nearly touched the toe of the Italian boot and was home to Germany's European partner. A flawed operation, the great Geoffrey Perret claims Sardinia could have been just as successful in delivering air power to better control the Italian peninsula; nevertheless, crushing firepower and the AWoF, including unprecedented mobility, allowed Americans to take this island.[244]

This first true opposed amphibious landing by the army almost seized disaster from the jaws of victory when the Germans counterattacked the beachhead. Navy destroyers filled the "**gunfire gap**"—the vulnerable stage of any amphibious assault between naval gunfire and the establishment of artillery ashore. Firing point blank and duking it out with German tanks, America's fighting navy saved the day. Opting to do a "**reconnaissance in force**," Patton harnessed the American aggressiveness (AWoF) and circumnavigated the island, attacking the enemy wherever it existed. He conducted this "reconnaissance" while the British General Bernard L. Montgomery continued to bang his head against the wall frontally assaulting the city of Messina. When roads proved unpassable, the brilliant use of amphibious shipping craft to leapfrog around the island enabled Patton to use the best elements of American staff planning, accomplishing the mission at minimal cost. Patton's use of shipping would be replicated in New Guinea by MacArthur the following spring. Just like at North Africa, the Americans made plenty of mistakes in Sicily.

A tragic **fratricide** occurred when glider/airborne troops, accidentally believed to be Germans, received American naval anti-aircraft fires. Finally, the ultimate mistake of the battles for Sicily might have been the Navy's also. The German Army escaped across the narrow Strait of Messina where Italy can actually be seen from Sicily. These German troops would fight a long and bloody contest up the Italian Peninsula.

The Italian Campaign

The Italian Campaign went from September of 1943 until the end of the war. This heartbreaking theater never really achieved success and cost precious American lives throughout its virtually unending campaign. Several factors worked against Allied successes in Italy; the most important probably being geographical. Controversial to this day, the Italian Campaign offers lessons to students of military history today and fighters for tomorrow.

The Italian Campaign largely was a result of the shape of the Italian peninsula. Maneuver would necessarily be limited on the long, rocky stretch of land, and the dreaded bloody frontal assault would often be required. To make matters worse, planners should have noted the direction and nature of the rivers. Fast-flowing rivers would drown many American soldiers who became desperate under fire. The Germans used vast groups of forced laborers to dig defensive lines, one of the more famous being the Gustav Line. Finally, from a geographic standpoint, the failure of armies can depend on simple dirt. Rocky soils like Italy converted into flying death when artillery landed. This

---

243. Ibid., 388.
244. Ibid., 390.

same dry rocky soil turned to mud, forcing American mobility to spin out and slip along, both of which slowed them down and caused them to become vulnerable. The geography of Italy forced the death of many U.S. troops, but the army continued to learn.

The development of elite troops can loosely be correlated to the development of operations. The idea of hitting the enemy where it is most vulnerable with manpower creates scenarios appealing to the wildest ideas of the staff planner's imagination. What if a sniper had killed Hitler, for example? Such visions are decreasingly far-fetched with advances in technology. The army has always had **elites**, but the opportunities for these highly-trained experts to leave the traditional line to wreak havoc on the enemy has increased throughout the century. During the Italian Campaign, the recognition of the value of the Rangers and the creation of the 1st Special Service Brigade symbolized by the arrowhead would arguably be the descendants of the Special Forces received with much acclaim later in Vietnam. These "super troops," today called special operators, in many ways follow their lineage from 1943. Always a problem for military commanders to control while attempting to release them for special independent duties, elite troops nonetheless have always existed and always will be needed in the future.

Two major Allied assaults within the purview of this work are **Salerno** and Anzio. The idea of Salerno, as did the idea for Italy in general, sprang from the minds of the British. Salerno represented another near disaster for the army as it learned the amphibious assault role. So questionable was the prognosis for success that leadership remained at sea and prepared to jettison the mission. Paratroopers actually landed on the beach, and according to Mr. Perret, "green troops fought as veterans" while artillerymen set fuses for 4/10 of a second, essentially firing point blank into the enemy. Frontally assaulting across the forbidding terrain of Italy, the 5th Army under General Mark Clark exhausted itself. Facing the Gustav Line built by forced Italian labor and protecting the Lire Valley leading to Rome, the price of geographic ignorance forced many lives to a wasted end.

Assaulting against the line, Mark Clark betted a landing at **Anzio** could force the Germans thin so that the Gustav Line or the penetration from the Anzio beach—better yet, both—would open the road to Rome that shone like a diamond in Clark's mind. Drowning in the Rapido River, the medieval abbey-turned-fortress of **Monte Cassino,** loomed like Frankenstein's castle. Using **carpet-bombing** against this historical treasure, the Germans merely used the rubble as cover and demonstrated the bombers' limitations for clearing the ground. Relying eventually on the Goumiers, North African mountain troops, Monte Cassino was cleared not with modern firepower, but with old-fashioned silent infantry on mules. Meanwhile the beachhead of Anzio provided the Germans with a shooting gallery of targets.

Crowded on the beach, armor plugging gaps, the Germans once again used the topography of Italy to their best advantage. Bound to hit, they relentlessly shelled the American positions from the surrounding high ground. The arrival of the 1st Special Service Force brought increased patrols that successfully forced the German artillery back from firing on the beachheads. The overwhelming numbers of Americans enabled a breakout and the mixture of the 1st Special Forces and the 1st Armored Division would eventually result in Clark's dream of liberating Rome. Helped by the use of strafing and bombs from medium bombers such as the **B-26 marauder**, the train yards had long since been neutralized, but at a terrible cost in terms of lives and time. The Italian Campaign remains controversial to this day, and though it is easy to second guess decisions by commanders working under combat conditions, we would be remiss to not note the lessons of history. We should dread forcing soldiers to one day suffer from the failure to learn these lessons. The terrain of Italy proved almost as deadly as the Germans.

The Air War over Europe

The path to a successful deployment of bombers followed a tortured path across Europe. Before the war, Allied production under George Marshall received first priority, so when the war did begin, the numbers existed to fight. The Axis initially had the advantage in technology, but they sat on their lead. Americans would learn painful lessons over the skies of Europe but did many things correctly as well. The B-17 bomber, though representing a breakthrough in strategic bombing, nevertheless did disappoint.

Unable to outrun enemy aircraft as pre-war theorists had imagined, this four-engine bomber nonetheless could go great distances. The problem was it couldn't hit when it got there. At Midway for example, 337 bombs did not produce a single hit on a Japanese ship. Nevertheless, Allied production proved superior to the Axis. Moreover, by 1943 at the height of the air war over Europe, the difference had increased to four to one. Axis pilots died in large measure simply because they saw themselves so outnumbered.[245] The B-17's problems would be even greater over Europe.

Hap Arnold, general of the Air Forces, brought General Carl "Tooey" Spaatz, commander of the 8th Air Force. Eighth Air Force Bomber Command would be led by Ira Eaker. In 1942 these leaders believed bombing success could be achieved in tandem with ground forces. In short, air power complemented other forms of military power, but in themselves were not expected to be decisive. By April 1942 the British Prime Minister Winston Churchill saw the merit in bombing cities and attempting to destroy civilian morale in the German police state, and by May was attempting to use massive numbers of bombers against cities. Abandoning costly **daylight bombing**, the British looked at the Americans as if they had gone crazy for continuing daylight operations with increased vulnerability to anti-air assets. No sense of fair play bothered the British after the German bombings on their island during the Blitz of 1940 to 1941. The British believed massive bombing against large targets represented the ideal means of breaking the public. The Americans continued to believe precision bombing could end the war.

With a maritime climate, much of Northern Europe is rainy, or at best overcast, with a rare sunny day. The **Norden bombsight**, which was designed and promised to provide the most accurate tool for high-level bombing to date, failed. Unable to penetrate the often overcast weather, the gunsight frequently presented a very blurry target at best. With pathfinders dropping flares and leading the way, attempts were made to knock out German industry in the Ruhr valley, ending finally with the horrible bombing of Hamburg, Germany, where high explosives weakened structures. In between, incendiary or fire bombs hit anything between the falling walls of structures. During August of 1943, facing furious waves of German fighters thick as bees, the Allied forces hit the ball bearing factories at **Schweinfurt**. An expensive and painful lesson of airpower is to be noted here: the enemy must be hit relentlessly. Simply an attack or two is insufficient. The Germans continued to produce war machines despite their ball-bearing stock (necessary for movement in machines such as aircraft engines) being depleted to the extent that bags of the stock had to be carried to the assembly line in backpacks, thereby slowing down production.[246] As Patton raced around Sicily, the air forces continued to hammer Germany, not winning the war as bomber theorists like Billy Mitchell no doubt would have believed possible, but slowing German war production down at a time when the Russians were pushing west and the American war machine continued into high gear. The final struggle for the perfection of the bombing campaign would emerge.

The attacks on Berlin from August 1943 to March 1944 would see 19 Allied attacks waged against the big city. Despite the use of dreadful **incendiary bombs**, the casualty rate of Allied flight crews during the bombing of Nuremburg alone reached 20.6 percent. Such unsustainable tolls of men and machines would force the Allies from industry to civilian centers, using terror to break morale. By 1944 target lists would see both oil and synthetic oil production targets by the 8th and now the 15th Air Forces. The American forces knocked German industrial production in half, but interestingly, the targets added to the usual industrial lists now included railroad assets. Perhaps the most valuable lessons from the Italian Campaign had been the bombing of railroad marshalling

---

245. Ibid., 405.
246. Randall Hansen, *Fire and Fury* (New York: NAL Caliber, 2008), 137.

Major General William L. Mitchell (Billy)

Courtesy of the United States Air Force

Soldiers are expected to display the Christian characteristic of obedience. General William L. (Billy) Mitchell in fact demonstrated honor by accepting the consequences of his disobedience. In his determination to prove the validity of air power theories, Mitchell received a court martial after sensational media accompanied proceedings against him when he received a verdict of guilty and received suspension of rank and half-pay for five years. Standing up for what he believed to be right against the system and, most importantly, willing to be punished for his views, Mitchell showed great honor when he resigned from the service. He continued to serve the nation by publishing various articles describing the future impact airpower would have. His prophetic views came to fruition in World War II when titanic flotillas of bombers taking hours to cross their targets obliterated cities from the face of the earth. In the spirit of Generals Pershing and Marshall, Mitchell would himself develop the next generation of Air Force leadership with Carl "Tooey" A. Spaatz and Henry (Hap) H. Arnold who would lead the Air Force into the business of interdiction and bombing.[247] The only soldier to ever have an aircraft named after him—the B-25 Mitchell bomber—Billy Mitchell demonstrated honor in doing what he knew to be right for a cause greater than himself. The American Air Force maintains supremacy over the airs of the Earth to this day due to the tremendous honor and self-sacrifice of General Billy Mitchell.

---

yards and its attendant success. By D-Day, the Army Air Force would be hitting both oil targets—pursuing the dreams of the bomber advocates and giving in to the demands of Ike to pursue the Transportation Plan. By the time of D-Day, the Supreme Allied Commander would have won the battle to force the Air Force to bend to the role of a Transportation Plan, focusing air efforts on tunnels, bridges, roads, and anything that rolled. Particularly suited to this mission, the B-26 Marauder bristled with twelve .50 caliber machine guns could fire effectively on the long axis of railroads and highways, wreaking havoc on German attempts to respond to the American invasion on D-Day.

D-Day

By the summer of 1944 the United States embarked on the greatest amphibious assault in history. General Marshall had been left by President Franklin Roosevelt to decide who would lead this great endeavor, and he chose to delegate his authority to Ike. As the reader is probably aware, one can always delegate authority, but never responsibility. The willingness to trust a subordinate and stick with that individual even when they make mistakes is the sign of a great leader. By the summer of 1944 Eisenhower had learned from his mistakes and so had the army. The next year and a half would see the U.S. Army moving with rapid speed in converging columns across Europe and into the pages of history. A greater and more efficiently mobile army never crossed the Earth's surface.

---

247. Geoffrey Perret, *Winged Victory* (New York: Random House, 1993), 12.

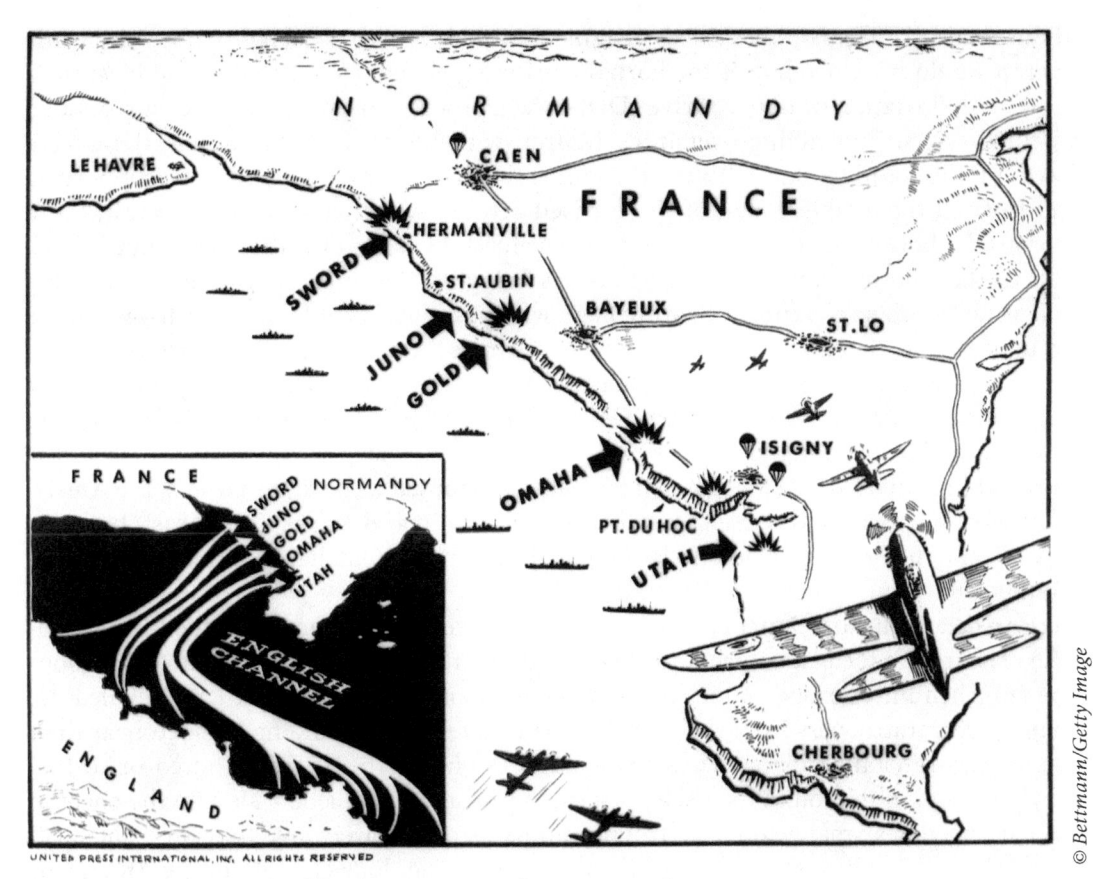

Figure 6.3 Map of Allied invasion of Normandy.

Adolf Hitler, unlike Marshall, tended to micromanage and require control of subordinates. Paranoia and the influence of medications may have contributed to Hitler's decision to ignore the advice of his Field Marshall Erwin Rommel who insisted on massing his firepower at the beach, knowing American airpower could kill anything that moved inland. General Heinz Guderian (father of the blitzkrieg, or "lightening warefare") believed massing such troops to be folly in light of the Sicilian and Salerno landings where American naval vessels had battered German tanks. Guderian thought like a man about to fight the Russians. Hitler ignored both of his subordinates; according to Steve Ambrose, "Just as he could not trust people, neither could he trust one plan over another. He split his resources and invited defeat in detail."[248] To be able to trust others one must not fear. Ironically, some historians now think Hitler's great passion for minute details had led him to the conclusion that the Allies would land at Normandy on the basis of similar hydrographic and geological similarities in beach substrates. Regardless, the Allies conducted a massive counter-intelligence operation using signals and misinformation, and Hitler's disregard for his generals and failure to follow Rommel's advice probably resulted in German failure. Hitler's belief in man's abilities and National Socialism gave him an inability to exercise a strong faith, and the need for him to personally control the minutia of planning stood in great contrast to the Allied plans for D-Day.

The plans for D-Day called for employing the lessons learned in the Mediterranean and the Pacific with a few modifications. Paratroopers would be dropped behind the lines the night before to secure the vital roadways and causeways leading up to the hills overlooking the beaches. Bombs to be dropped on the hills and cliffs would be timed with the use of underwater

---

248. Stephen E. Ambrose, D-Day: *The Climactic Battle of World War II* (New York: Simon & Schuster, 1994), 114.

demolitions teams (UDT). Highly skilled "**frogmen**" would clear the beaches of obstacles while landing craft would travel from over the horizon, bringing assault troops that would blast their way ashore with floatation or duplex drive (DD)—waterproof twin-propeller tanks surrounded with air-filled skirts. Resembling oversized children with life rings at the beach, these were intended to fill the "**gunfire gap**" between the vulnerable phases of landing between supporting naval gunfire and the establishment of shore-based artillery. Amphibious landing craft, those unglamorous flat-bottomed boats with letters such as LSTs, LCIs, and LCMs, would shuttle back and forth to the "mother ships" like water beetles bringing the infantry ashore. To resupply troops, floating "**mulberry**" ramps—floating piers with vast flotillas of landing craft—would be required to project force onto the continent. The "mulberries" represented the British ticket into the war; no mulberries—no British troops. Such were the plans. The great military philosopher Carl Von Clausewitz called the unexpectedness the "friction" or "fog of war." At Normandy on D-Day there would be friction indeed.

British and Canadian Allies landed north relatively unopposed while to the far west the American 4th Division successfully traversed Utah Beach with minimal damage. To the east, however, between Utah and the British/Canadians, lay Omaha Beach. It is at Omaha that the 29th ID and the 1st ID would land.

American delays due to weather had plagued Ike and forced him to postpone the June 4 landing and to plan around the fickle storms so likely to hit the treacherous English Channel as troops would be launched into Europe. The chaos of dropping paratroopers at night largely failed. Of more than 6,000 paratroopers from the 101st Airborne, barely a thousand had landed near their objectives to secure vital roads on causeways behind the lines. The fifteen hundred or so that missed by over eight miles found themselves German prisoners or killed.[249] Despite the chaos at the LZs (landing zones), mangled glider troops and paratroopers were able to form from small groups, and the end result was that they held vital road crossings long enough for the Americans to lightly grasp at the beachheads.

Naval gunfire generally proved inadequate, hitting mostly above the beach according to observers coming in. The bombardments did not consist of the round-the-clock amounts used so freely in the Pacific. To keep the Germans guessing where the main effort would be, the naval gunfire was planned for a short blast just before the landing. Additional concerns to the Allied fleet came from Hitler's toy box of new and frightening weapons. He had been using jet aircraft since the year before, displaying fearsome might from not just the V-1 rockets, but now the new V-2's which guided anti-ship missiles hurtling overhead against the cities of Northwest Europe that landed like exploding freight trains. The Fritz-X glide bomb that had sunk a U.S. cruiser off Salerno would lead the navy to explore electronic identification signatures resulting in countermeasure teams able to jam within 10 seconds. Still, the nervous grey ships off the coast could not help but keep one eye back over their collective steel shoulders just in case.[250]

If it could go wrong at Omaha, it generally did. Tides and winds took every unit except E up to about a mile and a half off their objective. Waves up to six feet caused by northwest winds pushed landing craft from right to left. Seasick soldiers in at least ten of the 200 boats in the first wave had been swamped with water and were saved by Coast Guardsmen.[251] The flotation tanks sank. The DUKWs (rolling transport vehicles able to propel through the water) carrying vital 105 mm howitzers flipped over and sank in the waves, eliminating much needed gunfire once ashore. In some cases dazed coxswains simply circled, lost and confused due to being blown off course from the incredible distance they had to travel. Other sailors simply accelerated towards shore, exploding themselves and showing the other craft where the mines no longer existed! Such was the chaos that it appeared this assault would be a total disaster. Entire units were wiped clean by German machine

---

249. Rick Atkinson, *The Guns at Last Light: The War in Western Europe. 1944–1945* (New York: Holt, 2013), 47.
250. Ibid., 55
251. Ambrose, *D-Day*, 325.

guns with narrow beaten zones from the heights above. Elements were liquefied before they could escape the landing crafts. As at Sicily, the navy came to the rescue again, brushing the ocean floor and firing point blank into the cliffs above while optimistic German reports of victory over the Americans sent follow-on forces to other areas.[252]

The few American troops who could get ashore shook off the shock, misery, and sea-sickness and gathered near the slippery stones called the shingle and began the tortuous ascent up through the mine-strewn draws to take out the German gun positions. By the narrowest of margins, the Americans had been able to grasp victory at Omaha in what may have been the hardest amphibious assault of the war. The beachhead secure, the Americans now must break out.

Surrounding the French coast is countryside, where thousands of years of farming left natural fences called **hedgerows**. These ancient shrub- and tree-lined knolls favored the German defense. Providing natural cover and concealment, it took an enterprising enlisted American soldier to weld some of the German beach defenses onto the front of a tank to break through. Simultaneously with the American air effort using air panels to direct close-air support from **napalm** dropping aircraft, the Americans found themselves able to finally break out of their month long stay in Normandy. The use of **carpet-bombing** flattened German attempts to defend against the breakout, while the Transportation Plan of tank killing aircraft from XIXth Tactical Air Command blasted anything that moved. Germans couldn't believe the deadly pinpoint precision and preponderance of firepower coming from the Americans. The Russians had never been able to deliver such fires!

War in Europe

By the end of July 1944, Operation Cobra had launched Patton's 3rd Army south in attempts to extend supply opportunities. Never really able to solve the supply problem, the army headed toward Paris, narrowly missing an opportunity to seize the city. Many in the American command structure blamed Montgomery because of his close relative location to the vital resupply ports. A single Mulberry supplied Allied soldier consumed up to 66.8 pounds of supply, while U.S. forces consumed up to 30% more than normal allocations. American dependence on rapidly moving vehicles burned a million gallons of gasoline per day.[253] Typically wasteful, Americans had discarded fuel cans across France, and the requirement to replace these was unrealistic. The port of Marseilles in France brought the 7th Army into the fight and some supply relief to accompany the goods finally moving from Cherbourg by late summer, but still Antwerp beckoned as the port most likely to aid the U.S. combatants as they slugged their way across France, into Germany. Logistics, the management of the flow of goods from production to consumption, proved important in World War II, and it will always be an extremely important, if somewhat unglamorous, function within the military.

By August, as Patton's Third Army rolled across France, Hitler continued to disregard the advice of his generals who wanted to fight in successive lines using five river lines on the road to Germany.[254] Attempts to secure Antwerp as a supply base failed when geography conspired to give the Germans positions on the Scheldt estuary, making use of the port impossible, as no ships would enter the port city. By September, with fuel shortages desperately causing the tanks to slow down, the **Red Ball Express** made heroic attempts to relieve supply problems and attempts to build railroads across France; however, time and relative location still served the German defenders. From August 26 to September 11, 1944 the British armies on the left and the American Army Group led by Bradley tried to advance together while separated by some fifty miles. However, the Americans essentially outran the British who could not fight over such distances with such speed. With over 30 **V-1 rockets** being hurled by Hitler in desperation to keep Antwerp under German control and

---

252. Perret, *Country*, 411.
253. Atkinson, *The Guns at Last Light*, 240.
254. Perret, *Country*, 414.

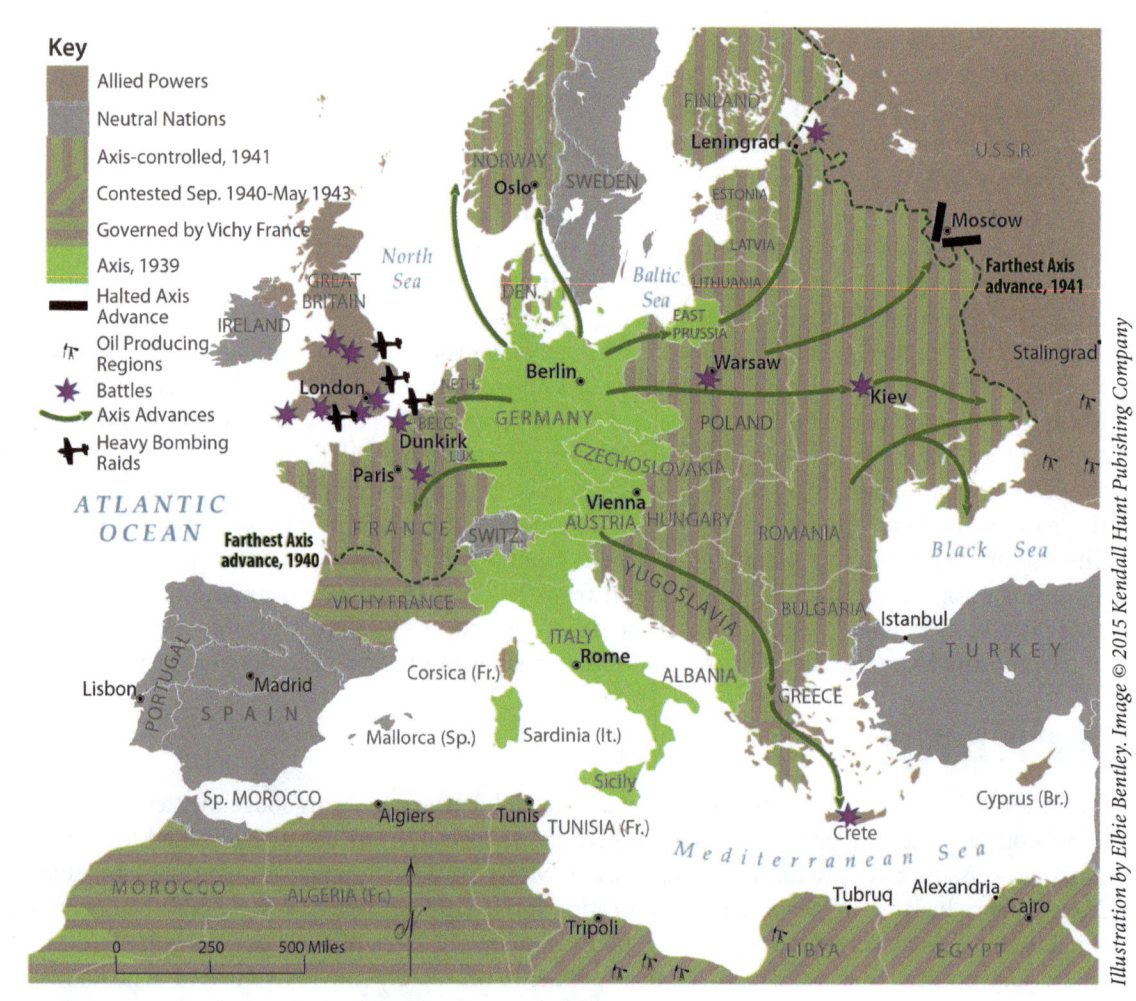

Figure 6.4 Map of German progress during the early years of World War II before the Americans enter.

with a mortified London shivering under the shadow of these unbelievable V-2s angels of death, something had to be done.[255] Suddenly an emboldened Montgomery proposed a bold attempt to solve supply problems once and for all with Operation **Market Garden**.

The audacious attack seemed to be doomed from the start, as the British-led operation depended on a single column advanced by motorized troops up a road surrounded by high ground that Max Hastings said was "steeply embanked, enabling German defenders to fire upon advancing British tanks as if they were being presented to them on a rifle range."[256] Failing to effectively use indigenous peoples—in this case the Dutch resistance—the mobile division, which was sent to relieve paratroopers who held various bridges, delayed while the Germans systematically rolled the British up. Ignoring intelligence, oblique photography had revealed the existence of a German Panzer Division. Clinging desperately to the bridges, more than 20,000 paratroopers held on to the very end. Any hopes for bagging a gigantic number of German prisoners and the new silent but more deadly **V-2 rocket** launching sites died along with an early 1944 victory. The inability to take the bridges continued to exacerbate the supply problem plaguing U.S. and British forces to this point. With the destruction of Mulberry B back in Normandy and with more German troops loading up more than ever on the artillery to Antwerp, the Scheldt Estuary—the passage of resupply ships through Antwerp—stopped. Eisenhower finally began to lose patience with Montgomery. With the

---

255. Atkinson, *The Guns at Last Light*, 332.
256. Max Hastings, *Armageddon: The Battle for Germany, 1944–1945* (New York: Knopf, 2004), 55.

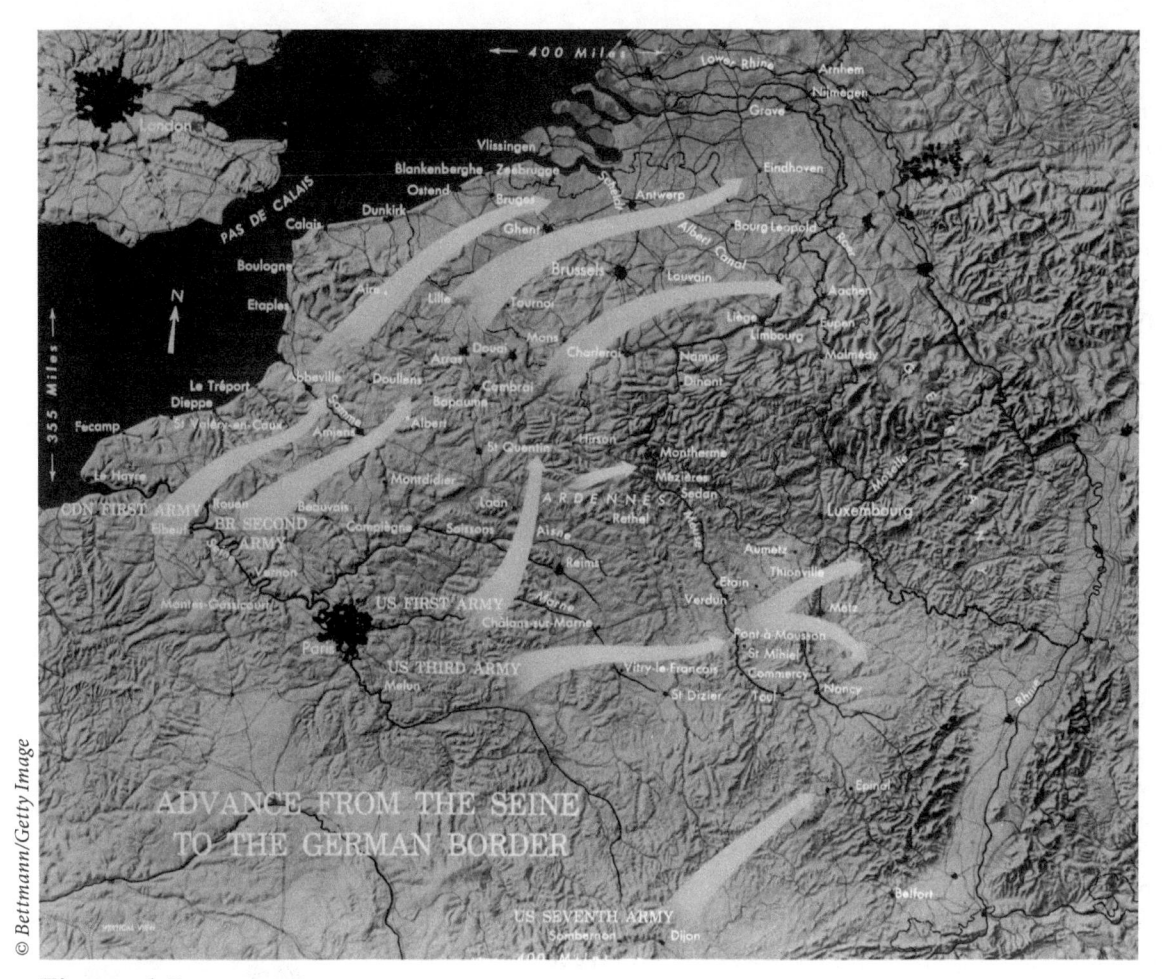

Figure 6.5

loss of nearly 12,000 airborne (some of the best troops in the army), never again would Eisenhower trust Montgomery in quite the same way. Subsequent claims by Montgomery that he could take other objectives would be ignored, and supply priorities would eventually go to Americans fighting an American war.[257]

The war would not after all end in 1944. In fact, Hitler, in a drug-enhanced trance, continued to try to fight World War I. In his vision he saw the Allies being pushed back to the sea with a new twist of the Ludendorff Offensive that had come so close to winning World War I. It is always a bad situation when a leader does not listen to his subordinates. Safe and sound in air-conditioned offices with thick carpets, it is easy to lose touch with the realities of the dirty, dangerous world of the battlefield. The confederate president in the Civil War and President Harry Truman both had been military men and both ran the risk of trying to fight wars their own ways without seeking the advice of their proven military leaders. America always does better when its presidents and leadership trust and hold subordinates responsible without micro-managing. Hitler simply could not do this. But the "**Miracle in the West**," as the Germans referred to it, would give Hitler a chance to launch the counterattack of this man's dreams.

On the eve of Market Garden with the British 21st Army Group tucked up in the northeast of the Allied lines, General Omar Bradley's 12th Army group consisted of four U.S. Armies pretty much on line with General George Patton's 3rd Army slugging it out in Alsace-Lorraine to the south. Coming to join the fray from the Vosges Mountains was General Alexander Patch's 7th Army just

---

257. Atkinson, *The Guns at Last Light*, 288.

up the Rhone Valley from Marseilles. The Germans most feared Patton of all the U.S. commanders, and here Hitler sent his best tanks. Despite the bombing of his factories, Hitler matched Americans in firepower. Crashing repeatedly against the Siegfried Line and barely penetrating the west wall of Germany, American troops after Market Garden became bogged down in the type of static warfare that was loathsome to Americans and reminiscent of World War I.[258]

With winter weather causing loss of transportation as roads turned to mud, and with clouds blocking the battlefield from the Allied air forces, Hitler boldly gambled away the German army on the western wall of defenses. German paratroopers in American uniforms and trained soldiers speaking with American accents created havoc in the rear of America's lines while a simultaneous thrust of spotlights from German tanks hit the Americans who had run low on fuel. As American prisoners surrendered in large numbers, many chose to escape and join tank-hunting bazooka teams who stood and fought with cooks and clerks. A secret weapon according to Geoffrey Perret, the **proximity fuse** made its appearance, exploding in lethal downward angles into the spines of dug-in troops. This secret weapon had been used in the Pacific where it was safe from falling into Axis hands, but it arrived with thunderous and devastating force in the Hurtgen Forest, popularly called the Bulge battlefronts. Patton's 3rd Army made a heroic turn and traveled a record 100 miles to the rescue of besieged troops trapped at Bastogne surviving off resupply dropped by way of parachutes.[259]

Second Lieutenant Audie Murphy

Second Lt. Murphy ordered his men to withdraw to prepared positions in a woods, while he remained forward at his command post and continued to give fire directions to the artillery by telephone… With the enemy tanks abreast of his position, Second Lt. Murphy climbed on the burning tank destroyer…and employed its .50 caliber machinegun against the enemy. He was alone and exposed to German fire from three sides… For an hour the Germans tried every available weapon to eliminate Second Lt. Murphy… [they] reached as close as 10 yards, only to be mowed down by his fire. He received a leg wound, but ignored it and continued the single-handed fight until his ammunition was exhausted. He then made his way to his company, refused medical attention, and organized the company in a counterattack, which forced the Germans to withdraw…

(Near Holtzwihr France, 26 January 1945)

excerpt from Congressional Medal of Honor citation

Courtesy of the United States Army

With Hitler's failed offensive and virtually every division he owned now broken, the way was open to Berlin. The American Army crossed the Rhine River ahead of schedule to the south and east while the British, with supply priority and American troop reinforcements, failed to advance. Reinforcing the American breakthroughs, Ike gave Berlin to the Russians, deciding the prize of Berlin simply not worth the American lives that the amount of desperate house-to-house fighting would be required to take it. If the Russians wanted it so badly, let them have it. Much criticism during the Cold War would be directed at Eisenhower for not taking Berlin, but in purely military terms, he probably made the right decision.[260] Other criticisms of the American military, particularly by British historians, point to the poor aggressiveness of certain U.S. units. Not taken into

---

258. Perret, *Country*, 420.
259. Ibid., 422.
260. Ibid., 424.

account, however, is that the same peaceful culture's work ethic, capable of enormous industrial production, simply did not rape and pillage to the extent the more socialist and statist European Allies did. Killing is simply not something that comes easy for a Christian people, and America in these days had not yet turned from Scriptures to government propaganda or hatred of the Germans to the extent the Europeans had. In the Pacific we would see a different level of ferocity displayed by individual riflemen, and eventually by the American government. Even tougher decisions would be forced upon American leadership after a brutal series of battles across the Pacific.

Key Terms:

Daylight bombing	**Hedgerows**	**V-2 rocket**
Norden bombsight	**Napalm**	**Miracle in the West**
Schweinfurt	**Carpet-bombing**	**Proximity Fuse**
Incendiary bombs	**Red Ball Express**	**Hedgehog**
Frogmen	**V-1 rocket**	**Bizerte**
Gunfire gap	**Fighting withdrawals**	**Kassarine Pass**
"Germany first"	**Corregidor**	**"Reconnaissance in force"**
Triton	**Anzio**	**Fratricide**
B-26 Marauder	**Monte Cassino**	**Elites**
Mulberry	**Market Garden**	**Salerno**

Thought Questions:

How did the AWoF hurt and help American attempts to break out of Normandy and race across Europe?

What are the advantages of delegating authority to subordinates, such as George Marshall did with Eisenhower? What are some of the risks of not doing so, such as Hitler with his Generals?

Chapter VII

WORLD WAR II: THE WAR IN THE PACIFIC

James 4: 1-3 "Where do wars and fights come from among you? Do they not come from your desires for pleasure that war in your members? You lust and do not have. You murder and covet and cannot obtain. You fight and war. Yet you do not have because you do not ask. You ask and do not receive, because you ask amiss, that you may spend it on your pleasures." NKJV

Check out an animated map of the events of World War II in the Pacific at this link: https://www.khpcontent.com/

1941
Japan attacks Pearl Harbor; United States enters war

1942
Doolittle Raid
Battle of Coral Sea
Battle of Midway
Battle of Cape Esperance
Guadalcanal Campaign

1943
Attu and Kiska Campaign
F6F Hellcat debuts
Gilbert Islands Campaign (Tarawa)
Operation Cartwheel

1944
Operation Cartwheel continues
Marshall Islands Campaign (Kwajalein, Eniewetok)
Marianas Islands Campaign (Saipan, Guam etc.)
Battle of Peleliu
Battle of Leyte Gulf
Landing at Leyte

1945
Battle for Iwo Jima
Battle for Okinawa
Atomic Bombs dropped on Japan

Go to www.khpcontent.com to watch a video introduction for this chapter.

After Pearl Harbor the Japanese suffered from the same disease most nations do that win opening victories—**victory disease**! The overconfidence accompanying success is like human pride. Whatever their mistakes or sins, the Germans and the Japanese would pay for them dearly. Anyone who believes World War II was a "good war" needs to study the war in the Pacific. Robert E. Lee's admonition, "It is well that war is so terrible—lest we should grow too fond of it," certainly is true here. The war in the Pacific is treated separately here for convenience sake, but remember the war in Europe pursued a victory as the war in the Pacific raged.

The Japanese failed abysmally in the Pacific. Why a nation dedicated to achieving a naval empire would ignore **ASW**, or anti-submarine warfare, against a potential enemy is still confusing to many. With an economy at the war's beginning less than 20 percent than that of the United States, Japan simply could not defend its entire empire, particularly later in the war when bombing would take its toll. The fury unleashed at Pearl Harbor would see American production reach unprecedented levels. Utilizing converging columns, the marine and navy team would battle across the Central Pacific and through the Southwest Pacific. Developing the amphibious assault while improving and learning new techniques of fighting, the army would meanwhile advance under General MacArthur. The marines/army would isolate and encircle the Japanese fortress at Rabaul by taking the islands of Bougainville and New Britain. MacArthur then turned toward New Guinea, and the two giant arrows, one blue and one green, would soon converge at the Philippines. With the newly developed B-29 bomber, by 1945 the mostly—U.S. war would be knocking on the door of the Japanese home islands from Okinawa. At about the same time the U.S. Army would be camped outside the Elbe River in Germany with President Roosevelt's passing. Throughout the Pacific War the United States constantly innovated its methods with new weapons and the means of employing them in varying geographic environments.

Ignoring **land-based airpower** and attempting to seize the separated ports in the Southwest Pacific at distances of about 600 miles, the Japanese attempted to take **Port Moresby** in New Guinea and the tiny island of Tulagi in the Solomon Islands. Rebuffed by carrier-based air, the Japanese withdrew to lick their wounds. Some say this **Battle of the Coral Sea** represented the first naval battle fought by opposing fleets unable to see. Carrier air now ruled battles for the ocean's surface. With Australia temporarily saved from the Japanese, a new threat emerged from Japanese airpower located at Port Moresby, New Guinea and the island of Tulagi in the Solomon Islands. Launched from these airfields, the Japanese would be able to use their airpower to cut off Australian shipping from the United States. Land-based airpower is superior to carrier air, but, in tandem, the use of aircraft and the aircraft carrier had forever changed warfare and military strategy.

Armed with intelligence analysis, the American carrier pilots hit the Japanese at the great naval **Battle of Midway**, where waves of torpedo-dropping dive bombers hit the Japanese fleet. The Japanese stayed one punch behind the U.S. in this desperate brawl at sea. The U.S. hit the Japanese carriers in waves of attacking; dive-bombing "wildcats" and torpedo dropping "avengers." Japanese ships buckled in the water cracked in half by the dropping bombs. The Japanese carrier decks marked with red bull's-eyes like rising suns made perfect targets for swarms of attacking U.S. aircraft plummeting at speeds of over 200 mph. The Japanese ships fatally exposed their vulnerability with torpedoes and fuel scattered over their decks. The Japanese desperately attempted to load aircraft with armor-piercing bombs and fuel in futile attempts to rearm themselves as they exploded under an onslaught of American fury. This "turning point" of the Pacific War represented the beginnings of the Japanese going on the defensive, but it had also demonstrated the power of intelligence. Whoever could find the enemy first would get the first punch in future fights. Airpower's eye in the sky capability partially explains why airfields remained so important throughout the Pacific fighting.

Most Americans are unaware that the Japanese had actually attacked and occupied the United States. In the Aleutian Islands the Japanese had hoped to distract the Americans from Midway Island in the Central Pacific. Code breakers and traffic analysts had begun to understand the Japanese Purple Codes and would flash messages called **Ultra**, warning commanders about probable Japanese actions;

sometimes taking up to two hours to get from Hawaii to the South Pacific.[261] Throughout the war these codes, along with the help of indigenous peoples (AWoF), would help determine victory. Radio traffic analysis—the wading through countless messages and documents attempting to get a picture of the battlefield—along with cryptanalysts or code breakers, would produce the dramatic killing of Admiral Isoroku Yamamoto when his aircraft was shot down over the island of Bougainville. Demonstrative of the sensitive nature of this sort of intelligence work, use of Ultra often required the acceptance of preventable American losses for fear of alerting the enemy that their codes had been broken. In fact, analysts feared the killing of Yamamoto, the architect of Pearl Harbor, would alert the Japanese to just this![262]

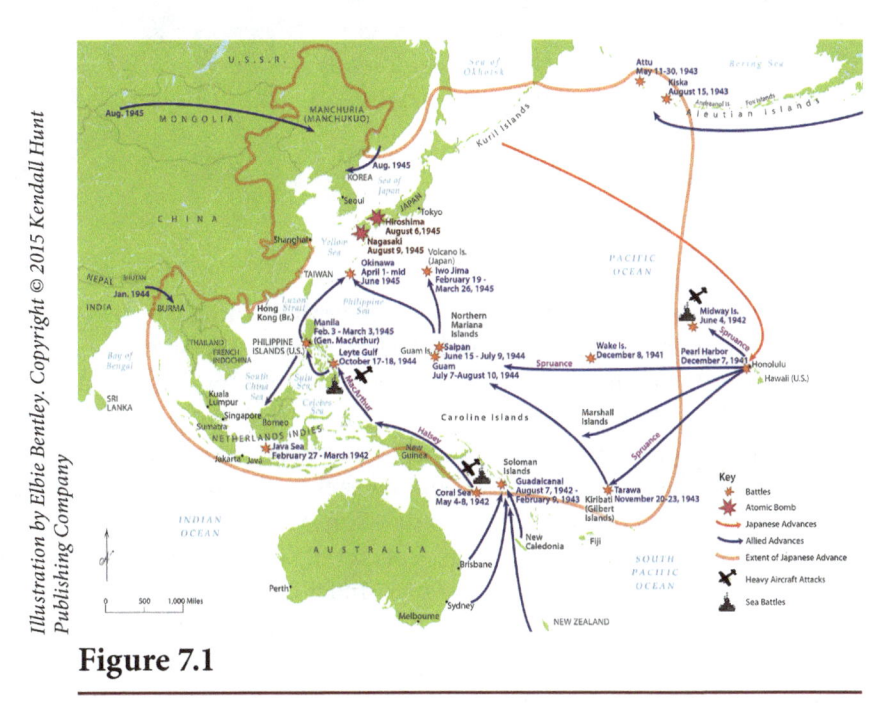

Figure 7.1

Illustration by Elbie Bentley. Copyright © 2015 Kendall Hunt Publishing Company

World War II: The Pacific Theater

The First Marine Division landed at **Guadalcanal** in an attempt to prevent the Japanese from securing a newly built airfield capable of isolating Australia. This resulted in an epic series of naval battles extending far off of shore. The Japanese owned the night, and with their spotlights they could fire with incredible accuracy upon the U.S. naval ships that were attempting to intercept these Japanese ships coming down "the slot." The Battle of **Savo Island** only two months before—the worst in U.S. Navy history with more than 1,000 sailors dead—would be followed by the naval Battle of Santa Cruz Islands in October 1942. Both battles represented terrible initial defeats. Learning from their mistakes, however, American naval power still grew in the South Pacific. Meanwhile on Guadalcanal on August 7, 1942, a somewhat amateurish attempt at an amphibious landing presented a somewhat bumbling affair with broken, smoking outboard motors and men who required their floundering boats to be towed ashore. Idle marines shot coconuts from trees and swam while shorthanded shore party chiefs worked without adequate numbers of troops.[263] Reality soon would set in with disease and deprivation as the Americans and Japanese continued to battle each other in the seas offshore, all while the Japanese attempted to funnel in supplies and troops far out of proportion to the importance of the island. Several deadly naval battles including the struggles for Cape Esperance and the Santa Cruz Islands would, in many ways, serve to bleed the Japanese dry

---

261. Richard B. Frank, *Guadalcanal* (New York: Random House, 1990), 29.
262. Ronald Spector, *Eagle Against the Sun* (New York: Free Press: New York, 1985), 454.
263. Perret, *Country*, 375.

Platoon Sergeant Mitchell Paige

…When the enemy broke through the line directly in front of his position, P/Sgt. Paige… continued to direct the fire of his gunners until all his men were either killed or wounded. Alone, against the deadly hail of Japanese shells, he fought with his gun and when it was destroyed, took over another, moving from gun to gun, never ceasing his withering fire against the advancing hordes until reinforcements finally arrived. Then, forming a new line, he dauntlessly and aggressively led a bayonet charge, driving the enemy back and preventing a breakthrough in our lines….

(Solomon Islands, 26 October 1942)

excerpt from Congressional Medal of Honor citation

Courtesy of the United States Marine Corp

in terms of valuable naval resources and pilots. Many believe the irrational Japanese attempt to grip the U.S. forces in mortal combat in the Solomon Islands of the Southwest Pacific ultimately represented as important a turning point in the war as the Midway and Coral Sea battles.

Island-hopping would be the means of achieving victory in the Central Pacific. Beginning with the Aleutian Islands in May of 1943, the Americans attacked Attu, skipping over Kiska 250 miles to the west. "Withering on the vine, like grapes with cut stems," the Japanese would be left on the islands to slowly starve as U.S. forces continued to drive on. While looking for airfields to extend the radii of deadly force from the new aircraft carriers coming off the American assembly lines of dry docks, the American air power of the 5th Air Force under diminutive General George Kenney struck the Japanese fortress at Rabaul. Softening Rabaul up for MacArthur's ultimate invasion, the unintended effect was to kill precious Japanese aircraft including Zeros, said to be the finest fighter aircraft available at the beginning of the war. A captured Zero was used as the prototype for the design of a new fighter that would become the new champ—the F6F **Hellcat**. As the Japanese robbed Peter to pay Paul, so to speak, taking their precious fighters from the Central Pacific to defend the fortress of Rabaul, Americans proceeded to hit the scantily-protected islands, seeking the deep water anchorage of Eniewetok about 1500 miles west of Hawaii.[264] To get Eniewetok, the navy-marine team needed to secure the seaways from the Central Pacific and take the key atoll of **Tarawa** and the island of Betio, where an important airfield lay.

Minesweepers proceeded the invasion forces of marines, but underwater demolitions teams (UDT) had not arrived in this part of the Pacific yet. Well-armed with big guns, including 127 and 75 mm guns, the notoriously poor coordination between the army and navy would reemerge to haunt the Japanese throughout the war. Simply unable to report defeat, reports lacking truth often would go back to higher headquarters, confusing leaders as to the actual conditions on the battlefield. Regardless, at Tarawa the Japanese had the moon on their side.

Sailors have known about neap tides for ages. Occurring twice a month when the moon is in its first or last quarter, the effect of the moon on tides is basically common knowledge. What constituted the unknown at Tarawa, however, is the apogean tide. Occurring with a neap tide, this rare event only occurs a couple times per year when the moon is closest to the earth. The tides at Tarawa were as Julian C. Smith called them, "freakish!"[265] Freakish or not, the tides spelled death for many men trying to get across the lagoon to the beaches. Wading in against enemy grazing fire

---

264. Ibid., 395.
265. Joseph H. Alexander, *Utmost Savagery: The Three Days of Tarawa* (Annapolis MD: Naval Institute Press, 1995), 77.

at distances of 700 yards and confronted by sea walls and peers, Tarawa is rightly a Marine Corps legend to this day. A horrified public, informed of over 3,000 casualties for an area roughly half the size of Central Park, was shocked. Even worse was the fate of the Japanese, forced to live on a coral reef without fresh water. Unable to bury communication lines at one foot of sea level on coral, the Japanese simply could not coordinate a winning defense. Lessons learned from Tarawa would see UDT teams and hydrographic surveys instituted within the operations orders of future assaults, as well as the use of rocket-propelled artillery to increase the velocity of incoming rounds sufficient to pierce reinforced concrete. Tarawa served as a bloody school for amphibious operations. Still, the navy-marine team swam on to Eniewetok.[266]

Eniewetok, by December of 1943, fell easily as Japanese forces continued to dwindle in the Pacific. A flat island is also a difficult platform to defend since visibility is limited by the curvature of the earth—sixteen feet for every five miles of distance. The defenders therefore could not tell which direction the marine punch would come from until almost too late. Now the navy had an anchorage from which it could continue to push the attack across the Pacific: and attack they did. Fuel ships acted as floating gas stations, refueling the fast carriers and battleships which, in turn, would fuel the cruisers and destroyers. Submarines stalked prey beneath the ocean's surface, further providing a layer of protection. Bristling with new variants of anti-aircraft guns, American ships constituted floating platforms forcing up a wall of lead around carriers.[267]

Why did the Americans want the Marianas, and why, in particular, Saipan? Five-star General of the Air Force Henry A. Hap Arnold had a new bomber, the **B-29**, and with it he could not only win the air war over Japan, but he could hit Japan directly. To fly off of the island though, Saipan must be taken by the marines. After the marines attacked, they found themselves clinging tenuously to a thin shoreline. The lack of coordinating arms support would almost cost the Americans this island. Naval gunfire liaison teams could not call in adequate support from gunships because of the devastating accuracy of Japanese artillery fires. The Japanese had, indeed, been learning, too. Instead of fighting the Americans at the beachhead, they had come to realize it was better to let the American troops land and then tie them down with interlocking fires. Saving time for space, the Japanese would execute this strategy from the end of 1943 to the end of the war. Forced to deploy the reserve division, General H.M. "Howling Mad" Smith eventually would fire the 27th Division (Nat Guard) under the command of Ralph Smith. A marine named Smith firing a soldier named Smith caught on in the press back home and caused interservice bitterness for years. Regardless, the beachhead finally held sufficiently for the Americans to drive inland, meanwhile the **Battle of the Philippine Sea** waged between contending navies.

Deployed in almost identical fashion, the Japanese launched their carriers at the U.S. forces, which nervously stood off the contested Marianas beachheads. The difference was the Japanese used the carriers to protect their battleships and cruisers, while the Americans had learned to let the "old ships of the line" protect their carriers. Throwing themselves into the walls of lead, the Japanese broke themselves on the American battleships firing their 40 mm Bofors and 20 mm exploding rounds. As Geoffrey Perret said it, "The Battle of the Philippine Sea was the greatest defensive naval triumph of the war." The Japanese carrier war was over.[268] This failed attempt to project force represented the last of the five great World War II naval carrier battles. The carrier battles may have been over, but the naval war had not ended.

The unglamorous lurking submarine is believed by many historians to be the one weapon system most responsible for victory against the Japanese in the Pacific. Initially starting the war with malfunctioning steam-propelled torpedoes, returning to hit the ship that fired them, the American submarine force almost represented an embarrassment. Remember, Japan is an area about the size of California, consisting of four major home islands. As an island, Great Britain in World War I

---

266. Perret, *Country*, 401.
267. Ibid., 400.
268. Ibid., 403.

faced grave vulnerabilities. Once again the author who provides so much of the inspiration for this book, Geoffrey Perret said for every submarine lost, about 100,000 tons of merchant shipping sank. A total of 52 submarines per year never to surface continued throughout the war.[269] Such losses to the Japanese put them at a state of general food rationing as early as February of 1942 with the average daily intake of calories at less than 60 percent of that of Americans.[270] The silent submarine service nearly starved the Japanese into defeat by themselves.

Air War against Japan

The **Doolittle Raid** of April 1942 had demonstrated American resolve after Pearl Harbor and gave an encouragement to the American people during a time of fear. Launching B-25 Mitchell medium-bombers against Tokyo and other targets on the island of Honshu, aircraft carriers demonstrated the need to maintain morale. Often overlooked by leaders in a computer-staring culture, morale is an intangible quality that can bring out the best in fighters. Though the Doolittle Raid represented only a series of miniscule pinpricks, morale at home soared. By seizing the offensive, the Doolittle Raid may have persuaded Yamamoto to have launched the Battle of Midway, and, as we have seen, this resulted in the high-water mark for Japanese naval power with America going on the offensive in the Pacific for the rest of the war. The lesson here for the student is clear: never lack courage, and always strike as fast and often as possible when in a fight. Always attempt to take the initiative with the enemy and never give up. After the Doolittle Raids, the Americans kept the offensive going by flying from the Aleutians to the **Kurils** (to the north of Japan) in horribly dangerous conditions. Perhaps, once again, this represented very little of strategic significance; the fact that the Japanese possessions could be hit from nearly 700 miles across the Northern Pacific speaks volumes of the difference between how Americans fought in World War II; by thinking "outside the box," unlike today where things are too often kept predictably neat and spreadsheet organized. An additional bonus of hitting the Kurils would be to force Japanese air defenses to continually stay on the alert to the north spreading their defensive lines thinner.[271]

We have mentioned the 5th Air Force (more on them in a moment), but the 20th Air Force initially operated out of China. By the summer of 1944 the **Marianas** Islands, consisting of Tinian, Guam, and Saipan, had been taken. In American hands, the islands provided an opportunity to not just defeat Japan, but to punish it with the B-29 Superfortress. Air Force raids on Tokyo in late 1944 saw continued prohibitive losses to U.S. aircraft and men. Even the United States, with its industrial machine humming so loudly, could not sustain nor replace such losses. After the hellish decimation of Dresden, Germany, Curtis LeMay reflected upon the idea that **terror bombing** could effectively shut down industry in Japan. Perfect flying conditions existed over Tokyo from March 9–10th in 1945 for a practice run to see if this horror would work.[272]

The silver-skinned angel of death that was the B-29 first rolled off the assembly lines in September 1943 while Americans still dried out from landing in Italy and continued to sharpen their teeth around Rabaul. The Japanese knew roughly what the capabilities of the B-29 would be and had assumed it would hit the islands around June of 1944, but, frustratingly for them, there was little they could actually do to prevent its becoming operational. Perhaps this was in part due to the aforementioned submarine successes and such thinned defenses the result of such "out of the box" operations flown by the Doolittle Raids.[273] General William T. Sherman once said, "War is Hell." The B-29 proved him right.

---

269. Ibid., 425.
270. Barret Tillman, *Whirlwind: The Air War Against Japan 1942–1945* (New York: Simon & Schuster, 2010), 40.
271. Ibid., 273.
272. Ibid., 142
273. Ibid., 40.

On March 9–10th of 1945, the B-29s hit the Japanese cities with their incendiaries designed to hit, penetrate, and explode for up to 150 feet. Firebombs destroyed the traditionally-built wooden and paper walled buildings (remember, Japan is a series of volcanic islands on potentially violent tectonic plates). A firestorm occurred the likes of which has probably never been witnessed by human eyes. Mr. Perret again:

> The bombers dropped up to 70 tons of incendiaries per square mile, first creating huge rings of fire, to be filled in by succeeding currents rose from the fire storm with such force they hurled the bombers two miles overhead up and down like yo-yos. Smoke forced the last bombers to attack blind. Silver B-29s flew back to Tinian as black as ravens, coated with soot.[274]

So violent were the updrafts from the hell below that crews became injured; one aircraft pitched so violently that one crewman actually received a Purple Heart.[275]

The Japanese received the ultimate nightmare. The flames continued to spread with the western winds, and, as they could, the lucky survivors leapt into water towers and canals that were boiling and evaporating in the 1800 degree Fahrenheit storms; even the Imperial Palace would be burned. Clothes burned off people, leaving them fleeing in bare skin while others nearby simply exploded into spontaneous combustion as southeasterly winds blew embers and pushed flames across neighborhoods.[276] The result would be a loss of up to 90,000 people's lives and more than a million left totally homeless; subsequent raids would hit many other cities in like manner. To his dying day, an unrepentant Curtis Lemay never expressed remorse or regret for doing what he believed to be his duty. The business of war is frighteningly serious and must never be entered into lightly.

For all of the weaknesses of the Japanese home islands, the losses in B-29s continued to be too high. The marines would eventually be forced to take Iwo Jima for the purpose of securing airfields for the P-51 Mustangs with their new 108 gallon **drop tanks**. The tanks enabled the pursuit/fighters to escort the B-29s and keep them safer as they continued to systematically erase Japanese cities from the map.

Douglas MacArthur is, without question, one of the most peculiar figures in modern American military history. Competitive and vain, in his later years he surrounded himself with sycophants and yes-men. MacArthur's vanity displayed itself when a subordinate received his picture on the cover of the premier newsmagazine of the day. The old general had him brought into his office and reminded the popularized figure that he could be fired. Despite his vanity, MacArthur achieved results. When the Marines fought their way ashore in Saipan, MacArthur harshly pushed his subordinates for land victory in the Southwest Pacific. Throughout 1944 MacArthur had demonstrated a measure of genius using high mobility and by passing enemy strongholds to take the huge island of New Guinea during **Operation Cartwheel**. Utilizing the awesome airpower of the 5th Air Force and an intricately planned use of transport shipping, MacArthur had already pushed his troops to the limit. Announcing the end of the campaign after landing in **Biak**, he would later eat those words after it took up to three months for Americans to dig the Japanese out of the caves surrounding the airfield, keeping aircraft from flying. Biak is located about 75 miles from the northwest coast of New Guinea; what MacArthur really wanted sat in Manila about 1500 miles away. One can only imagine why the man who had been the youngest major general and the youngest chief of staff held such a fierce fascination with the Philippines. A man of proven courage decorated with the Medal of Honor like his father had been hurt badly by the derisive nickname of "Dugout Doug" given to him by the troops after he had been ordered from the Philippines. What General MacArthur really sought appeared to be his reputation and vindication!

---

274. Perret, *Country*, 433.
275. Tillman, *Whirlwind*, 155.
276. Ibid., 1v49.

When Admiral William "Bull" Halsey discovered during his patrols off of the Philippines that the Japanese aircraft had fallen back to Taiwan in their attempt to better defend the Japanese home islands, the Joint Chiefs of Staff decided not to go into Taiwan but to let MacArthur have his dream—an invasion of **Leyte**, an island in the Philippines. With no real resistance, the landing proved a cakewalk, but MacArthur, not content to secure just the necessary air fields, failed when he decided to take the entire island. Here he ran into the enemy of all armies, mud.

Mud must be experienced to be understood. Seemingly simple, it ruins all objects attempting to move. MacArthur's men found their morale plummeting. The end of 1944 found its leader Lt Gen Robert Eichelberger of the 8th Army in an attempt to motivate them saying, "Infantry is the arm of close combat, it is the arm of final combat; supporting arms are of great assistance; it ultimately becomes the task for the small infantry units to dig them out."[277] By the end of the grueling Leyte experience, one of MacArthur's trusted subordinates, Eichelberger, said, "This theater has been a victim of over-optimism."[278] General Krueger had worked for General Otis during the Philippines War and had chased after Aguinaldo. This older officer would be slated to command his 6th Army in the final invasion of Japan and was another trusted subordinate to MacArthur. Berated for a delay in the attack on Manila, Krueger believed until his dying day that MacArthur was more interested in obtaining the city on his birthday then he was in destroying Yamashita's army.[279] Krueger and Eichelberger together are somewhat unsung heroes of the Philippines fights during World War II and may have prevented a disaster by refusing to be rushed into the trap Yamashita had set for them. Listening to subordinates is important for any successful officer, but this certainly was not MacArthur's strength.

General of the Army Douglas MacArthur

Historians have generally been unkind to General Douglas MacArthur. Gifted and brilliant, MacArthur's character seemed to vary from the Christian attribute of meekness. In World War I, MacArthur received seven Silver Stars and two Distinguished Service Crosses for bravery. Ironically, he rarely wore his decorations and it seemed MacArthur forever lived in the shadow of his father Arthur MacArthur, who had performed brilliantly in the Philippines and who had received the Medal of Honor in the Civil War. MacArthur's mother even followed him to West Point where she lived on the edge of campus as if to shadow him! Perhaps vanity caused MacArthur to often fail to listen to and to remain critical of both subordinates and seniors alike. It is no accident the magnificent generals who served under MacArthur are still virtually unrecognized by many to this day. MacArthur once even said George C. Marshall was the most "overrated soldier in the Army."

(Cont.)

---

277. Kevin C. Holzimmer, *General Walter Krueger: Unsung Hero of the Pacific War* (Lawrence: University Press of Kansas, 2007), 205.
278. Max Hastings, *Retribution: The Battle for Japan, 1944–1945* (New York: Knopf, 2007), 191.
279. Holzimmer, *General Walter Krueger*, 224.

> MacArthur also seemed to display a cyclical contrasting pattern of actions ranging from being caught off guard to one of a decisive action for the purpose of protecting his reputation. MacArthur's self-confidence fed a complacency that infected those around him and possibly explains the disasters that befell his forces such as in the Philippines, reaction to the CCS decision to bypass Rabaul, and when the Chinese invaded in Korea. Unfortunately, in the Philippines and in Korea, an obsessed MacArthur would act independently of his superiors, flirting with disobedience, and ultimately needlessly sacrificing his men in Manilla and by approaching the Yalu River in Korea. In World War II, he would claim premature victories as if defying the calendar itself to preserve his reputation. In Korea, as if desperate to regain his reputation after the catastrophic Chinese invasion, MacArthur's use of political contacts to argue for a broadened war against the directions of President Harry Truman and MacArthur's subsequent relief draws obvious parallels to President Lincoln and his ambitious General, George B. McClellan, after the battle of Antietam in the Civil War. In both cases, we are reminded of the importance of military obedience to civil authorities and the need for civilian leadership to trust their subordinates.
>
> It is said unrewarded talent is proverbial. MacArthur's career proved that he had great physical courage and even the spirit of temperance and calm when facing great odds, but his loyalty seemed to fall short. Nonetheless, those who had served under MacArthur had learned to tell their superiors what they wanted to hear, and this thread of ambition would continue to demonstrate itself sadly within the American military to the present day.[280]

Fresh from smashing the Japanese forces in the **Air Battle over Taiwan**, where he had swatted the Japanese land-based air forces, the impetuous and recklessly bold Admiral William F. Halsey took the bait on October 25, 1944. With the invasion of Leyte, only a week along and leaving no security behind during the **Battle of Leyte Gulf**, Halsey chased empty decoy Japanese aircraft carriers off to sea. As the Japanese worked this ruse, they brought their navy through the Archipelago in two strikes; one through San Bernardino Strait and the other through Surigao Strait. Japanese ships desperately running out of refined fuels hit American forces with ten to one odds, but the numbers didn't reveal the truth. The Americans boldly attacked, launching destroyers against battle ships and cruisers while the American fought with the fury of an avenging angel. The other Japanese probing attack coming through Surigao Strait ran into a wall of steel laid down by many of the battleships from Pearl Harbor refurbished and fit to fight. If the Philippine Sea had seen the end of the Japanese carriers as fighting forces, then the battle of Leyte Gulf represented the end of the fleet fighting as a team. Both Japanese attempts at Leyte had failed, and their navy limped back home, increasingly desperate to die for victory.[281]

Moving into the northern island of **Luzon**, MacArthur launched a bold plan using converging columns to seize and secure the island. Again, either his ego or his past (perhaps both) put MacArthur into hot water. Ignoring JCS instructions, he played into the hands of Lt. Gen Tomoyuki Yamashita, the "Tiger of Malaya," who authorities argue represented the best Japanese General of the war.[282] Going into the highlands after Yamashita and determinedly focused on securing the city of Manila, MacArthur wasted the use of airborne drops and maneuver for his ego's sake. He allowed his forces to become sucked into the steep hills and mountains in an operation reminiscent

---

280. Geoffrey Perret, *Old Soldiers Never Die* (New York: Random House, 1996), 562.
281. Perret, *Country*, 428.
282. Hastings, *Retribution*, 122.

of Italy.[283] Foreboding of another city in the future (Korea) where MacArthur would waste time to secure a symbolic capital, he made matters even worse by attempting to liberate the entire archipelago before Luzon had even fallen, and proceeded to send away valuable and much needed manpower. Manila would be one of the most destroyed cities of World War II and perhaps represented a sad legacy of one man's ego. Indeed, the man who had brilliantly used a bypassing strategy up until the Philippines found himself discarding it once he came home, according to the famous British historian Max Hastings, who further said, "Japanese barbarism rendered the Battle for Manila a human catastrophe, but MacArthur's obsession with seizing the city created the circumstances for it. Indeed it seems MacArthur's ambitions had grown more important than the necessary strategy to win the war".[284]

The island of **Iwo Jima** represented the last major marine operation of the war. With numbers so large, armies swallowed up amphibious corps, making the rest of the Pacific War an army-run operation. The Japanese, as we have already seen, had learned the lessons of the textbook perfectly-run operation of Guam where ten days and nights of continual U.S. bombardment had made defeating the marines at the water's edge almost impossible. Now the enemy instead would draw the Americans in, making them trade space for time. Described by one veteran of Iwo, it was like crossing a pool table.

Iwo sat about 700 miles south of Tokyo. This island shaped like a porkchop had air bases for disabled B-29s and, due to its proximity to Japan, was able to service fighter aircraft, too. The name Iwo Jima is Japanese for "Sulphur Island," and the smell of sulphur permeated the still semi-active volcanic island. Landing at the beach, the real trouble did not begin until the Americans came inland. Receiving fire within 200 yards of the beach showed the real genius of General Tadamichi Kuribayashi. Reputed to be the finest Japanese commander of the war, Kuribayashi proceeded to lay out the battlefield in advance using scientific-like methods of interlocking fields of fire from an underground bunker complex running for miles under the island.[285] Sinking into the ash, marines depended upon shell craters for protection. The real problem on this "pool table," as the veteran described it, was the mortars. They couldn't be dodged and would hit you in the hole. Iwo in English could have meant "death." Few Americans who have seen the iconic photograph of the marines raising the flag understand how few of these men actually survived the battle. Half of the six men seen raising the flag in the famously recreated picture would die on Iwo. The recreated picture had to be taken after the initial flag raised proved to be too small to be seen on the beach. Morale is an intangible but serious element in war. While roughly half of the island fell to the advancing marines in the first three days, it took more than two weeks to secure the northeastern side of the island and to get the much needed airfield.

Often the Marine Corps has been criticized by those with more firepower and defense revenues as uncreative or lacking in imagination. Part of this unfair criticism may come from the island fighting experience on Iwo Jima. Maneuver advocates of the 1980s would cite the Marine Corps as deficient in its ability to maneuver around the enemy, though subsequent wars would reveal otherwise. The truth is, fighting on an island simply did not allow for the type of sophisticated planning or use of converging columns as in Europe. Instead, innovation came from the small unit level. The rudiments of current fire team tactics emerged as individual acts of heroism became commonplace. Using satchel charges, or C2 plastic explosives, to take out enemy pill boxes and trenches, other marines began to organize systems whereby on command grenades and automatic fire would be aimed at the firing slots, while the brave rifleman maneuvered with his weapon, explosive charge, or flame weapon closer to the offending structure. What kept these men going? In many ways, Marine Corps training and the sublimation of the individual to the team bore fruit on Iwo Jima. Courage ruled on Iwo, but not everyone was a hero.

---

283. Spector, *Eagle Against the Sun*, 529.
284. Hastings, *Retribution*, 246.
285. Spector, *Eagle Against the Sun*, 527.

According to Lt Col Robert Cushman, a future commandant of the Marine Corps, his battalion went through two complete changes of platoon leaders. Once when the battalion was reduced to 200 men, he ordered a charge. According to Cushman, "Nobody got out of their foxholes. So I picked up a rifle and bayonet and went round and got everybody out the hard way, and eventually they got moving along with the tanks."[286] Iwo Jima will always be a legacy to the marines, but it took over five weeks, about 6,000 dead, and 20,000 wounded to take the island. One can only imagine the bitter satisfaction of March 4, 1945 when the B-29 "Dinah Might" landed in crippled condition. According to an eyewitness, four or five members of the crew jumped down and fell to their hands and knees and kissed the runway. What a contrast to the marines still fighting who thought, "its ground not even good enough to spit on."[287]

If Iwo represented an attempt to more securely conduct B-29 operations against Japan proper, **Okinawa** received selection on the basis of its potential as an anchorage for sea power and a platform for both airpower and invading troops attacking the home islands. A 60-mile long island about 350 miles from Japan, this large axe-shaped island would be supported by over 40 aircraft carriers and 18 battleships. This army-run operation would face the Japanese led by Lt General Ushijima, who followed the Japanese burgeoning strategy of allowing the enemy to come ashore. Building upon a network of rings coming out of Shuri Castle to the south of the island—about where the ax head connected with the handle—Ushijima believed that by placing his forces out of reach of naval guns, he could delay and bleed American troop strengths, and hopefully the Americans would be forced to discard their invasion plans. Although the Japanese could never effectively hide from the crushing American naval gunfire, the Japanese use of artillery represented a masterpiece of planning.[288]

Everything was quiet on April fool's day of 1945 as Americans went ashore on Okinawa, but it would not be quiet for long. Within a week, soldiers and marines would be in a fierce death grip of fighting, attempting to secure the deadly heights and ridges. Blasting Japanese out of caves and going in with flame tanks, brave men ran hoses hundreds of feet up to caves and fighting holes, burning the Japanese while fighting occurred at point blank range. "Zippo" tanks burned the Japanese out as fighting like World War I saw men packed into fighting lines with little room for maneuver. Grenades rained down as General Simon B. Buckner (son of the Confederate general who had surrendered Fort Donelson in the Civil War and was ironically killed on Okinawa by the last Japanese artillery firing) saw "**Corkscrew Tactics**" being used, with infantry speaking to tanks and directing them as they went around and up the hills, blasting and burning their way.[289] Still a daytime killing force, the U.S. military continued to do its best work by day and not very efficiently using the night.[290]

To add to the horror, on April 9 the first Kamikaze hit. Essentially human-operated cruise missiles, in hindsight they were a natural attempt by an under-gunned enemy to even the odds against the U.S. Navy; busy rearranging the geography of Okinawa with unceasing fire from well over a half million naval shells ranging up to 16 inches in diameter. Between April 6 and June 22, ten mass attacks by numbers ranging from 50 to 300 aircraft came up against the fleet surrounding the island of Okinawa. Many of the targets would be the radar picket destroyers, two of which sank in one day, killing 100 U.S. sailors. Fighting for its life against 20 inbound suicide craft, the destroyer USS *Laffey* took out nine of them before six smashed into the ship. Easily lost in these numbers is the horror experienced by a largely Christian culture that viewed suicide as a great evil. As the Americans began to contemplate the invasion of Japan, planners reflected in horror on what these numbers foretold. The Japanese people simply would not surrender no matter what we threw at them.

---

286. Ibid., 255.
287. Richard Wheeler, *IWO* (New York: Lippincott & Crowell, 1980), 201.
288. Hastings, *Retribution*, 379.
289. Perret, *Country*, 431.
290. Hastings, *Retribution*, 379.

The results of Okinawa had powerful ramifications. Operation DOWNFALL consisted of two operations, one against the southern-most island of Kyushu. The other was to invade the main home island of Honshu. Krueger's 6th Army was given the task of taking Honshu. Calling for a classically American converging columns action, three-fourths of the entire Marine Corps landed. With FDR's death in April of 1945, Harry S. Truman was forced to make the tough decisions. The horrific specter of Okinawa hung over the invasion planning for the Japanese home islands, and the fear of a non-stop blood bath was only enhanced by listening to the Japanese government that ordered, "All able-bodied Japanese, regardless of sex, should be called upon to engage in battle . . . on enemy armored forces. Each citizen is to be prepared to sacrifice his life in suicide attacks on enemy armored forces."[291] As we will see in the first Iraq War, Americans hate killing. George Patton's famous statement that the American soldier "is willing to die, but not to kill," contained some truth.[292] The Truman administration possibly believed the Japanese might be willing to surrender, thereby preventing more bloodshed if their sacred emperor could be allowed to sit on the throne at war's end. The Potsdam Declaration, carefully worded so as not to offend Americans, represented an attempt to wave an olive branch to the Japanese. The Japanese cabinet refused this and continued to hope Soviet aid would be forthcoming.

The Americans had hoped for Soviet assistance against the Japanese during the planning to invade. With the development of an atomic bomb, however, hope became a fear of Soviet invasion. When Truman mentioned at the Potsdam Conference the existence of a new weapon of unusual destructive force, the Soviet leader Josef Stalin replied casually that "he was glad to hear it;" to observers it appeared obvious that Soviet intelligence had long been aware of the bombs development. Any reservations about using the weapon seemed not to trouble Truman. Memories of Pearl Harbor's sneak attack and the bloody fighting of the Pacific and the recent experience with the kamikazes and Okinawa may have led Truman to say, "When you deal with a beast you have to treat him as a beast." (These words written shortly after Nagasaki.)[293]

On August 6, 1945 the United States, with one B-29 bomb, hit **Hiroshima** with the impact of 150 bomb loads, killing up to 100,000 people. A second bomb would be necessary to finish the war on August 9, wiping out the most historically Christian city in Japan. Japan had been so ravaged by the firebombings and ceaseless attacks of the war that target planners were hard-pressed to find cities to demonstrate the ferocity of the bombing.

World War II would officially end on the deck of the **USS Missouri** in Tokyo Bay with General MacArthur approaching demi-god status as he accepted the surrender. The cost in lives was 325,000 Americans dead and nearly one million wounded. Still America had been blessed relative to the other world powers.[294] This most terrible war to date had resulted in the end of the European colonial empires and a new awakening in the Arab world, as well as India, where nationalism would begin. Perhaps most importantly for future generations was the incidental discovery of evil when American troops entered Germany. The discovery of the Holocaust and the killing camps quickly spread throughout the army, and gruesome details revealed through the war crimes trials gave a new American Empire a sense of righteousness. In the process of inheriting the status previously reserved for the United Kingdom, an American Empire emerged more determined than ever to wipe out wickedness abroad. This new empire, led by the man who had ordered the bomb dropped, would see its armed forces as agents for projecting force for political and humanitarian purposes. In addition to a perceived moral vindication for going into this global war would be an

---

291. Spector, *Eagle Against the Sun*, 544.
292. Perret, *Country*, 436.
293. Spector, *Eagle Against the Sun*, 555.
294. Perret, *Country*, 436.

almost spiritual belief in the demonstrated power of force from the air. Almost as if a premature rapture had occurred with winning the war, the Air Force and all things technical would be seen by Americans as the solution to the messy business of war and killing.

The American domestic scene had changed as well. For the first time in American history, the work force had learned the fulfillment of bringing home a pay check from both husband and wife; but until war's end the workers had nowhere to spend it. The days in America when black people would be willing to stand at the back of the line had gone; after all, how do you tell a decorated combat veteran he doesn't count? Consumerism would flood into America, as would things plastic, further increasing an American reliance on oil. The electronics industry and a new invention called the computer would capture the imagination of futurists and military men alike. And education? The armed forces continued to represent the smarter and healthier elements of society and almost eight million of them elected to take advantage of college benefits under the **G.I. Bill** at war's end, beginning a tradition of higher education and an advancement of the middle class. You probably would not even be reading this book if it hadn't been for World War II. The university had previously represented only the well-off, privileged, and the brilliant. And a home? Most Americans had never dreamed of owning their own homes, but, with the G.I. Bill, you could get an affordable home loan, and, with military civil engineers throwing up suburban neighborhoods separated by green yards as uniform as any military barracks, you could live in it and watch your new T.V. The United States had overcome a lonely and isolated frontier experience and emerged at least temporarily as a team that had sacrificed to overcome evil through technology and air power. Why not continue this cleansing force throughout the entire world wherever evil may be?[295]

The Medal of Honor was awarded to 473 of the approximately sixteen million members of the U.S. Armed Forces who served during World War II.[296] Due to the large scale of this war, the actions that merited the Medal of Honor were varied. From Captain Richard Fleming, in his damaged dive bomber, following his bombs into the *Mikuma* during the Battle of Midway to Staff Sergeant Henry Erwin carrying a malfunctioning phosphorus bomb, with his bare hands, before throwing it out of his B-29, the Medal of Honor recipients highlight the most courageous Americans who fought for freedom worldwide.[297]

Technology of World War II

For the American military, technology once again dictated the tempo of war and its final results. Though studying technology is important, it is just as important to understand how military doctrine and tactics caught up with the technological changes that had occurred over the past three decades. The American military continued its fundamental ways of war, mobility, power, defense, and accuracy in World War II by creating technology that improved older versions of weapons. Tanks, aircraft, machine guns, artillery, and other technologies of World War II were neither new in concept nor new to the battlefield. Essentially, they were more capable versions of earlier technologies that were tested in battle and improved incrementally through the interwar period. This process of improving from past battlefield failures continues in the American military today. Below are a few of the technological advancements of the American military during WWII.

---

295. Ibid., 439
296. "Archival Statistics," The Congressional Medal of Honor, https://www.cmohs.org
297. The Boston Publishing Company, *Above and Beyond,* 205, 237.

M4 Sherman

Plans for the M4 Sherman tank were submitted to the U.S. Army Ordinance Department on August 31, 1940. This was the iconic American tank of World War II, and was employed in all theaters of the conflict by the U.S. Army and Marine Corps. Considered a medium tank at the time, the Sherman initially mounted a 75mm gun and had a crew of five. During the June 1944 landings in Normandy, the Sherman's 75mm gun was incapable of penetrating the front armor of the heavier German Panther and Tiger tanks. Due to the gun's ineffectiveness in battle, there was rapid introduction of the high velocity 76mm gun. Even with the new 76mm gun, the M4 Sherman was only capable of defeating the deadly Panther and Tiger at close range or from the flank position, which was made possible by its advantage in speed.

The average M4 Sherman was approximately 19 feet in length, 8 ½ feet in width, 9 feet in height, and weighing in at a total of 33 tons. The Sherman was equipped with a 400 HP Continental R975-C1 gasoline engine that could reach speeds of 24 MPH for a total of 120 miles at a time.

Tactical Bombing

During WWII, tactical bombing was a great success. It was influential in disrupting enemy supply lines as well as supporting ground forces. Though direct attacks were important, tactical bombing was critical in the tactical and operational level of WWII. Air superiority and the ability to attack at long distances was defined by the United States as they forced Japan to surrender after the atomic bombings of Hiroshima and Nagasaki.

Rocket Systems

In WWII, rocket systems were used in the air, land, and sea, allowing for a new level of firepower for the American military. The American bazooka was a tube-launched 2.36-inch rocket system. This weapon mastered speed and mobility. It was a stabilized, hand-held system that could be loaded and fired within minutes. Once armed with an armor piercing tip, an infantryman was equipped to engage a tank on the battlefield. In 1942, most ships were equipped with shipboard, rocket-launched, anti-submarine depth charges, also known as mousetraps, as well as Barrage Rockets. A Barrage Rocket had a range of a thousand yards and could be launched from a landing craft. By 1943, air-launched rockets were equipped on most airplanes. This increased the use of an aircraft's firepower against submarines and unarmored vessels. After this invention, in 1944, armored vessels could now be penetrated due to the improvements of 5-inch high velocity rockets. Rockets had proven to be a great example of the AWoF by combining speed, mobility, and firepower for the American Navy, Air Force, and Army.[298]

The M1 Garand "The Gun That Saved the World"

This American rifle was a .30 caliber, gas-operated, air-cooled, clip-fed, semi-automatic gun that weighed about 10 pounds. Some experts would argue that the M1 Garand is the most important weapon in all of modern American history. This was the first semi-automatic rifle issued in battle that gave a sizable advantage over the enemy who were mostly using WWI style rifles. General George Patton called the M1 "the greatest battle implement ever devised." Beyond

---

298. Hacker, *American Military Technology*, 98.

its firepower, it was durable. It was said that "in surf and sand, dragged through the mud and rain of tropical rain forests, sunbaked, caked with volcanic ash, covered with European snows that melted, then refroze inside the breech, beset by rust and mildew, mold and dirt, the Garand still came out shooting."[299]

As noted, technology changed greatly from WWI to WWII. The concepts of the AWoF did not change, however, but dictated the success of the advancements in the field. The preeminent example of success with the new technologies was on D-Day. This is where all the technology, tactics, and operations advancements over the past thirty years came together and allowed for a victory in Normandy.

Key Terms:

Victory Disease	**Eniwetok**	**Air Battle over Taiwan**
Land-Based Airpower	**Tarawa**	**Battle of Leyte Gulf**
ASW	**Biak**	**Leyte**
Battle of Coral Sea	**Marianas**	**Luzon**
Port Moresby	**Doolittle Raid**	**Iwo Jima**
Battle of Midway	**Kurils**	**Okinawa**
Ultra	**Terror bombing**	**Corkscrew Tactics**
Guadalcanal	**B-29**	**Hiroshima**
Savo Island	**Drop tanks**	**USS Missouri**
Island-hopping	**Operation Cartwheel**	**G.I. Bill**
Hellcat	**Battle of the Philippine Sea**	

Thought Questions:

What intelligence helped Americans as they sought to advance towards Japan in the Pacific War? What AWoF did these represent?

Did airpower enthusiasts get it right? Did airpower actually win the Second World War?

---

299. Kyle, *American Gun*, 198.

Chapter VIII

THE KOREAN WAR

Luke 12:4-6 "And I say to you, My friends, do not be afraid of those who kill the body, and after that have no more that they can do." NKJV

Check out an animated map of the events of the Korean War at this link: https://www.khpcontent.com/

1947
Greek Civil War

1948
NSC-68 "Containment" begins

1949
Chinese Civil War ends

1950
North Korea attacks South Korea
Task Force Smith
River Battles
Battles for the Pusan Perimeter
Incheon Landing
Seoul Retaken by the UN
Wonson landing
Diverging Columns" X Corps and 8th Army advance north to reunify peninsula
Chinese enter war
Battles of Chongchon
Marines retreat to Hangnum

1951
Ridgway replaces MacArthur
Meat grinder tactics
Battle for Chipyong ni
Battle of Bloody Ridge
Battle for Heartbreak Ridge

1952
Eisenhower elected

1953
Battle for Pork Chop Hill
Korean War Armistice

Go to www.khpcontent.com to watch a video introduction for this chapter.

The Korean War found an American global power with a Manichean worldview that saw the world basically in black and white with a few shades of gray. American foreign policy would soon be committed to the preservation of this perceived light versus dark. The light, defined as a commitment to capitalism and the freedom of democratic government and human spirit, would surely be able to restrain the darkness of totalitarianism and communism. The Korean peninsula represented a gray type of frontier and established a precedent, beginning a series of costly and undeclared wars fought by the United States with self-imposed limitations administered through various international governmental bodies. The unfortunate propensity of Americans to use military force without any declaration of war also started in Korea. Fighting wars expeditiously had occurred throughout time; the British had notoriously used butcher and bolt operations throughout the 19th century, but essentially America in the short-run would successfully contain communism, but in the long-run would commit itself to use its newfound strength after World War II for the purposes of fighting ideological conflicts it could never quite win or finish. The Korean War generally remains in the shadow of knowledge today, but the sacrifices made in American blood and treasure must be understood in a time when Americans continue to launch military force with good intentions. The Korean War remains largely overshadowed by the Second World War and Vietnam; any visit to the local library will find the student hard pressed to find 20 books on the subject, thinly sandwiched on the shelves between the Second World War and Vietnam.

With Nagasaki still warm from the dropping of the atomic bomb, Soviet forces entered Northeast Korea, as the nearest U.S. forces remained about 600 miles away on Okinawa in a brutal form of total warfare. A couple of U.S. Army colonels with a national geographic map drew a line randomly along the 38th parallel and to the surprise of many in Washington, the Soviets accepted this as a temporary administrative division. Ignoring geographic realities, the line tended to favor any force from the north seeking to control the south. Like the "Iron Curtain" drawn across Europe soon after, this administrative division not only ignored geographic reality, but it ignored history.

Korea is historically a unified culture. The peninsula has not truly been divided since the ancient period, and Koreans are generally united to this day on one fact—their hatred of the Japanese. Brutally colonized by this sea power from the east, Korea has historically looked to the West in terms of culture and relations with China. With a long history of using other nations to counterbalance invaders, the Koreans during World War II had been long exploited in about every way imaginable by the Japanese. It's little surprise then, in light of history, that the Koreans would divide themselves along different camps in their attempts to employ a divided world to help them in their liberation. Essentially two different views of Korean freedom would emerge very different but unified on one thing—their hatred of the Japanese.

General John R. Hodge had the tough task of taking a devastated Korea on as a military governor after the surrender of the Japanese. Because of the chaos in the area, the United States attempted a gradual transition from Japanese control, and actually used some of the Japanese police forces to continue to maintain order until a transition in government could occur. As a result, the Koreans began to see the Americans as another colonial invader in league with the hated Japanese. Any rising Korean leaders who had associations with the Japanese had pretty much been killed or run out of the country.[300] With people's committees seemingly springing up spontaneously over Korea seeking confiscation of Japanese property, limiting rents, and attempting to create a minimum wage and an eight-hour work day, U.S. military occupiers took little interest or ignored these movements, ignoring the homegrown KPR political party and instead dealt with the conservative KDP (Korean Democratic Party).[301] As the writer's father once said, "It is easier to win a war than it is to win the peace afterwards." The importance of civil affairs must never be ignored in any military operation.

---

300. Michael J. Seth, *A History of Korea: From Antiquity to the Present* (UK: Rowan, 2011), 307.
301. Ibid., 309.

Figure 8.1 The Korean Peninsula

Into this atmosphere of distrust came **Syngman Rhee**. A true Korean patriot, Rhee had been in the United States and had a family background like so many of our Korean friends in the Christian community in Korea. As early as Versailles at the end of World War I, he had sought recognition of Korean independence and self-determination. Backed by the United States as "one of our type of Koreans," he stood in contrast to another Korean patriot, **Kim Il-Sung**.

Kim Il-Sung emerged onto the tumultuous scene in North Korea. The North Koreans had many veteran troops who had served in the Soviet Army, and with these fluent linguists the Soviets commenced to create a smooth transition to power in Pyongyang in marked contrast to American efforts in the south. Kim Il-Sung, the son of a Christian mother, fought with the Soviets in Manchuria as a relatively junior officer. Leading attacks and raids against the Japanese, he had the backing of the Soviets, who themselves seemed to have many advantages in contributing to a new post-war Korea. The Soviets had the advantage over the Americans in terms of location as well as the Red Army's ranks full of Koreans who could fluently speak the language; moreover, a void left by the execution or exile of Korean communists to China seemed to indicate a smooth transition to power in Pyongyang in marked contrast to the chaotic South with the United States increasingly identified with the Japanese, whom they had unwittingly embraced, unaware of Korean bitterness.[302]

---

302. Ibid., 311.

By 1946, as Kim Il-Sung's portrait began to be displayed alongside Stalin's, the Soviets began to push for communization of the North and the immediate redistribution of wealth and property. Prohibiting contrary views, the attempt at trusteeship in an American-Soviet Joint Commission failed to resolve problems of electrical infrastructure from north to south or removal of road blocks. The Soviets' refusal to allow representatives of any organization not supporting their proposed trusteeship to participate essentially created unforeseen separate states under military occupation.[303]

Rhee, meanwhile, had used an anti-trusteeship movement to take power, and potential adversaries either had been assassinated or simply were too old to compete. The United States fruitlessly sought a more moderate leader with perhaps a bit less nationalistic leadership, but this would be to no avail. The United States had furthered its own position through the employment of police forces throughout the raucous, free-speech south, tainted by Jap associations.[304]

Typical of totalitarian states, the initial successes of government control helped to consolidate central power. As the north continued to smoothly consolidate power in Pyongyang, North Korea, the southern capital at Seoul crushed rebels at Cheju (Korea's Hawaii). Without electric power from the northern Korean hydroelectric plants, a confident Kim Il-Sung traveled to see the head of international communism, Stalin, in Russia. Pleading for help and pointing out the disparity with the south, Kim confidently promised to unite the peninsula with his 150 T-34 tanks and his thousands of artillery pieces. A combat-proven army of up to 135,000 mounted up and ready to move had been probing the south for years looking for weak spots. Stalin gave the go-ahead but only under the condition that the Soviets would not be lending assistance; this would be the job of the Chinese.

American officials never really trusted Rhee. His forces had been limited in strength somewhat in an attempt to prevent him and his nationalistic cronies from attacking the north. When the North Koreans hit the south on June 25, 1950, they faced a South Korean army with zero tanks and only about 90 small artillery pieces.[305] Mao was angry from a loss of face when the Truman administration had earlier blocked China from having a seat on the United Nations Security Council and referred to Chinese communists as being part of the USSR. More recent attempts by the South Koreans to seize the high ground behind the strategically important city of Kaesong and the Ongjin peninsula that formed a natural highway into Seoul overlooked by the folks who drew lines on maps may well have led Stalin to order the attack and for Mao to participate in the war.[306]

The previous January, Secretary of State Dean Acheson had declared that both Korea and Taiwan stood outside the American defense perimeter. Most historians today believe this signaled to Stalin and Mao to support the invasion of the south, but the truth goes a bit deeper into the American view at the beginning of the war.

Eve of War

Just as thinkers of the day tended to see the world in black and white or good vs. evil, students like yourself throughout the 1920s and 1930s had been taught the geographic Heartland Theory of Halford Mackinder. Viewing history as cyclical, the view permeated that an apocalypse would occur between East and West with eventually only China remaining as a decadent West collapsed. Always aware in a time of classical emphasis of the collapse of the Roman Empire, 19th century historians neglected the means by which the Romans had bled themselves during the empire by the continual deployment of troops to a frontier rather than relying upon a reserve force and using natural geographic features to ease transport and defense.[307] By the time the students of the early

---

303. Ibid., 313.
304. Ibid., 316.
305. Perret, *Country*, 449.
306. Geoffrey Perret, *Commander-In-Chief* (New York: Farrar, Straus and Giroux, 2008), 142.
307. Edward Luttwak, *The Grand Strategy of the Roman Empire* (Baltimore: The John Hopkins Univ. Press, 1976), 132.

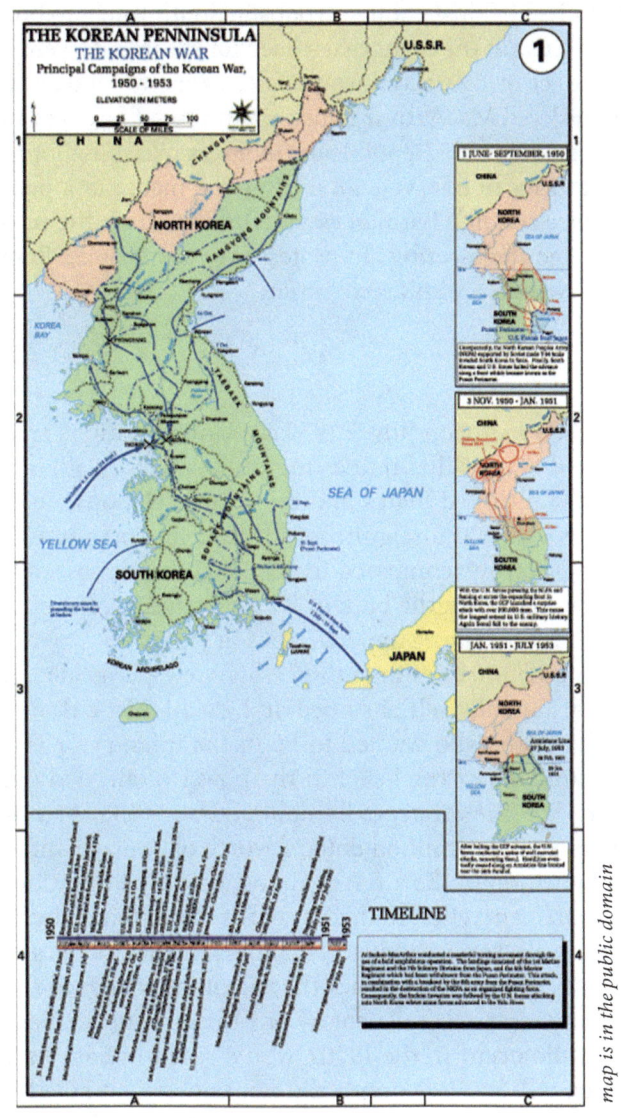

Figure 8.2 The Korean War.

20th century had ascended to positions of authority in government, a belief in a somewhat inevitable apocalypse between the United States and the Soviet Union would be the greatest challenge to the West since the Romans had fought Carthage.

The **Greek Civil War** of 1947 had demonstrated how communist expansion could be stopped. General James Van Fleet had successfully trained and equipped a Greek army with more than a ten to one advantage over a guerrilla force. The famous terrain provided natural advantages to a defense; the same that had allowed philosophers the luxury to pontificate rather than sweat in fields may have led Americans, in general, and President Harry S. Truman, in particular, to believe Korea could be another Greece.

The Korean War marked a turn from a post-WWII **offshore defensive strategy**—one that believed America should defend from the Bering Strait to Australia: "Defense at a minimum cost, moreover it would be generations if not centuries before its offshore position might be seriously threatened." In a knee-jerk reaction, possibly due to health issues, President Truman responded decisively to the North Korean invasion by ordering MacArthur into Korea.[308]

---

308. Perret, *Commander-In-Chief*, 131.

The American military had left just enough troops in South Korea to both advise and, in some ways, act as a trip wire or excuse in the event that a need for future intervention should occur. With the explosion of the Han River Bridge, Seoul would fall in a matter of days. Immediately and decisively, President Truman ordered MacArthur to use air and naval forces to support the Republic of Korea. Truman avoided trouble with a Republican Congress by asking for a resolution that would give the United States authority to intervene. Asked by the media in a possibly planted question if he would call this a "police action," Truman essentially agreed.[309] The resolution passed quickly since the USSR had boycotted the meetings in protest over the People's Republic of China's being denied admission to the UN and Taiwan's recognition.

War Begins

As the North Koreans pushed south, on July 7, 1950 the United Nations created a unified military command under the United States. This interesting rank structure, giving U.S. military leaders parallel positions between the United States and the United Nations, enabled a small return in assistance. By spring of 1951, 40,000 foreign troops would support the United Nations' effort.[310] Less than 600,000 were in the army (compared to 508,000 today); most of which were in Europe. The troops in Japan, who would form the bulk of 8th Army, were softened by peacetime garrison duty, army cutbacks, and lack of training opportunities in Japan.

After the bomb who needed armies anymore? This view permeated American society and blended in neatly with a historically self-absorbed and isolationist culture. In this "push button age," with unprecedented wealth, who wanted to be in the infantry or even be a soldier? Army cutbacks, in large part a function of the belief in the power of air, had overlooked the strategic bombing survey after the war. The Strategic Bombing Survey (SBS) had determined that it had taken about a million dollars to do a million dollars' worth of damage, indeed what Geoffrey Perret referred to as a war of attrition in the air. It is almost as if the formation of the Department of Defense from the War Department reflected the fear of the atomic bomb by those who had dropped it. Advances in the radar and electronics industry and the return of pilots after World War II to the commercial airlines industry all seemed to mark the end of the soldier in the dirt or the marine in the mud. The absence of any reserves and a cut by one third of the artillery through reorganizational attempts, such as would occur in the 1990s, would result in East Asian forces going to war weak and mentally unprepared. Soldiers simply did not understand how Korea was important to the folks back home.[311]

The River Battles

The North Koreans continued to push south in armored columns. The confused South Koreans blew up the Han River Bridge full of fleeing citizens as the ill-prepared army continued to fall back on the successive natural defensive lines the rivers of Korea presented. By early July, the city of Taejon fell, but not until the first pathetic attempt by U.S. troops of Task Force (TF) Smith to stop the advancing North Koreans had failed. Firing their undersized bazookas harmlessly off at the advancing tanks, TF Smith would become a future rallying cry in the army for the need for preparedness and funding in the years ahead.[312] Brushing by the American "speed bump," the North Korean forces by early August had taken much longer than expected. Facing the fury of the Far East Air Forces that were beginning to hit the overextended lines, the North Koreans showed their inability to make independent decisions—the soldier's rationale was that it was far better to be slow

---

309. Seth, *A History of Korea*, 324.
310. Ibid., 324.
311. Stanley Sandler, *The Korean War: No Victors, No Vanquished* (Lexington: Univ. of Kentucky, 1999), 62.
312. Ibid., 56.

than to be executed for making a mistake! Han River Bridge was blown as confusion reigned in Seoul. The stupidity of the North Korean communists in committing atrocities quickly resulted in the resolve of Americans to not surrender. Documented by the North Koreans, death marches— like in the Philippines during World War II—broadcast emaciated prisoners.[313]

At the Kum River as North Korean momentum grew, U.S. troops presented a poor performance as more bridges exploded. Yet help from the Air Force soon arrived to hit the advancing enemy hard.[314] By July 19, Taejon fell, but every 24 hours gave U.S. forces space for time to resupply the Pusan Perimeter. General William F. Dean of the army's 24th Division wanted to do a delaying action, but the Second Infantry Division (ID) would be due by the end of July. By early August, the marines received orders to hold. Dean was taken prisoner, and the highest ranking American held would not be freed until the war's end. Still he had bought time. An attack by the communists opened with Yak fighters and would be the last time any communist aircraft would be seen by communist soldiers over the battlefield again in the war. At this point American airpower had started to dominate. Napalm was dropped on the advancing enemy. With no U.S. armor yet available, the enemy again flanked and went around the desperately fighting Americans. The North Koreans continued to advance but at decreasing speeds as 3.5 inch rockets slammed successfully against T-34 tanks. American Mustangs and C-47 transports flew in from Japan. Sensitivities exist to this day about the supposed "bug outs" of the 24th and the 25th ID black troops. If the black troops did run, they were not the only ones in Korea at this point to do so. As the North Koreans brushed by Taejon, time had been bought for the arriving troops behind the Naktong River.

Pusan Perimeter

Kim had ordered an August 15 victory. At the Battle of the Naktong River, the North Koreans crossed the river in shoulder-deep water and used underwater bridges. Upon seizing a beachhead of sorts on the bank of the river, the army's 27th "Wolfhounds" of the 24th Division arrived after being ordered to hold. Carpet-bombing on August 16 by B-29s achieved debatable results, but the North Koreans were dying from an increasing lack of medical treatment. Walker desperately launched the 1st Marine Division into gaps created by the final North Korean in total desperation and used up all available reserves.

Unknown to the Americans, by early August at the Pusan Perimeter, China had decided it would intervene if U.S. forces were to cause a reversal. Mao had begun the process of sending his forces from southeastern China on the march towards Manchuria.[315] While the Chinese were secretly moving, morale began to swing against the North Koreans. Unlike the Americans, the North Koreans understood why they fought; they wanted to unify their nation. But air power and the stiff resistances on the Naktong had taken their toll. The use of napalm and increasing amounts of steel and phosphorus met the advancing North Koreans head-on, while lack of medical supplies and supplies in general began to cause despair. American C-119 "flying box cars were dropping ammo and supplies while the arrival of the F-80 'shooting stars,'" (the first jets) began firing rockets at anything moving down the roads. In just a couple of days, the 27th had knocked out six of eight North Korean tanks.

The Pusan Perimeter saw a series of grueling fights where General Johnny Walker's 8th Army troops had been forced back into what seemed like a goal line defense. Demanding that troops fight, he declared there would be no Dunkirk evacuation. The troops must fight and die. Fight and die they did, but once again they were aided by the use of intelligence that somehow managed to plug gaps just about the time the North Koreans would hit. Telling a junior officer he didn't want to see him again unless it was in a casket might motivate troops for the short-term, but success is necessary in a fight to improve morale. A future Chief of Staff of the Army, Harold K. "Johnny"

---

313. Ibid., 60.
314. Ibid., 65.
315. Ibid., 325.

Johnson, would take out company-sized patrols run ragged and much reduced in numbers. Though he was later accused of not standing up to a future president over the war in Vietnam, in Korea he and his men at the Pusan Perimeter had indeed stood up, fought hard, and succeeded.

By August 18, 1950, almost two months after attacking South Korea, the North Koreans had thrown everything at the Americans they had. Attacking on five different fronts, the communists frittered away their force in piecemeal attacks. The United States lost more troops in the first half of September than at any other time in the war. A close affair, MacArthur would launch a masterstroke of military planning and maneuver. After two weeks of ferocious fighting, out of 20,000 total casualties, 4,280 had died. South Korea had been saved![316]

Incheon

President Truman had begun a war and proceeded to clean house. Firing his Secretary of Defense and replacing him with the great George C. Marshall, Truman then went on to alienate the marines by insulting them, calling them a police force and generally acting somewhat quixotically.[317]

By mid-August, **Operation Chromite** planners had created an X Corps from the 7th ID and 1st Marine Division under the command of MacArthur's Chief of Staff, Major General Ed Almond. Almond, who demonstrated impetuosity as a commander, seemed in many ways to match MacArthur in terms of vanity. The landing of Americans would be assisted by Japanese sailors driving LSTs and other amphibious landing craft, since most of these watercraft had been lent to the Japanese for ferry transport service since the end of World War II; wisely, this remained a secret kept quiet for political purposes. The 1st Marine Division would have little time to rehearse and would actually be landed at the last possible minute, as it was a vital "fire brigade" to the Pusan battles raging. Many historians wonder if the future of the U.S. Marine Corps depended on a successful invasion, despite its World War II successes. Such was the depth of Truman's antipathy for the marines; he even refused to give them credit for success after the Incheon landings.[318]

Diversions to Kunsan and counter information shouted on docks by marines in front of Korean civilians marked the preliminary phase of Operation Chromite. Actual operations barely made it ashore before Stalin could mine the harbor. The Soviets had raced to get there before the Americans, so sure of the landing site. Security had indeed been compromised, but the communists couldn't move fast enough according to Bruce Cumings.[319] Chen Jian argued Mao could not respond in time for Incheon due to the instability of the NE Border Defense Army. Arguing for success of American security, Jian stated that it was unlikely Mao knew the September schedule and, "It is likely that Mao would have further pushed Chinese military preparations."[320] Unbeknown to American analysts, by mid-August Mao had begun mobilizing the entire nation. Kim had basically ignored China and resisted overtures of military intervention.[321] The historical pattern of a unified peninsula using outsiders continued. Pyongyang had not coordinated Chinese involvement with Moscow as so many Western analysts to this day believe.[322]

For all MacArthur's difficulties and shortcomings as a leader, Incheon represented his best moment. Even going against the advice of the navy and marines, he decisively turned the war into a potential victory by invading Korea mid-way up the western side of the peninsula at the port of

---

316. Bruce Cumings, *The Korean War* (New York: Modern, 2011), 19.
317. Perret, *Commander-In-Chief*, 158.
318. Sandler, *The Korean War*, 89.
319. Cumings, *The Korean War*, 19.
320. Chen Jian, *China's Road to the Korean War: The Making of the Sino-American Confrontation* (Ithaca, NY: Colombia Univ. Press, 1998), 155.
321. Ibid., 157.
322. Ibid., 2.

Incheon, the beginning of the road to Seoul. The difficulties in this amphibious assault consisted of difficult tides, an urban environment, sea walls, and armed islands off the mouth of the estuary.

The navy was facing the difficulty of the neap tides as well as a dire shortage of LSTs; the navy needed 47 but only had 17. Thirty had been lent to the Japanese to improve their economy through economic trade.[323] Landing with little land-based air in support, Far East Air Force (FEAF) instead served as a diversion to the fake landing at Kunsan.[324] Wolmi-do guarded the port of Incheon and sat "studded" with Russian artillery. Mud flats would see ships laying on their sides. To get out of the port, a sea wall loomed higher than ever.[325] Evidence exists that the North Koreans thought Kunsan would be the American objective and Incheon simply represented a diversion! Was Incheon a masterstroke? Recent scholarship indicates 8th Army had begun to bust out of its perimeter, and MacArthur's publicity did typically smack of the dramatic.[326] Regardless, the commander can delegate authority, but never responsibility, and MacArthur put it all on the line at Incheon. Even the Joint Chiefs of Staff (JCS) had asked MacArthur to reconsider because of concerns about Pusan and the deploying of troops to Incheon. When asked if he thought the operation would succeed, MacArthur responded, "There is no question in my mind."[327] Unfortunately, after brilliantly launching troops ashore and breaking the back of the North Koreans, the pattern of Luzon began to reassert itself. A legend in his own mind, MacArthur would again become obsessed with a city and would manage to seize defeat from the jaws of victory while an intimidated president and JCS stood back and gave him the rope necessary to hang himself.

Seoul to Wonson

After achieving a stunning victory behind North Korean lines, a simultaneously launched invasion, or **break-out,** by Walker to the south created the perfect hammer and anvil to crush the fleeing North Korean Army. Instead, MacArthur became obsessed with Seoul as he had with Manila in the last war. Bloody house-to-house fighting ensued, and even a rare United States vs North Korean tank battle saw U.S. M-26 tanks defeat North Korean T-34's. Marines and soldiers were disgusted to hear peace declared while they were still fighting. As late as September 22, NKPA showed no signs of withdrawing. Ordering the X Corps' commander LTG Ned Almond to take Seoul, MacArthur proceeded to engage in grandstanding and received the key to the city on September 29, giving back the glorious victory of Incheon as the enemy fled north. Instead of cutting the peninsula in half and destroying the enemy, he seemed to seek the publicity to accompany the liberation of Seoul. After Incheon, no one dared to challenge the great man and as North Koreans continued north, MacArthur coolly called for an invasion at Wonson on the other side of the peninsula. Not to worry—MacArthur is in charge! The result would be the port of Incheon being unable to offload fuel and supplies to the advancing 8th Army, subsequently forced to a crawl.

Unfortunately, no one had realized that a lack of minesweepers for the harbor of **Wonson** would force the re-embarked marines to take over a week to get to Wonson and an additional week to land. Old mines from earlier in the century still lay off shore. The embarrassment created much distrust between the marines and their army leadership in X Corps. With impending elections, Truman and MacArthur met at Wake Island on October 15, supposedly to discuss strategy. This meeting, reminiscent of that between Lincoln and McClellan at Antietam during the Civil War, supposedly concerned future strategy. The truth probably lay closer to a consideration of the upcoming elections in November. With little probably achieved, MacArthur would receive instructions to unify

---

323. Robert D. Hienl, *Victory at High Tide* (New York: Lippincott, 1968), 64.
324. Ibid., 60.
325. Sandler, *The Korean War*, 91.
326. Ibid., 93.
327. Hienl, *Victory at High Tide*, 64.

the Korean peninsula. The mission, therefore, had changed from liberating to conquering. Only one qualification remained: the American forces must not approach the Yalu River. They were only allowed to cross the 38th parallel. Only a short time before, the Chinese had warned the Americans through the Indian ambassador (India considered itself non-aligned and therefore totally gray in this black and white world) they would enter the war if the Americans entered North Korea. Surrounded by yes-men and sycophants, MacArthur's intelligence chief pretty much told him what he wanted to hear: there simply was no threat.

Meanwhile some of the most experienced soldiers on Earth moved into North Korea, crossing the Yalu. Overconfident and suffering a bit from "victory disease," MacArthur moved north in what Geoffrey Perret called "**diverging columns**."[328] Separating his forces by over 70 miles, to MacArthur's and Almond's irritation, the marines only slowly advanced north, clinging to the comforting coastline where their carriers and battleships lay. Lacking supplies due to the debacle of debarkation at Incheon, Walker's 8th Army halted at the Chongchon River about 50 miles south of the Yalu River. The marines reached the Chosin Reservoir, a source of hydroelectric energy under the Japanese. There they discovered Japanese uses for a nuclear program labeled "Top Secret," that has to this day never totally been shared. American troops had moved over 300 miles in less than six weeks and into the dragon's mouth.[329]

China Enters the War

The initial goal in Korea had been the liberation of South Korea. Had the United States stopped after liberating Seoul, the war could have been said to be won. Instead, with new orders the definition of victory changed to liberating the entire peninsula. With the change in definition, America lost the war in October of 1950. With Europe beginning to recover from the Second World War and Japan likewise emerging, the communist leadership in the Soviet Union cheered when China entered the war. Still chafing from the decision of the United States to support Taiwan and while fighting to secure coastal islands with a junk navy, the Chinese leadership had been caught flat-footed by Kim's decision to enter South Korea. Still, with Soviet assistance the threat from atomic reprisal was virtually eliminated, and it seemed like a good time to restore face by attacking Americans.

After a failed attempt by the 187th Airborne to drop and block the North Korean's fleeing north, the army continued to follow them, and on October 24 some United Nations Command (for the purposes of this narrative the term US will be used) troops reached the Yalu River. The Joint Chiefs of Staff (JCS) questioned MacArthur about this but did not countermand the order they had given previously that no non-Koreans were to cross.[330] The old George C. Marshall had grown tired and did not ride MacArthur with the same energy he would have as a general in World War II; instead he sent a loosely-written memo leading MacArthur to feel unhampered above the 38th Parallel. Attempts by the Soviet Union for a cease-fire at the United Nations met with a riled up President Truman telling MacArthur to use his own judgement if "action by forces now under your control offers a reasonable chance of success."[331]

Restrictions on air over the Yalu River explained the lack of intelligence that over 60,000 Chinese troops had crossed over the river while another 240,000 waited on the Chinese side.[332] Infiltrating at night, using creek beds and concealment, one of the greatest intelligence failures of all time had occurred. Amazingly similar to the Japanese invasion of Korea during the 16th century, the American forces simply became spread too thin and separated by frighteningly difficult terrain. The Japanese had

---

328. Perret, *Country*, 458.
329. Sandler, *The Korean War*, 106.
330. Ibid., 112.
331. Perret, Commander-In-Chief, 166.
332. Ibid., 116

Captain Carl Sitter

… Assuming the responsibility of attempting to seize and occupy a strategic area occupied by a hostile force…he reorganized his depleted units the following morning and boldly led them up the steep, frozen hillside under blistering fire…During the night when a vastly outnumbering enemy launched a sudden, vicious counterattack…he fought gallantly with his men in repulsing and killing the fanatic attackers in each encounter. Painfully wounded in the face, arms, and chest by bursting grenades, he staunchly refused to be evacuated and continued to fight on until a successful defense of the area was assured with a loss to the enemy of more than 50 percent dead, wounded, and captured…

(Hagaru-ri, Korea, 29 and 30 November 1950)

excerpt from Congressional Medal of Honor citation

proposed a similar action against the Russians in the Russo-Japanese War. Understanding history is a large part of military intelligence, and here the historians had failed as well.

With his having ignored Chinese warnings throughout October, thinking he could simply brush away any potential resistance with air power, and ill-informed with poor intelligence, MacArthur's troops saw their hopes dashed of being home by Christmas when the Chinese hit in the first Chinese Offensive.

The Chinese hit everywhere, and they hit hard. Flanking American troops in night attacks with bugles blowing obliterated an entire battalion of the 1st Cavalry Division. For a week, the marines took fire to the northeast around the Chosin Reservoir. Like a bumble bee bumping into its intended victim before the sting, these basically amounted to China's last warning. One wonders in the frighteningly cold, unusually early winter how this threat could be ignored. One of the most common mistakes in military history is a commander being unable to change his mind. Determined on a course, evidence is stacked up and summarily discarded by the yes-men that the boss had previously hired often on the basis of their "can-do" and "good attitudes" in peacetime. In this case, the "can-do" attitude prevailed, and evidence was gathered to make MacArthur believe that the Chinese simply did not have the strength or will to fight the United States—after all, everyone wanted to be home by Christmas. Meanwhile the Yalu froze, and by November 1, 1950 the Chinese could drive supply trucks and artillery across it.

After the debacle at Wonson, the silver-haired, rail-thin commander of the marines, General O.P. Smith, had refused to move farther into the interior of North Korea, and this may have saved the marines. During fantastically cold weather approaching 30 degrees below zero in some places and 16 below near the Chosin Reservoir, the marines and elements of the army's 7th Division desperately worked their ways south to the safety and warmth of the coast where the navy waited like a beckoning angel. With the Yalu frozen and with temporary air superiority from Soviet Mig-15s, the Chinese pushed hard south with a five to one advantage in manpower over the Americans. The marines successfully held the high grounds along the roads running to the Hungnam. Watching intensely through the media, the American people were shocked at what had happened to their army and found solace in the marines' orderly withdrawal to the coast, ultimately mauling the Chinese and bringing back their dead. The luxury of an organic air force, specializing in close-air support, flying themselves around the clock into the thick of the Chinese positions in many ways saved the day. After ten days of continual fighting and protected by a wall of Pittsburgh steel surrounding them from naval gunfire, the marines broke free from the Chinese who had begun to give up and in some cases simply freeze to death.[333] Meanwhile, the army to the west on the other end of the "diverging column" faced utter ruin.

On the night of November 25, the Chinese had up to 300,000 soldiers in Korea. Crashing into the right flank of Walker's 8th Army, three divisions of South Koreans (ROKs) splattered into the night. An open flank, Walker's attempt to withdraw turned into a panic. The same army that had not fled from the Nazi's at Kassarine Pass during the Second World War now neared an uncontrollable mob. Fleeing faster than the Chinese could keep up, they ran south, in some cases merely dropping loaded weapons as they went. Too many convoys sat road-bound while the Chinese controlling the high ground stitched the roads with lead, killing lead and rear vehicles, and systematically mortaring and killing Americans who lay on the sides of the road or in their vehicles waiting for orders. The AWoF of speed and maneuver also had created an army, at least in the 2nd Division, addicted to transport. Meanwhile, the light Chinese infantry began freezing to death, but as their appendages fell off they still continued to grind up ROK units and the widely spread U.S. forces.[334]

A shaken MacArthur told the JCS, "We face an entirely new war." As late as November 28, Walker was still advocating the offensive even after his forces received such a mauling on the Chongchon that the artillery had abandoned its guns. As Walker's forces continued the longest military retreat in history, one wonders if higher headquarters was not out of touch.[335] Meanwhile bullet wounds mercifully froze, saving lives, while medics kept blood next to their chests to keep it from freezing. Oil turned to honey as vehicles froze and would remain where they sat until spring. The Chinese suffered terribly; up to a third of one Chinese Corps suffered from frostbite.[336]

Meanwhile, 8th Army continued in disorder to burn supplies, even after no Chinese had been seen since November 30. Pyongyang would be abandoned on December 5, and in the chaos General "Johnny" Walker would die in circumstances remarkably similar to those that killed his old boss Gen. George Patton—in a head-on collision. Into this chaotic scene stepped LTG Matthew B. Ridgway. A scholar and a fighter who had been with the 101st Airborne in Europe, Ridgway was given total control to do as he felt best. Ridgway cancelled a planned offensive and learned his command. Finding demoralized troops wandering aimlessly about and headquarters in disarray, Ridgway would incorporate a flair for the theatric with his unmistakable hand grenade attached to his battle gear, and would immediately begin inspecting the front lines. He did not like what he saw and began to order commanders up with their forward units—such as Division Commanders with their forward battalions, etc. He maintained a schedule that saw him popping up unexpectedly on the front lines, and he ordered a slow withdrawal back to Seoul. MacArthur, who had a week earlier termed the Eighth Army's situation as untenable, now agreed the army could hold in Korea—in large measure a tribute to Ridgway's leadership.[337] On March 14, American troops reentered Seoul, but this time with little fanfare.

Ridgway also personified operational success. Recognizing the material strength of his army and how it contrasted with the Chinese in terms of resupply, Ridgway began to trade space for time using **meatgrinder** tactics. Using techniques perhaps learned from the Germans, he set about pushing the Chinese through patrols, launching Operation Killer. When the Chinese would mass and attack, he gave ground using FEAF to pummel their meager supply lines. When the Chinese would withdraw, he would do the same thing again and again. Committing suicide against American firepower, the Chinese pathetically launched three more invasions into the late spring of 1951. Each time the army would counter with operations such as Ripper. With names like Killer (began

---

333. Perret, *Country*, 462.
334. Perret, *Country*, 462.
335. Sandler, *The Korean War*, 122.
336. Ibid., 121.
337. Ibid., 133.

18 Feb), Ripper (began 17 Mar) and Strangle (air interdiction), the army meant serious business. The day of the American Army running had quickly passed.

MacArthur had not just now become a problem for Truman, he represented a problem for the nation. After being instructed in a December 6 memo from the JCS instructing military officers not to comment on serious issues, he proceeded to give a press interview stating the UN Command should not halt "short of its true objective, the 'unification of Korea.'"[339] Finally on April 5, a letter was read on the floor of Congress quoting MacArthur's now famous statement, "No substitute for victory."[340] Truman and MacArthur had never gotten along. Truman had contempt for senior military officers and identified himself as the common man who could relate to the common soldier. He had presented MacArthur with a third award Bronze Star in a paper bag years before, and the old general never forgave him. This latest disregard for political considerations by MacArthur indicated to Truman it had become time for him to retire. Also, the ground had changed. One of the last five star generals, Omar Bradley, now Chief of Staff of the army said Korea was "the wrong war at the wrong place, at the wrong time, with the wrong enemy." By implication, the right war was against the USSR and in Europe.[341]

General Matthew B. Ridgway

General Matthew Ridgway set the example. Ridgway had caught the eyes of both MacArthur and Marshall after World War I when he served on the faculty at West Point and used his fluent linguistic skills as a master communicator. Avoiding stages when speaking to soldiers, Ridgway combined an aggressive daring nature with a personal example that demanded he looked his people in the eye to better understand their needs and to share their sufferings. Leading the 82nd Airborne in World War II magnificently, Ridgway would be brought up to replace General Walton Walker during the Korean War after Walker's untimely death in an automobile accident. Immediately sensing the despair present throughout Eighth Army, Ridgway approached the front lines with dangerous closeness, popping up unexpectedly to inspect units, handing out socks to soldiers, and wearing grenades on his war belt as if to remind soldiers of their missions to fight. The epitome of the operational warrior, throughout 1950 to 1951 Ridgway utilized "meatgrinder tactics," and used his strengths against the Chinese weaknesses. With MacArthur's relief by Harry Truman, it would seem this consummate leader and commander had achieved a perfect career. Putting the Army ahead of self, Ridgway resigned as the Army Chief of Staff after only one term in protest over cuts to personnel and budgets during the Eisenhower administration. Ridgway had irritated his bosses by giving his considered opinion that a war in South East Asia would be a disaster. The old expression "good guys finish last "could be used to explain the career of the man who, in many ways, saved the army in Korea. The Christian concept of self-sacrifice for others certainly described the leadership by example of Matthew Ridgway, one of the greatest fighting generals ever produced by America.[338]

Courtesy of the United States Army

---

338. Thomas E. Ricks, *The Generals* (New York: Penguin, 2012), 179.
339. Ibid., 136.
340. Ibid., 136.
341. Ibid., 138.

With Ridgway moving up to the Far East UN Command, he was replaced by James Van Fleet at 8th Army, a general who had achieved success in the Greek Civil War. The third Chinese Offensive on April 19, 1951 was no surprise. American artillery annihilated North Korean forces while the "Epic Stand" of the British Army's Glosters upset the attack schedule of the Chinese. Seoul was fought for house by house. Ridgway was again using the advantage of the defense against the Chinese while giving ground in other areas. Into the meatgrinder went the Chinese, finding out too late that spirit was no replacement for firepower. A late April (fourth offensive) attack by the Chinese left nearly 45,000 dead as they melted back to the north. A final pathetic attempt by the Chinese on May 5 would see them mauled for the last time, as even medics killed Chinese seeking to escape and Americans coolly calling for fire on their own positions. The smell of rotting Chinese from previous offensives still hung over certain battlefields as the pathetically supplied Chinese soldiers often stopped the attack to check the corpses for ammo and goods. With Chinese laid crisp and pulverized on surrounding hillsides, Mao would finally begin to listen to his military leaders and see that further attacks against the U.S. lines would be fruitless. He began to settle in on a strategy of limited fighting while negotiating to wear down the Yankee imperialists.[342]

By May of 1951, General Van Fleet at 8th Army requested to conduct a converging column attack on the Chinese by again landing the army at Wonson. The JCS had no stomach for further war at this point, and the two armies, like tired heavyweights, would watch each other over trenches instead. Ordered on May 1, 1951 to go onto the defensive, nearly half of the casualties that occurred in the Korean War happened after the peace talks began. To his dying day, Van Fleet remained bitter, insisting he could win the war. It probably did not help that he also lost his son in a B-26 crash during the war. President Truman said something about Van Fleet that he never said about MacArthur or Ridgway: "He was the greatest general we have ever had."[343] By June, when Operation Pile Driver drove a spike into the heart of the dragon at the "Iron Triangle," an intersection of roads and towns in Central Korea, Chinese morale would drive the Chinese to the peace talk table in June.

Air War in Korea

The Korean War witnessed the first use of military jets. Air force hopes of replicating a dramatic victory in World War II would leave them as frustrated as the ground forces. The aluminum air bridge of cargo transport came through, as did naval forces. Finally the bombing campaign would leave war planners further concerned about the futility of fighting future wars in Asia. The helicopter would also make its debut in the Korean War.

The F-80 shooting star appeared on stage as the North Koreans pushed south, but, in the beginning at least, jets left something to be desired. Traveling too fast to really see the enemy, they lacked use as close-air support platforms. The marines had stuck with their time-tested prop aircraft, the F4U Corsair, and many airmen much preferred using the old F-51 Mustangs for close-in work. Despite their vulnerabilities, the prop aircraft enabled the eyes in the sky to see the ground better.

Then came the F-86 Sabre. Designed to pursue Russian bombers in Europe, the swept-winged **F-86 Sabre** included wide wings for the thin atmosphere it was expected to reside in. Where the old guard propeller craft could not go—into the fighting ring with the Mig—the F-86 went and won. Racking up approximately a seven to one kill ratio, the F-86 demonstrated American superiority in aviation engineering. An air conditioner prevented the bubble canopy from steaming up and young pilots, taught to turn their heads to see over the opposite shoulder, used the nifty air break and sliding rear stabilizers, features that compensated for the Mig's maneuverability. Strangely, the air force did not begin aerial refueling until the last years of the war. Stranger still is the fact that refueling in the air had been proved decades before, and how those jets could suck down fuel!

---

342. Ibid., 143.
343. "Hero Exalted by Truman," *Los Angeles Times*, (September 24, 1992): A28

Often limited to mere minutes on station due to their thirst, eventually mobile teams of jeep-riding airmen and pilots would serve as Tactical Air Control Parties, using FM broadcasts to bring in circling aircraft with precision strikes.

The use of bombing as a tool for interdiction fell short. Against an army of 300,000 requiring a mere fifty short tons a day, bombing simply proved insufficient.[344] **Operation Strangle**, launched by the United States after the Chinese entered the war, tried to stop traffic from the north by dropping roofing nails over the roads, but the Air Force still could not halt the enemy. In frustration, later in the war attempts to bring the enemy to the peace table would lead to attacks on Pyongyang with firebombs and even attempts to blow dams with the hope of ruining the rice crops with flooding. Meanwhile, the fighting went on in the static trenches war below the clean cockpits of the aircraft. Although somewhat lacking in glamour, air power did find areas of success in Korea.

Since Korea is a peninsula, by definition it is surrounded by water on three sides. Naval forces from various task forces on station contributed their share to the war effort, and marine air continued to serve as "flying artillery" to frontline troops, both army and marine. The Marine Corps also continued its legacy of 20th-century innovations when the first use of a helicopter in combat augmented the medical use of vertical lift. In November of 1951, 950 troops arrived at the frontlines and, thanks to the helicopter, relieved troops likewise returned to the rear. As of the first day of the same month, over 8,000 wounded troops had been evacuated by helicopters. The helicopter had quickly made itself indispensable on the post-World War II battlefield.[345]

The Russians and Chinese had begun to call for peace talks out of need. The Chinese had realized they could not liberate the entire peninsula, and the Russians had started to demand cash payments for supplies and weapons.[346] Likewise, cracks in the UN alliance with MacArthur's stated request for nuclear warfare continued with comments made by Syngman Rhee about the British, who he claimed had had MacArthur dismissed.[347] Chinese began to see they could not take all of Korea, and their dreams of war ending by winter/spring were going up in smoke. Russians began demanding cash payments for supplies and weapons. The alliance was strained by Rhee's anti-British statements, accusing them of contributing to MacArthur's dismissal.

Cultural strains between Korean and American troops according to John Toland reached "a pattern to become bleakly familiar later in Indochina." The American public's lack of support for the war soon after 1951 also worked against the morale of troops. In marked contrast to the Second World War, but just as tough, many of the troops were galled and embittered until their deaths. John Toland quoted a vet as saying, unlike later in Vietnam, there was "nothing to do but fight in the Korean War."[348]

The Static War June 1951–July 27, 1953

And fight they did, bleeding while newspapers moved the fight in Korea to the back pages of the first section, but by the summer of 1951 U.S. planners sought the Kansas Line as the best defensive line for the United States to force the success of peace talks. Peace talks had set forth the concept of a 20 mile no man's land to be divided with 10 miles of enemy control and 10 miles of U.S. control. It was at this phase of the Korean War that American attempts at containment began to take on the characteristics of a larger war of containment, and became less like the bold lines of advancing troops in World War II. A brutal phase in American history had started.

---

344. Perret, *Country*, 467.
345. Stanley Sandler, *Encyclopedia of the Korean War* (London: Routledge, 1995), 129.
346. Hastings, *The Korean War*, 230.
347. Ibid., 235.
348. Ibid., 271.

Many precedents would establish themselves in this mostly unknown phase of the Korean War: the inability to force a breakthrough, the beginning of a numbers game, and the beginning of a new relationship between the military and civilian leadership. Like World War I, neither enemy could quite finish off the other. The Chinese had demonstrated that American air power in itself simply could not destroy the Chinese war machine. The ability of the Chinese to utilize defensive terrain and the lack of American resolve at home resulted in an American inability to maneuver or hit on a scale likely to do much more than produce casualties for little gain. On the Chinese side, the American artillery (again like in World War I) simply proved impossible for the Chinese troops to penetrate. A brief survey of some of these brutal hilltop fights is in order here.

The Battle of **Bloody Ridge** took place west of the Punchbowl from July to September 1951, and was followed up by the Battle of Heartbreak Ridge, northwest of the Punchbowl from September to October 1951. Attacking J Ridge to the southeast, American advances to Bloody Ridge saw delays until August. Eventually five bloody days of see-saw type fighting back and forth for the mountain tops occurred. This characteristic of advancing U.S. troops using enormous firepower to blow away Chinese positions resulted in exhausted troops—low on ammo and unable to consolidate these high grounds so sought by artillery observers. The inevitable Chinese counterattacks would push U.S. and South Korean (ROK-Republic of Korea) troops off of the recently seized objectives and so it would go, on and on. Headquarters tended to find itself farther back in the rear, and delays in deployment of reserves and attempts to keep casualty numbers down contributed to the inability of the increasingly demoralized Americans to do more than fight, bleed, and sweat in the dust.

Fighting continued throughout the summer as the 9th U.S. Infantry aided the South Koreans in taking J Ridge back from the Chinese. The X Corps Commander ordered marines up from J Ridge to the northeast while, simultaneous attacks from the army's 2nd ID regiments attacked the south and east with the ROK's coming from the north in a classic converging columns squeeze operation. In addition to casualty numbers, the initiation of a rotation program started pulling front lines out of the forward ranks after a year, artillery men after 18 months, and support personnel after a couple of years on the basis of points assigned for each month—36 being the winning number ensuring a return to the United States. This system would plague U.S. commanders through Vietnam, and while it made things easier for personnel officers in terms of providing experience and increasing troop morale, it did little to win the war. Soldiers found themselves most likely to be killed or injured at the beginning of their tour, and by the time they had mastered their trade of fighting and killing, they became cautious for fear of dying before going home. Units suffered from this manpower drain, and morale and team work declined.

In contrast to the Americans, the Chinese had no such problem with troop morale since they rotated their troops by units (as the United States does now). In fact, the Chinese rewarded units for fighting hard by rotating them out for rests, and giving individual awards for how many of the invading imperialists the Chinese killed. American awards tended to recognize injuries. In addition to the preoccupation with numbers during a post-war time of increased use of computers and attempts to quantify efficiency, finally the assault upon Bloody Ridge succeeded after three weeks of fighting and over 2,700 casualties sustained by ROKs and Americans, while the communists supposedly sustained about 15,000.[349]

As Rudyard Kipling wrote about in the *Arithmetic of the Frontier*, here we see the real beginning of the numbers game. The problem is the numbers don't tell the whole story. The Chinese regarded loss of manpower in quite a different way than did the American people. Van Fleet was given the go-ahead by Ridgway and attacked the next ridge, a mere 1,500 meters to the north. The 2nd Division was ordered to attack **Heartbreak Ridge**, and essentially it suffered similar casualties to Bloody Ridge. The North Koreans had merely fallen straight back into another labyrinth of dug positions, and the Americans, politically unwilling to follow Van Fleet's proposal to widen the war

---

349. Bevin Alexander, *The First War We Lost* (New York: Hippocrene Books, 1986), 442.

by landing at Wonson, essentially consigned their fighting men to frontal assaults into the enemy's fangs. By mid-October, more than 3,700 casualties had been squeezed from the 2nd Division, and for what? Another mountain, and behind it lay another, and behind that another.[350] The lines above the Punchbowl had been slightly straightened up in time for peace talks. As the peace talks dragged on for two more years and as American airpower valiantly attempted every trick it could to hasten peace, an embarrassing POW uprising occurred.

An American general held hostage by prisoners who themselves were surrounded by armed American guards in a standoff presented an amazing picture. When wars are not fought to be won, strange things do occur. Another bizarre aspect of the Korean War was that advancing Chinese soldiers wanted to continue advancing straight into American lines so that they could surrender. Nowhere did we see evidence of Americans even on the defensive attempting to go to communist lines. The embarrassment caused by a propaganda exchange, whereby Americans pointed out the fact that so many communists did not even want to return home, may have contributed partly to the irony of the POW hostage issue. Eventually quelled by early 1952, with the prison secured at Koje-do, the Chinese continued to accuse the Americans of committing germ warfare and for dropping lice and fleas on the Chinese countryside as biological warfare. Counter charges of the "brain washing" of American prisoners accompanied the frustrating hill battles and provided ongoing drama during the static phase of the war.

When Dwight D. Eisenhower won the election during the fall of 1952, the war began to wind down. Ugly hill battles continued with brilliant infantry advances by the Chinese at night against inexperienced and recently rotated American troops, utilizing enormous amounts of firepower with killing fields such as Pork Chop Hill; but by this time the real show had ended. At Ike's inauguration, the new 280 MM tactical nuclear cannon found itself center stage in a not so subtle reminder that America remained the only power to use the atomic bomb. MacArthur must have smiled, because by the summer of 1953 the Korean War had settled into an armistice destined to last at least another 60 years. Ike's simple statement, "I'm going to Korea," must have persuaded the Chinese to finally stop war by other means during the peace talks.[351] The result of the Korean War is summed up in the words of Geoffrey Perret, who said "Americans don't cheer a tie."[352] Popularity for the war effort hovered around 35 to 37 percent of the American public, while soldiers and marines returning from literal hell on Earth found that many Americans did not even know where Korea was located.[353] A harbinger to Vietnam, many of these veterans smoking Camel cigarettes and carrying "church key" can openers for their beer cans wondered why they had even served. Bitterness aside, the contributions of the men and women in Korea had demonstrated American resolve. An expensive abandonment of the pre-war offshore defensive strategy by Truman had created a situation where American lives, blood, and treasure would be, in some places, wasted, while an inability to finish the war successfully seemed to continue. But in Korea a free people continued the explosion of the economy recently seen in neighboring Japan. Not only did Korea become more wealthy and powerful then its previous Cold War enemy, the Soviet Union, but the willingness of Americans to make a stand in Korea may have eventually played a powerful role in the growth of capitalism in China. Perhaps Mao thought clearly when he attacked in Korea for fear of Taiwan, since today the explosion of the coastal Chinese economy is a function of Taiwanese and Hong Kong capital. This occurred because of the boost to East Asian industry that came from the Korean War.

---

350. Ibid., 447.
351. Perret, *Commander in Chief*, 176.
352. Melinda. L. Pah, *In the Shadow of the Greatest Generation* (New York: New York Univ. Press, 2014), 30.
353. Ibid., 185.

Key Terms:

Syngman Rhee	**Operation Chromite**	**Meatgrinder**
Kim il-Sung	**Break-out**	**F-86 Sabre**
Greek Civil War	**Wonson**	**Operation Strangle**
Offshore defensive strategy	**"Diverging columns"**	**Bloody Ridge**
Pusan perimeter	**Entirely new war**	**Heartbreak Ridge**

Thought Questions:

Can America only win wars fought with limited objectives? Why or Why not?

Should MacArthur have been allowed to attack China?

Chapter IX

VIETNAM

Romans 1:18 "For the wrath of God is revealed from heaven against all ungodliness and unrighteousness of men, who suppress the truth in unrighteousness." NKJV

Check out an animated map of the events of the Vietnam War at this link: https://www.khpcontent.com/

1954 — Battle of Dien Bien Phu

1957 — Sputnik launched

1962 — Cuban Missile Crisis

1963 — Battle of Ap Bac

1964 — Gulf of Tonkin Resolution

1965
- Operation Rolling Thunder begins
- Battle of Ia Drang
- Marines begin Combined Action Platoons/Companies

1966 — Battle of Attleboro

1967
- Operation Cedar Falls
- Operation Junction City
- Gen. Westmoreland addresses Congress
- Battle of Dak To

1968
- Tet Offensive
- Mini Tet Offensives (May, August)
- Johnson halts bombing campaign
- Nixon elected

1969 — Battle of Hamburger Hill

Vietnam 151

1970
Cambodia invasion
Kent State shootings

1971
"Pentagon Papers" released
My Lai trials see Lt. William Calley convicted

1972
Operation Linebacker
Last U.S. maneuver elements leave Vietnam

Go to www.khpcontent.com to watch a video introduction for this chapter.

Intro and Events up to JFK

The Vietnam War changed America politically and left a still unhealed scar. This undeclared war represented a continuation of the action in Korea in that the American people did not really understand the nature of the war they had entered. Over time a series of presidents used their irresistible newfound power to deploy military force, but found they also had increasingly become unable to achieve a decisive victory. Throughout the war, the fear of Chinese intervention floated over Southeast Asia as it had in Korea. The true nature of the times and place could only barely be seen by American historians and analysts, as once again the best our country had to offer responded to the call of their duties.

Vietnam is not Korea. Korea is a temperate zone peninsula surrounded by water on three sides. Vietnam is a tropical attenuated coast line (the parallels here with the 13 colonies are amazing), stretching generally south and southwest and on the edge of a mainland region. The cultures of Korea and Vietnam represented two different cultures as well. Whereas the Koreans, it has been argued, essentially are a unified culture, historically seeking to manipulate outside forces for their own preservation over time, Vietnam offers a different picture altogether. Since most global cultures tend to spread lattitudinally, or east to west, an attenuated and tropical nation-state will have vast differences between the north and south. Vietnam had never really experienced a unified nation or culture, and about the time the state emerged at the end of the 18th century, the French came in and artificially divided it. Vietnam offered the United States a quagmire of social forces; ranging from a north fighting a south in a conventional and guerilla civil war as well as a social political revolution. Like the British in the American Revolution, the Americans in Vietnam floundered from one brushfire to the next and never really had a coherent strategy.

America by the late 1950s and early 1960s had seen its military maintained at a war-time footing for the first time in its history. President Eisenhower believed global communism offered a planetary threat to freedom and in its nature represented evil. Nevertheless, Ike knew America ran grave risks running a global military force and recognized the strength of the American people came from their freedom and independence. Attempting to merge through Dual Use Science and Technology (DUST), the advantages and potential of free-market capitalism, and the arrival of bright immigrants (many from Germany) helped America continue her technological prominence. Ike also sought to use the technology militarily to contain communism. This "**New Look**," as Ike characterized his defense policy, reflected the American propensity for speed and gadgets. The 1950s represented a time where the air force dominated defense budgets, and it seemed everything was made bigger, faster, and designed to fly higher!

The Space Race with the Russians had started to ramp up. Eisenhower's tendency to ignore the army like a teacher whose classroom contains his rowdy son or daughter, the president sought to show he did not have favoritism for the army he had previously led. By attempting to encourage the navy with its solid-propellant rockets, the Russians had beat the Americans into space when the first satellite, **Sputnik**, launched into space in 1957. The creation of almost all war weapons in the 1950s followed the familiar pattern of bigger, faster, higher. The army assisted in planning as former Wehrmacht officers planned to prepare for the inevitable real war of good vs. evil bound to come in Europe against the Russians. As the military in general and the army in particular grew increasingly frustrated with the former four-star general now president, other threats emerged.

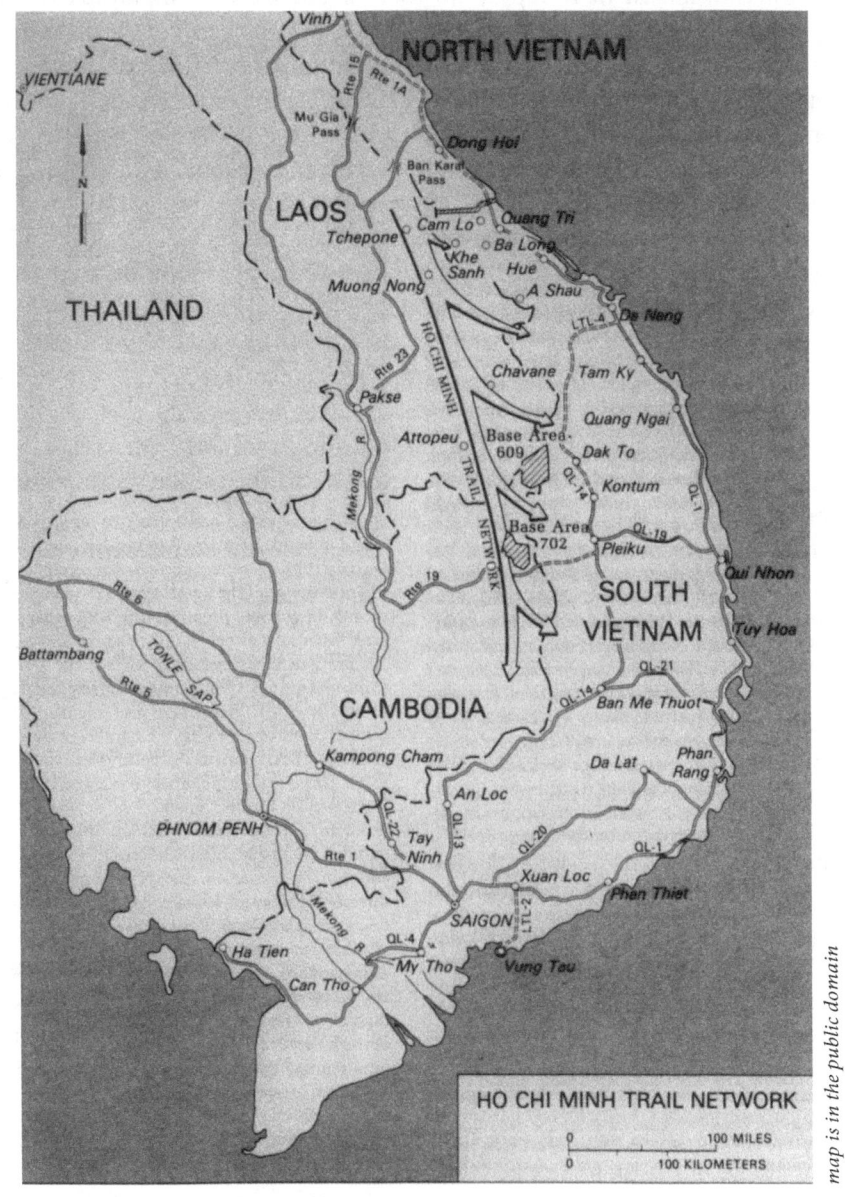

Figure 9.1 Vietnam and the Ho Chi Minh Trail

map is in the public domain

The old general knew a threat when he saw it, and the threat to Southeast Asia would be Laos and the strategically important Plain of Jars. A pathetic attempt to forge another UN-type justification for the defense of Southeast Asia came in the form of SEATO. As the French continually lost to the Vietminh in the countryside of the North, the United States came to support a French attempt to return to their colony after the Japanese defeat in World War II. The United States continued funding the French at levels of 80 percent of the cost of running the Diem government and 98 percent for the cost of its armed forces by the late 1950s.[354] In part, U.S. aid represented a fear of France

---

354. Perret, *Country*, 491.

becoming communist as a result of its weakened status after World War II. The French increasingly experienced great frustration with the time-proven North Vietnamese tradition of attacking, then in a disciplined manner breaking off the attack, living to fight another day. It was the same frustration the Romans faced against the Parthians in Mesopotamia, and once again in Southeast Asia the Western way of warfare was stumped until the French identified the **Ho Chi Minh trail**.

The Ho Chi Minh trail consisted of a supply line that was successfully employed to resupply troops to the south for years and would continue throughout the next two decades as well. Seeing an opportunity to defeat the Vietminh, the French sought to shut the trail down. Instead, the French garrison at Dien Bien Phu in 1954 found itself surrounded and cut off. As the American JCS advised President Eisenhower, General Matthew B. Ridgway stood his ground and declared the war in Vietnam not worth American intervention. To his dying day Ridgway remained proud of his standing up and telling the truth. If only others had followed. The army general who would replace Ridgway had himself served earlier in Korea—Maxwell Taylor. Developing new concepts such as the "pentomic division," and many innovations that frustrated the army, he would eventually retire on somewhat less than popular grounds. Following Ridgway and Taylor would be Lyman Lemnitzer.

The army had long stated after Korea, "**No more ground wars in Asia**." Nevertheless, Eisenhower did not appreciate the general standing up to him—a former five-star general himself—and when Ridgway subsequently resigned from the army in protest over budget cuts, this action was inevitably noted by other ambitious senior officers. The hardest thing a military officer can do is to sometimes tell the truth about a particular mission. Regardless, it is the military's responsibility as the experts to tell the truth when asked and then to follow orders to the best of their abilities. Ridgway demonstrated great honor by standing his ground for the army and then resigning on a principle, as some wish current Chiefs of Staff would also do. America allowed France to fall but continued to fund a man with strong connections to the Roman Catholic Church in America and possessing strong anti-communist credentials named Ngo Dinh Diem. Not only had Ike left the legacy of a war fought by France and largely funded by Americans, following a strategy of containment, he continued to support and lend the weight of American prestige now to Diem.

With Kennedy's arrival into the White House, a new, more telegenic "**Camelot**," as it was known, appeared in Washington. The old "brown shoe" military types seemed to be little more than relics of a bygone era in this world of the new. Facing the charismatic and handsome John F. Kennedy were a host of quite ugly problems. Cuba and Vietnam represented challenges to the world's peace. Finding himself with a CIA plan to invade Cuba during the first half year of his presidency in April 1961, JFK gave approval to support an attack on Cuba using expatriates to invade. The problem was the military did not know what the plan consisted of. In contrast to Eisenhower, who had led by consensus, Kennedy only had a few trusted advisors. When things went wrong on the beaches of Cuba, as they needed to do with no air support available, Kennedy and his young entourage blamed the old military types. In Camelot there existed little room for the old or the ugly. Who did these young protégés of the president actually consist of?

Leading the group, Robert C. McNamara had been responsible for contributing to a statistical control group that analyzed maintenance, logistics, and operational problems in various theaters of the Second World War. Not often well received by military officers who did not believe numbers won wars, McNamara had left the army a true believer in the need for statistical management and control over the military.[355] Soon, joined by others of his ilk known derisively by the military as "**whiz kids**," McNamara faced a military very hurt by what it perceived as unfair criticisms after the aborted Bay of Pigs mission in Cuba. Heading up these generals, the Chairman of the JCS (CJCS), the same Lemnitzer who had replaced Maxwell Taylor, determined to stand his ground against JFK who considered going into Laos. Arguments put forth by the military reeked of the bitter Korean War experience and the often heard expression, "no land wars in Asia," struck the wealthy and young president as somewhat indicative of the lack of a "can-do" or "good attitude." The Army Chief of Staff by 1960 was General George H. Decker. The CJCS Lemnitzer would be promoted out of his recent position for

---

355. H.R. McMaster, *Dereliction of Duty* (New York: Harper Collins, 1998), 2.

arguing against Laos, but still Decker held his ground. Doing like Ridgway, Decker told the president that the army could not win a war in Southeast Asia and that nuclear weapons might be necessary. Decker's attitude expressed the views of a man who had served as Krueger's Chief of Staff in Operation Cartwheel in New Guinea under MacArthur. Decker was nobody's "yes-man," and had served with plenty of them. Regardless, a new world had dawned with computers, and oldsters who had served in Southeast Asia soon found themselves dismissed. Ridgway's resignation after being denied a second term as Army Chief of Staff firmly signaled the lesson of the consequences of telling the truth to the military's leaders. Never really trusting the military, JFK found himself more comfortable instead with the confident young McNamara and the increasingly empowered "whiz kids."

By 1962 the Cuban Missile Crisis had resulted in Kennedy showing the Russian leader Nikita Khrushchev who really had guts. Previously pushed around by Khrushchev, Kennedy at last had a foreign policy success when he bravely stood the Soviets down from resupplying what U-2 intelligence aircraft had revealed to be a building program. Using a technique since called **Gradual Escalation**, the whiz kids and Kennedy had used sea power to offer a picture of increasing force to solve a problem. The fact that the Soviets had never been a naval power and that fighting anti-colonial wars in the jungle presented two different pictures mattered little to these men in clean air-conditioned offices. The only Roman Catholic nation in mainland Southeast Asia, Vietnam had long fascinated the Roman Catholic Kennedy since his political career as a Senator. Increasingly surrounded by a chorus repeating what he wanted to hear, Maxwell Taylor, now an author and patron of the arts, would be brought out of retirement to be the new Chief of Staff and would be responsible for reigning in any troublesome service chiefs who might disagree with the administration's line. This precedent thereby created an obvious affront to the military and began a process whereby Kennedy, using McNamara, could bypass those troublesome Chiefs of Staff. Without the military there to stand up to the president, the way soon opened to increase the number of soldiers, euphemistically called "**advisors**," to Vietnam. By appearing tough on communism, Democrats had learned since Korea they needed to take a stand. With Richard M. Nixon of the Republican Party waiting in the wings with impeccable anti-communist credentials and an obsequious JCS, Kennedy proceeded to pass the point of no return in Vietnam.

Using a staff that believed in Graduated Escalation after the Cuban Missile Crisis, Kennedy supported Maxwell Taylor's belief that flexible response necessitated the need for a military to be ready to fight in several types of varying levels of conflict, not just conventional warfare. This was seen as the perfect antidote for Khrushchev's wars of national liberation, and Taylor and McNamara together argued for the increase of "advisors" to 16,000, and aid to Diem increased dramatically.

By 1963 Diem lost his grip in Vietnam. His brother had persecuted Buddhists, and the Roman Catholic Diems never had been able to successfully claim the Mandate of Heaven—the Confucian ideal of obedience to one's leadership as the rightful leader. This time-honored concept stood at odds with American ideology and sense of fair play, and represented another terrible failure by Americans to understand the nature of the Vietnamese. As Buddhists responded by burning themselves to death, the president's brother's wife exacerbated tensions by referring to her willingness to provide more matches for "Buddhist Barbeques."[356] The situation in Vietnam continued to decline despite rosy reports from Maxwell Taylor, Paul Harkins, and his new protégé William Westmoreland. By October it seemed Kennedy was about to give up on Diem who, like Syngman Rhee, had demonstrated a measure of nationalistic independence by possibly opening up talks with the North Vietnamese. By November, drastically changing direction, Kennedy gave the signal to the CIA to let Diem's military know the United States would not be averse to a change, and that the United States would pledge to spend funds to ensure the survival of the government of the Republic of Vietnam (RVN). Diem and Kennedy would both be dead by the end of November, and as Larry H. Addington says, "By making a pledge on behalf of the United States that obligated him and his successors in office to defend the post-Diem government, he would make it more difficult for later administrations to find an honorable way out of the Southeast Asian tangle."[357]

---

356. Larry H. Addington, *America's War in Vietnam* (Bloomington: Indiana University Press, 2000), 63.
357. Ibid., 67.

General Maxwell Taylor

General Maxwell Taylor, more than any other individual, is probably responsible for the quagmire of the Vietnam War. Representing a new type of military officer, Taylor the "yes" man came to power by getting the attention of President John F. Kennedy when he criticized the U.S. Army in his book *Uncertain Trumpet*. Once brought back from retirement, Taylor proceeded to surround himself with men who supported his and the president's view that the Vietnam War represented an opportunity for the United States to contain communism. Highly political, unlike the Marshall tradition of rendering advice when asked for, Taylor oversaw the removal of the Joint Chiefs of Staff from the decision process in the Vietnam War. Taylor's clever ambition would see the division of the services to a degree where the civilian leadership could alone direct the Vietnam War.

Johnson's War

President Lyndon B. Johnson, the consummate politician, fought war the same way he ran a political campaign. With very little military experience, he and his inherited advisors would proceed to direct the United States into war and then would attempt to fight it as if we could not lose. Backing a failed strategy on the ground and in the air, the president would wreck his presidency and, in many ways, the United States on the coast of Vietnam. Assuming a rational enemy, the president and his inherited advisors proceeded to fight a war using logic.

Democrats, as we have seen already, feared accusations of being soft on communism. Ever since China became communist after World War II, and since the administration of FDR, the Democratic Party has been very sensitive about accusations that they were not tough in terms of foreign policy and in dealing with the nation's enemies. The newly appointed president, upon Kennedy's death, sought to be elected in his own right in 1964. To be elected against a tough-talking conservative Air Force Reserve Major General, Barry Goldwater, Johnson's opportunity came in the Gulf of Tonkin mere months before the November elections.

OPLAN 34A represented the blueprint of operations consisting of secret raids into Vietnam. Ever since the United States had failed to require the RVN to live up to its agreements at the Geneva Accords by conducting an election in 1956, North Vietnamese fighters had been infiltrating into the south. Under MACV, the Military Assistance Command in Vietnam, the Americans had sought to aid the South Vietnamese endeavors to conduct a counter-insurgency. The failed **Strategic Hamlets Program** had seen the familiar pattern going back to Cuba in the Spanish-American War where possibly well-intentioned government programs forcibly moved populations into areas where they could be "protected" from the sometimes brutal counterinsurgents. Achieving little more than alienating the villagers who were forced to move, OPLAN 34A represented an attempt to use raids along the coast of North Vietnam to harass and keep the advancing north guessing.

This attempt to gain the initiative would provide an opportunity for the United States to appear tough and to enter the war in terms easily seen and demonstrably anti-communist.

The first of several incidents occurred in the gulf when U.S. ships conducting DESOTO (DEHAVEN Special Operations off Tsingta—an acronym describing coastal operations off the coast of China) patrols off the coast arrived shortly after an RVN attack occurred on an offshore island in adjacent waters. During this first incident, North Vietnamese PT boats (light, fast, nimble raiders) attacked the *USS Maddox,* a destroyer. Aircraft from the nearby carrier, *USS Ticonderoga*, pursued the craft, and the DESOTO patrols continued with understandably nervous crews. A supposed second incident may have resulted from ghostlike radar images that were never really confirmed, and the Johnson Administration immediately implied an unprovoked attack in international waters. The American public reacted with outrage, and, similar to Truman at the UN, with a 98-2 vote in the Senate along with a unanimous decision by the House, a resolution was given to pass the **Gulf of Tonkin Resolution** enabling the president to "take all necessary measures to repel armed attack against the forces of the United States and to prevent further aggression: … to take all necessary steps, including the use of armed force, to assist any member or protocol state of the Southeast Asia Collective Defense Treaty requesting assistance in defense of its freedom."[358] In testimony before Congress, Defense Secretary McNamara said the ships were merely conducting routine patrols.

The way to war into Vietnam continued the Korean War pattern of utilizing force against a nation that had not attacked the United States directly. The long road to the Vietnam War had been paved by Truman, who committed the United States to global containment against communism in the Greek Civil War, had abandoned an inexpensive off-shore defense strategy, and had established a precedent for using military force without a declaration of war. President Eisenhower had attempted to support French colonial endeavors in Vietnam and had continued support for Diem despite the Geneva Accords' call for elections in 1956. Finally there was President Kennedy's decisions to deploy "advisors" in large numbers into Vietnam and committing the United States to support Diem's assassination and, by extension, subsequent regimes in South Vietnam. The AWoF had changed, as had American society. With prayer now outlawed from public schools and with dramatic social changes impending, President Johnson, having achieved the landslide victory he sought, would, in 1965, take America into another undeclared war.

The last month of 1964 would see the last of the American chiefs advising the president to either "go all in" into Vietnam or to get out. Such negativity simply remained intolerable, and the whiz kids convinced Johnson to ignore them and instead to launch Operation Barrel Roll against the Ho Chi Minh trail in December 1964. As 1965 dawned, Curtis LeMay, the famous architect of the 20th Air Force's attacks on Japan during World War II, argued against Gradual Escalation, reflecting air force doctrine hard earned during the war when it was learned that piecemeal attacks did not work; bombing hard and fast seemed most likely to bring an opponent to the peace talks. One of the key reasons Johnson and McNamara would not listen to LeMay was fear of Chinese intervention. CJCS used Maxwell Taylor's ally, the new army Chief of Staff General Earl Wheeler, a career staff officer, to support him against the opinions of LeMay and the Marine Commandant General Wallace Green. LBJ silenced General Wheeler when he attempted to explain the marine position on Vietnam; moreover, Ridgway's earlier assessment to Ike resulted in the general being silenced. Sadly, senior officers had begun to understand the futility of disagreeing with a civilian leadership who simply would not listen.[359] **Gradual Escalation**—increasing the use of force gradually until the enemy saw the futility of their actions—had now become the policy for the war in Vietnam against the best judgement of proven military advice, and rested on the shakiest of legal foundations with the merest of public support. In such a confused manner the war grew hot.

---

358. Ibid., 78
359. McMaster, *Dereliction of Duty*, 70.

Air War in Vietnam—Rolling Thunder

As B-52s lumbered down Guamanian airfields in the Central Pacific headed towards the Ho Chi Minh trail, a series of tit-for-tat type operations would ensue as the United States gradually increased its effort and now sought a strategy. Beginning with the attack in February of 1965 at the base in Pleiku, retaliation in Operation Flaming Dart would strike the North Vietnamese military bases up to 40 miles north of the DMZ (Demilitarized Zone, or no man's land). As the communists hit Qui Nhon, Flaming Dart II launched in reprisal, erasing any doubts Johnson had about unleashing Rolling Thunder. Operation Barrel Roll was moved to northern Laos to support a secret American-backed army fighting against the communist Pathet Lao. Operation Steel Tiger moved over to take on the Ho Chi Minh Trail.

Operation **Rolling Thunder** would be a civilian-run program broadened and conducted in the absence of a coherent military strategy. Military leadership essentially stood by, basically mute, as civilians picked and chose operations at lunches in the White House. This "Tuesday Lunch Bunch" epitomized the extremes of civilian control in this war and the inability to articulate a concise mission. Civilians in air-conditioned buildings decided what air targets should be selected in tandem with ground forces forced to slug their way through tropical heat under triple canopy jungle. The micromanagement occurred out of the fear that a bumbling military might create another Chinese intervention, such as occurred in Korea, and represented one of the most pathetic moments in American military history.[360]

1965

By the spring of 1965 the marines had landed to defend Danang Airfield. As their trousers drip-dried, General William C. Westmoreland stood by to greet them. A handsomely chiseled man, Westy, as he became referred to as, obeyed LBJ's directive to place virtually no limit on troop requests. Judged by historians as a man who did not demonstrate exceptional brilliance, seldom did the general miss a photo opportunity, nor did he stand up to the civilian leadership. Not a well-read student of military history, he represented a man without formal schooling who had achieved his position in large measure due to associations with Maxwell Taylor, and he was certainly not the type of general to make problems by asking too many questions.[361] Led by the strategic thinking of the civilians, troops were increasingly requested throughout 1965, and in April, Taylor agreed to an Exclave Strategy whereby U.S. forces would populate coastal areas and the ARVN (Army of the Republic Vietnam). They would attack into the interior. Seizing the strategic initiative by June of 1965, Westy would be asking for more troops and sending U.S. teams into the countryside to attack offending communists, essentially killing the Exclave Strategy.[362] The North Vietnamese would maintain this ability to continue laying punches while the United States would respond throughout almost the rest of the war.

Westmoreland's strategy essentially created enclaves in coastal cities (modification of exclave) and from there, envisioned search and destroy missions—classic hammer and anvil attacks—guaranteed to generate negative publicity because of their bellicose names to destroy communist forces in the rural countryside. Then training the ARVN to fight and hold the nation themselves, the United States could declare victory and leave. Requesting 165,000 troops by the end of 1965 and 34 maneuver battalions, the war would be totally "Americanized." Attempts by the JCS to mobilize the reserves were blocked and rejected by LBJ who seemed to increasingly see Korea as an example of a democratic success. If ever there was an excuse needed to study the Korean War, here it was; long forgotten was the bloody trench fighting of the 1952–53 years when American support waned.

---

360. Perret, *Country*, 509.
361. Lewis Sorely, *Westmoreland* (Boston: Houghton Mifflin Harcourt, 2011), 109.
362. Addington, *America's War*, 86.

Meanwhile Johnson was determined to pursue a Great Society and to eliminate poverty in America. Essentially a New-Deal politician, LBJ's first love appeared to be domestic politics. Why he continued to feed men and materials against the advice of so many generals is as strange as the burgeoning social unrest and use of drugs within just a few years of the Supreme Court's decision to take prayer out of public schools. Could pride have resulted in clouded judgment at the highest levels of American leadership and explain the acceptance of Westmoreland's shaky strategy? Regardless, Westmoreland's hopeful strategy would be tested at Ia Drang.

The use of helicopters for the combat role had been pursued by the army since Korea. Maxwell Taylor had forced the army to accept Special Forces, a Kennedy initiative, and the use of **"Sky Cavalry"** helicopter forces, but the army's doctrine remained in Europe where terrific army task forces would destroy the advancing Soviet "hordes" as they tried to roll their way into Western Europe. The North Vietnamese attempted a smash-and-grab strategy led by General Nguyen Chi Thanh who, in August tried to springboard from the central highlands—the Damocles sword that threatened to split the long attenuated coastline in the middle—and had tried to attack boldly to the coast before the Americans could arrive in numbers. The marines crushed the North Vietnamese at Chu Lai with converging columns landed from sea—smashing against blocking forces on land—but Thanh massed to try again.[363]

By October 1965, American intelligence had located the NVA at the Chu Massif, a large cliff valley area in the **Ia Drang** Valley. Using the 1st Air Cavalry division that had recently arrived from the United States, some of the boldest, fastest-moving infantry in the world jumped off the "slicks" and into battle, outmaneuvering an enemy they had practically landed on top of. Now outnumbered, the Air Cav fought back using the new M-16 rifles, known among the troops as the "mighty Mattels." These strange new stubby rifles without wooden stocks fired at unmatchable rates of speed with unbelievable muzzle velocities. Using B-52 ARCLIGHT strikes to release more than a hundred 500 pound bombs directly on the enemy, strategic bombers demonstrated deadly close-air support, hammering thousands of Vietnamese to their deaths. Over a four-day period, Americans held ground while the enemy mysteriously disappeared into the jungle, springing their deadly ambushes on subsequent American movements, harbingers of the pattern of the ground war to come. An overjoyed Westmoreland asked for 100,000 more troops above the 300,000 already promised and received even more than this request.[364] Had victory disease been piled on a shaky, legal and strategic foundation?

By the fall of 1965, McNamara had just read the results of war game **Sigma II-65**. An emerging picture of a war of attrition, the limited impacts of Rolling Thunder, and the prospect of waning American public interest in the war began to creep into McNamara's mind. Perhaps the results of the war game gave birth to his doubts about the ability to actually win the war. He nevertheless continued to say in public that America could win.[365] Possibly the fall of 1965 bombing pause orchestrated by McNamara represented the realization that Westmoreland's strategy and Rolling Thunder were insufficient to achieve victory. Either way, the pause gave the North Vietnamese the opportunity to reinforce their aerial defenses and seek outside aid. Fighting the opposite type of air war than what LeMay had wanted, LBJ had produced the opposite results. Spurned again for the second year, LBJ's hopes to see the North Vietnamese make a deal continued to fade.

---

363. Ibid., 90
364. Perret, *Country*, 506.
365. Addington, *America's War*, 94.

1966

The year 1966 had arrived. Operation Rolling Thunder continued to plod along. The war appeared increasingly broadcast as being won on the basis of numbers. Achieving a noteworthy four-to-one kill ratio over enemy Migs may, for example, have represented a pyrrhic victory. The diminishing returns for a modern combat force and the cost of war today is captured magnificently in Rudyard Kipling's poem as the "arithmetic of the frontier." In this poem Kipling used the backdrop of the loss of a British soldier over an untrained adversary in one of the numerous military operations the British Empire conducted during the 19th century. Though the numbers coming from Vietnam (and the present war) seemed to reflect a sports-like outcome of victory, the cost in warfare is not always accurately portrayed by the numbers. Nevertheless, just as fighter-bomber aircraft represented the bigger, faster, heavier, higher mentality of engineers in the 1950s and 60s, the nature of the war in Vietnam would continually befuddle the "bean counters" who waged war from computer terminals. Lost in the numbers is a truth-morale. If morale is not maintained, and if a rapidly impatient American people (AWoF) do not see an ultimate goal fulfilled, numbers will ultimately mean nothing. Additionally, as the North Vietnamese began to place SA-2 missiles, essentially phone poles with fins on them, at the border to hit American jet aircraft, the arithmetic of the frontier tended to produce a sum intolerable to the American people.

As sex, drugs, and rock and roll began to litter the American cultural landscape, throughout 1966 the United States continued pumping men and money into a faraway place of very little interest to the average American. Misreading the lessons of the Korean War, a democratic president could still believe by 1966 that holding the communists in Vietnam would project strength at home and abroad. By the end of the year the marines had initiated institutional attempts to fight a counter insurgency with the formation of **Combined Action Platoons** and **Companies** (CAP, CAC). The brilliant marine, Lieutenant General Victor Krulak, who has already been discussed, had been a key developer of amphibious warfare in the years leading up to World War II and had overseen the first use of the helicopter by the time the war in Korea flared up. A proponent of the CAP in Vietnam, he essentially employed the concepts learned and perhaps forgotten by the army in the Philippines at the turn of the last century and merged them with ideas incorporated by the marines into the Small Wars Manual still remembered by the marines of 1966. The idea consisted basically of using small teams, living within, fighting, and, when necessary, dying for the local population. The marines would win the hearts and minds of the local population and represented the USMC's best hope for winning the Vietnam War—essentially putting out the fires of revolution and providing the military security necessary for the Vietnamese to determine their own directions.

President Johnson, not accustomed to listening to military men, gave Krulak a cool reception at best, and the little general possibly received a violent eviction from the Oval Office when he tried to convince Johnson he had been ill-served by his civilian aids and military leadership.[366] Nevertheless, Krulak had sons in this war and he stood his ground heroically. Westmoreland never did like the marines' program; he wanted clean, neat numbers, and probably did not want the marines stealing the show from the army as they had so often done in previous wars.[367] Krulak lost an opportunity to receive a fourth star—he had been greatly expected to become the marines' next commandant—and represented another military casualty of truth. Westmoreland later claimed, in response to charges, that he should have followed the marines with the argument that he did not have the troops to follow the marines' ideas on counter-insurgency, but the record generally shows he had a very low opinion of U.S. Marine strategic thought or maybe he just had a distrust of any new ideas not his own.

---

366. Robert Coram, *Brute* (New York: Little, Brown and Co., 2010), 314.
367. Ibid., 290.

Lieutenant General Victor Krulak

Given the nickname "Brute" due to his diminutive size by the Marines he served with, this tiny but intense officer demonstrated few of the Fruits of the Holy Spirit, but embodied many of the selfless service recognized in the Army values, thereby procuring a permanent record of his contributions to the AWoF. While General William C. Westmoreland and most of the Army depended upon the use of firepower and maneuver such as used in World War II and Korea to win the war in Vietnam, Krulak thought creatively instead. Krulak, the innovator who had overseen the initial development of amphibious landing craft in World War II and who had pioneered the use of the first helicopters in Korea, realized that the key to victory in Vietnam remained the population, remarking, "The Vietnamese people are the prize."[368] Robert Koram relates a story illustrating the difference between the Marines' approach and the "Big Army" approach favoring the use of firepower so characteristic of General William C. Westmoreland.

"Around Da Nang, the Marines found that numerous Vietnamese suffered from rashes and sores that in many instances could be cured simply by keeping the infected areas clean. The Marines ordered tons of soap to pass out locally as part of CAP. About the same time this was going on, when Westmoreland was asked about how he planned to win the war, he responded, 'Firepower.'"[369]

As related in this book's narrative, Krulak had confronted the President about the need to undertake a population centered approach or counter insurgency effort in Vietnam. The leadership trait of moral courage was on full display here as it appeared that the Army leadership bowed to executive pressure in preventing Krulak from being promoted to full General, or Commandant of the Marine Corps. When, however, Creighton Abrams succeeded Westmoreland as the head of Military Assistance Command Vietnam (MACV), Abrams revealed he was not beguiled by the sorcery of numbers, body counts, or Westmoreland's single-minded obsessive reliance upon firepower. Krulak's ideas of opting to fight a counterinsurgency would be adopted under the name CORDs in a joint-run Army and CIA program designed to reward former communists for coming forward, using American small unit patrols as in the Philippines, working in tandem with indigenous leadership, and finally Operation Phoenix.

(Cont.)

---

368. Ibid., 268.
369. Robert Koram, Brute (New York: Little Brown & Co., 2010), 290.

> Krulak, a true man of action who had faithfully served his nation with his gifts of innovation, lived to see his ideas implemented in Vietnam, and though he himself denied terminal rank, he lived to see his son receive the fourth star his wife had bought decades before. In the same office where Krulak had been thrown out for stating his innovative ideas forthright, he lived to see his son Charles become the Commandant of the Marine Corps. As the Marines' leader in the late 90s, General Krulak personally led Bible studies or devotionals and surrounded himself with Christians and those who held to Christian values.[370] A creative thinker like his father, General Charles Krulak would contribute to the Marine Corps' emphasis on urban combat and the need for Marines to follow a "three-block" war, whereby within an area of three blocks the combatant may be expected to go from full-scale operations mode to peacekeeping and humanitarian efforts.[371] Maintaining the long tradition of seeing the enemy as a person, the Krulaks together anticipated and possibly contributed to the work of General David Petraeus who, in 2006, would implement many of the ideas using counter insurgency developed and maintained by the Marines over the last century.

1967

By 1967 the U.S. Army continued to use the conventional methods so characteristic of Westmoreland's Chief of Staff William Dupuy who saw warfare as a linear-type function of attrition. The previous November had seen the largest battle of the war at **Attleboro**. American forces had devastated the North Vietnamese enemy in both maneuver and firepower by liberally using bombing strikes and killing thousands of the enemy (2,130 killed) while only losing 155 themselves. Still, as DePuy noted, the enemy just backed off, and, in fact, "They controlled the battle better; they were the ones who decided whether there would be a fight."[372] This trend would continue throughout 1967.

The year 1967 opened with the army in **Cedar Falls** in January attempting to clear the ground only about 20 miles north of Saigon by clearing the forest with spiked bulldozers, essentially resurrecting the old failed French strategy of *quadrillageor*, which is clearing squares off the map, but Westmoreland called it a spreading oil spot. As Geoffrey Perret says, "A flop by another name is still a flop."[373] Anyway, tunnel complexes uncovered in the area represented a degree of determination and sophistication beyond the wildest military imagination. The tunnels marked miniature towns living underground, safe from American bombs, and included hospitals and living areas. The tunnel networks represented such an extensive area in many cases that the only way to secure them involved rolling giant boulders over the tunnel entrances. The dangerous term "turning point" first emanated from Westmoreland's Chief of Staff at the end of Cedar Falls and would be quickly grasped by numbers people. According to Spencer Tucker, "Cedar Falls was hardly a 'turning point' . . . and a blow from which the VC in this area may never recover."[374]

By February, at **Junction City**, American forces found themselves engaged in heavy fighting against enemies motivated to win. Firing from the hip while carrying wounded comrades, the North Vietnamese pushed the assault, while at Fire Base Gold artillery fired point blank into the attacking infantry. The familiar pattern returned: when firepower favored the Americans, the enemy simply melted away into the jungle or crossed the border back into Cambodia.

---

370. Ibid., 333.
371. Ibid., 332.
372. Spencer C. Tucker, *The Vietnam War* (Lexington: The University Press of Kentucky, 1999), 130.
373. Perret, *Country*, 510.
374. Tucker, *The Vietnam War*, 130.

By spring and summer, II Corps[375] was hit from Pleiku to the Central Highlands. Surrounding a large force at **Dak To** using close-air support and the road from Kontum, the battle for Hill 875 was won by the Americans with four-to-one losses to the enemy incurred. As the marines sat dejectedly on the defensive at Con Thien, bombardment from North Vietnamese fires over the DMZ took its toll on the marines' patience and resembled World War I. Sent by Westmoreland into Khe Sanh in the general area of the French defeat at Dien Bien Phu and near the Ho Chi Minh trail, the marines fought a fierce series of hill battles that raged for weeks to maintain an open supply route. McNamara decided to initiate Operation Dye Marker, a series of sensors and defenses running the length of the DMZ. Attempts by marines to provide security resulted in numerous fire fights and one catastrophic ambush that left only 28 of 300 marines able to return to their own lines. By the end of summer the project to build the McNamara Line, as it became known, laid abandoned. The aggressive marines had not been best deployed according to their capabilities and now sat static, essentially without a mission.[376]

As the war waged on the enemy's terms throughout the year 1967, the flood of Americans in and out of the country changed the nation dramatically. Damaging Vietnamese culture, the 12-month tour continued to destroy military cohesiveness as it had in Korea. An obsession with body counts and numerical efficiency had essentially begun the process of destroying the army and marines; all the while leadership insisted the United States continued to win the war. In fact, by the end of 1967, Westmoreland, speaking in the United States possibly to raise support for the war effort, declared on NBC's *Meet the Press*, "We are winning a war of attrition now." In November Westy said, "We have reached an important point where the end begins to come into view."[377] The problem with numbers and computers as once related by a Special Forces veteran is, "Junk in; junk out."

Body counts had become inflated. As American military leaders found it increasingly difficult to stand up and tell the truth, so too did junior officers learn to inflate casualty numbers. Often time after a firefight, what had been a dead enemy or two became more when reported by higher levels. Junior officers often times received instruction to go back and count blood trails and so on until the numbers justified what the boss at the op wanted to hear. Men who had fought valiantly in World War II watched helplessly at the loss of integrity within their beloved army.

1968

By 1968 racial tensions in America had come to Vietnam to the extent that many white officers found themselves afraid to arm black or African-American troops. There was a fear of "**fraggings**," or the unlawful use of weapons, to kill unpopular leaders (exploded grenades rarely show finger prints). Drug problems began spreading through drug-rich Southeast Asia as traditional values in America seemed as antiquated as the old brown shoe military types who had said to stay out of Vietnam in the first place. Still Americans and their families gave and embodied service to a somewhat ungrateful nation that, increasingly like Korea, just wished the war would end. Meanwhile the draft had become a contentious issue and an unfortunate tradition of punishing local "hippie type-protestors" by their often being selected for service first, thereby turning the whole enterprise into a type of punishment. McNamara continued to demonstrate his brilliance at manipulating numbers and data by attempting to help LBJ wage his war on poverty by forcing the Armed Forces to take many troops it never wanted—sort of a fighting-employment agency. In short, the military in general, but the army in particular, continued to waste away. Perhaps melt would be a better term as the jungle and tough terrain tended to sap energy and cause men to become less alert to the ubiquitous booby-traps used

---

375. For administrative purposes Vietnam is divided from North to South, which consisted of the marines at I corps in the North and the U.S. army exercised responsibility for II and III Corps heading south. IV Corps to the far South saw ARVN in charge.
376. Addington, *America's War*, 94.
377. Sorely, *Westmoreland*, 155.

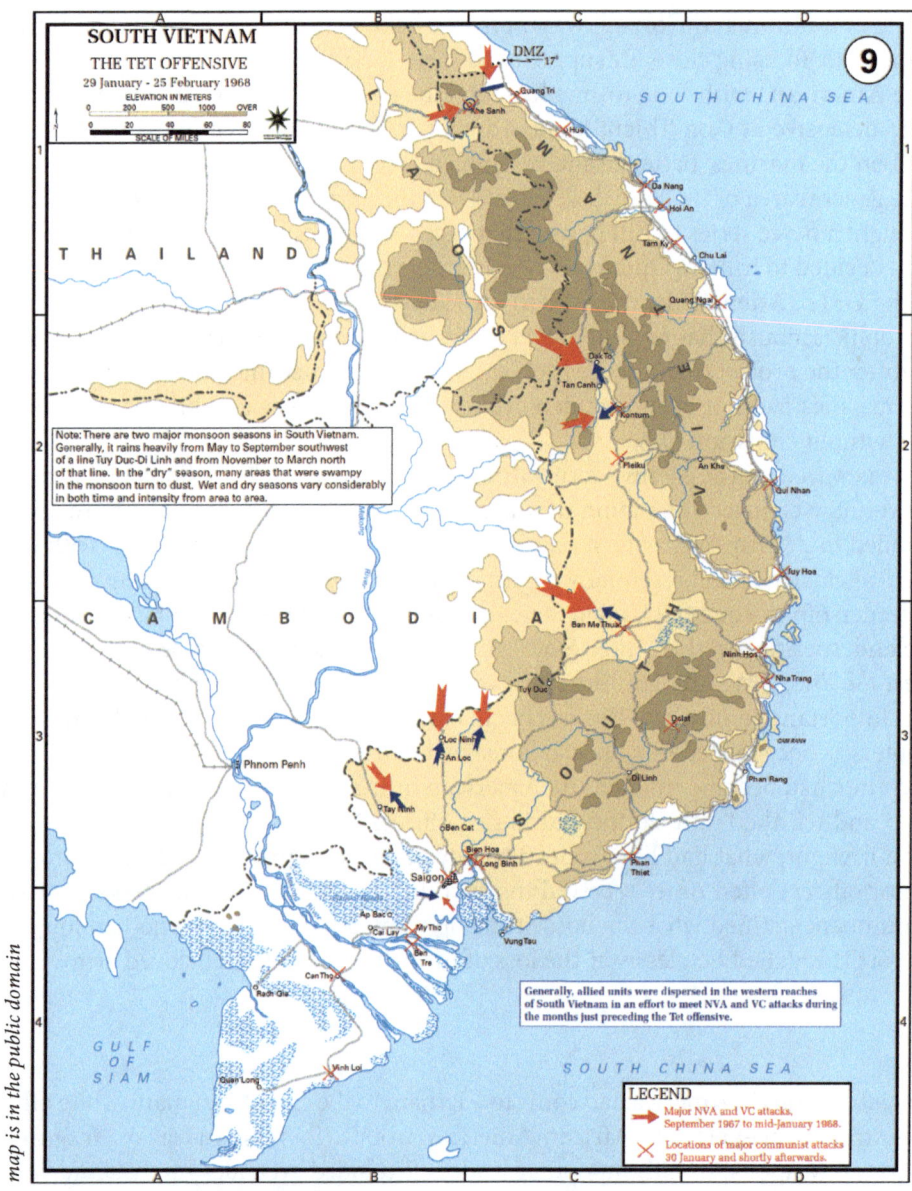

Figure 9.2 The Vietnam War: The TET Offensive of 1968

with artfulness by an enemy using the concealment of vegetation to its advantage. Bumbling around in pursuit of numbers had punished the valiant, taken a toll on Vietnamese culture and society, and ground down the American fighting men.[378]

By the end of 1967, the North Vietnamese had come up with their own strategy. The first phase of raids had been conducted. These were designed to throw the United States off balance while drawing the Americans into the countryside. Recruiters and propagandists would infiltrate the coastal cities, and, on signal, the people would rise up with the liberating communists, and the Americans would be destroyed. The communist strategy had been the exact opposite of the exclave strategy originally proposed in Honolulu in 1965, where it had been envisioned that Americans would initially pacify the cities. Like a fighter falling for a fake punch, the Americans had allowed the North Vietnamese to seize the strategic initiative in the countryside by luring the Americans out. The marines had seen the problem, but no one would listen. Now the Politburo led by Le Duan, over the wishes of General Vo Nguyen Giap, decided to attack the Americans on the lunar New Year of January 1968, and to leave behind the peripheral fights of Attleboro, Junction City, and Dak To the previous summer.

---

378. Perret, *Country*, 515.

Aware of an impending offensive, American intelligence knew an attack would come, but not specifically where. The **Tet Offensive** only represented a tactical victory and one the Americans quickly recovered from and won. This was not a Pearl Harbor or Nazi offensive in the Ardennes; but the American public, lukewarm from the beginning, suddenly saw images in their living rooms showing the dead around the U.S. Embassy in Saigon. The number of cities the north would hit, 40 alone in the Mekong Delta area, including the major fighting at Hue and Saigon, could not be anticipated.[379] The strategic effect on America as Mr. Perret says, was like a "kick in the shins and a dazzling light in the eyes."[380] An American public instructed over and over that the end was in sight, received a considerable psychological blow from the Tet Offensive way out of proportion to its military victory. The American war effort would never really recover. Ironically the South Vietnamese (ARVN) did fight! Typically city boys, the ARVN actually succeeded in defeating the communists in many street fights, and the brutal fight at Hue stood in marked contrast to the cowardly atrocities the North Vietnamese committed when they realized they had failed. Still, the numbers didn't matter; in war, morale is what wins.

The Tet Offensive saw the experienced and battle-hardened army of North Vietnam mismanaged to near destruction. Never again would a great offensive be waged, but for the United States time had started to run out. Broken by the criticisms, LBJ, after seeing the early primary victory of Robert Kennedy who had decided to run against the war, announced to the American public he would not run for reelection. This consummate politician now had faced the inevitable. His nerves strained by Tet and the drama of the marines besieged at Khe Sanh, the president had actually asked the JCS to sign a document pledging the garrison would not fall. As for Westmoreland, he soon would be promoted to Army Chief of Staff where he remained basically ignored. He gave many the impression that his mind remained on trying to vindicate his record in Vietnam.[381] More often than not, Westmoreland tried to salvage an army besieged by absenteeism, drug-abuse, and crime—in part a manifestation of his willingness to follow orders from the number counters.[382]

President Nixon, at the end of 1968, would inherit an unwinnable situation, but managed to leave a free Vietnam behind. He almost lost America, though. Years of presidential abuses against civil liberties and lies about the war's progress had jaded the nation and, in particular, the youth. Attempting to initially use a madman approach in dealing with Hanoi, Nixon attempted to replicate his former boss Ike's success in Korea by insinuating he would use nuclear weapons. Rebuffed in what had become an annual tradition for American presidents since 1964, the Vietnamese flatly rejected American terms. Working diplomatically behind the scenes, Nixon brilliantly understood the communists did not represent a monolithic or block international force. Divisions between the Chinese and Soviets gave Nixon an opportunity he exploited, eventually resulting in a strategic-arms limitation treaty with the USSR and a triumphant visit to China, isolating the North Vietnamese. A strong argument could be made that Nixon managed to seize victory from the jaws of defeat, but how does one define victory when there has been no declaration of war?

1969–1970

General Creighton Abrams wanted to implement Vietnamization—the last phase of Nixon's strategy. While training the ARVN to take over the war effort from the Americans, an American effort led by the 101st Airborne launched an offensive into the Ashau Valley to hit the North Vietnamese staged there. The battle grew in intensity to the point where the United States took the hills in contention after battering the slopes for over 36 hours by artillery and air power. The U.S. victory on what soldiers began calling "**Hamburger Hill**" represented a public affairs failure as the media now

---

379. Phillip B. Davidson, *Vietnam at War* (New York: Oxford, 1991), 482.
380. Perret, *Country*, 516.
381. Sorely, *Westmoreland*, 222
382. Ibid., 224.

turned against the war effort and criticized the loss of life. The military command weakly reported the enemy had lost twice as many men (numbers die hard), but the end result would be Abrams' understanding that the United States could not tolerate any more such victories. The beginning of withdrawal planning from Vietnam began.[383] Between announcements of American withdrawals and with the ARVN increasingly taking responsibilities, a horrific murder occurred at the village of My Lai. Led by an incompetent lieutenant, a platoon of soldiers murdered 22 villagers. To make matters worse, the army had apparently dragged its feet investigating the matter. The trial became public in 1971—three years after the murders in 1968, and just in time for the most effective part of the growing anti-war movement.

General Creighton Abrams

General Creighton Abrams was a natural fighter. He inspired those around him and it was said he could "put fight into a begonia." His contributions to the Army, though generally unknown, would reemerge after his lifetime. As a tanker during World War II, he fought from the front hanging out of his tank hatch with a cigar in his mouth and possessing an uncanny ability to anticipate what the enemy would do next in a fight. Differing from his predecessor in Vietnam, General William Westmoreland, who embodied the corporate mentality of the Army in the decade after World War II, Abrams instead thought "outside the box." Imaginative and creative, whenever a subordinate would present a problem, Abrams reply inevitably was, "why not?" Inspiring those to think around him, Abrams would avoid the piecemeal battle plans or "search and destroy" approach of Westmoreland, and instead instituted imaginative plans to reward surrendering Viet Cong with financial rewards (Chieu Hoi) and through the use of Operation Phoenix to break up insurgencies within the rural areas of Vietnam. Abrams discontinued the obsession with numbers of enemy dead, so prevalent in the post-World War II army, and instead oversaw the institution of small unit patrols, more along the lines of those long advocated by the Marines. With the drawdown of available food for the enemy and by hammering enemy supply routes on the Ho Chi Minh trail, Creighton Abrams essentially oversaw a period of time where domestic dissatisfaction with the length of the war in Vietnam threatened the ability of policy makers to maintain the initiative. Overcoming Westmoreland's aversion to train and arm the South Vietnamese, Abrams effectively instituted the means to give time so desperately needed by the South Vietnamese to develop their own defenses. By inspiring others and through a creative approach to anticipating the enemy, Abrams bought the time to allow U.S. forces to leave Vietnam with a measure of honor. The life and leadership of Abrams would be a topic of intense study during the years in Iraq where time seemed to have run out. The only Chief of Staff to die in office (from cancer), this little known general was immortalized by the naming of a tank, the M-1, after him. A fitting tribute for a true tanker.[384]

---

383. John Prados, *Vietnam: The History of an Unwinnable War, 1945–1975* (Lawrence: University Press of Kansas, 2009), 349.
384. Ibid., 319

Student protests accompanied President Nixon's attempt to temporarily broaden the war to hit the communist sanctuaries over the Cambodian border. This book is written at a time in history when cross border incursions into Pakistan occur regularly. This particular violation shook the nation with intensity equaling or excelling the Tet Offensive. ROTC buildings were burned on campuses and bombs were exploded—the first domestic U.S. terrorism, while future White House leaders and their administration colleagues would cut their teeth on political leadership during these tumultuous times. One National Guard unit, called in to **Kent State** University in Ohio, accidentally killed four college students. The Republicans and conservatives had incurred the wrath for a war created largely by Democrats in one of the most amazing political transformations to ever occur. Still, Nixon must be given credit. He fought back by appealing to the "silent majority" of law-abiding Americans. By insinuation, those who did not support him demonstrated lawlessness. Congress, riding a wave of anger in May of 1970 following the **Cambodian Incursion**, repealed the Gulf of Tonkin Resolution, mostly for show, but demonstrated that the end in Vietnam neared. The Nixon administration realized it had inherited an unpopular war and there simply was too little it could do to bring it to a successful conclusion.

The Ho Chi Minh trail turned into a killing field as American gunships arrived. By 1969, the U.S. Air Force had launched the AC-130 Spectre gunship, a close-air support platform bristling with a 20 mm rotary cannon system, and used a 40 MM Bofors system. Truck traffic on the Ho Chi Minh trail was reduced close to a heart-thumping 1,000 fewer vehicles per month in January alone. The use of B-52 bomber "Arc Light" strikes resulted in the North Vietnamese being allowed only between two and four ounces of rice rations a day according to enemy documents obtained.[385] According to Ronald Spector, "for the hapless Vietnamese truck driver, there was only one defense against bombs, rockets, and shrapnel: keep moving."[386] Four AC-130s equipped with technology able to detect electrical emissions from automotive ignition systems took out about 40% of the enemy's trucks. As the air war raged, the North Vietnamese attempted to use more trucks and anti-aircraft guns, sometimes with fatal results to U.S. airmen. The desperate nighttime fights on the Ho Chi Minh trail and the use of sensors, airpower, and Special Forces troops had finally begun to choke the North Vietnamese, but the question remained: had the hourglass been running for the United States too long?

Just as in a later Iraq War, when the United States found the need to expand its efforts from Iraq into Pakistan, so too by 1970 the United States determined the need to expand the Vietnam War. Cryptographic breakthroughs and increased control of the Ho Chi Minh trail meant that the United States now could read the North Vietnamese playbook as intelligence analysts increasingly discerned the enemy's pattern. Nixon decided to defeat the enemy before it could launch counterattacks, and with the North Vietnamese nearly "on the ropes," Nixon decided the time had arrived to finally finish off the Communist threat. As in later years, the military and its civilian counterparts experienced a learning curve in the need to disregard certain rules of engagements (RoE). With the king of Cambodia overthrown while traveling in Europe, the time seemed right to finally cut the Ho Chi Minh trail, and more importantly, supplies coming through Sihanoukville—a key infiltration point in Cambodia. Of short duration and limited to only 30 km, the incursion uncovered a treasure of information, including one million pages of classified enemy intelligence as well as Vietnamese plans for invasion in 1970. The effect on President Nixon's and General Creighton Abram's strategy of Vietnamization appeared immediately as intelligent sources continued to appear and then often permanently disappear.

---

385. Lewis Sorley, *A Better War: The Unexamined Victories and Final Tragedy of America's Last Years in Vietnam* (New York: Harcourt Brace & Co., 1999), 101.
386. Ronald H. Spector, *After Tet: The Bloodiest Year in Vietnam* (New York: Free Press, 1993), 303.

1971–1973

Nixon had dramatically reduced American casualties from 1969 to 1970 and had begun pulling out the troops. In 1971 Vietnamization would prove to be a failure when ARVN troops sent into Laos facing possible encirclement fled disgracefully. In 1971, Daniel Ellsberg released the "**Pentagon Papers**" to the *New York Times*. The Nixon administration sought to prevent the *Times* from publishing them and even appealed to the Supreme Court who decided to deny the injunction, thereby allowing the paper to print. Ellsberg had been hired by McNamara to record a classified historical record regarding how decisions had been made in the Vietnam War.[387] President Nixon ordered the last maneuver battalion to leave Vietnam in 1972. Internationally, Nixon visited China and this, in tandem with the relentless Easter and Christmas bombings of 1972, kept the North Vietnamese both contained and at the bargaining table. By not backing down and standing against the popular tide of frustration with the war in Vietnam, Nixon managed to allow American forces to go on the offensive and, for the first time, take the fight to the enemy in North Vietnam. A combination of a skilled political opposition and a monopolized media scenting pay-back for Nixon's early days of prosecuting domestic communists, popular support for Nixon would eventually decline and he would face impeachment for his stated knowledge of a somewhat sophomoric break-in by overly enthusiastic political operatives into the headquarters of the Democratic Party. The war in Vietnam had broken traditional trust in leadership and political institutions. America had exhausted itself in Southeast Asia and in many ways had lost itself in the process of trying to win an undeclared war. The challenge for the military would be how to restore an institution so badly used by a succession of presidents who had neither the inclination to listen to military leadership, nor the wisdom to discern which military leaders should be ignored.

Staff Sergeant Jon R. Cavaiani

…While serving as a platoon leader to a security platoon… for an isolated radio relay site located within enemy-held territory…the entire camp came under an intense barrage…when the entire platoon was to be evacuated, S/Sgt. Cavaiani unhesitatingly volunteered to remain on the ground and…was able to direct the first three helicopters in evacuating a major portion of the platoon…On the morning of June 5…the superior size enemy force launched a major ground attack in an attempt to completely annihilate the remaining small force…He ordered the remaining platoon members to attempt to escape while he provided them with cover fire. With one last courageous exertion, S/Sgt. Cavaiani recovered a machine gun, stood up, completely exposing himself to the heavy enemy fire directed at him, and began firing the machine gun in a sweeping motion along the two ranks of advancing enemy soldiers. Through S/Sgt. Cavaiani's valiant efforts with complete disregard for his safety, the majority of the remaining platoon members were able to escape…

(Republic of Vietnam, 4 and 5 June 1971)

excerpt from Congressional Medal of Honor citation

Vietnam War Medal of Honor recipient retired army Sgt. Maj. Jon Cavaiani, left, chats with Marine Corps Sgt. Maj. Mark Allen of the 6th Motor Transport Battalion based in Red Bank, N.J., during the Marine Corps Law Enforcement Foundation's 10th Annual Invitational Gala in Atlantic City, N.J., June 12. Photo by Rudi Williams

Photo source: U.S. Department of Defense

---

387. Addington, *America's War*, 141.

Key Terms:

- New Look
- Sputnik
- Ho Chi Minh Trail
- "No more ground wars in Asia"
- Camelot
- Whiz kids
- Gradual Escalation
- Advisors
- Strategic Hamlets Program
- Gulf of Tonkin Resolution
- Gradual Escalation
- Rolling Thunder
- Sky Cavalry
- Ia Drang
- Sigma II-65
- Combined Action Platoons
- Attleboro
- Cedar Falls
- Junction City
- Dak To
- Fraggings
- Tet Offensive
- Hamburger Hill
- Kent State
- Cambodian Incursion
- Pentagon Papers

Thought Questions:

Did America actually win the Vietnam War?

How did the AWoF contribute to or fail to contribute to victory in Vietnam for the United States?

Chapter X
VOLUNTEER FORCES, NEW STRATEGIES, AND DOCTRINE

Psalm 144:1 "Blessed be the Lord my Rock, Who trains my hands for war and my fingers for battle." NKJV

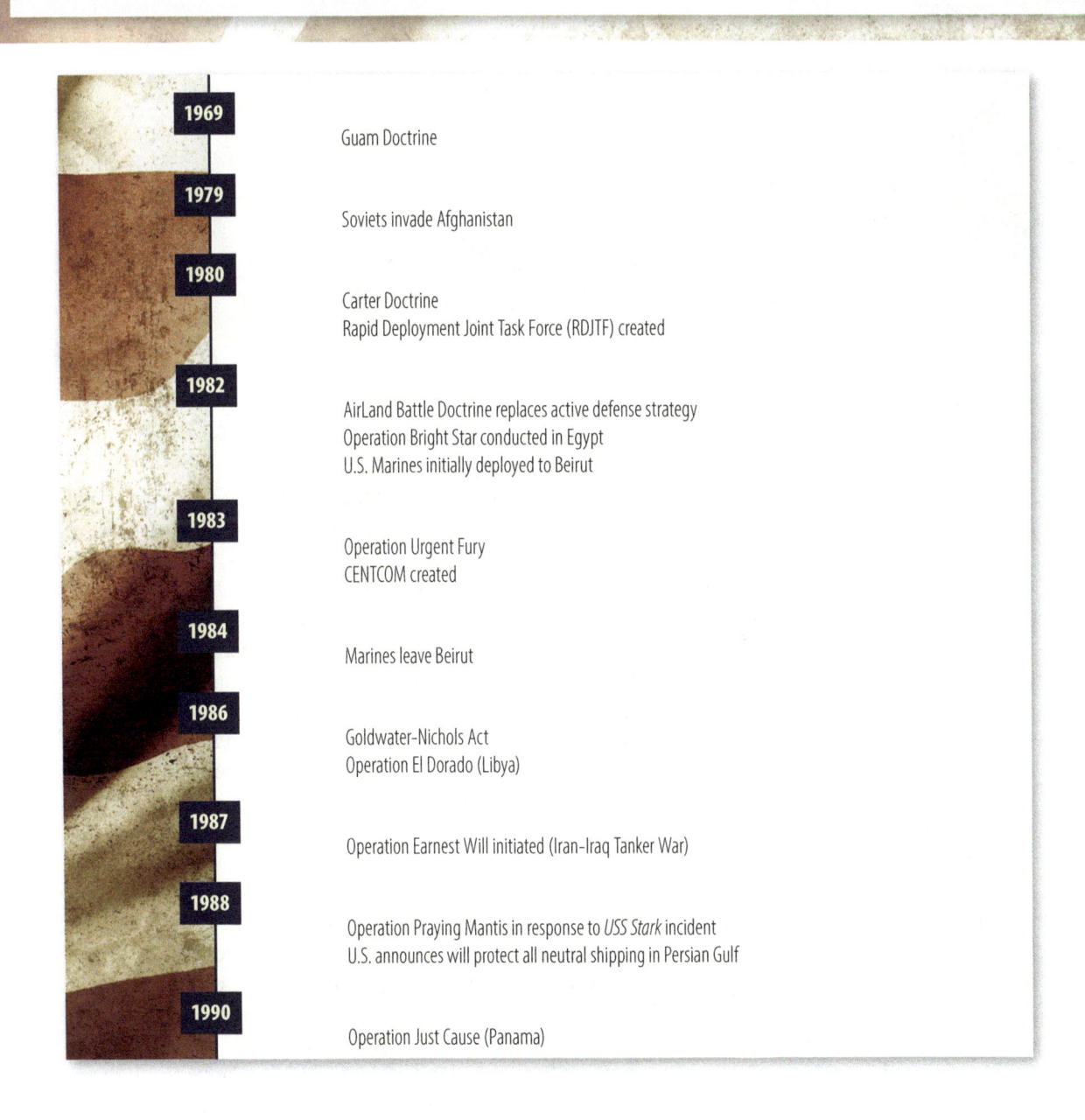

1969
Guam Doctrine

1979
Soviets invade Afghanistan

1980
Carter Doctrine
Rapid Deployment Joint Task Force (RDJTF) created

1982
AirLand Battle Doctrine replaces active defense strategy
Operation Bright Star conducted in Egypt
U.S. Marines initially deployed to Beirut

1983
Operation Urgent Fury
CENTCOM created

1984
Marines leave Beirut

1986
Goldwater-Nichols Act
Operation El Dorado (Libya)

1987
Operation Earnest Will initiated (Iran-Iraq Tanker War)

1988
Operation Praying Mantis in response to *USS Stark* incident
U.S. announces will protect all neutral shipping in Persian Gulf

1990
Operation Just Cause (Panama)

1992

Operation Restore Hope (Somalia)

1993

"Blackhawk Down" Battle
Operation Deny Flight (protection of Bosnians Apr 93-20 Dec 95)

1995

Operation Determined Force (NATO led air operation to protect Bosnians)
Operation Joint Endeavor (NATO peace enforcement enters Bosnia)

1996

Khobar Towers bombing

1998

Operation Infinite Reach (cruise missile attacks on in response to Tanzanian and Kenyan attacks probably by Al-Qaeda)
Impeachment Articles against President Clinton approved by House Judiciary Committee
Operation Desert Fox launched (cruise missiles against Iraq)

1999

24 Mar — Operation Allied Force
7 May — B-2 strike hits Chinese Embassy

2000

USS Cole attacked

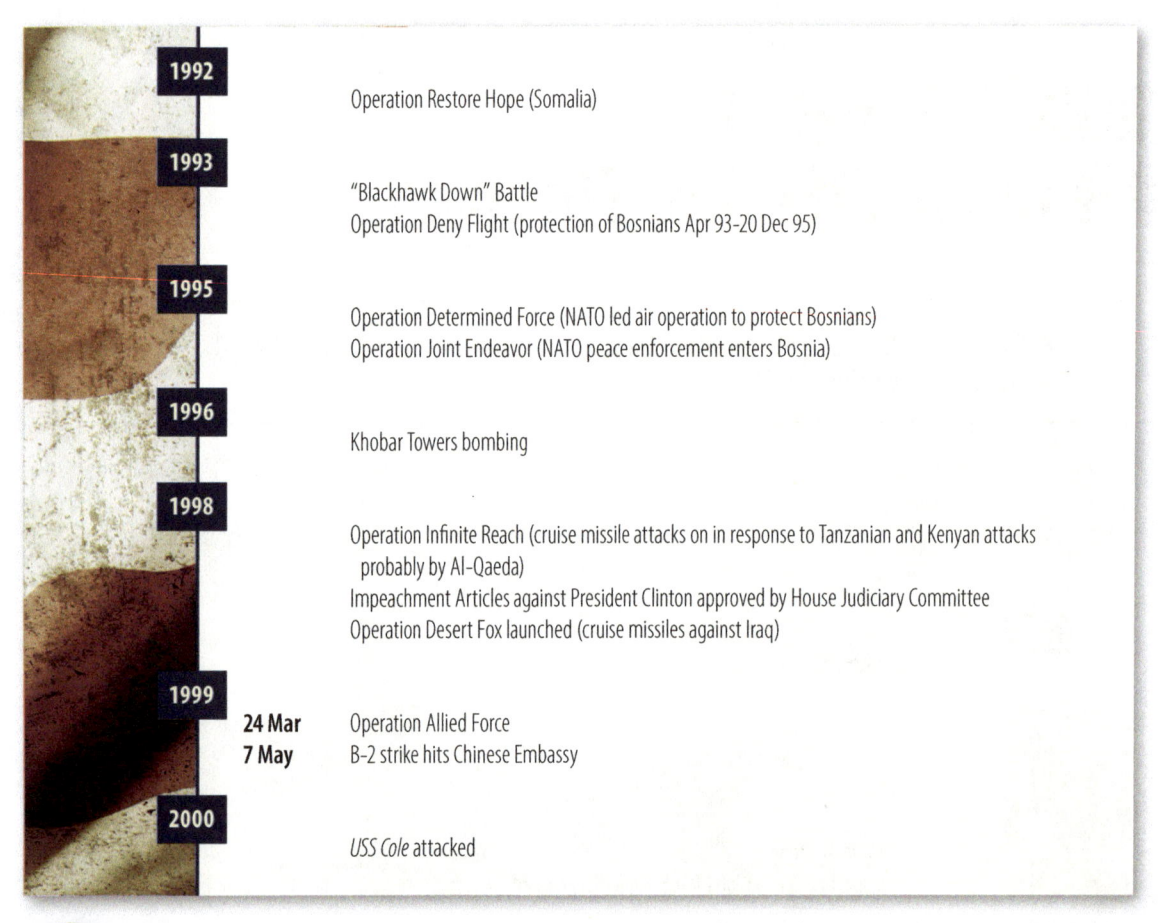

Go to www.khpcontent.com to watch a video introduction for this chapter.

The military would survive and continue to adapt to changing doctrines; ranging from a defensive force designed to fight in Europe, to a force seeking to employ the "operational art" by integrating supporting arms into a lethal, fast, mechanized force in the 80s, to a military that could achieve victory in a full spectrum of needs. Starting in 1969, President Nixon announced a **Guam Doctrine**, whereby the United States would be prepared to fight one and a half wars. With the beginning of a new all-volunteer force, the American Armed Forces increasingly depended on women to make its end strength goals. This continued a tradition of the military advancing social change.

Leadership in the post-war years reflected a variation of isolationism under President Jimmy Carter, an incredible and unprecedented military build-up under President Ronald Reagan, and an idealistic use of force to achieve a type of "New World Order" or "**Pax Americana**" under President George H.W. Bush's leadership. By the 1990s President William Jefferson Clinton, a creation of the Vietnam War era who had avoided the draft and protested the war, would attempt to use the military in new ways, providing relief derisively referred to as "Meals on Wheels." He would use the military in every conceivable role in over 40 different nations.

Greatly affected by the dramatic victories Israel had obtained in the 1967 and 1973 wars, the American military began to explore the potential of utilizing new communications capabilities into an **AirLand Battle** Strategy. General William DePuy, Westmoreland's Chief of Staff in Vietnam, created TRADOC as an institution to develop and promulgate new strategic ideas and to ensure the **doctrine** existed from which weapons procurement and training would derive. Soldier skills developed from the simplest movements to how corps and armies would be moved—all in an attempt to integrate America's perceived strengths and to focus them against the enemy's weakness.

Throughout the 70s and 80s doctrine developed with the idea of the United States fighting outnumbered against an enemy approaching a three to one advantage. Doctrine in 1976 favored firepower, while by 1982 maneuver held the key to winning future operations.[388] The first mention of threats from terrorism occurred by 1986, but by 1993 the Field Manual (FM) 100-5 emphasized "jointness" among the military branches and the term OOTW (operations other than war) was an acronym constantly argued under President Clinton's leadership. FM 100-5 represented a major departure from AirLand Battle; it had been greatly affected by operation Restore Hope in Somalia.[389] By 2001, shortly before the United States would be attacked in its worst case of domestic terrorism ever, the army had begun to recognize "full spectrum" operations—basically every imaginable operation.[390] It seems, in retrospect, the army in particular responded to the various challenges and a changing world by establishing its philosophy for war through doctrine. Recognizing political necessities and an institutional need to survive, one cannot help but wonder if the depressive post-Vietnam era did not result in a level of overconfidence and a new variation of "yes sir—we can do it all." The source of this overconfidence can be traced back to the successes of this period.

From scapegoat in Vietnam to a changing social landscape with women entering all aspects of the military, the first post-Vietnam trial occurred in El Salvador where the future of the army lay. "Manhunters," or special forces, trained and advised the Salvadorans to fight an insurgency. Their increasingly restored confidence would be reinforced in Grenada. **Operation URGENT FURY** occurred in October 1983 and essentially consisted of Army Rangers, the 82nd Airborne, and special forces attacking the island of Grenada in the Caribbean from the southwest, while a marine battalion landed in the northeast. Converging forces secured the small, approximately 20 miles long island, and a rapid and relatively bloodless success continued to give the American people and the military confidence in its abilities. Perhaps the greatest lesson learned from Grenada would be shortcomings in joint (interservice) operations. **Goldwater-Nichols** in 1986 would change this by strengthening the power of the chairman of the Joint Chiefs of Staff while creating the position of deputy chairman. The world would be divided into five zones, each headed up by a commander in chief responsible for the operations of the zone. Noticeably absent in 1990 was a North American command. No one aspiring to high rank could do so without attending joint education through other schools: navy officers going to army schools and vice-versa. By the time of **Operation JUST CAUSE** in Panama on December 20, 1989, a local war lord and his forces received rough justice after an eight-hour operation that saw the use of new weapons such as the neighborhood-leveling 40 MM MK-19 grenade launcher or the awesome lightning bolts hurled from the sky by the C-130 Spectre gunships capable of firing 105 mm guns-virtual tanks in the skies![391]

The inexperienced and somewhat soft President Clinton proved to be quite the deployer of troops. Sending the military to over 40 countries on his watch, he launched only one truly offensive ground operation; **Operation RESTORE HOPE** in Somalia on December 9, 1992. It failed miserably. Reflective of the confusion in a bifurcated role, the military attempted to assist peacekeepers from the United Nations to supply food. When a local strongman Mohammad Farah Aidid presented a threat, a "Snatch Operation" sent to get him failed when an RPG hit the inserting helicopter. Delta Forces and the 75th Ranger Regiment sent in found themselves trapped while a 10th Mountain Division convoy sent to relieve the besieged Americans ran into an ambush. Finally a heavily-armored convoy arrived to rescue what may have been one of the longest small-arms gunfights to ever occur, and America limped out of Somalia with 18 dead.[392] The seeds appeared laid by two opposing forces in Somalia-Al-Qaeda, which had probably launched the well-timed ambushes

---

388. Kretchik, *U.S. Army Doctrine*, 212.
389. Ibid., 226.
390. Ibid., 251.
391. Richard W. Stewart, *American Military History Vol. II: The United States Army in a Global Era, 1917–2003* (Washington DC: Center of Military History, 2009), 399.
392. Crocker, *Don't Tread on Me*, 386.

General William E. DePuy

© Associated Press

General William DePuy reflected the fruits of patience and faithfulness throughout his long military career. Despite criticisms of his conventional approach to warfare, like many of the leaders described here, his ideas and actions lasted long past his successful career. As the Vietnam War wound down, DePuy, who had served directly under Westmoreland, led a demoralized and, in many ways, broken Army into a new era where ideas on how to fight future wars would at times seem as brutal as the combat they described. While the Grant-like charismatic and hard-charging, drinking, and smoking Abrams attempted to inspire the Army during its dark years, DePuy sought to be the brains. In 1973 DePuy created the Army's Training and Doctrine Command (TRADOC). This new headquarters would anticipate the needs of the nation and the Army in the years ahead by researching and training the Army according to the established doctrine or objectives. Greatly influenced by the Arab-Israeli wars, DePuy and his successor General Donn A. Starry would attempt to implement the latest technologies to create a strategy capable of defeating the Soviets during the Cold War, assuming American forces would probably be greatly outnumbered. Developing the newest weapons platforms such as the M-1 tank, the Blackhawk helicopter, the M-2 Bradley fighting vehicle and the Patriot anti-air missile system in a mechanized environment, DePuy and Starry would set the Army on a path that would lead it into the Middle East and an apparent unprecedented military victory over Iraq. In large measure a feud between TRADOC and the Army Command and General Staff College at Ft. Leavenworth, Kansas eventually broke out because of DePuy's contributions to the AirLand Battle Doctrine. Historically, it had been the job of CGSC at Leavenworth to produce doctrine under the name of FM 100-5 Operations–a key manual that taught soldiers how to fight. Throughout the ensuing debate, the Army would find its intellectual center at the National Training Center out in the deserts of Ft. Irwin California and the short-term brilliance of DePuy and the organizational requirements to teach soldiers how to fight would be complemented by the long-term philosophical view that taught soldiers to see a bigger picture; thereby further enabling them to be able to better formulate doctrinal ideas and more properly advise civilian leadership on proposed future courses of military action. DePuy and Starry through their patience served in large measure to create standards that would enable the army to survive and seemingly win one of the most one-sided victories in human history with their emphasis on the "Jominian" approach to winning the decisive battle. Meanwhile, rival intellects in the tradition of Marshall and Ridgway would also be embodied by a future generation of generals who would find that the need to win conventional or big army operations did not necessarily alone represent the key to victory in the Middle East by 2004, and recognized a more "Clausewitzian" philosophical approach.[393]

---

393. Ricks, 345.

Master Sergeant Gary Gordon

Equipped with only his sniper rifle and a pistol, Master Sergeant Gordon and his fellow sniper, while under intense small arms fire from the enemy, fought their way through a dense maze of shanties and shacks to reach the critically injured crewmembers. Master Sergeant Gordon immediately pulled the pilot and the other crewmembers from the aircraft, establishing a perimeter, which placed him and his fellow sniper in the most vulnerable position. Master Sergeant Gordon used his long-range rifle and side arm to kill an undetermined number of attackers until he depleted his ammunition. Master Sergeant Gordon then went back to the wreckage, recovering some of the crew's weapons and ammunition. Despite the fact that he was critically low on ammunition, he provided some of it to the dazed pilot and then radioed for help…After his team member was fatally wounded and his own rifle ammunition exhausted, Master Sergeant Gordon returned to the wreckage, recovering a rifle with the last five rounds of ammunition, and gave it to the pilot with the words, "Good luck." Then, armed only with his pistol, Master Sergeant Gordon continued to fight until he was fatally wounded…

(3 October 1993, Mogadishu, Somalia)

excerpt from Congressional Medal of Honor citation

and RPGs in Somalia. The American military was increasing in confidence, but increasingly led by generals who had the taint of Vietnam about them; they simply could not say no. In the meantime, while budgets grew leaner, Clinton continued deploying troops.

The last half of the 1990s would see the American military deployed into the former Yugoslavia for the purpose of protecting Bosnians from the Serbs and then later in an effort to protect the citizens of Kosovo in their efforts to gain independence from the Serbs. The ultimate result would be to see the American military acting under the aegis of supranational organizations, the increase of global jihadism, and ultimately the rise of the autocratic powers of Russia and China.

The American military, along with an alliance of supra-national organizations, attempted to continue the long-term exhausting and expensive task of maintaining freedom of the air in the former Yugoslavia. As will be seen in Chapter XII, maintaining a no-fly zone—relying upon the American advantage in airpower—offered political leaders relatively bloodless opportunities to demonstrate efficacy and compassion to the American public. Despite dubious results, an image of American strength and a means of preventing atrocities such as in Bosnia nevertheless could be pursued. Operation Deny Flight continued the tradition of the no-fly zone concept and resulted in Serbian bombers being shot down. With air supremacy virtually ensured, designated "safe areas" were established under the watchful eyes of NATO (North Atlantic Treaty Organization) and UN authorities. With the end of the Soviet Union and the unprecedented successes of the United States in Kuwait years before, politicians feared voting against the use of military force at a time when multi-national organizations such as the UN still remained loath to take on belligerent roles. American thinkers viewed Bosnia as a predominantly Muslim nation more secularized than other nation-states in the Middle East, and the Serbians seemed to fill the bill of potential Nazis to post-Cold War policy makers. The eventual July 1995 discovery of genocide perpetrated by the Serbs against nearly eight thousand Bosnian men and boys occurred about the same time that increasing military developments in nearby Croatia, largely undertaken by American military contractors, had created an environment ripe for military intervention. Operation Determined Force now replaced Deny Flight and the mission changed from enforcing no-fly zones to direct intervention through bombing. By August 1995, a Croatian Offensive captured the vital Krajina territory on the Croat-Bosnian border forcing the Bosnian Serbs to surrender. Largely unnoticed were the large number of jihadists and vast amounts of money flooding into Bosnia from the Middle East. The Serbs had a long history of resisting the Turks and saw themselves as the frontier outpost for civilization in Europe; they still had a lot of fight left in them.

With a Croatian invasion recently finished, the hatred of the Serbs simmered like a pot. Stung by the lack of little international concern for the well-being of their peoples, the long historical tendency to view themselves as outcasts seemed to reassert itself when the Bosnian population of the emotionally-important city of Kosovo sought independence from Serbia. Recent successes in the Dayton Peace Accords seemed to vindicate the growing chorus of military interventionists who, despite the failures of peacekeeping in Somalia and Beirut, cried for the American military to continue to forge a New World Order (NWO) of peace free from genocides resulting from the breakup of nation-states after the fall of the Soviet Union.

If the New World Order represented an objective, the Revolution in Military Affairs (RMA) would be the language. The computer and the explosive growth of the Internet made the military and its network-centric efficiency simply irresistible to those who believed the world had ceased to be bound by history and for those who saw globalism, an increasingly smaller and faster world, as the chess board of the future. President Clinton's Secretary of State, Madeline Albright, wanted Serbia to leave Kosovo. The unintended result of the new militarism saw protection given by NATO to the terrorist KLA (Kosovo Liberation Army) at odds with the NATO anti-terrorist mission. The President, increasingly under pressure for an affair with an intern, had ordered Operation Desert Fox (see page 189) after a series of confrontations with Saddam Hussein. As the Serbs withdrew from Kosovo, the KLA quickly entered the area, and when the Serbs refused the February 1999 ultimatum to desert this city of supreme cultural importance, NATO began bombing on March 20, thereby initiating Operation Allied Force. With NATO credibility on the line in this New World Order, cruise missiles began to slam into Serbian targets while stealth bombers and fighters took out air defenses and key communications centers. A NATO operation, the United States flew two-thirds of the combat sorties.[394] A ferocious air campaign exceeding even that of Desert Storm failed to secure the ground. The long-stated claims of air power enthusiasts came closest to being fulfilled in Serbia but still the need for ground forces quickly became apparent. The disastrous attack by an Air Force F-15E on April 12, 1999 against a convoy of fleeing Kosovars proved made to order for the Islamic world that was failing to see the alluring prospects of a secularized New World Order. The May 7 bombing of the Chinese embassy by B-2 bombers flying from the United States proved to be utterly disastrous from a diplomatic standpoint. As retribution began to play out on the Serbian peoples, the American military and those who control it learned a couple of vital lessons with the final toppling of the Serbian President Slobodon Milosevic in the summer of 1999.

The lessons taken from Serbia continued to see technology and in particular air power as the key to destroying "future Hitlers." The idea that a bad guy's removal would solve the military challenges faced in the New World Order would shape interventionist policies that would eventually lead into the effort to topple Saddam Hussein. Without declaring war, the air campaign over Bosnia would be largely an American affair covered as an international effort.

By the late 1990s a beleaguered president faced impeachment, but unlike Nixon, Clinton was saved by a strong economy and looked to the military at a time when he needed political support. U.S. forces entered a war in Bosnia and Serbia in southeast Europe in a series of operations still misunderstood to this day. By 1995 when 20,000 American ground troops arrived in the former Yugoslavia, long gone were the anti-war activists of an earlier era; instead they were replaced by **CNN** (cable news network). Spectacular displays of guided munitions by generals on TV pointing

---

394. Andrew J. Bacevich, *America's War for the Greater Middle East* (New York: Random House, 2016), 186.

at TVs seemed to mesmerize a bored public and give sustenance to a beleaguered leader. How the NATO-led operation fit into the legal framework of the military experience still befuddles. It seems ultimately deposing the Serbian President Slobodon Milsoevic after a successful 78-day long air campaign did little more than end the Cold War peace, the Pax Americana or the New World Order—all names for the peace dividend marking the fall of the former Soviet Union. It would be another decade or so before American thinkers and war-planners recognized attacking the erstwhile psychologically Slavic-ally of the Russians (the place where WWI had started after all) and an accidental destruction of the Chinese embassy would portend a need to regain face by both nations and a subsequent unification of purpose in these **emerging autocracies**.

A Chinese or Russian threat would be a long way off in the future; however, of more immediate concern in the 1990s was the explosion on the scene of terrorism. Taking up where they had left off in Somalia, Al-Qaeda continued to refine its killing methods against Americans. Led by the rich **Osama bin-Laden**, former "freedom fighters" against the Soviets in Afghanistan funneled their hatred for the last remaining infidel power. They had defeated the feared Soviets; surely the soft Americans they had seen on TV could be defeated. Starting in 1993, an attempt to level the World Trade Center (WTC) demonstrated bin-Laden's resolve in destroying this cultural landmark that symbolized the new American empire of Internet, satellites, and world military reach. The cowardly Americans had fled Somalia after all. Other bombings occurred at Riyadh in 1993, and by 1996 in Dahrain, Saudi Arabia bombs killed 19 Americans. A fatwa in February of 1998 issued by bin Laden resulted in truck bombs very similar to the WTC and Oklahoma City Federal Building bombings (1995). By 1998 the killing spree continued in Nairobi, Kenya and Dar es Salam, Tanzania with virtually no reprisals by the United States. Finally the *USS Cole*, an American naval destroyer, was hit while refueling in Yemen, but after all the solemnity and speeches, there was a close election in 2000, and the president prepared to move on to other opportunities to make speeches, but perhaps at an increased price.[395] Osama meanwhile had two years to plot his next move.

Key Terms:

Guam Doctrine   **Operation Urgent Fury**   **CNN**

Pax Americana   **Goldwater-Nichols**   **Emerging autocracies**

AirLand Battle   **Operation Just Cause**   **Osama bin Laden**

Doctrine   **Operation Restore Hope**   *USS Cole*

Thought Questions:

What lessons had the military and its civilian leadership learned or failed to learn from Vietnam?

Did Vietnam influence the decision by Americans to intervene or not to intervene abroad militarily in the 1980s?

---

395. Daniel. P. Bolger, Why We Lost (Boston: Houghton, Mifflin, Harcourt, 2014), 12.

# Chapter XI

THE FIRST IRAQ WAR

> **Micah 6:8** "He has shown you, O man, what is good; And what does the Lord require of you But to do justly, To love mercy, And to walk humbly with your God?" NKJV

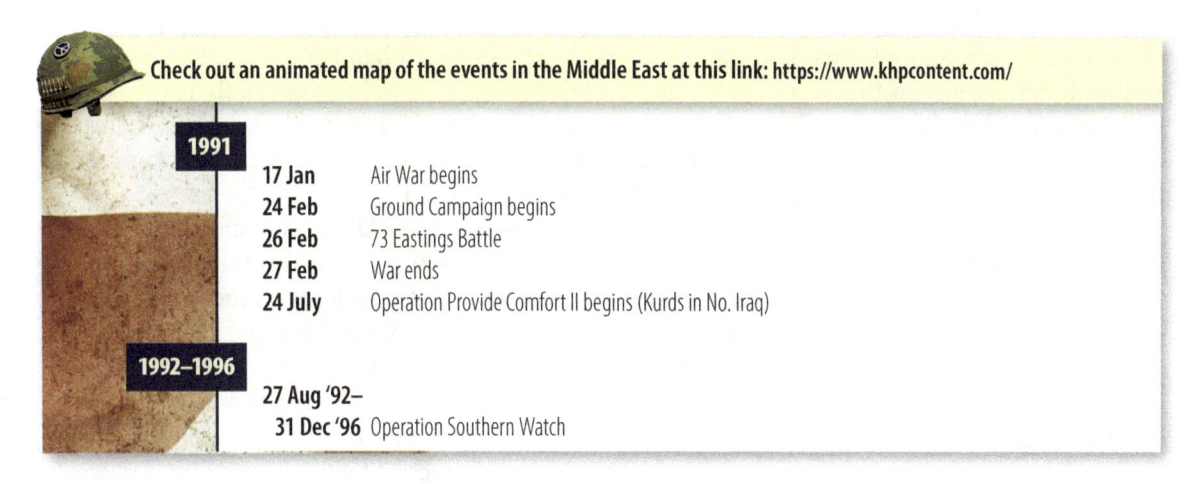

Check out an animated map of the events in the Middle East at this link: https://www.khpcontent.com/

1991
- 17 Jan — Air War begins
- 24 Feb — Ground Campaign begins
- 26 Feb — 73 Eastings Battle
- 27 Feb — War ends
- 24 July — Operation Provide Comfort II begins (Kurds in No. Iraq)

1992–1996
- 27 Aug '92– 31 Dec '96 — Operation Southern Watch

Go to www.khpcontent.com to watch a video introduction for this chapter.

A newly confident American military stood ready when on August 1990 Saddam Hussein invaded the oil-rich nation of Kuwait in an attempt to adjust his national borders and to pay off creditors from his decade-long war against Iran that had raged through the 1980s. With an unprecedented arms buildup, President Ronald Reagan had helped the army develop a number of new weapons platforms to include tanks, infantry fighting vehicles, helicopters, and missiles. With this new arsenal, America would cast off the Vietnam syndrome and begin to embark on military deployments at the end of the Cold War. These deployments would continue for at least a generation.

The M1A1 is the finest tank in the world. With an eventual upgrade to an A2 variant, it could fire a round almost three times the size and total firepower of a World War II Sherman tank. Because it could fire faster and more accurately at higher rates of speed, the days of stopping to range or seeing rounds bouncing off of the hulls of adversaries had passed. Instead, with laser range firing accuracy, guaranteed death at 4,400 meters gave a virtual victory to the first gunner who squeezed the hand actuator switch. The M1A1 would provide the main punch of the strategy of AirLand Battle.

The M-2 Bradley delivered earth-crunching infantry behind the shielding arrow head of armor. Close behind and able to maintain the new higher speeds, the Bradley delivered fires from a lethal 25 mm chain gun. Also capable of firing the TOW (Tube-launched, optically tracked, wire-guided) missile at over 4,000 meters with a 98 percent kill probability, the lessons of the Arab-Israeli wars as incorporated into AirLand Battle had clearly manifested themselves on the battlefield. Additional procurements of helicopters for fighting (the Apache) and transport (the Blackhawk) would further move air assault troops, like leapfrogging razors, into the enemy's rear areas, securing roads and performing vital cavalry functions. The Patriot missile system would replace the 1950s era HAWK (Homing All the Way Killer) and Nike-Hercules missiles, time-proven anti-air assets, but ones requiring tremendous maintenance and parts support. Other systems would include the MLRS (Multiple Launch Rocket Systems) as artillery and the replacement for the old jeeps with the HMMWV (High-Mobility Multipurpose Wheeled Vehicle).[396] America now had a new store-bought arsenal and a joint forces organization. The army and marines had trained for years in maneuver warfare at their desert training areas of NTC and 29 Palms, California. Focused on mission with a clear doctrine and led by a president not afraid to use it, the U.S. military only needed one thing; someone stupid enough to challenge it. The stage had been set for the most dramatic military victory since perhaps the Hundred Years' War of the 14th century.

Desert Shield protected America's vital ally Saudi Arabia from Saddam Hussein's invading army, but to liberate Kuwait, Desert Storm would need to be launched. The attack would total nearly a million armed combatants from 30 participating countries. The participating commanders were General Colin Powell, the Chief of Staff of the U.S. Army, and the CENTCOM (Central Command) commander General Norman Schwarzkopf. Both men had been officers in Vietnam, and both felt the loss of that war deeply. The so-called **Powell Doctrine** essentially reserved any military operations for only those areas of vital national interests or security, the use of overwhelming force to ensure victory, and finally an exit strategy. The war was fought by these criteria and, though undeclared, represented a well-thought out and executed victory.

A preliminary bombardment drew on the idea of **concentric rings**. Unlike Vietnam, the air force in the First Iraq War decided on targets and prioritized its target listings using the model of circles, as in a bull's eye. Modeled larger rings denoted targets in sequence of priority with more importance represented by those rings approaching the bull's eye. Eschewing a direct fight, the air force would instead choose key personnel and technological mediums such as fiber optic connectors as the intended targets, thereby knocking out the key "nerve center" of the enemy's operation. This air strategy essentially rendered the opponent's army motionless for want of communications and control. Keying American firepower (AWoF) against the enemy's weaknesses epitomized operational success. As electronic jammers hit radar networks, Apache helicopters fired radar-seeking missiles, opening electronic windows for American F-15 fighters led by EF-111 Ravens following the ground with radar. As Tomahawk cruise missiles flew by at eerily slow speeds to pummel leaders, the F-117 stealth fighter flew invisibly through the air, presenting false radar signatures to Iraqi gunners firing helplessly from below. Smashing the Iraqis starting on January 17, 1991, the actual ground assault did not begin until February 24, 1991—over an entire month of airpower. What overwhelming force indeed!

An amphibious demonstration and a bold frontal assault by America's Arab allies, a diplomatic windfall in a post-Cold War-forged coalition, accompanied by an armored VII Corps fist of over 146,000 troops and 50,000 vehicles, gave Saddam Hussein of Iraq a left hook he never forgot. While air assault units from the 101st Airborne and 82nd Airborne secured rear areas, the 24th Division rolled on the VII Corps' left, protecting its flank. The armored fist of America flew through the desert with clockwise precision, rapidly consuming or brushing aside any opposition it encountered. Using night-vision goggles (**NVGs**) and the new **GPS** (Global Positioning System) devices, the age of space had arrived on the battlefield. So fast and furious did Americans hit the Iraqis, prisoners could be seen standing in

---

396. Ibid., 385.

lines for great distances just waiting to surrender. So terrible was the rapid speed of American forces that the fleeing Iraqi army on the **Highway of Death** died by the thousands as U.S. aircraft hunted people and vehicles through the deserts without mercy, becoming virtual angels of death.[397]

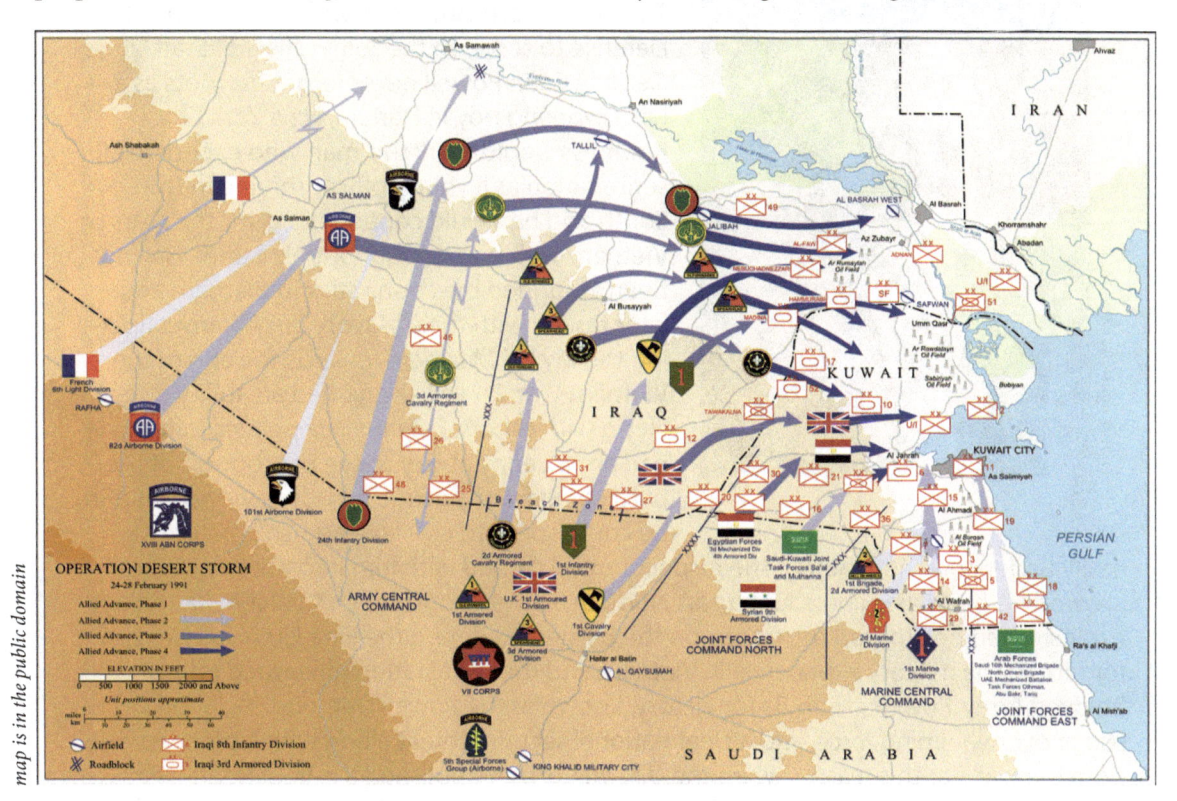

Figure 11.1

As General Colin Powell asked the president to consider halting operations for "humanity's sake," efficient mine breaching maneuvers and combined arms maneuver supplemented by supporting arms demonstrated the AWoF of creativity and learning. The military had developed AirLand Battle doctrine and honed the application of it through the sacrifices of endless hours of hard and dangerous training, conducted 24/7 in the delta corridor at 29 Palms, Ca. by the marines throughout the 1980s and at the National Training Center at Ft. Irwin, Ca. by the army; together these services had produced a deadly winning, mechanized, and combined-arms team. The Powell Doctrine had enabled the mission to be rapidly accomplished by focusing the effort on the defeat of the Iraqi Army and not ancillary or spin-off missions. Still, an uneasy feeling quickly set in as it had on the conclusion of the Meuse-Argonne Offensive. Something told the participants that despite an overwhelming victory, the war had not been finished. As is so often the case, it's easy to win the war, but hard to win the peace.

Deciding to stop combat operations, President George H.W. Bush inadvertently turned what might have been the most one-sided victory in history into a 30-year war. The Republican Guards who were loyal to Saddam Hussein had escaped to Iraq. At the peace table General Norman Schwarzkopf unintentionally frittered away a victory when the wily Arab negotiator asked for permission to maintain helicopters. The Americans appeared unaware these helicopters represented an armed threat to minority Shiites and Kurds that the United States had encouraged to rise up against the Saddam regime. Perhaps Schwarzkopf and his staff remembered as General Daniel P. Bolger suggests, the kindness Grant had shown Lee at Appomattox.[398] It is, after all, hard for Americans to think like non-Americans.

---

397. Bolger, *Why We Lost*, xli.
398. Ibid., xxxiv.

General Colin L. Powell

The first African-American and last Secretary of Defense to serve on the Joint Chiefs of Staff, General Colin Powell never forgot his roots as a hard-working boy in Harlem, New York City. Kindness would mark this man who experienced segregation as a young officer serving in the South and he would continue to carry the scars of Vietnam with him throughout his career. Having been wounded by a punji stick in Vietnam and later tasked with the unsavory duty of investigating the My Lai Massacre towards the end of the Vietnam War, Powell always had an ability to get along with others. Essentially a political officer, he had an uncanny ability to see the "optics" of the battle field from a political leader's viewpoint and he could speak to civilian leadership in terms easily understood and tactful. The respect Powell carried with him into the Oval Office allowed his hard-charging counterpart Norman Schwarzkopf, with his volatile nature and explosive temper, to lead the troops on the battlefield during the First Gulf war. Never forgetting the military experience in Vietnam and the devastation unleashed on his beloved Army, Powell's formula for victory, known as the Powell Doctrine, included the use of overwhelming force, and a clear national security threat along with a planned exit from the war. For this reason, when the U.S. VII Corps demolished the Iraqi Republican Guard in little over 24 hours, it was Powell who saw the danger in the overwhelming victory. As Iraqi forces bolted north on the "highway of death" in an attempt to escape the American armored juggernaut, it was Powell who asked Schwarzkopf to cease ground operations at the 100 hours mark. After Goldwater-Nichols had mandated a separation between the authorities of the various unified commands and the Joint Chiefs of Staff, Powell's tactful nature made him the last truly powerful wartime Chairman of the Joint Chiefs of Staff and his advice to the President went far in ensuring the avoidance of "mission creep" in the First Gulf War. Subsequent mistakes by the Commander of Central Command required the maintenance of no-fly zones over Iraq, but Powell's contributions and ability to see the big picture enabled him to continue service as the Secretary of State reminiscent of the great George C. Marshall. Brilliant, personable, tactful, and demonstrating kindness, Colin Powell in many ways represented the end of an era and the beginning of a new one.

Key Terms:

Powell Doctrine

Concentric rings

NVGs

GPS

Highway of Death

Thought Questions:

Is it wrong for the military leader to order death on the battlefield? Is killing the same as murder? By what moral framework or through what Bible verses do you defend this conclusion?

What is the relationship of doctrine and training? How does a declaration of war clarify the military's mission and the employment of forces? Did the Gulf War represent these concepts or did the United States find an enemy who blundered into our AWoF?

9/11, ENDURING FREEDOM, AND THE SECOND IRAQ WAR

Chapter XII

Romans 12:19 "Do not take revenge, my dear friends, but leave room for God's wrath, for it is written: 'It is mine to avenge; I will repay,' says the Lord." NKJV

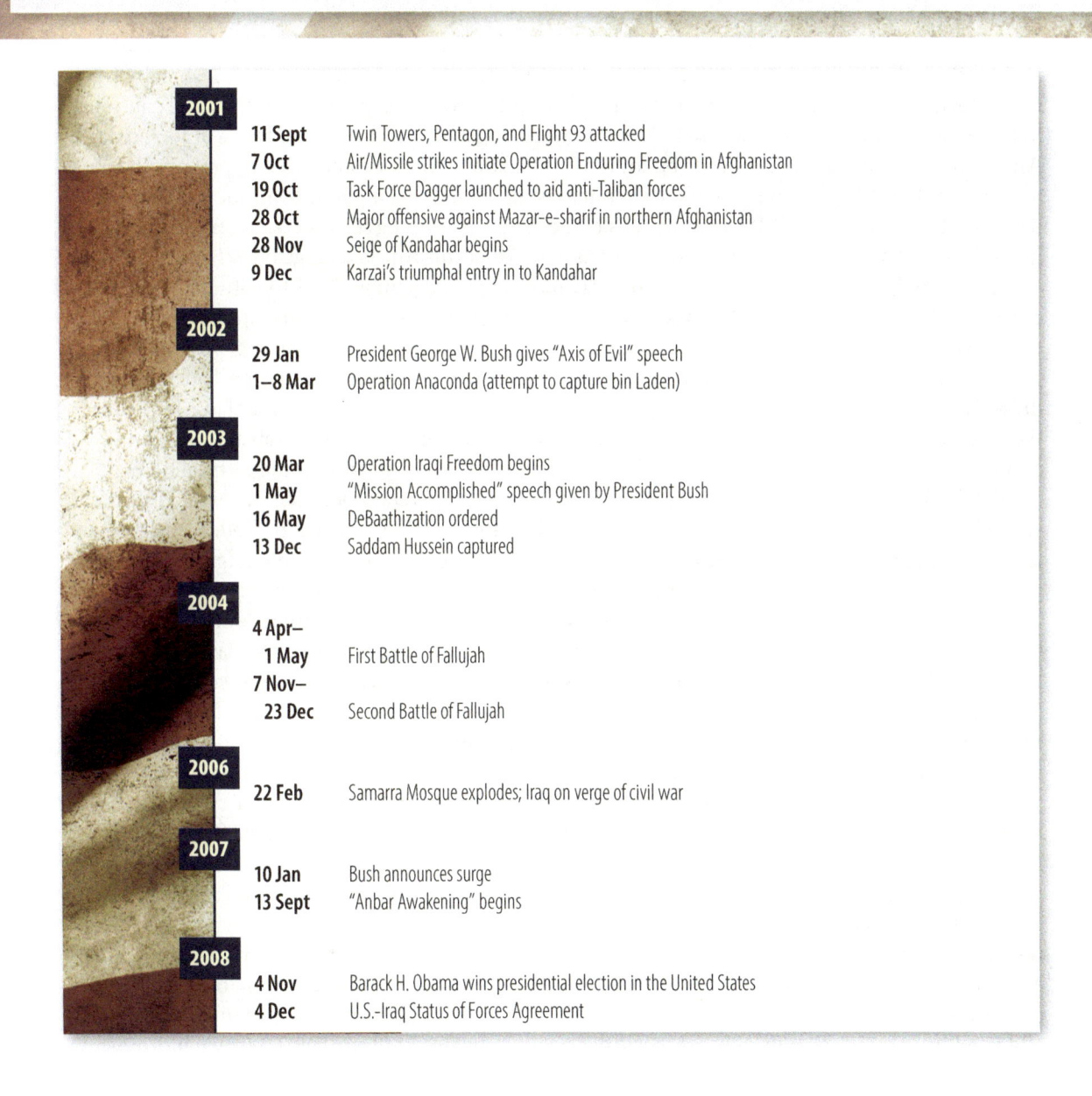

2001
- 11 Sept — Twin Towers, Pentagon, and Flight 93 attacked
- 7 Oct — Air/Missile strikes initiate Operation Enduring Freedom in Afghanistan
- 19 Oct — Task Force Dagger launched to aid anti-Taliban forces
- 28 Oct — Major offensive against Mazar-e-sharif in northern Afghanistan
- 28 Nov — Seige of Kandahar begins
- 9 Dec — Karzai's triumphal entry in to Kandahar

2002
- 29 Jan — President George W. Bush gives "Axis of Evil" speech
- 1–8 Mar — Operation Anaconda (attempt to capture bin Laden)

2003
- 20 Mar — Operation Iraqi Freedom begins
- 1 May — "Mission Accomplished" speech given by President Bush
- 16 May — DeBaathization ordered
- 13 Dec — Saddam Hussein captured

2004
- 4 Apr–1 May — First Battle of Fallujah
- 7 Nov–23 Dec — Second Battle of Fallujah

2006
- 22 Feb — Samarra Mosque explodes; Iraq on verge of civil war

2007
- 10 Jan — Bush announces surge
- 13 Sept — "Anbar Awakening" begins

2008
- 4 Nov — Barack H. Obama wins presidential election in the United States
- 4 Dec — U.S.-Iraq Status of Forces Agreement

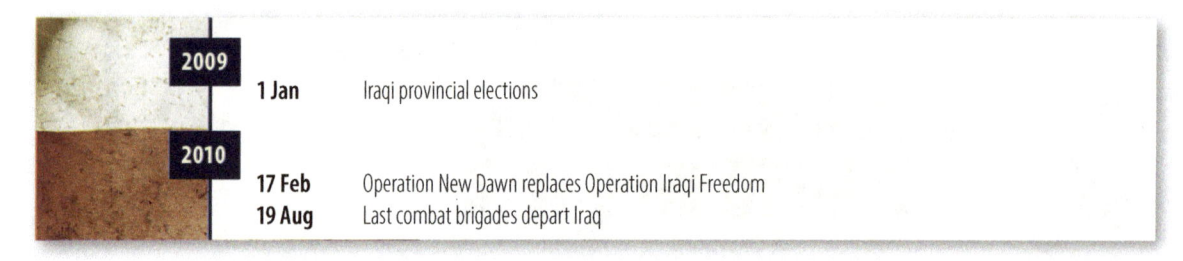

2009	1 Jan	Iraqi provincial elections
2010	17 Feb	Operation New Dawn replaces Operation Iraqi Freedom
	19 Aug	Last combat brigades depart Iraq

Go to www.khpcontent.com to watch a video introduction for this chapter.

Powell's apparent mercy and Schwarzkopf's willingness to display generosity to the defeated representatives of Saddam Hussein had left much undone and would contribute to the need for another war against Iraq. Continuing to overfly Iraq and engaged in one of the 1990s typically inane operations described as Operations Other Than War (OOTW), the United States, once again under an international umbrella organization, remained responsible for securing the overfly zones of northern and southern Iraq. Facing almost daily challenges with deadly cat and mouse games whereby Iraqis would turn on their anti-aircraft radar and American pilots would respond in kind, the bill continued to increase for America's willingness to hold the world together. As the United States enforced a silly American program designed to trade oil for food, the nation remained anchored in perhaps the most unstable and hostile place on planet Earth, purchasing Iraqi oil so it could continue to fly over and drop bombs on the Iraqis.[399] The inability to say "no" and a prevailing sense of overconfidence exuded from the ranks after Desert Shield and Desert Storm. All of this would change on **9/11**.

A confused nation awoke on a bright Tuesday morning in September 2001 to witness the senseless death of 2,973 Americans. Amid televised scenes of confusion, it quickly became apparent the attacks on the World Trade Center (again), the Pentagon, and an apparent near miss on the Capitol Building, had a common thread. Proudly taking credit for the attacks, the Saudi Osama bin-Laden hoped to draw the infidels into war with the Dar-al-Islam, or "world of submission." Memories last a long time in the Middle East, and while anguished Americans asked why, elements in the Arab and Muslim world awaited the next round of the Crusades—the same Crusades that had ended in the 14th century.

Boldly claiming a new type of war, President Bush and his Secretary of Defense, Donald Rumsfeld, excitedly witnessed the virtual overnight collapse of the Taliban ("the students," or "cadets") in Afghanistan who they blamed for serving as an Al-Qaeda breeding ground. Entering into Afghanistan after a prep fire of long range missiles, SOF operators and their Northern Alliance allies quickly devastated their Taliban enemies. The **RMA** (Revolution in Military Affairs) was represented by the use of the Tactical Air Control Parties (TACPs) and special forces detachments with air force personnel who "lazed and blazed" their way, often on the back of draft animals across Afghanistan within a month. Similar to the Soviets, British, and a host of other invaders, the Afghans faced rapid defeat, but would reemerge from these same ashes and unify on the basis of an ancient warrior ethos. Taken in by the rapid victory, it had appeared that Americans had accomplished in eight weeks what the Russians had failed to do with 100,000 troops in nearly a decade.[400] Apparently the new "super soldier" armed with a laser pointer could rain death from above with an accuracy that would have taken waves of bombers to have equaled from World War II. Like First Manassas in the Civil War or Ia Drang in Vietnam, a type of "victory disease," or overconfidence quickly set into the minds of military planners. Today Afghanistan, tomorrow the world!

Donald Rumsfeld didn't seem to make many friends. Possessed with an irritating habit of returning questions with questions, he had been greatly encouraged by the apparent Revolution in Military Affairs (RMA—see page 176) manifested in the rapid and apparent victory in Afghanistan. Rumsfeld believed private contractors and technology could allow a cost-savings by deflating a bloated military. A big fan of recent writings arguing against a "big army" approach, Rumsfeld

---

399. Crocker, *Don't Tread on Me*, 389.
400. Max Boot, *War Made New* (New York: Gotham, 2006), 382.

Figure 12.1 Ground Zero after 9/11

probably micromanaged the military more than any Secretary of Defense ever had. The **neo-Cons**, or neo-conservative movement, reflected the views of many in the George W. Bush administration. To many thinkers in the neo-Conservative movement, the relatively easy victory in Afghanistan would justify war in Iraq, Syria, or just about anywhere some Hitler wannabe type seemed to threaten. The horrors of the Holocaust had not been lost on this community, and after a mysterious series of letters circulated around the United States and through Washington, D.C. containing weapons' grade anthrax, the intelligence community became open to suggestions for potential enemies. The American intelligence community that had been weakened after Vietnam in its ability to employ human intelligence assets now went from a reactive to proactive search in an attempt to desperately follow any potential terror lead that might involve weapons of mass destruction (**WMDs**). The president had spoken forcefully and passionately after 9/11 when a desperate search for potential enemies had commenced. The extent to which Iran, long covetous of the post-colonial border with Iraq and flanked by friendly Shia Muslims to the oil-rich south in Iraq, encouraged this through disinformation has never been publically explored.

U.S. prewar planning continued to be sacrificed to time and political expediency. Rumsfeld forced Chief of Staff of the Army General Eric Shinseki into retirement when he had the temerity to announce that he thought too few troops had been deployed for the job. Voices of other generals such as Marine Anthony Zinni likewise argued unsuccessfully that it would take up to 100,000 troops to hold a post-war Iraq, and CENTCOM's (Central Command) operations planners called for three corps and some 380,000 troops in all, not counting support troops, and an anticipated 10-year occupation. Rumsfeld pushed Zinni's replacement, General Tommy Franks, to get his army ready to fight quickly. Rumsfeld wanted to use what he called a Running Start, because he believed a light force of as few as 18,000 troops could do the job, particularly in light of the wonderfully rapid fall of Afghanistan. Franks tried desperately to create his own Generated Start strategy which involved a 72-hour air campaign before pushing on to Bagdad after a slower buildup of 250,000 troops.[401] Such old school talk sounded "big army" and irritated Rumsfeld, who had peered into the future since Afghanistan while resurrecting a return to the Kennedy administration's culture of disdain for a brown-shoe military opinion. Rumsfeld insisted the new military could and should go into Iraq lighter and faster. Particularly disturbing seemed to be Rumsfeld's propensity to scrutinize troop lists, micromanaging as if he had remained in the civilian sector. Alteration to the

---

401. Michael R. Gordon and Bernard E. Trainor, Cobra II (New York: Pantheon, 2006), 54.

TPFDL represented a particularly egregious mistake and one that would leave the military short-handed in personnel and weapons after its brief campaign to take Iraq.[402]

General Tommy Franks

Courtesy of the United States Department of State, Office of International Security Operations, January 8, 2003

A profane man who seemed to see the world in terms of the present, many today are critical of General Franks, the man who succeeded in destroying Saddam Hussein. As the Commander of CENTCOM, Franks was worn down by the incessant micromanagement coming from the Secretary of Defense's office. Beguiled by both the "transformation" and "revolution of military affairs," civilian leadership more than ever needed a strong and respected voice of moderation to stand up and speak for military realities based on a broad world view of study. Military leadership owes it to civilian leaders to sometimes say no. The moral courage in this requirement may mean the end of careers and missed opportunities for promotion, but it is the Christian principle of the long-term view of eternity that enables one to rest on the fruits of the Spirit. It is the love of nation and the trait of self-control that enables us to be able to take the rejection of our leadership ideas in the short-term. The necessary patience, temperance, and faith to keep working in sometimes utterly thankless conditions is a function of the hope that is within us. General Eric Shinseki of the Army Chief of Staff had openly expressed concerns about troop numbers to be used in Iraq before the invasion and, as a result of his honesty, became ostracized and retired shortly thereafter.[403] A return to the dysfunctionality of the Vietnam era seemed apparent and though General Tommy Franks served his country well in a tough environment, in the end his vulgar persona left him brutally criticized by subordinates. His seeming inability to push back against Secretary of Defense Donald Rumsfeld left the Army in a precarious position without the numbers necessary to either guarantee victory in Iraq or to exit gracefully as seen previously with the Powell Doctrine. Frank's hesitation in securing the border with Pakistan and the decision to not utilize the equipment and forces prevented by Turkey from crossing their border further placed the American military and the mission at risk. In his memoirs, Franks claims the War in Iraq ended as he had expected, but Lt. Gen Ricardo Sanchez who replaced Franks on the ground in Iraq claimed he had been told by Franks that American forces would be out of Iraq by 2003. Basically outplayed by Secretary Rumsfeld, Franks would end up retiring almost immediately upon conclusion of initial combat operations in Iraq, while victory still seemed certain. The contributions of General Franks would, indeed, place a victory in the win column of Modern American military history, but the fact that American forces are still engaged in Iraq and Afghanistan as of 2016 indicates he probably should have fought harder for the forces necessary to secure the peace and to demand the implementation of an exit plan. Sometimes when we win, we lose, and sometimes when it seems our careers are over, we have actually won. Throughout the modern American military history experience we have seen the thread of selfless service from General Pershing to the present. The ability to see the big picture while conducting the real fight is the key to effective military leadership, and whether a star is received or not, the contributions each member makes in service will have eternal ramifications for good or bad. After all, being a servant is what the military is all about.

---

402. Ibid., 97.
403. Ibid., 403.

President Bush, in response to a February 27, 2003 UN proclamation of non-compliance in dealing with UN weapons inspectors, warned Hussein with an ultimatum. Saddam ignored Bush and within 48 hours bombs began exploding over Baghdad.[404] Saddam Hussein had probably gotten rid of most of his weapons of mass destruction. Operation DESERT FOX, launched over a period of four days in December 1998, had probably convinced Hussein to get rid of these chemical weapons. Fear of the Iranians might have led him to be so stubborn. Some authors contend he never believed the Americans would actually attack Iraq.[405] Instead, the more likely foe would be the Iranians. Hadn't the Americans showed they feared entering Iraq at the end of Desert Storm? Saddam continued to believe he remained safe behind the sand and deserts of the Middle East, where those Americans with their dependence upon air power could never launch forces with the stomachs to fight. If they could, they would have. The solution would be the **Fedayeen**. Like a home guard, various weapons caches planted throughout the Iraq countryside would soon become the real threat to invading American forces.

A simultaneous advance through Iraq would follow a very short bombing campaign. Unlike the air war in Desert Storm, Operation COBRA II, the attack into Iraq, would not be a long preliminary attack, possibly because of the numbers depleted by the Secretary of Defense's desire for quick action. Because of Turkey's unwillingness to allow American forces to converge on Bagdad from the north and south, the marines generally advanced from the southeast, going north up the Tigris River in a campaign reminiscent of Xenophon in 400 BC.[406] The army's 3rd ID would attack from the southwest up the Euphrates River. Like a simultaneous right-left punch, a mostly **freeway war** ensued. At Nasiriyah, marines attempted to secure bridges the army had already crossed, and traffic jams slowed maneuverability.[407] The danger of being hit in the grill doors at the vulnerable rear of the tanks necessitated the depletion of combat strength to guard underpasses and on-ramps for fear of being hit in the rear. Here the failure to properly pre-war plan the numbers in the interest of haste caused nervous officers to worry that the force may not have the inertia to continue. The arrowhead had begun to erode. Nevertheless, by the second day's advance and halfway to the objective, sandstorms hit. Foolish Iraqis thinking the buttoned up U.S. tanks and Bradleys could not see them, forgot the thermal optics could still see them and received an instant pass to the afterlife.

At **Samawah,** during a disastrous Apache raid against the Republican Guard, Medina Division saw its security compromised by a system of lights turned off and on reminiscent of Somalia. Cell phones used to warn defensive positions of an impending attack resulted in walls of small-arms fire and S-60 missiles fired high to force the choppers down into the flying lead. Virtually every helicopter in 1-227 returned with bullet holes, and seven aircraft remained lost to enemy fire.[408]

Amazingly efficient but at odds with the AWoF of self-reliance and innovations, the Blue Force Tracker made its combat debut in Iraq. Officers could risk micro-management while easily observing on a computer screen the exact locations of troops. The use of technology, though, revealed American vulnerabilities when the United States had to negotiate with other nations for satellite space to be able to use its amazing network centric approach to Baghdad. Marine air continued to pummel the enemy with breathtaking accuracy and a 10 X 10 mile **tab system** which allowed commanders within a 30 X 30 mile kill box to open and close them. No longer did a cumbersome Fire Support Coordination Line mark the beginning of close-air support or supporting arms. The battlefield could be finessed now—down to where an attacking force could face a front line in almost any direction.

---

404. Crocker, *Don't Tread on Me*, 394.
405. Ibid. 65.
406. Robert D. Kaplan, *Imperial Grunts* (New York: Random House, 2005), 308.
407. Gordon and Trainor, *Cobra II*, 280.
408. Ibid., 274.

Figure 12.2

Flying aircraft tankers bravely risked a fiery descent by flying over the enemy with nothing but courage and fuel. As the much-feared Karbala Gap loomed ahead and while brushing aside small arms attacks, the advancing juggernaut of exhausted soldiers sped through the last natural obstacle on its approach to Baghdad. Advancing on Baghdad, the airport was secured by exhausted troops who held against counterattacks, while "**Thunder Runs**" out into the city and into the airport proper projected what commanders hoped would signal to the Iraqis an American victory, and the result would be a stand down. A swift and conclusive 21 day campaign ended with 138 Americans dead; the time would have seemed ripe for leaving such as in the earlier Iraq War, but alas, ideology replaced strategic necessity.

Over-optimistic diplomatic successes after Operation **Cobra II** would see Libya surrendering weapons of mass destruction. While a global media shifted in their studio chairs uneasily with the idea of an American victory, a post-Vietnam type of distrust of American military force decried what seemed to be the unraveling of Iraqi society because of the American intervention. Other thinkers gushed with excitement at the entire world being cleansed by future American military operations. The American propensity to see the world in black and white had led to overconfidence. The beginning of widespread looting and disorder seemed at odds with the liberation of "good people." Like the Union Army advancing through the South followed by the newly-freed slaves, no one had really thought through what to do next. Slowly the question emerged, where were all of the cheering crowds?

Sergeant First Class Paul R. Smith

...When his Task Force was violently attacked by a company-sized enemy force... Sergeant First Class Smith quickly organized a hasty defense consisting of two platoons of soldiers, one Bradley Fighting vehicle and three armored personnel carriers. As the fight developed, Sergeant First Class Smith braved hostile enemy fire to personally engage the enemy with hand grenades and anti-tank weapons, and organized the evacuation of three wounded soldiers...Sergeant First Class Smith moved under withering enemy fire to man a .50 caliber machine gun mounted on a damaged armored personnel carrier. In total disregard for his own life, he maintained his exposed position in order to engage the attacking enemy force. During this action, he was mortally wounded...

excerpt from Congressional Medal of Honor citation

Courtesy of the United States Army

General Tommy Franks and General Jack Keane both quickly retired after Cobra II, which marked the ending of the invasion of Iraq. Neither felt the United States should remain, but Rumsfeld's aura of invulnerability may have stayed their opinions at this point. The military thought the mission had been accomplished as in the First Iraq War. It was time to go home. Events would prove otherwise, however. A bumbling attempt at de-Baathification of the new Iraqi military again left historians thinking of the American Civil War where former Confederates had been prevented from serving in political positions due to an "iron-clad oath." Forgetting most Arab males had a proud tradition of military association, many with the former Hussein regime found themselves blocked out of future service. To make things worse, the unfortunate name given to the new military in actuality represented an Arabic profanity! Increasingly, the disenfranchised Iraqi veterans remembered those weapons stashes located throughout the country by Saddam who had relied on his Fedayeen to protect them from the real enemy—Iran.

Landing triumphantly and cheerfully piloting himself aboard the aircraft carrier *USS Abraham Lincoln*, President Bush made a speech praising the military. Unfortunately behind him was a banner that read, "Mission Accomplished." The banner had been hung celebrating the end of a naval deployment, but the imagery chosen delivered an unfortunate sense of completion at odds with the message delivered by the president to the effect that the United States "will stay until our work is done . . . and we will leave behind a free Iraq"; it guaranteed failure. Well-intentioned ideals reminiscent of the Union during the Civil War reflected an idealistic desire, but one akin to a type of mission creep. Without a declaration of war and with no stated pre-war goals, the military would be groping for a strategy for the rest of the war while the American public and political leadership would be increasingly beholden to images broadcast by the media.

Such an image came, luring Americans into a fight and leading to defeat. Fallujah saw U.S. forces deployed in response to the grisly killing and desecration of Blackwater contractors over a bridge. This image demanded results, and the marines would kick doors down on their way into the **First Battle for Fallujah**. The attack launched on April 5, 2004 by four marine battalions initially made solid progress, but the opposition had invited Al Jazeera into the city. Terrible images of reputed atrocities at the hands of the infidels managed to unite the Sunnis and Shias who had been at each other's throats up to this point. Within days of finishing off the enemy, the order to stand down came. Marine Commander Jim Conway is quoted as saying, "Al Jazeera kicked our butts."[409] Breaking on top of the fight in Fallujah came reports of detainee abuse at Abu Gharib prison. As

---

409. Bolger, *Why We Lost*, 179.

Figure 12.3

General George Casey Jr. of Multi-National-Force Iraq said, "The last week of March and the first two weeks of April 2004... were a strategic disaster for America's mission in Iraq."[410]

By November 2004, it seemed American resolve had returned just in time for elections. With troops sent back into Fallujah, this time there was no backing out. Marines and soldiers fought house to house in the Second Battle of Fallujah, using tanks as snipers and essentially destroying anything in their way. LTG Daniel Bolger in *Why We Lost* compares the marines in Fallujah to their predecessors on Peleliu and Okinawa.[411] As the American military ground on in Iraq in its attempt to hand over a "free nation" to the Iraqi people, the decision to rotate troops by units may have proven instrumental in preventing another post-Vietnam disaster. As Americans worked side-by-side with Iraqis in Operations Forward I and II, attempts to pacify failed abysmally and the nation continued to teeter into civil war between Sunni and Shia Muslims. With the elections of 2006, however, the **Iraqi surge** began.

General David Petraeus had assisted in the revised Field Manual 3-24 entitled *Counterinsurgency*. Petraeus represented the best of the military's thinkers and had a political knack for gaining a following from both academia and the media. Authors previously critical of the efforts of the George W. Bush administration found a general somewhat reminiscent of Maxwell Taylor that they could appreciate. Armed with a surge in manpower (a credit to the decisiveness of the president, as in the Philippines) soldiers and marines would patrol and fight! Entering neighborhoods, putting up high platforms with cranes at night, often using SEAL sniper teams, and bringing in Jersey barriers to surround teams of soldiers who would patrol, the Americans demonstrated that they had entered the fight to stay. As soldiers used handheld identification devices and sometimes retinal scans, records of neighborhoods allowed the Americans to displace the growing al-Qaeda

---

410. Ibid., 179.
411. Ibid., 188.

insurgency that had emerged under the sometimes unfair Shia civilian leadership. The "Sunni Awakening," as it would be called, increasingly saw al-Qaeda driven out as Arabs turned toward the Americans. By 2006 the United States not only had become bogged down in a seemingly hopeless pacification program, it began to experience deadly, explosively formed penetrators (**EFPs**) proven to be of Iranian manufacture.[412] The **IED** (improvised explosive device), a distance-activated bomb or mine, usually activated by a cell phone, now had been replaced by something even deadlier and capable of throwing armored vehicles over on their backs. Eventually, through a messy process carried on the back and through the guts of America's terrific military members, a "**Strategic Framework Agreement**" would euphemistically pass for a treaty (a stated treaty eluded policy makers in the same mysterious way a declaration of war did). A "Sunni Awakening" saw Americans fighting their way into Baghdad and, as Bing West said, the Sunni Arabs of Ramadi made common cause "with the strongest tribe."[413] The decision to stand and fight at the **Second Battle for Fallujah** and the hard-won respect of the Arabs earned through countless violent patrols had paid dividends it seemed.

With only the United States remaining in Iraq, by 2009 it had become time for the Americans to also leave. A new president had arrived and he had determined combat would end by 2010 and that all American forces would leave by December 31, 2011.

Essentially trapped between sectarian violence between the nation's **Shia** majority (viewed by the Arabs [**Sunni**] as inferior pawns of Iran to the south) and the Sunni, mostly Arab minority, the United States succeeded in holding a post-colonial drawn nation-state together while battling an al-Qaeda insurgency. America and its troops gave their all—blood and treasure—and would leave Iraq behind with a semblance of order. On November 14, 2011 the last U.S. soldier died from the blast of an IED. The epitome of the Christian ideal of service, this single life—largely unnoticed in its passing—personified the sacrifice, sweat, and deprivation suffered by the best America and its families had to offer.[414]

Key Terms:

9/11	Samawah	EFP
RMA	Tab System	IED
Neo-Cons	Thunder Runs	Strategic Framework Agreement
WMD's	Cobra II	Shia
TPFDL	First Battle for Fallujah	Sunni
Fedayeen	Second Battle for Fallujah	
Freeway War	Iraqi surge	

---

412. Michael R. Gordon and Bernard E. Trainor, *The Endgame* (New York: Pantheon, 2012), 319.
413. Bolger, *Why We Lost*, 251.
414. Ibid., 275.

Thought Questions:

How would a declaration of war simplify or complicate pre-war planning?

What AWoFs were demonstrated in the Second Iraq War? Were these strengths, weaknesses, or both?

Chapter XIII
AFGHANISTAN

Corinthians 1: 6 "If we are distressed, it is for your comfort and salvation; if we are comforted, it is for your comfort, which produces in you patient endurance of the same sufferings we suffer." NIV

2009
- 6 July — Gen. Stanley McChrystal (Cmdr ISAF and U.S. forces-Afghanistan) promulgates Rules of Engagements; calls for "courageous restraint."
- 12 July — McChrystal orders Nuristan operations
- 1 Dec — President Obama announces Afghanistan "surge"

2010
- 23 June — General David Petraeus replaces McChrystal

2011
- 10 July — General John R. Allen replaces Petraeus

2012
- 2 May — Osama bin Laden killed by Navy Seals

2013
- 10 Feb — General Joseph F. Dunford Jr. replaces Allen
- 18 June — Afghans assume control of Afghanistan

Go to www.khpcontent.com to watch a video introduction for this chapter.

Waxed by the Americans, the Taliban remained quiet for many years. Afghanistan didn't take center stage as had Iraq, and Nixon's old Guam Doctrine of one and half wars seemed to occur within CENTCOM (Central Command). By 2006, while Iraq witnessed a thousand attacks a week, Afghanistan only had about a hundred. **NATO** (North Atlantic Treaty Organization) led the International Security Assistance Force (**ISAF**) and avoided fights and contact.[415] The utilization of Provincial Reconstruction Teams (**PRTs**) sought to improve living conditions throughout Afghanistan in a manner reminiscent of British India where dedicated civil servants worked with local officials and the military. The U.S. military had not resolved whether its strategy in Afghanistan involved nation-building or security, and time had started to run out.[416]

---

415. Ibid., 289.
416. Francis J. West, *The Wrong War* (New York: Random House, 2011), 242.

Sergeant First Class Jared C. Monti

…While Staff Sergeant Monti was leading a mission aimed at gathering intelligence and directing fire against the enemy, his 16-man patrol was attacked by as many as 50 enemy fighters. On the verge of being overrun, Staff Sergeant Monti quickly directed his men to set up a defensive position behind a rock formation… While still directing fire, Staff Sergeant Monti personally engaged the enemy with his rifle and a grenade, successfully disrupting an attempt to flank his patrol. Staff Sergeant Monti then realized that one of his soldiers was lying wounded in the open ground between the advancing enemy and the patrol's position… Determined not to leave his soldier, Staff Sergeant Monti made a third attempt to cross open terrain through intense enemy fire. On this final attempt, he was mortally wounded, sacrificing his own life in an effort to save his fellow soldier. Staff Sergeant Monti's selfless acts of heroism inspired his patrol to fight off the larger enemy force…

(Nuristan Province, Afghanistan, June 21, 2006)

excerpt from Congressional Medal of Honor citation

In the 2009 surge decision, President Obama sought recommendations from all the top admirals and generals, then made up his mind and ordered a different solution than the ones the military wanted.[417] Upon arriving in office, President Barack Obama received advice from a former CIA undercover that largely guided his thinking with an inherited war in Afghanistan. The strategy proposed to Obama identified a threat to the United States from Pakistan and would necessitate expanding the war from Afghanistan into Pakistan, where drones would be a part of the "carrot and stick" strategy to be employed.[418] Like Nixon drawn into Cambodia in 1970, Obama found himself attempting to plug security gaps made obvious by the cooperation of the Pakistani ISI (Inter-Service Intelligence), which had a vested interest in maintaining a continuing American presence in Afghanistan, thereby allowing the Pakistanis to focus their total attentions on their real perceived enemy—India. Following his advisors' logic, Obama's use of the new predator drone to hit high-profile targets offered a way for the Obama administration to finish its inherited commitments in Southwest Asia. Unlike Bush, President Obama had never wanted to be in Iraq; he had campaigned against the war in Iraq as a candidate and believed Afghanistan represented the real war. American forces attacked **Marjah** in Helmand Province to the south, the home of the Pashtuns. While all preparations for an attack seemed to be in full view of the media, which seemed to increasingly cast a watchful eye during Obama's War, the Taliban observed from the surrounding heights. The marines chose to clear the town from the inside out, employing helicopters to hop over possible IED's (improvised explosive devices). Parachute flares from circling aircraft revealed nothing to those on the ground without NVG's (night vision goggles). Battling through the streets and liberally using firepower from A-10 Warthog aircraft with 30 mm Gatling guns and the 9 inch (227 mm) HIMARS (High-Mobility Artillery Rocket System) similar to a JDAM (Joint Directed Attack Munition), a current generation "smart-bomb" used GPS to increase accuracy. Nevertheless, some civilian casualties did occur as a result of the Taliban shielding themselves with civilians.

---

417. Bolger, *Why We Lost*, 430.
418. Bob Woodward, *Obama's Wars* (New York: Simon & Schuster, 2010), 106.

General McChrystal hoped Marjah would represent another "Sunni Awakening" such as happened in Iraq.[419] Regardless of what would happen in Afghanistan, McChrystal would not be there to see it.

Throughout the Obama administration, military generals came and went at record rates. The magazine *Rolling Stone* quoted some loose talk that painted an unflattering picture of General Stanly A. McChrystal and his staff after he attempted to open up to the media, perhaps in a manner indicative of Petraeus' success in the Iraq surge. The media seemed to be calling the shots in the promotion and dismissal of military leadership. McChrystal's long service to the nation as a leader of special operations and "man hunters" would be replaced by the author of the Iraqi surge and a growing political prospect, General David Petraeus. By July of 2010, Petraeus would be brought to Afghanistan and would implement an **Anaconda strategy**, in part similar to that proposed by General Winfield Scott on the eve of the American Civil War. The strategy was intended to squeeze the various disparate elements of Afghanistan through a determined effort, but never had time for implementation.

Using elite "man hunters" or special operators and carefully-obtained intelligence as well as observation drones, Obama ordered the killing of Osama bin Laden in Pakistan. The men who killed the murderous mastermind belonged to SEAL Team Six and, in conjunction with the CIA, conducted a combined, multiservice effort, carried out by the Joint Special Operations Command (JSOC) called Operation Neptune Spear.[420] Since President Teddy Roosevelt, progressives and Democrats seemed comfortable using naval forces. This trend would continue with the use of SEALs under Obama in vital areas of the long Middle Eastern wars. Despite issues with helicopters reminiscent of the disastrous Operation Eagle Claw or Desert One in the Iranian desert a generation and a half ago in Iran, which started the long U.S. involvement in the Middle East, this mission succeeded. A painful lesson emerged. Mission creep continued to plague the military under Obama; now the war had spread to Pakistan and the military remained transfixed on the idea of killing a villain as a means of destroying the enemy. The need for special operations troops in what seemed to be an unending war certainly attracted more men to the ranks of these elite, while on the other side of the globe the continuing war in the Middle East seemed to be a magnet with different polarity. Frighteningly, it seemed the more of the leadership the United States killed, the more individuals who flocked to join the extremists.

Determined to be out of Afghanistan, Obama announced the end of the surge on June 22, 2011 and ordered 10,000 troops out by year's end, and the rest by July of 2012. The entire mission would conclude by December 31, 2014. President Obama, by virtue of setting a date, doomed any lasting counterinsurgency (CI) effort. CI demands assurance by the host government that the Americans are in the fight to stay; setting an arbitrary date may have made sense politically, but not militarily. In contrast to the Iraqi surge, which had not saved Iraq but had given time for the United States to leave with its head up, the Afghan surge of 2010 seemed reminiscent of the attempt by Westmoreland to resurrect the strategy of *quadrillage* at Cedar Falls in 1967—so empty had the military footlocker of ideas apparently become. Though cheated of glory in Afghanistan, Petraeus would be promoted to Director of the CIA and would be replaced by the quiet General John R. Allen USMC.

With some sad cases of substance abuse and suicide beginning to show up, the man who would end the show in Afghanistan was General Allen, a marine somewhat reminiscent of Eisenhower, and who likewise represented a smart officer who had survived various staffs and loved numbers.[421] A marine who served until the end, he was attacked in another mysterious media assassination with ungrounded accusations of impropriety emerging when e-mails were traced by the CIA to General Petraeus and an affair he had with a biographer. Perhaps most remarkable here is the convenient elimination of so many high-ranking generals at the end of an American war. Potential political purges aside, Americans remained confused by the long war in Afghanistan, now the longest war in the American experience.

---

419. Ibid., 329.
420. Chuck Pfarrer, *Seal Target Geronimo* (New York: St. Martin's Press, 2011), 1.
421. Ibid., 389.

General David Petraeus

Courtesy of Eric Draper, White House Staff Photographer

General Petraeus represented the scholar-soldier ideal. A synthesis between TRADOC's (see pg. 114) view of operational proficiency and the CGSC big-picture approach converged in the leadership of General David Petraeus. In essence, Petraeus represented the culmination of a generation of Army intellectual self-searching since the Vietnam War.

Following up on the Iraqi successes of General George Casey compared by Thomas Ricks to General Walton Walker in Korea, Petraeus would similarly achieve temporary success.[422] Petraeus would return to Iraq in 2007 with the newly-printed counterinsurgency manual FM 3-24 he had overseen production of at Ft. Leavenworth. The Army in Iraq drastically changed its approach under Petraeus' leadership in a manner again referred to by Ricks in Korean War terms as being like Matthew Ridgway (see pg. 85).[423] The truth is, America's Army has always been a learning army and the change of strategy from a conventional approach to that of a counterinsurgency during conflict, such as in the Philippines, nevertheless remained unprecedented at such a large scope. Like Krulak (see pg. 101) in Vietnam battling with President Johnson and General Westmoreland in an attempt to change strategy from conventional to counter-insurgency, Petraeus, seeking strategic change, came to the attention of President George W. Bush through a retired general. A master of using academia (he held a PhD from Princeton University) and the media to his best advantage, Petraeus also followed through on a counter-insurgency approach similar to that used by and argued for by the Marines in Vietnam; moreover, he used the same recipe for success seen by Generals Arthur MacArthur and Henry Lawton in the Philippines: with increased small unit patrols, the increased use of indigenous peoples through a newly trained Iraqi Army, and transitioning soldiers from kicking down doors, into building relationships with the people. Petraeus, in tandem with his subordinate LTG Odierno, would see civilian casualties in Iraq declined by 45 percent; thereby Petraeus served primarily to buy time for the policy establishment in the United States to catch its breath as President Obama came to office.[424]

By 2011 President Obama would also attempt to use the charismatic nature of Petraeus towards a surge in Afghanistan in another effort to buy time. The results in Afghanistan reflected a marked difference from those in Iraq because of different cultures and geography. The Army in the last year of George W. Bush's presidency had seen total casualties in Afghanistan of 798 per year but by the time of the Obama surge, this would exceed five thousand killed.[425] President Obama, who avoided military opinions had, as

(Cont.)

---

422. Ibid., 431.
423. Ibid., 435.
424. Andrew J. Bacevich, *America's War for the Greater Middle East* (New York: Random House, 2016), 284.
425. Ibid., 317.

> a presidential candidate, described Afghanistan as the "war we needed to win." Like John F. Kennedy, Obama turned grudgingly to the army for help and it was here Petraeus best served his nation by presenting a scholarly and non-threatening voice of wisdom predicated on years of service in various military commands, battlefields and schools. Though a seemingly unwinnable war in Afghanistan, Petraeus, through leadership and stated opinion, gave cover to major withdrawals of troops.
>
> Though General Petraeus's later service to his country as CIA director ended abruptly from personal failings, his contributions to the American military tradition are indelible. Audacious and bold in creatively applying the lessons of history, perhaps the best comparison to Petraeus with his flamboyant personality and use of the media would be Douglas MacArthur (see pg. 64), who could think outside the box on occasion, exhibited tremendous physical courage, and saw his career cut short due to political considerations. Petraeus also is reminiscent of the great George C. Marshall in his long service to his nation and ability to communicate with political leadership in an effort to ensure the American Army would remain the world's greatest Army for at least another generation.

After the blitzkrieg-like taking of Baghdad and Kabul, it seemed almost heretically un-American to suggest that the wars in Iraq and Afghanistan could still be lost. After all, had not both political parties come together after 9/11 in a spirit of cooperation? An examination of the historical record would have revealed the AWoFs described in this book, and one of these is impatience. Who and what was the actual enemy? By entering into nations with borders drawn during the European colonial experience, first by the British in the nineteenth century (Afghanistan) and for simple expediency in managing oil-rich resources in the Middle East during the early 20th century (Iraq), America found itself attempting to provide freedom to people in nations not truly reflecting the nation-state. Were the Pashtuns to control Afghanistan or the Shia in Iraq? The question of who the good guys were should have been asked in the very beginning and spelled out in a declaration of war that the people and the media would have understood. Our troops deserved better.

In retrospect, perhaps military leadership should have spoken up and recommended leaving the nations of Iraq and Afghanistan after initial victory. Instead, America increasingly faced a rapidly growing Fedayeen (Iraqi militia) and a nation essentially split along sectarian lines on the verge of civil war. Afghanistan, a nation proved unworkable since its inception, eluded American attempts at unification. As LTG Bolger suggests, if the United States had pulled out of Iraq at this point, these fights would have been the model of U.S. wars. Instead, the American military between Iraq and Afghanistan tried to police the Middle East and south central Asia, and had essentially spread itself too thin. Inherent in the creation of an all-volunteer military is the danger of a burden increasingly laid on the shoulders of the service people, their families, and potential failure of a protected political elite to recognize the limits this segment of society can bear.

Despite dysfunctionality in the decision making-process (a legacy from the Vietnam era), a major lesson learned in Vietnam involved the use of the Reserves and unit rotations. Improved morale for American troops came in various forms involving recognition by a grateful public; ranging from simple thank-yous to media coverage of units returning. Nevertheless the burden of a global peace continued to take its toll on a smaller segment of the population. PTSD and dreadful suicide rates plagued the segment of the American population carrying the load for so many. In part, the increased weight on the shoulders of this smaller population resulted from increased accuracy of munitions as well as increased deployments of these systems in a new type of fight.

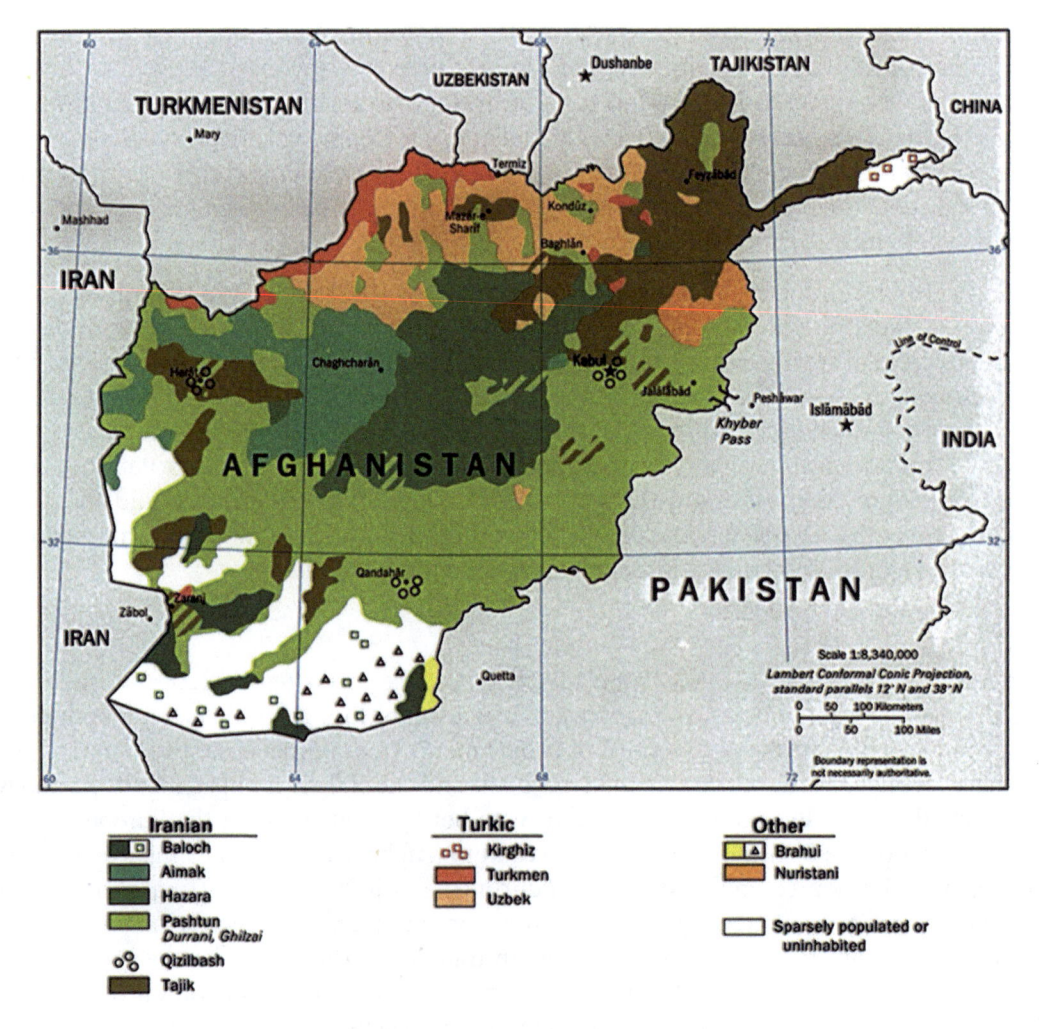

Figure 13.1 Afghanistan Ethnolinguistic Groups, 1997

The American military has always embodied the best aspects of American society. Sadly, the relative intelligence, health, and clean records of our service members have become increasingly unusual amongst those in our society of military age. Future leadership will be challenged as never before to provide unity in an increasingly divided society. Foreign policy will continue to demand legions of men and women willing to get in the dirt, squint with exhaustion at another sunrise during an aerial refueling, or try to remain standing on a frozen and pitching deck far from home. These servicemen and women deserve a vision clearly articulated and put into writing. They deserve leadership with the courage to vote on future actions, putting their own political futures on the line.

As Americans, we must pray for our leaders to exercise wisdom in the deployment of our precious remaining military assets and for the intelligent development of doctrine to ensure that they are trained to meet the demands of conventional war so atrophied during the recent military missions. Hopefully, American military leaders will, in the future, only advocate any military deployment that utilizes the American strengths or ways of warfare, and hopefully we will have political leaders with the good sense to listen to those charged with executing the military arts—the generals. Our military deserves public support. To maintain this public support in an era of instant media and conflicting images, American political leadership owes our military a declaration of war before deploying military forces, thereby identifying the enemy and clearly spelling out the terms for victory in advance and the requirements for a lasting peace to follow.

Key Terms:
NATO
ISAF
PRTs
Marjah
Anaconda Strategy

Thought Questions:

Who actually led the effort in Afghanistan militarily and how did the sublimation of U.S. forces to the UN in the Korean War establish a precedent for the effort in Afghanistan that would occur over a half century later?

What differences in war time Presidential leadership in this book can you identify and how have these helped or hurt the military efforts of the wars they represented? Should the generals have spoken up more forcefully in these wars or was America better served by their obedience?

Chapter XIV
THE WAR CONTINUES AND SPREADS

Proverbs 14:34 "Righteousness exalts a nation, but sin condemns any people."
NKJV

Go to www.khpcontent.com to watch a video introduction for this chapter.

When General Stanley McChrystal arrived in Afghanistan, he seemed to represent the emergence of a new type of warrior. The "golden age" of the special operator had arrived as we have seen with the killing of Osama bin Laden in the previous chapter. The ability to use UAVs offered the American military new challenges and broader responsibilities, many within the purview of the U.S. Special Operations Command (**SOCOM**).[426] If the American military can see it, it can be hit and killed, but the problem remained of having someone on the ground to direct this fire. The training of special operators, while expensive and necessitating another level of recruitment, offered the United States a converging global mission between conventional warfare and unconventional, utilizing the revolution in military affairs occurring with the proliferation of information and technology. The institutional challenge is to see doctrine developed that can standardize, within the legal framework, a global war. The global challenge facing today's military consists of the Middle East and the edges of the Islamic world, from Somalia to West Africa. The South China Sea continues to test the limits of American resolve and resources while UAV strikes have become a common occurrence without either the American public's knowledge or support.

The war in Iraq has grown, and the reintroduction of American "advisors" into the battlefield would imply another Iraq War has begun for the United States. The complications arising from the growth of ISIS have implications far beyond Iraq, however. To understand what is happening in Iraq, one must travel back to 2011 into Libya with Operation Odyssey Dawn, another attempt to use American force to effect regime change in the Islamic world.

In 1986 Operation El Dorado Canyon had marked American willingness to use force to change leadership in the Arab world. Representing the one nation that agreed to get rid of weapons of mass destruction, Moamar Gadaffi, the Libyan leader, actually responded to President G.W. Bush's call for nations to turn in these terrible weapons. Under the Obama administration, however, a new ideology seemed to be sweeping through the Middle East that appealed to the President and his Secretary of State, Hillary Clinton. The Arab Spring represented an uprising against autocratic authority, and following the precedent established back in 1986, the Obama administration used military force to take out Gaddafi with **Operation Odyssey Dawn** on March 19, 2011. A predator aircraft badly injured the Libyan dictator, but the result was similar to Iraq with Al-Qaeda's arrival to take advantage of the chaos. The same "**Arab Spring**" seemed to offer a democratic alternative to the backwards leadership

---

426. Ibid, 325.

of the nations in the CENTCOM area as responsibility began to spread into Syria where, by 2013, the Obama administration had made a deal with the Russians whereby the Russians secured the important Syrian port of Latakia in 2015. The Russians, after achieving immediate air superiority, began bombing the very rebels the United States had tried unsuccessfully to recruit and train at a cost of roughly $100 million each.[427] It appeared Al-Qaeda now had morphed into something even more sinister: **ISIS**. The Islamic State in Iraq and Syria emerged like a dark phoenix from the ashes of Al Qaeda and further threatened to rock the world through its creative use of torture and death; broadcasting its actions using social media. After Iran was bombed by the Russians and at war with the United States in Iraq, by 2015, it appeared American efforts since the Carter Doctrine of 1980 had only continued to unify the Islamic world against the West and had caused military force to continually be expended into areas not only in the Middle East, but beyond into Africa.

You read about Somalia in Chapter X and might recall how Operation Restore Hope had devolved into the long gunfight during the early 1990s popularized in the film *Black Hawk Down*. By 2007, the U.S. Air Force attempted to control acquisition and management of unmanned aerial vehicles in a pattern somewhat reminiscent of earlier inter-service power struggles between the World Wars to ensure primacy of air power and established roles with the advent of the aircraft carrier (or the fight for transport aircraft and helicopters during the late 1950s). Therefore the Air Force continued to police the skies off of the vital Horn of Africa with the AC-130 Spectre gunships, the same awesome platform that had been used to squeeze the North Vietnamese use of the Ho Chi Minh Trail after the Tet Offensive (see Chapter IX). The United States in Somalia again attempted to curb another Al-Qaeda offshoot called Al Shabab, in what increasingly appeared to be a bloody international contest of whack-a-mole. The American propensity to try to find a technical solution to what appeared to be a Middle Eastern morass led to increased reliance upon the UAV/Drone.

The **MQ-1** unmanned aerial vehicle has become America's weapon of choice since 2001. Initially used in the air war over the former Yugoslavia in the late 1990s, the drone and its counterpart, the Hellfire missile, have been used in increasing numbers. According to Colonel Andrew J. Bacevich, to whom much of this chapter is indebted, "Between 2004 and the day George W. Bush retired from office, the annual tally of U.S. drone strikes in Pakistan reached double digits only once. During Obama's first term, UAV (unmanned aerial vehicle) attacks in that country averaged 75 per year, peaking at 128 in 2010."[428] Colonel Bacevich again said, "Of the 99 confirmed U.S. drone strikes in Yemen that occurred between 2002 and mid-2015, all but one occurred on Obama's watch."[429] Obviously, the war had not just spread to Pakistan, but the UAV and the Hellfire missile saw further employment in the Global War on Terror to Obama's renamed **Overseas Contingency Operation** in 2009. The problem of American assassinations and targeted kill lists did not seem to be preventing the emergence hostile enemy leaders. As the American military in 2016 fought what Chairman of the Joint Chiefs of Staff Martin Dempsey called "the decisive battle in the ground campaign" in Mosul, Iraq,[430] the Chairman had earlier stated an opinion that America had entered into a long war, or a "generational problem."[431] The considered opinion and expression of a long war seemed

---

427. Ibid, 331.
428. Ibid, 334.
429. Ibid.
430. Ibid, 348.
431. Ibid, 356.

to be predicated on the view that chaos had been unleashed from Afghanistan to Africa. The appearance of an American military quagmire had emerged.

While the American military continued to see drone strikes and special operations troops fighting in various locations from the Philippines to Northwest Africa, concerns about the ability of American forces to fight a stand-up conventional fight emerged, particularly in light of the naval challenges faced by the United States from Russia and China.

As Russian control of airspace over Turkey in 2016 continued to heighten international tensions, an unfortunate series of bellicose events in the Baltic served to remind the United States of the need to remain strong conventionally, and served to remind military thinkers of the need to avoid becoming bogged down in unconventional conflicts around the globe. AFRICOM (Africa Command), one of the newest of the U.S. Department of Defense Commanders' areas of responsibilities, has been the scene of largely unsuccessful attempts to train and encourage democracy. Recent attempts to ensure "security engagement" and to stabilize nations in western and central Africa have resulted in the Pax Americana attempting to counter Islamic insurgencies in Chad, Mali, Mauritania, Niger, Nigeria and Cameroon. Groups such as Boko Haram have largely been unsuccessful, while the defense establishment has worked to see "partnerships" formed between National Guard units in various states with mentor armies from Botswana to Djibouti. The American military has gone from attempting to create order in a post-Cold War world, to attempting to secure oil supplies and managing the Middle East, working to protect Saudi Arabia while balancing the various powers and threats emerging in this "generational war." What might the future hold?

In addition to the aforementioned violations of Turkish airspace, the Russians have, as of this writing, engaged in what the Pentagon calls "aggressive simulated attacks" in the Baltic Sea. Russian jets and helicopters flying dangerously close to an American destroyer, if not being intentional harassment, could qualify as a danger due to the series of international events a simple mistake or accident could cause. After Russian movements into Ukraine earlier in the decade, the historical expansion pattern of the Russians to deep water sea port access seems once again to have emerged. The potential of Russia coming into conflict with NATO in the Baltic or Turkey would be dire to the United States, which is bound by the 1949 treaty made during the Truman administration to collective and mutual defense where "an attack on any one nation . . . shall be considered an attack against them all." As we saw in Chapter X, the emerging autocracies coming out of the NATO-led war in Bosnia and Kosovo also included China.

Railguns firing electromagnetic projectiles at miles per second and light energy devices blasting targets at the speed of light may make their appearances someday in the South China Sea—should diplomatic efforts fail. The Chinese have been moving with historical patience and deliberation towards a blue water navy capable of projecting force to defend the growing interests of Chinese investments around the world. The Indian Ocean appears to be of primary significance, as well as penetrating the offshore barrier island chains important for American military strategy until the Korean War. The Chinese have worked hard to control the electromagnetic spectrum necessary for drone flights over the Maldives and into the vital and sparse South African port areas around Zanzibar and Dar es Salaam in Tanzania for the purpose of exploiting the abounding mineral resources of the South African interior. Again, as in the Baltic, American forces need to remain vigilant and knowledgeable in the face of what has become a forgotten conventional mission for the global American projection of force.

American military action today continues to result in unexpected missions and increasing commitments around the globe. As America runs the risk of imperial overstretch in this Pax Americana, it seems an increasing burden is placed on the fewer and fewer Americans who possess the requisite loyalty and commitment, as well as sobriety and honor to serve their nation. A plethora of social changes such as allowing homosexuals, and most recently transsexuals, to contribute to the enlarging need for military personnel continues a long tradition of using the military as a source for social and cultural change. Most of the world's nations are held together through a centripetal force that is called militarism. It is the long tradition of the American military to exercise restraint

> The Congressional Medal of Honor is the highest medal awarded for valor to members of the military. It is distinguished from other medals by being atop the pyramid of honor. Even how the medal is worn, around the neck as opposed to the chest, sets it apart from other medals. It is also the only medal that is awarded by the president in the name of Congress.[432] As a sign of respect and gratitude for their sacrifices, all Medal of Honor recipients are saluted regardless of rank. The Medal of Honor has progressed to attempt to adequately recognize true American heroes. As one Medal of Honor recipient, Specialist Peter Lemon, stated, "Whenever you see the medal, you see millions of people who have given their services and sacrificed for your freedom."[433] Of the 3,508 recipients, only sixty-seven are currently living.[434] The Congressional Medal of Honor serves as a reminder to American citizens of the cost of freedom.

and to submit to civilian authority. Transforming from a frontier constabulary to an imperial force with global ramifications, we have seen in this book how the Americans contributed to the defeat of fascism and ultimately communism after becoming a global power capable of projecting force in World War I. In Korea the trend towards beginning a fight beckoned irresistibly to political leaders, but consequentially they found it impossible to "close the deal," or to emerge victorious. The dysfunctionality of civil-military affairs led to a strategy that served to run out the clock and ensured the permanency of American military involvements abroad of questionable legality and suffocating rules of engagement. Emerging from the post-Vietnam experience with renewed confidence and technological efficiency, the American military learned it could please its political masters by effecting regime change and drastically changing offending nations through the profligate and inexpensive, at least in terms of manpower, use of air power, cruise missiles, and UAVs. The sad experience in the generational war that has consumed the United States in the larger Middle East has been to increasingly lay the burden on the shoulders of fewer and fewer who are willing to go into harm's way. Attempting to use the best of the best to eliminate leadership and continuing head long into war, the American people now face tough decisions involving even more ruthless adversaries and conventional giants. As the military continues to brace itself for the task of doing even more in the years ahead, it is the sincere hope that America's men and women will be granted the full measure of American support as evidenced by law to ensure either complete victory, or better yet, a final peace.

Key Terms:

SOCOM

Operation Odyssey Dawn

Arab Spring

ISIS

MQ-1

Overseas Contingency Operation

---

432. The Boston Publishing Company ed., *The Medal of Honor*, 95.
433. "Recipient Detail- Henry, Erwin," The Congressional Medal of Honor, https://www.cmohs.org
434. "Archival Statistics," The Congressional Medal of Honor Society, https://www.cmohs.org

Chapter XV
CYBER WARFARE

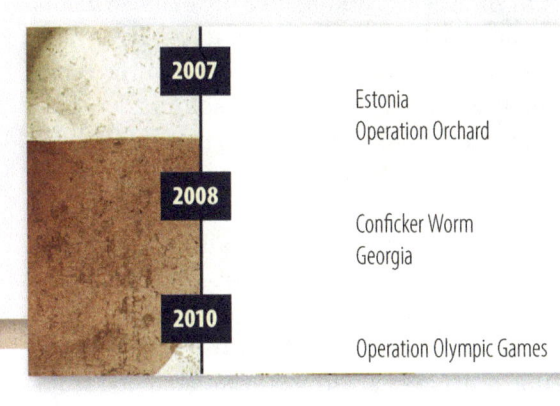

2007
Estonia
Operation Orchard

2008
Conficker Worm
Georgia

2010
Operation Olympic Games

Go to www.khpcontent.com to watch a video introduction for this chapter.

Warfare has entered space. The two types of space under consideration here are cyber space and outer space. Cyber space is invisible; where events occur at the speed of light, in many ways similar to outer space. To better understand cyber warfare, one must understand the current organizational structure of the military and where Cyber Command fits into the overall effort.

Currently, the Department of Defense has direct authority over the nine unified commands. These unified commands involve six areas of responsibility, or geographic areas around the world, and three functional commands. One of these functional commands is known as Strategic Command. Strategic Command has, among other missions, C^4SIR (command, control, computers, communications, security, intelligence, and reconnaissance). Within Strategic Command we find today's cyber warriors.

Cyber Command is a sub command within Strategic Command. The philosophies and approaches used to train for potential contingencies are currently spelled out by the Joint Chiefs of Staff in joint publication 3-12R. JP-312. Although such directives give guidance on how to train and coordinate forces, it remains up to the unified force commander to employ such assets as deemed necessary. Each service (Army, Marines, etc.) has its own component command; the Army, for example, has the United States Army Cyber Command.

Many feel Cyber Command should now be a separate component, like the Army or Air Force. Recall the historical parallel of how the Army Air Force achieved independence, becoming the Air Force in 1947. Evidence of potential change exists within the Department of Defense's budgets between 2013 and 2014. Within both budgets, the mention of "cyber" and the amount of money appropriated for Cyber Command headquarters grew exponentially.[435] Offensive missions seemed to parallel the attitudes of the Imperial Japanese when they took over vast amounts of territory quickly during the beginning of World War II. Just as the Japanese military tended to discount defensive considerations such as anti-ship-warfare (ASW) to prevent U.S. submarines from penetrating their defenses (see World War II: The War in the Pacific), likewise an American emphasis on the offensive leaves concern today about the possible neglect of defenses. A survey of the Department of Defense's Cyber Strategy Fact Sheet shows defense is in the second and third places behind offensive operations in its list of strategic goals and key implementation objectives.[436] A history of

---

435. Singer, P.W., & Friedman, Allan. *Cybersecurity and Cyberwar.* Oxford, NY, 2014, 134
436. U.S. Department of Defense Fact Sheet on Cyber Strategy, April 2015. https://www.defense.gov/Portals/1/features/2015/0415_cyber-strategy/Department_of_Defense_Cyber_Strategy_Fact_Sheet.pdf

cyber-attacks could explain this current posture and reveal the difficulty of defense in an invisible playing field.

The recent history of Cyber Operations reflects the model of linear massive fires we have seen since the time of the musket and the precision fire of the rifleman. As of this writing, something akin to social hysteria has gripped the United States since the election of 2016. A fear of an outside force meddling in our elections has created a narrative in some ways, taking on a life of its own. It is important to note that until recently there had been no deaths directly attributed to cyberwarfare, yet increased reliance on computer systems will, without question, cause catastrophe in the event of compromise. The first step is to recognize the true nature of the threat and the source.

Determining the source is no easy task. The military implications to the growth in technology is a function of globally changing social relationships. The somewhat bungling diplomatic confusion over how to handle the Iranian "Green Revolution," or the Arab Spring in 2011, reflected a dawning awareness of just how powerful the use of Social Media had become with the ability to maintain security with overlay networks that provided security from government control. Meanwhile, as government officials still struggled to understand how to maintain and delete email accounts, the real problem emerged: when does a government cease to be a government? In other words, what is the source of a cyber attack; who is actually shooting at us? Has an attack been launched from a government or from private individuals? What would appear to be a seemingly easy question to answer highlights the difficulty of properly determining just whom to blame.

Further determining who has attacked in cyberspace can also be determining if the offending party is a lone criminal, a gang sponsored by a hostile government, or a government itself. Earlier in the text (see the Air War over Serbia in Chapter X), the bombing of the Chinese embassy in 1999 seemed to mark the beginning of the end for the post-Cold War or New World Order period. A possible Chinese need to save face in response to the disastrous American bombing mistake may have led to the Hainan Island incident in 2001, when the Chinese forced down an American spy plane (Navy P-3 Orion). The Communist Party then encouraged non-governmental computer-smart citizens, or "**hacktivists**," of China to attack American websites in mass. Thousands of young Chinese, mostly teenagers, happily participated in a type of international attack.[437] How can such an army be held accountable—who is in command and how are they to be demobilized?

An instructive example demonstrating the challenges of determining who actually is "shooting" at us is the 2007 Russian attacks upon Estonia. The book, *Cybersecurity and Cyberwar* by P.W. Singer and Allan Friedman, demonstrates the difficulty in laying blame for such a cyber-attack. During the 2007 Estonian cyber invasion, in reaction to accusations by Estonia of Russian involvement, parliamentary leader Sergei Markov with an apparent lack of concern, said, "About the cyber-attack on Estonia... Don't worry, that attack was carried out by my assistant."[438] In fact, patriotic groups of Russian youth loyal to Vladimir Putin had conducted the attacks, following the Chinese model of creating sub-state armies. The point is, there is no international law or precedent to establish definitively when an individual acting with malice or if a government can be implicated in cyber space.

An example of the permanency and abstract nature of this new threat is the **Conficker worm**, released in November of 2008. The worm infected more than twelve million computers worldwide, creating a botnet (robot network) army of computers still awaiting commands. The creator of the worm now only needed to wake the computers up. The botnet never did wake up, fortunately, but a new frontier with an invisible threat now faced our cyber warriors. Someone somewhere had proved an ability to take over a large portion of the internet, instantly rendering the world system as a sort of hostage. President Obama, having just moved into the White House, immediately recognized the problem and said cyberspace is "real... and so are the risks that come with it." Cyber Command emerged from the Conficker experience. Intense interest in cyber capabilities would

---

437. Singer & Friedman, *Cybersecurity*, 114.
438. Ibid., 110.

constitute one of the first military initiatives of the Obama administration.[439] The new Cyber Command needed a strategy and had to determine where to defend and fight the war.

Just as it took centuries for rules of war to define what constituted proper and legal rules for fighting amongst belligerents, we have likewise entered a new phase in history. Nation-states must determine not just who is shooting at them, but how to determine the rules for the borders of this new invisible realm. For example, at what point does one become a hacker? Is it okay to watch someone in cyber world, but not touch? At what point has one transgressed or trespassed against a corporation, a bank, or a national intelligence office? Operations in Estonia in 2007 marked the beginning of the use of cyber operations to achieve specific state goals offering future guidance on what can be expected and tolerated amongst nation-states.

The problem for **Estonia** started with its decision to move a controversial statue dating back to World War II. Russians, upset at Estonia, initiated a botnet of a million computers from seventy-five nations;[440] it turned out twenty-five percent of the computers used to attack Estonia had been American based.[441] Estonia called out for aid, citing Article 5 of the Washington Treaty, calling for the collective defense of NATO, essentially arguing an attack on one is an attack on all. The nations of Europe then proceeded to ignore Estonia since geographic borders remained intact. The failure to mobilize helped illustrate the difficulty of collective cyber defense and determining precisely when an actual attack has occurred only in cyber world.

Apparently emboldened, in 2008 Russia similarly attacked **Georgia**. A denial of service attack virtually isolated Georgia in a way similar to Estonia. Focused attacks on key websites halted the government's ability to function, as Russian tanks rolled across the border. It seems the physical crossing of the border constituted the legally recognized violation of laws dating back to the Treaty of Westphalia in 1648. Though the computer attack came first and constituted an integral part of the attack, how a nation could respond to attacks and defend itself remained unclear. All fighters have to seize the initiative or offensive at some point to achieve victory. Israel illustrated how future war might seize the cyber offensive in response to a threat or perceived attack.

Operation Orchard in 2007 saw Israeli fighter aircraft crossing into Syrian airspace—a cyber-operation with a military result. Operating across the border through networks, the Israelis broadcasted false images on Syrian radar screens. Syrian operators did not even know of the Israeli attack until the first bombs dropped.[442] The Israelis, like the rifleman on the American frontier, had developed a smaller force armed with increased accuracy and had opted to violate recognized borders after securing the cyber environment. For the first time, the use of the cyber truly proceeded the associated use of physical military force.

Operation Olympic Games in 2010 saw the first use of a cyber-weapon that used the cyber space to produce actual direct physical damage. A "worm" crawled globally through the world's computer systems and focused on Iran. Using secret signing keys, which are very valuable codes that allow one to enter into and rewrite device drivers, the worm aimed for a specific target. An industrial controller served as the precise target of the worm, thereby making a small adjustment to the Iranian centrifuges, altering speeds and causing mechanical problems.[443] The damage to the Iranian nuclear program, still classified, resulted in untold damage. Israeli and perhaps a U.S.'s ability to enter into Iran's network actually caused a physical change to the consistency of plutonium in Iran's burgeoning nuclear arms program. Now cyber warfare had produced tangible results and consequences.

The idea of creating change that people could not control has always caused fear. The entire American military experience has always been one of an uncontrolled frontier offering continuous challenges. Americans tamed a hostile frontier and had employed the rifle in tandem with the musket to win its borders. The time-proven method of implementing new technology in concert

---

439. Bowden, Mark. *Worm: The First Digital World War.* Atlantic Monthly Press: New York, 2011.
440. Singer & Friedman, *Cybersecurity*, 122.
441. Ibid., 73.
442. Singer & Friedman, *Cybersecurity*, 127.
443. Ibid., 117.

with the old has insured American victories for centuries and continues to offer a way forward using the inherent American traditions of initiative, imagination, and creativity.

Charity Barker is a brilliant young undergraduate who embodies the American tradition of "thinking outside of the box" and is typical of the cyber warrior of today. Delightfully, but deceptively unassuming, the traditional countenance of a soldier is missing; replaced instead by an innocent smile. What catches one's attention quickly, however, is her focus. In her paper entitled Precision vs. Volume, Charity argues there are Two Types of Cyber-attacks, the Denial of service and the Advanced Persistent Threat. The description of these dual approaches to a cyber-attack remind us of why American military history is so important.

The **DOS** attack, or Denial of Service, is analogous to the musket line putting out a maximum amount of firepower with a minimum of accuracy and control. A denial of service attack is very "noisy," creating massive amounts of network traffic or volume. Think of explosions on the linear musket volley type of conventional battlefield. The use of these types of attacks, as we have seen, will continue to dominate any future military aggression. DOS attacks can serve to be a feint or deceptive move to keep an enemy off balance while we maneuver in for the kill.

The **APT** or Advanced Persistent Threat, on the other hand, reflects a precise attack somewhat analogous to the frontier woodsmen with his rifle deployed as a skirmisher. The APT relies upon a precise attack by an individual or a group working together using a very low network traffic volume in order to evade detection.[444] By evading detection, the source of the attack remains unknown, ensuring further lethality in future operations. In other words, the APT utilizes an ambush using cover and concealment in the invisible global battlefield of today's cyber realm. The historical comparisons to the American style of fighting developed on the frontier are obvious: we must continue to be open to new and affordable concepts of warfare, but only to the degree these changes can be purposefully planned and integrated with the successful time-proven principles of the past.

Since it is quite possible one will never know they have been cyber-attacked, a need for balance of both types of attacks must be considered in future planning as well as the defense. The American propensity to move quickly and to pursue "progressive" techniques often neglects the lessons of the past. For example, **DARPA** (Defense Advanced Research Projects Agency) had funded the creation of the internet, but had essentially abandoned the Internet security field during the Bush Administration; instead it focused its energies upon "network centric warfare."[445] Sacrificing security for glamour and quick gain is easy to do in a competitive environment—but one usually destined to end with disastrous results.

Space Warfare

The idea of outer space has excited American imaginations for generations. Though probably not as exciting as the science fiction many of us grew up on, outer space is inseparable from the study of cyber space. Space Command is a major command of the United States Air Force (itself a component) and the Army also has a space and missile defense command, (a major specialized command for the Army component) demonstrating the competitive nature for military institutions out in the "final frontier."

The similarities between the two invisible forms of space: cyber space and outer space, while obviously different, have many similarities since both have borders defined with difficulty and both represent the use of integrated technologies. Without the satellite networks circling the Earth, the "high ground" of operations on the surface of the planet could not operate since internet, for example, depends in large measures on satellites. The problem is like parking spaces on a college campus, there simply are not enough of them.

As of mid-2016, a count of 1,419 satellites operate around the globe. The current numbers have more than a 3:1 advantage to the U.S. in terms of numbers over China, with Russia in third place.

---

444. Barker, Charity. Email message to author, May 4, 2017.
445. Clarke, Ric.hard, & Knake, Robert K. *Cyber Warfare*. Harper Collins: New York, 2010, 132.

Bear in mind the first anti-satellite rocket successfully fired by the U.S. in 1985 demonstrated an ability to destroy satellites, and resulting debris could eliminate the others. With twelve nations currently in the space business, the ability of space command to protect American assets is more important than ever.[446] In 1995 the first "magic moment" occurred when GPS and unmanned systems merged; the United States advantage revealed itself clearly. Since then, the advantages of global positioning near the equator or control of locations in orbit have become secondary to the need to prevent jammers from ground systems capable of electronic bubbles that block GPS signals. The Russians demonstrated this technology to disable a Ukrainian drone in 2014.[447]

The American ways of fighting have conquered frontiers and remain strong even today. The love of the offense must, however, be balanced with security. For example, the Germans set the standard for offensive warfare when they took France in only forty-four days with only twenty-seven thousand dead. In the Iraq War it took half the time, and with .005 percent of the cost in terms killed—most of these by deadly fire. As dramatic as these results may be, the real danger may be the American preoccupation with the new. A lack of historical awareness today presents the risk of Americans forgetting older and less glamorous, but nevertheless time-proven, systems and practices. A desire to rapidly attack in Iraq in 2003 revealed dangers of poor planning on the high-tech battlefields of today.

The United States in Iraq found it had to borrow bandwidth and even batteries to continue the attack.[448] Future planning to integrate new platforms and systems must build upon those already proven. If the average 12-volt BA 5590 battery weighs 2.25 pounds and is required to power everything from radios to missiles, one would wonder why the Marines used 3,028 per day, but had no stockpiles of this vital war material in storage during the Iraq War. If the average truck can carry 2.5 tons, this means 6,813 pounds of batteries, or about three transport trucks per day, must be assigned specifically to this mission alone, thereby lengthening supply lines and increasing vulnerabilities to the enemy.[449] The real invisible danger facing the American military today in a time of rapid changes is not an enemy with newer cyber techniques or spacecraft, but the cost of uncontrolled acquisitions without taking into account the timeless proven principles of the past of integrating new technology with the old.

Key Terms:

Hacktivist

Conficker Worm

Estonia

Georgia

Operation Orchard

Operation Olympic Games

DOS

APT

DARPA

---

446. davidignatius@washpost.com. War in space is becoming a real threat. Article from *In Military*, March 17, 2017. http://inmilitary.com/war-space-becoming-real-threat/?utm_source=IME&utm_medium=newsletter&utm_content=war-space-becoming-real-threat&utm_campaign=20170317IME
447. Ibid.
448. Singer & Friedman, *Cybersecurity*, 188.
449. Ibid., 190.

Chapter XVI

HYBRID WARFARE AND POTENTIAL FUTURE CONFLICTS WITH CHINA AND RUSSIA

Matthew 7:3 "And why beholdest thou the mote that is in thy brother's eye, but considerest not the beam that is in thine own eye?"

Introduction

God created the world through time and space. The world's nations emerge from that space with characteristics that can be used to model and anticipate culture. Warfare is an aspect of culture, and while it changes over time, it presents broad patterns allowing one to anticipate future developments. Spatial considerations in the physical realm seldom change, but history is fluid. Particularly today, new technologies present themselves daily. The Russians and Chinese have long patterns of history, which give them unique perspectives and a **historical memory** that is often at odds with the United States—the military leader of the West today. The dangers and consequences of failing to see changes in the human context of culture and the potential consequences are apparent throughout our history. One example occurred in 1940, when Adolf Hitler misjudged the French building the West Wall and, in fact, found himself surprised at the relative ease of the blitzkrieg's success. The resulting overconfidence in large measure led to Hitler's disastrous decisions (from a German standpoint) to attack Great Britain in the air and to eventually turn on his former ally, the Soviet Union. Hitler's actions further persuaded Japan to enter the war without telling their German allies. Likewise, by misreading foreign cultures, the United States has found itself on the global stage in a postcolonial world. The United States has certainly served as a force for good, but the cost of failing to consider the cultural perceptions of other nations before acting has resulted in unintended consequences, such as the Russian and Chinese military resurgence. After the long costly encounters abroad indirectly in Eastern Europe and through direct interventions into East Asia, it is imperative for the United States to forge both a new way forward and a new approach to warfare.

Many military thinkers today believe the United States may have already lost this new type of war without realizing it. Oftentimes something as subtle as the simple display of a new national coat-of-arms can be instructive to the area analyst. In Russia, for example, the displayed return of the **two-headed eagle** holding three crosses, unseen since the time

The Russian two-headed eagle.

of the Czar in 1917 at the end of a war arguably started in Serbia, during 1993 caused little concern in the West, although in retrospect it probably should have.

As the remaining superpower, America's well-intentioned attempts to enforce world order since the end of the Cold War resulted in an overreliance on technology, subsequent military mistakes, and a lack of awareness of geographic and historical realities. As a consequence of these mistakes, Russia and China appeared ready to emerge as autocracies, thereby developing a unique type of hybrid warfare in response. **Hybrid warfare** can be defined as the blending of conventional and unconventional forces into the strategic, operational, and tactical levels of warfare. Russian military failures would lead to an introspection and a new doctrine attempting to stay "below the radar," or what is now commonly referred to as hybrid warfare. Over time, China transformed from a land power to a near peer threat mirroring American forces while pursuing a global strategy of expansion to its perceived borders both to the east and south, with a regional anti-access and area denial (**A2/AD**) strategy, as its economy thrives. China has remained fixated on Taiwan and has grown in conventional operations while exercising a horizontal form of warfare across the spectrum. The United States, weakened in large measure from decades of maintaining a permanent war-footing, is searching for a new strategy. The historical precedent for a Byzantine Defense Strategy exists.

Wars never end. The United States, historically an isolationist nation, seems intent on recreating the liberation of France in 1944. The Russians and Chinese, in contrast, have developed perspectives at war beyond the United States' conventional approach.

The Grand Strategic Dilemma

Led at various times by each of its major political parties, America has sought to transform the Greater Middle East into a reflection of itself through developing various democratic states, largely following colonial borders, while ignoring the region's cultural differences from the West. Perhaps more importantly, considering its skyrocketing national deficits, rival states have emerged and have grown more prosperous by seeking to maintain a constant fight against what appears to be a Pax Americana effort to create an American global empire relegating ancient and proud civilizations into secondary statuses.

The unintended consequences of warfare in the Greater Middle East at the beginning of the 1990s, and the air war over Serbia by the end, would lead to the rise of autocracies in Russia and China.

Rapid victories and the **Highway of Death** during the 100-hour Gulf War of 1990–91 eventually led to a decade of nonstop deployment in which the military was used to proactively combat injustice and evil. Neoliberal utopianism (maybe define what exactly this term entails) found a military counterpart in the Revolution of Military Affairs (RMA), which argued that information technology was transforming war's very nature in the same way the internet had changed the way business was viewed.[450] Airpower, the military language of neoliberalism, combined with a belief in war on the cheap eventually led to the United States' inextricable role in the Greater Middle East. Perhaps an intervention with far worse consequences occurred in Kosovo—the very region where World War I started. The Russians and Chinese, still recovering from their losses at the end of the Cold War, were alarmed by the rapidly growing and indiscriminate use of American military power throughout the 1990s and found themselves involved in a new type of war arguably born in the former Yugoslavia.

The Highway of Death: Operation Desert Storm, March 4, 1991.

---

450. Bacevich, 178.

> "The Road to Hell is paved with good intentions."

General Wesley Clark appeared to be a true believer in the power of RMA and led the U.S. effort into Bosnia and Kosovo, which would forever alter its relations with Russia and China. As Supreme Allied Commander Europe (SACEUR) or the military head of the **North Atlantic Treaty Organization (NATO)**, Clark led a movement that many, including the State Department, classified as a terrorist organization and in the process alienated followers of Islam as well as former allies. According to Andrew J. Bacevich, for the Serbs, "Kosovo possessed a significance akin to that which many Americans accord to Gettysburg."[451] In an attempt to stop the Kosovo Liberation Army (KLA), the subsequent flood of two hundred thousand Kosovar refugees represented a public relations disaster. Led by the Clinton Administration's Secretary of State Madeleine Albright, the media narrative issued ultimatums against the Serbs, who now represented the "bad guy" in the 24/7 news cycles.

The air war in Serbia, while ostensibly a NATO endeavor and therefore terrifying to the Russians, was actually a primarily U.S. effort, one rife with unintended consequences. In all, 83 percent, or 2/3, of the munitions dropped and sorties flown originated from U.S. aircraft. General Wesley Clark characterized the Allied Force as "the most precise and error free campaign ever conducted," but as Andrew Bacevich argues, ". . . his assertion mistakes tactical measures of success for actual victory." In other words, an operational success does not ensure a victory like Hitler experienced in France in 1940. General Clark himself wrote, "The operation in Kosovo violated almost every one of these principles [Principles of War] as it began. . . . This was not the first time that a military campaign departed from its original ways and means, but it may have been the most far-reaching adaption in decades."[452] The effects of this undeclared and generally unplanned conflict, which was arguably a "wag the dog" operation designed to cover a scandal-ridden president, are still felt today.

As Republicans regained power in America, they also increasingly turned to the now "anesthetic" use of force offered by the RMA and airpower. These so-called "NeoCons" saw the RMA as an opportunity to preemptively anticipate potential holocausts. If the hallmark of an empire is a religious-type view with a destiny to spread a way of life abroad, then Secretary of State Madeline Albright's statement made in February 1998, "If we have to use force, it is because we are America.

Map of Kosovo.

U.S. Air Force enforcing no fly zone over Southern Iraq.

---

451. Bacevich, 180.
452. Clark, 426.

We are the indispensable nation. We stand tall. We see further into the future," epitomizes this.[453] Sadly, the administrations of George W. Bush and Barack Obama sustained this view of the inevitability of American triumph, reinforced by an intellectual quoting of terms such as an "end of history" and a "flat world." Ultimately, U.S. military attempts led by General Clark to halt the Serbian "ethnic cleansing" of Kosovo through the threat of air power during *Operation Allied Force* created a situation whereby NATO appeared threatening to the Russian perspective and simultaneously weak and dependent on the United States.

During the air war and occupation of the former Yugoslavia, a convoy of fleeing Kosovars was destroyed, angering the Muslim world. Air operations caused the ultimate offense to the Chinese, when B-2 bombers lifted the **Chinese Embassy** off of the ground with explosions on May 7, 1999. Instead of ensuring the peace through a U.S.-led collective-military effort, bombing the Chinese Embassy was an unbelievable and unmitigated disaster. From the Russians' standpoint, the paternalism felt for Serbia as in 1914 had been offended. America simply did not understand the geographic perspective the Russians felt toward the Serbs. In a manner akin to America's support for democracy abroad, the Russians also felt a historic paternalism toward Serbia.

B-2 Stealth Bomber

"Just because you are paranoid doesn't mean they aren't out to get you!" —unnamed sage

Physical map of Russia.

---

453. David Kilcullen, *The Dragons and the Snakes* (Pub City: Publisher, year), 230.

The Russians viewed the end of the Cold War as a defeat; in response, they developed hybrid warfare. A perspective of geographic determinism and theories have provided language for a way forward for Russian expansion since the end of the Cold War. **Sir Halford J. Mackinder** first coined the concept of the "heartland or pivot area" of the "world continent" consisting of Eurasia and centered in large measure on the key areas of Western Russia and Ukraine as well as the areas of Eastern Europe formally in the Soviet sphere of control.[454] The influence that Mackinder and a larger school of geographic determinists had on the early twentieth century is difficult to overstate. Establishing the idea for control of the world continent (Africa, Asia, and Europe) on the basis of the control of the heartland, Mackinder's ideas have been expanded upon in Russia since the fall of the Soviet Union.

Aleksandr Dugin expanded Mackinder's thinking by arguing a "whale vs. lion" theory, noting that the Russians, because they naturally have occupied the key pivot area, essentially have a right to occupy, since land powers (lions) are essentially supported by authoritarian regimes with large standing armies (as opposed to coastal or naval powers such as the UK or the United States, which are more liberal).[455] Therefore, the Russians are destined to see the rise of someone like Vladimir Putin to lead their rejuvenated military force. Not surprisingly, Putin's political party has embraced Dugin's deterministic views.[456]

Russia's geographic perspective of the world can be understood in the light of Putin's rise to power. As a thirty-six-year-old intelligence officer with the GRU (The Soviet military intelligence office—not to be confused with the KGB or political police) stationed in East Germany at the time of the collapse of the USSR, Putin perceived betrayal by NATO and saw the subsequent expansion of the Western power during the 1990s as a threat. Putin had served as prime minister to Boris Yeltsin, and by 2000, supported with an army honed by fighting that had been developing for nearly a decade, Putin rose to power. In a pattern reminiscent of the Germans' anger after Versailles following World War I, a new Russian leadership emerged, feeling angry and betrayed. Putin's embrace of Dugin's geographic theory developed in part from a geographic perspective that would clash with the expansion of NATO.[457]

The well-intentioned humanitarian interventions into the former Yugoslavia left yet another trauma to the minds of "greater Russia."[458]

NATO: Flags of members of the North Atlantic Treaty Organization.

© Maxx-Studio/Shutterstock.com

> "If you know yourself but not the enemy for every victory gained you will also suffer a defeat."—Sun Tzu

---

454. Kilcullen, *The Dragon and the Snakes,* 135.
455. Kilcullen, *The Dragon and the Snakes,* 134.
456. Kilcullen, *The Dragons and the Snakes,* 135.
457. Kilcullen, *The Dragons and the Snakes,* 127.
458. Kilcullen, *The Dragons and the Snakes,* 133.

History Post-Cold War Decline and Reemergence

The Russian people faced utter humiliation at the end of the Cold War. The former Soviet Army of 3.4 million troops found themselves in some cases forced to harvest crops for mere survival. Large numbers of troops were released from service due to lack of funding and became homeless on the streets. Adding to this humiliation, during the First Chechen War of 1994–96, the poorly supplied and trained Russian troops were annihilated by many of their former fellow Soviet soldiers in **Chechnya**. During these years of the "end of history" and post-Cold War euphoria in the West, the Russians began to stew with anger and fear.[459] In addition to the shaping of Russian culture by geography, Russia needed a leadership schooled in the "gray world" of intelligence, armed with military leadership capable of self-evaluation, and guided by doctrine to bring them out of the misery left by the collapse of the Soviet Union.

As if the defeat in Chechnya and the divisions of the Russian Black Sea fleet were not enough, the classic Russian paranoia of an enemy on the doorstep was vindicated by events in their long history that reemerged with NATO's apparent rise.

Map of Chechnya.

Ukraine's desire to join NATO in the 1990s threatened the Russians. This was further exasperated by the United States, when they foolishly, albeit with the usual good intentions, entered into Yugoslavia—the failed former client state of the USSR. Similar to the interventions in the Middle East, these events proved to be untenable. To this day, the Chinese have never forgiven the United States for this questionable and possibly illegal war. However, the Russian geographic perspective of Serbia, the horrible flashpoint that ignited World War I, went unnoticed to an oblivious West, who were ignoring history and culture in the post-Cold War years.

In 1991, NATO established the North Atlantic Cooperation Council, which drew former east-bloc Soviet client states into the Western orbit.[460] By 1992, the Baltic States joined NATO's Partnerships for Peace Program. They also began policing Bosnia by 1996 under NATO's command, which is discussed in greater detail later in the section on China. The Russian historical memory of threats seemed to manifest themselves to the present view of the United States and the West, and the typical strongman appeared.

Under Putin's leadership, the **Chechen operations** led to the organizational development of the battalion tactical groups (BTGs), which would prove vitally important in later deployments to Georgia, Ukraine, and Syria.[461] Additionally, the development of nuclear artillery or conventional nuclear weapons were not intended for deterrence, but rather for the offensive in the spirit of "deep operations," a Soviet doctrine successfully used in World War II and later to influence German and U.S. war planners during the Cold War.[462]

As early as 2008, Putin warned NATO that plans to expand membership into Ukraine and **Georgia** "would be taken as a direct threat to the security of our country."[463] By the summer of

---

459. Kilcullen, *The Dragons and the Snakes*, 131.
460. KIlcullen, *The Dragons and the Snakes*, 133.
461. Kilcullen, *The Dragons and the Snakes*, 137.
462. Kilcullen, *The Dragons and the Snakes*, 139.
463. Kilcullen, *The Dragons and the Snakes*, 143.

2008, Georgian forces entered South Ossetia, and in response Russian Spetsnaz forces operated deep into Georgian territory, while combined-arms forces maneuvered rapidly into the tiny nation-state. A new domain of warfare had emerged onto the world stage—cyber and information warfare. By eliminating Georgian command and control (C2) with directed denial of service (DDOS) attacks, the Russians were able to exercise power more efficiently over time in a classic example of the decision-making cycle.[464]

Russian Spetsnaz armed with a Kalashnikov.

Perhaps more interesting than Russia's improvement from the dark days of the previous decade was its honest introspection. The focus on improvements within the Russian military establishment led to the **"New Look,"** a name describing the Russian self-examination and search for a way forward militarily. The New Look, according to Dr. David Kilcullen, the world's ranking authority at this time, represented the "most radical military reform since the creation of the Red Army following the 1917 Revolution."[465] The technique now known as hybrid warfare played an inherent role in these developments. The Russians would further develop more specialized troops capable of cyber and electronic warfare with a focus on network vulnerabilities. Potential disruptions included electromagnetic pulse (EMP) weapons.[466]

The term *hybrid warfare*, first used in 2007 by retired Marine Colonel Frank Hoffman, identified Hezbollah as a key example of warfare in 2006 with Israel.[467] Ironically, from the Russian perspective, hybrid warfare is most useful in training minds to understand the true complexity of modern conflict today.[468]

While the view of hybrid warfare incorporates broad strokes of the various domains and actors in warfare today, David Kilcullen describes liminal warfare in his groundbreaking book, *Dragons and Snakes*. Liminal warfare is an "... ability to ride the edge, operating right on the detection threshold ... not enough to trigger a military reaction."[469] In a similar manner to the geographer Dugin, who provided the impetus for a return to Russian power from a geographical standpoint at the end of the Cold War, the language for the Russian war machine continued to grow quietly, apparently without the notice of the West. During the Aleppo offensive of December 2016 in Syria, the Russians demonstrated what they call the **"Gerasimov Doctrine,"** in which hybrid warfare was used through a model of vertical development.

General of the Army Valery Gerasimov's doctrine in May 2014 advanced ideas that essentially sought to use political, diplomatic, economic, and other nonmilitary measures in combination with the use of military forces.[470] David

Chief of the General Staff of the Russian Armed Forces—First Deputy Defense Minister, Army General Valery Gerasimov.

464. Kilcullen, *The Dragons and the Snakes*, 146. *For more on the decision-making cycle see the OODA loop in the MAMH.*
465. Kilcullen, *The Dragons and the Snakes*, 149.
466. Kilcullen, *The Dragons and the Snakes*, 148.
467. Hoffman, *Conflict in the 21st Century*, 8.
468. Sean McFate, *The New Rules of War: How America Can Win-Against Russia, China, and Other Threats* (New York: Harper-Collins, 2019), 237.
469. Kilcullen, *The Dragons and the Snakes*, 150.
470. http://www.understandingwar.org/report/russian-hybrid-warfare

Kilcullen again notes, " . . . one key aspect of Gerasimov's framing is that while the West considers these nonmilitary measures to be ways of avoiding war, Russia considers them part of war."[471] Probable Russian attempts to interfere in the U.S. election of 2016 as a means to cover their advance into Syria indicated the use of temporal approaches to shaping operations that allowed liminal or "beneath the radar" approaches to success.

The stealth approach to war favors the asymmetric or weaker force in a confrontation. This reflects an absorption of the lessons of the world's postcolonial military history by using a protractedly slow approach while confusing the superior opponent. While playing on "fake news" and spreading disinformation as cover, the Russians were able to move into an objective area and quickly stand down before NATO or the United States could even respond. Essentially operating within the decision-making cycle of an opponent's force, the objectives of securing the battlefield, such as occurred in Ukraine and Syria, might even be a nearly bloodless endeavor.

Unlike Americans who plan for war as a seasonally defined period for conflict, an organized type of activity planned within the open-air market of ideas and politics with defined lines marking areas of legal responsibility, the Russians view hybrid warfare as a type of continuous warfare. U.S. strategic thinkers, in contrast, tend to discuss hybrid war as below the threshold of conventional forces and conflict that the Russians have most famously used. Gerasimov looked for a 4:1 ratio of nonmilitary to military forces in his use of the aforementioned measures in combination with military forces.[472] The National Defense Strategy (NDS) of the United States gives primacy to the use of military power for deterrence of major conventional conflict between great powers. However, Russia also seeks to avoid major conventional wars between great powers even as it designs a way of waging war that would achieve its objectives and enable it to win despite being weaker than the United States.[473]

Arguably, the ultimate age-old military problem is one of the balances of economy of force and mass, or metaphorically, the decision to use the fingers or fist. Lately, operations in Afghanistan reflect the balance between forces to cause an enemy to amass, at which time conventional forces can eliminate them, but also provide enough forces to be able to thinly spread them over a greater area, preventing hostilities from locals offended by their presence. (M&M 293) In Ukraine, the Russians operated short of activating the feared American war machine. For example, American watchers seemed to focus more on the Russian soldiers without insignia ("**green men**") who helped seize Crimea in 2014 than the proxies Russia used in Eastern Ukraine in attempting to decide on an approach to war.[474] While Americans remained focused on the soldiers themselves, events transpired short of Americans pulling the American trigger.

In short, hybrid warfare today represents an iceberg to military planners that largely remains below the surface. It is a smart and all-encompassing attempt to defeat a superior enemy while focusing on the increased importance of information. According to a Nielsen Company audience report, during the first quarter of the year 2016 the average American spent about ten hours and thirty-nine minutes each day consuming media.[475] It should not be surprising that a great nation who traces its history to the fall of Rome and that has been threatened throughout history would maintain an intellectual edge in the areas of intelligence and military thought. The recognition of an asymmetric and confrontational relationship with the United States served to shape a series of military adventures that resulted in the introspective examination of strengths and weaknesses in the Russian military. The result is hybrid warfare specifically employed in various frontier regions with vulnerabilities.

---

471. Kilcullen, *The Dragons and the Snakes,* 162.
472. Kilcullen, *The Dragons and the Snakes,* 162.
473. http://www.understandingwar.org/sites/default/files/Russian%20Hybrid%20Warfare%20ISW%20Report%202020.pdf
474. http://www.understandingwar.org/sites/default/files/Russian%20Hybrid%20Warfare%20ISW%20Report%202020.pdf
475. https://www.cnn.com/2016/06/30/health/americans-screen-time-nielsen/index.html

It would be ironic indeed if the American propensity to take a manipulative media at face value, which started with a 24/7 news cycle at the end of the Cold War, in fact resulted in warfare antithetical to an American ability to project peace. Mason Clark of the Institute for the Study of War stated that Russian analysts claim NATO previously "chose a victim" and forced other states to join large-scale military operations, as in Yugoslavia and Iraq, to eliminate unwanted states.[476] Russian analysts project their own mindsets when they claim the West now uses hybrid wars to achieve its goals. In March 2016, Gerasimov stated that the "falsification of events [and] restriction of activity of mass media . . . can be comparable to the results of large-scale use of troops and forces."[477] Such an emphasis on pre-conflict shaping, with the need to remain hidden for as long as possible, then to rapidly seize objectives after the decision is made to reveal yourself, and then just as quickly to engage in de-escalation that is simultaneously negotiated from a superior position represents the ideal of the Russian view of hybrid warfare. None of the boasting and announcements of planned dates to attack that are so characteristic of American warfare since Vietnam are involved in the process of hybrid warfare.

The degree of Russian successes in terms of "flying beneath the radar" can be seen in U.S. domestic political discourse. In the 2012 U.S. presidential election campaign, for example, Republican candidate Mitt Romney suggested a Russian threat, which President Barack Obama dismissed. The president's comments are instructive in of themselves, as events during Obama's second term would soon reveal the Russian ability to "fly below the radar" in both Ukraine and Syria.[478] From the vantage point of recent history, the Russian's proven ability to combine conventional and nonconventional assets to defeat an adversary prior to actual combat would be decisive. During actual combat, the Russians also showed an ability to rapidly secure objectives and then just as quickly de-escalate during negotiations.[479] The Russian military had apparently correctly self-examined and was led by a new strongman Putin, who emerged in 1999, the very year the United States conducted the air war over Serbia. With hybrid warfare, other global vacuums would soon be filled.

Russian aircraft in Syria.

Aside from the political element, there's always a human element. Far removed from any of the hot spots mentioned in this work so far are fields of rotting potatoes in Russia. Planted as soon as the snows of winter melt, long after the permafrost beneath the earth's surface melts, and subsequently as the muds of Russia's vast interior dry, a single growing season combined with a paucity of ice-free Russian ports requires the use of extensive agriculture. There is a need to exploit increasingly large numbers of acres of arable land to provide the sustenance so desperately needed but robbed by the short growing season and the choking muds of spring. As a result, the Russians will probably

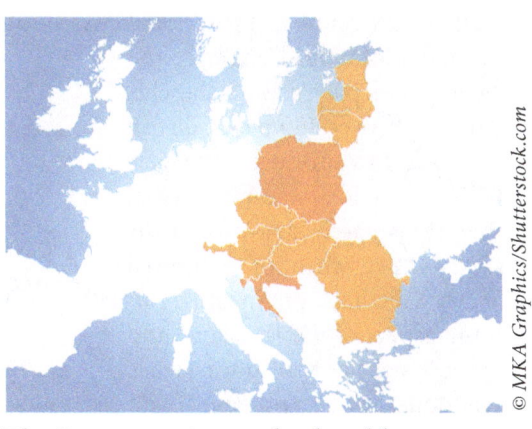

The Intermarium: the land between the Baltic and Black Seas.

---

476. http://www.understandingwar.org/report/russian-hybrid-warfare
477. http://www.understandingwar.org/sites/default/files/Russian%20Hybrid%20Warfare%20ISW%20Report%202020.pdf, p. 17.
478. Kilcullen, *The Dragons and the Snakes*, 163.
479. Kilcullen, *The Dragons and the Snakes*, 164.

require expansion into the **Intermarium,** or region between the Baltic and Black Seas in Eastern Europe, particularly between Poland and Ukraine. In fact, recent events in Belarus show similar patterns preceding the Russian advance into Ukraine. Another such "bubble" or frontier may be occurring in Finnmark today.

Russian leadership, shaped historically by paranoia, saw a manipulative enemy to the West armed with the latest technology poised precariously close to perceived Russian space. They felt use of below-the-radar type "liminal" warfare and multidomain hybrid warfare represented a response from a nation angry from perceived recent exploitation, which could potentially prompt a headlong collision with the West. The necessity of plausible deniability and the consolidation of key real estate within a favorably shaped environment against a superior foe will probably continue. In other words, the Russians have already identified key areas they can neither afford to have closed nor even threatened, and by the time the United States identifies these areas they will have been largely secured. One particular area is on the extreme northeastern border of Norway and Russia. The Cold War deployment of U.S. Marines here essentially resumed in 2018.

In **Finnmark,** the use of Syrian refugees to overwhelm border crossings demonstrated a Russian ability to test how quickly Norwegian forces could respond to a border challenge. This vital area, located regionally near the port city of Murmansk, demonstrates an area Russia identified and prepared, utilizing various aspects of human geography for a strategic or military purpose. When one considers that the Baltic States in the Intermarium are only sixty hours from this region, and in light of the need for Russia to expand simultaneously to secure a vital northern port, hybrid warfare is in full display.[480] By the time the West responds to the refugee crisis and realizes what has occurred, the Russians will have continued to use a full spectrum of forces and information operations to keep the West distracted. They successfully demonstrated this when they engaged in cyber and information warfare during the U.S. election of 2016. Proactive use of all means available to secure an operational environment, all hallmarks of hybrid warfare, and the global deployment of the U.S. military to over 800 bases abroad currently has produced the perfect catalyst for ongoing Russian operations barely detected in the West—the essence of a liminal strategy. Perhaps the most frightening aspect of the Russians' and Chinese's use of hybrid warfare is it is done legally and reflects an understanding of the U.S. system.

When the Russians bombed Syria and secured the deep warm-water port of Latakia in 2015, they achieved even more through

Map of Finnmark.

Latakia, Syria.

---

480. Kilcullen, *The Dragons and the Snakes,* 119.

the displacement of peoples (an old Stalin trick) legally. European law requires all countries to absorb refugees; however, the open-hearted crafters of the law never anticipated millions arriving. Germany alone spent $6.7 billion in resettlement costs and accepted a million refugees. The European political backlash to Russian manipulation resulted in the unthinkable return of neo-Nazis as well as other nationalist groups. Arguably, the immigrant problem contributed to the British exit (Brexit) from the European Union. Thus, by weaponizing **Syrian refugees,** Putin's Russia essentially achieved in one stroke what conventional forces training throughout the Cold War had failed to do—contribute to the breakup of the European alliance. The destabilization of a perceived dangerous nuclear-armed Western adversary in a frontier of extreme value for Russian expansion represented a masterstroke of mayhem.[481] In essence, the Russians used the very displaced people the Russians had largely caused to be homeless, then continued to use the movement of these same desperate people into areas to overwhelm and test defenses the Russians coveted.

The Russian conception of hybrid war is much more expansive. It covers the entire "competition space," including subversive, economic, information, and diplomatic means, as well as the use of military forces extending above the upper threshold of the "gray zone" concept that more accurately captures the Chinese approach to war. The Kremlin considers conflicts including Belarus, Ukraine, Syria, Libya, and Venezuela to be hybrid wars.

While Americans view themselves as tasked with correcting global injustice as a type of crusader spirit since the end of the Cold War and have attempted to financially aid the poorer nations of the world through such organizations as the International Monetary Fund, the opponents of the United States have perceived wildly unpredictable emotionally guided military responses. A failure to uphold the agreement at Bretton Woods when the United States left the global gold standard in 1971, and an apparent infatuation with rapidly executed military exercises often unnecessary for U.S. national security, alarmed the burgeoning autocracies. As the United States became focused on the Greater Middle East from the 1980s to the present, the Russian military shifted into gear with an introspective approach leading to the New Look series of military reforms. After poor performances in Chechnya in 1994–96 and Georgia in 2008, the Russians focused on developing anti-access and area denial (A2/AD) in regions particularly important to them such as the Baltic and Finnmark.[482] President Vladimir Putin brilliantly executed a smart game of using weaker forces with precision to return Russia onto the world stage to be taken seriously in various locations ranging from securing the periphery of the Russian borders (Ukraine) to achieving a Mediterranean deep and warm-water port in Latakia, Syria, in 2015, therein fulfilling a Russian goal for centuries—all done under the nose of the United States. Russia has further established itself as the regional diplomatic power in the Caucuses today (Nagorno-Karabakh).[483] The 1980s are not calling for their foreign policy back anymore, at least not in Russia, where the effectiveness of the hybrid warfare doctrine threatens the Intermarium.

Hybrid Warfare in China

Since the end of the Vietnam War, the Chinese have sought to use a multidomain approach by creating a comparable A2/AD system to the Russians but focused on the East and South China Seas. Since the United States' decision to intervene in what arguably was an illegal NATO war in Serbia in 1999, the Chinese have followed informal and formal approaches to an expanded vision of warfare, while simultaneously attempting to weaken the West and secure safe transport of vital resources.[484] In Washington DC, the Chinese are now viewed as a challenge to the United States' historical presence as the leading military power in the Western Pacific.[485] The various Taiwan Straits Crises illustrate a lack of understanding by *both* the United States and China in understanding each other's

481. McFate, *The New Rules of War,* 105.
482. Kilcullen, *The Dragons and the Snakes,* 222.
483. Kilcullen, *The Dragons and the Snakes,* 164.
484. Kilcullen, *The Dragons and the Snakes,* 223.
485. Kilcullen, *The Dragons and the Snakes,* 193.

viewpoints. The air war launched against Serbia and the Belgrade resulted in the embassy bombing in 1999, and demonstrated the need to firmly reflect on history and geography in future operations.

The February 1999 release of **Unrestricted Warfare (URW)**, a book presented and read by Jiang Zemin after the Third Taiwan Strait Crisis but before Kosovo, revealed an official Chinese acceptance of a new military strategy and the synthesis from a debate that had existed within the People's Liberation Army (PLA) since 1991. This foundational paper conveys the idea that the United States, as a post-Cold War power, found itself constrained by a rules-based order of its own self-imposed creation while enemies were not. According to David Kilcullen, the most salient feature of the book is to define war beyond winning on the battlefield and suggesting "using all means to include both armed and non-armed force."[486] Also noted was that U.S. network-centric warfare may create an "electronic Maginot line that is weak because of its excessive dependence on a single technology."[487] Kilcullen further remarks this is amazingly prescient considering that when *URW* was published, the internet and GPS had just been created and social media and smartphones had yet to arrive. Both the degree of "addiction" since then and the tendency to spend is obvious in American society today. The authors of *URW* note that the ostentatious battle style of "attacking birds with golden bullets" represents the fact that, as a nation, the American-style extravagant warfare contradicts with the nation that has never been willing to pay the price of life. Obviously, the echoes of the U.S. Civil War escaped the ears of Chinese thinkers, but the perspective presented is chilling.[488]

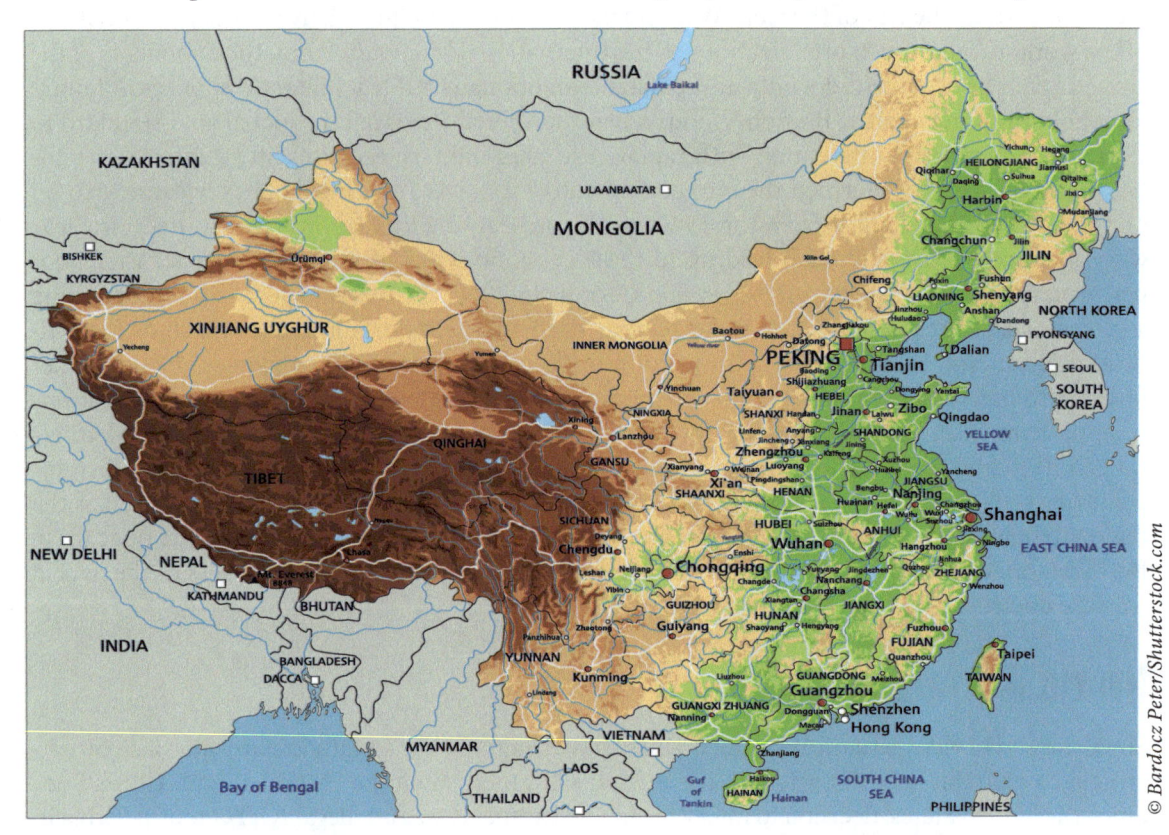

Physical map of China.

The focus of *URW* is a modification of the age-old Chinese principles of combat as a last resort, and only after forces have gained a winning position by surrounding a target. On the ground in Korea, China would engage in giant pincer movements following the historic Chinese model of

---

486. Kilcullen, *The Dragons and the Snakes*, 203.
487. Kilcullen, *The Dragons and the Snakes*, 203.
488. Kilcullen, *The Dragons and the Snakes*, 203.

"boxing-in" an opponent, but since the Gulf War of 1990–91 and with a recognition of the American "addiction" to technology, the use of envelopment takes a different form. The Chinese military displayed its recognition of a lack of lines such as the West follows (see Operations diagram); from a Chinese perspective, the blurred lines between what is war and what isn't allows an expanded definition to include military, transmilitary, and nonmilitary aspects.

The conception of war for the Chinese military included conventional forces from all domains; however, the transmilitary list of wartime tools not only included unconventional items but also an emphasis on diplomacy and information warfare aspects. The nonmilitary aspects include everything from financial to resource control, up to and including the use of regulations, drugs, and the media to box-in an opponent and attempt to surround them. By the time the circle is complete, the foe has not realized they have been attacked. For example, Kilcullen ponders the use of fentanyl, mass-produced in China, and shipped in industrial quantities directly to the United States, often disguised as legal pharmaceutical supplies; it is also sent through Canada and Mexico, where it is illegally trafficked into the United States. In 2017 nearly thirty thousand deaths occurred from the drug, and despite promising to reduce production, indications are that a reverse "Opium War" has been waged."[489]

Another key aspect noted in the *URW* paper is the importance of resources. In the current race for global hegemony of 5G technology, the use of "rare earth elements" will prove decisive. China currently has a monopoly on these sources, but in its traditional "Side-Principle Rule" has chosen to expand attacks from different directions, be it the support of a coup in Zimbabwe for the control of mineral resources or the use of weak American borders to smuggle drugs. The point is a full spectrum of military, nonmilitary, and transmilitary approaches are used and stand in direct contrast to the American operational view of a closed synergistic system divided into clear parts.[490]

Americans misread Chinese reactions to the horrific bombing of their embassy. Chinese officials never accepted the U.S. apology nor the explanation for the bombing of their embassy. To this day, the bombing in China is regarded as deliberate. Alleged storage of a wrecked F-117A stealth fighter aircraft being studied by the PLA technical intelligence teams in the embassy would indicate the United States attempted to prevent the pieces of the aircraft from being transported to or studied by the Chinese. Further credence for the accusations of U.S. intentions were tied to the fact that the flight had been directed from Langley alone.[491] Regardless, the near blind faith in the American military successes in the Gulf and the self-evident righteousness of the American efforts as expressed by Secretary Madeleine Albright go far to explain how the United States failed to properly gauge the level of anger felt by China from the accidental bombing of the embassy.[492]

January 12, 2015: A monument dedicated to the dead members of the Chinese Embassy attack in Belgrade.

Consequent interactions with the United States resulted in the Chinese military transforming *URW* into a new doctrine guiding military efforts. In 2001, when an American F-8 collided with a P-3 Orion over Hainan, there were similar patterns of apologies. There was no apology by the United States, only face-saving sorrows expressed.[493] By 2003, the *URW* paper had morphed into a **Three Wars Strategy**, and included psychological warfare, public opinion warfare, and legal

489. Kilcullen, *The Dragons and the Snakes*, 206.
490. Kilcullen, *The Dragons and the Snakes*, 211.
491. Kilcullen, *The Dragons and the Snakes*, 187.
492. Kilcullen, *The Dragons and the Snakes*, 187.
493. Salaam Khan, *Haunted by Chaos* (Pub City: Harvard, 2020), 194.

warfare. China's military, similar to Russia's, had developed new strategies to counter the conventional excellence of the U.S. military since the Gulf War. The Three Wars Strategy, along with the emergence of the Gerasimov Doctrine in Russia, led to the U.S. creation of Cyber Command in 2009.[494]

The Chinese are aware of the American tradition to see war and peace, probably more than most Americans. A digital view of conflict means the Chinese will attempt to keep from activating the U.S. war machine through two means, brinkmanship and nonmilitary tools. Like the Russian use of "green men" mentioned previously (soldiers without markings on uniforms), the Chinese recognize that if they can disguise themselves as noncombatants, they will not risk the ire of the American armed forces. The Three Wars Strategy builds on the ancient teachings of Sun Tzu and views psychological warfare through information operations to incorporate "lawfare" and cyber/information warfare as a means to defeat the West. The incorporation of a wide or "horizontal range of information," as described by David Kilcullen, was developed by two Chinese colonels who wrote the book **Unrestricted Warfare** in 1999.[495] By 2003, the Chinese Central Military Commission and Communist Party recognized this new version of an ancient way of fighting.[496] The essential goal is to defeat an enemy without them realizing they are even in a fight.

Lt. General H. R. McMaster, who served as President Donald Trump's National Security Advisor from 2017 to 2018, believes problems with China began during the 2008 financial crisis. The appearance of a weakened United States can be traced to changes in Chinese approaches to the creation of exclusion zones in the Pacific. Besides appearing weak, Chinese leadership, armed with an enumerated strategy, also shared the age-long fear of a Chinese peasant rebellion. Rebellions feature prominently throughout the rise and fall of Chinese dynasties as far back as the Han, and they represent a fearful specter in areas such as Hong Kong; moreover, they pose a threat, possibly leading to Chinese aggression.[497] Perhaps the real Chinese problem is the distribution of wealth both within and on the periphery of the nation. Within the current pattern of distribution, one sees less than 1 percent of the leadership controlling over 90 percent of the wealth. Conflicting loyalties and corruption could potentially present a situation of unrest—the ultimate Chinese nightmare. As a result of this fear, McMaster believes the Chinese leadership then could seek war to demonstrate their grip on China:

> Chinese Communist Party leaders will become more anxious about losing their exclusive grip on power. What they will do to reduce that risk is to intensify the establishment of the Orwellian surveillance police state internally, and they will begin to aggressively pursue "national rejuvenation" externally with maybe a move on Taiwan. We already see threatening behavior toward Taiwan and attacks against India on the Himalayan frontier."[498]

The key word in the previous quote is *anxious*. The need to control their nation from within drives the Chinese to look toward the border and any indication of foreign attempts to undermine authority, real or imagined. The need to prevent such an infection from entering the nation requires vigilance and a need for further buffer space along the arc of vulnerability from Korea to Taiwan. Chinese attempts to expand control of their contiguous borders, therefore, will likely become more intense in light of the perception of a weakened United States. As it has since 1949, the Chinese determination to maintain their grip on the nation through a move on Taiwan will likely continue

---

494. Kilcullen, *The Dragons and the Snakes*, 211.
495. Kilcullen, *The Dragons and the Snakes*, 176.
496. McFate, *The New Rules of War*, 65.
497. David R. Petriello, *A Military History of China* (Yardley, PA: Westholme, 2018), 90.
498. https://www.csmonitor.com/USA/Foreign-Policy/2020/0922/Strategic-empathy-H.R.-McMaster-on-foreign-policy-and-China?utm_source=Hoover+Daily+Report&utm_campaign=df398e0d3d-EMAIL_CAMPAIGN_2020_09_23_05_59&utm_medium=email&utm_term=0_21b1edff3c-df398e0d3d-72843637

to be conducted through a subdued, largely legal effort. How then does the present day contrasting distribution of wealth on the periphery or frontier of China present a threat?

The barrier surrounding southern and central China poses a contiguous threat to their egos and security at the present time. A new Chinese strategy utilizes information, and the use of various means of coercion and distraction ensure cover for China to achieve its true objectives. America awoke to the dangers presented in the Three Wars Strategy by 2008 and shortly thereafter created Cyber Command. Some even believe the epidemic of deaths caused by fentanyl represents Chinese attempts to weaken the United States. Meanwhile, attempts to distract the United States by employing forces into the Taiwan Strait could provide cover for more surreptitious attempts to control America and the West. For example, by controlling large portions of Hollywood, the Chinese ensure they are never cast in a negative light, while the grooming of anti-war party organizations and the spin of news stories to cast a pro-Chinese view before other media sources can develop a counter narrative feed a steady stream of information to a screen-addicted U.S. culture.[499]

Lawfare is the use of the law in a nefarious way to achieve Chinese objectives.[500] For example, if, as history indicates, the true objective of China is Taiwan, the means utilized may be to flank this vital region using Economic Exclusion Zones (EEZs) as a justification for the building of bases in the South China Seas, as opposed to the strategy of claiming a historical right to these areas in a Middle Kingdom type perspective. Despite the laws disagreeing with China's claims, it is as if by using information and telling a lie over and over again they can convince themselves and others in Hitlerian fashion that the "big lie" is true.[501] An end to using the bubble of A2/AD within the realm of law by claiming over and over a right to these vital areas while engaging the United States in a costly arms race may ultimately prove successful at achieving the neutralization of an American ability to respond to future advances by the mainland against Taiwan.

A precursor of expanding into contiguous areas gradually without alerting the West was seen when the People's Republic of China (PRC) declared in 2013 an air defense identification zone had been established in the South China Sea. Americans responded by flying through the zone, but like the Russians in Finnmark resolve is tested with responses studied.[502] The resolve of Japan has likewise been tested in the Senkaku/Daiyou Islands, where using a type of "People's Warfare," Mao

Map of Taiwan.

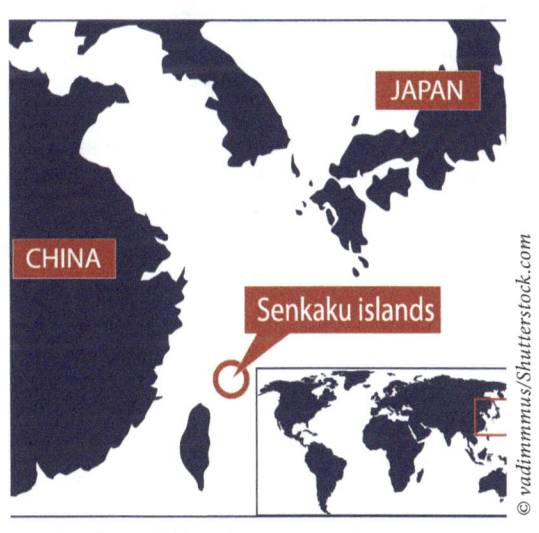

Senkaku Islands map: Japan and China territorial disputes.

499. McFate, *The New Rules of War*, 67.
500. McFate, *The New Rules of War*, 65.
501. McFate, *The New Rules of War*, 68.
502. Khan, *Haunted by Chaos*, 226.

would recognize armed fishing boats controlled by China sent out to test the Japanese coast guard.[503] One wonders how the eventual Japanese tradition of maritime excellence will eventually respond institutionally. The potential reemergence of the Samurai spirit represents a transcendental return of militarization as an expression of Japanese unity, perhaps even starting an arms race.

While the West has sought to counter the Chinese attempts to secure international territory through legal means, one high profile case was presented before the United Nations. With the recent United Nations Convention on the Law of the Sea (UNCLOS) decision in 2016 in the South China Sea and despite initial indications of success, the eventual results may not have been as positive. The president of the Philippines (the first ever from Mindanao to serve) surprised many with a clear pivot toward China after winning the case in a court of law. Suspicions of financial corruption suggested themselves to area analysts who have long counted on the Philippines as a stalwart of support.[504]

As of 2016, eight of ten container ports are located in China, have their financial backing, or are at least partly owned by them.[505] Djibouti represents the first Chinese overseas base from which the PLA Navy (PLAN) can send warships into both the Red Sea and the Gulf of Aden; these two areas are responsible for 12 percent of world maritime trade.[506] Global outreaches on Okinawa include support for Japanese separatist movements in the Ryukyus and standing in direct opposition to American forces in the area.[507] The attempt to vertically escalate or focus on a given location and specific type of competition while remaining "below the radar" is the hallmark of Russian actions, but must include geographically expansive plans of Russia due to physical geography. Both these types of hybrid warfare represent different challenges and are the natural results of geography and history.

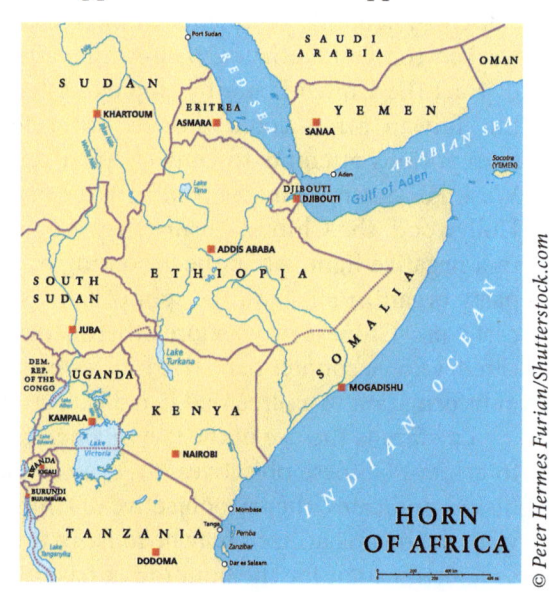

Map of Djibouti in relation to both the Red Sea and the Gulf of Aden.

"Blessed are the peacemakers: for they shall be called the children of God."—Matthew 5:7

The United States must work toward peace by remaining strong. Strength, however, requires understanding an adversary. Gone are the days of a threat to the mainland from Taiwan. The threat now is a two China's model. The Taiwanese today increasingly support independence: As of 2015, only 9.1 percent of the population supported some type of eventual unification with China. Those identifying themselves as "Chinese" reached a low of 3.3 percent. An earlier poll found that more than 80 percent think Taiwan and China are separate nations. The same percentage would secure permanent separation if it would not cause war. Further polls revealed 43 percent of those under 40 supported independence even if it resulted in a Chinese attack.[508]

---

503. Khan, *Haunted by Chaos,* 226.
504. Khan, *Haunted by Chaos,* 228.
505. Kilcullen, *The Dragons and the Snakes,* 173.
506. Kilcullen, *The Dragons and the Snakes,* 173.
507. Kilcullen, *The Dragons and the Snakes,* 174.
508. Ian Easton, *The Chinese Invasion Threat: Taiwan's Defense and American Strategy in Asia* (Manchester, UK: Eastbridge Books, 2019), 6.

Therefore, the Chinese Communist Party (CCP) today views a democratic Taiwan as its greatest threat to its political legitimacy. The PLA prepared to protect the political legitimacy of the CCP by creating the "Joint Island Attack Campaign." The plan covers the entire spectrum of the modern battlefield and all domains, with information operations and media outlets as the primary targets.[509] In essence, this is hybrid warfare! Information favorable to China, ranging from positive publicity through Hollywood to the message "Taiwan is a lost cause—resistance is futile," is commonly broadcast through information operations.[510]

In the present, the risk of war has increased instead of decreased, primarily due to a divergence of Chinese views between the mainland and Taiwan supported often by the United States. As evidenced by the freezing of various weapons programs, the PRC has succeeded in isolating Taiwan from American support during both the Bush and Obama administrations. The enforcement wing of this strategy is the PLA. The PLA only continues to grow stronger, reflecting simultaneously the wealth of China and the insecurity felt by its leadership. According to Ian Easton, an expert on Taiwan, Chinese literature from within the PLA states that a future invasion of Taiwan is probably inevitable. While the timing may be uncertain, it is felt without question a "historic meeting" will not be put off forever. "Taiwan is a 'splittist' regime," and China's national territorial integrity remains under severe threat until Taiwan is returned to the ancestral "Fatherland."[511]

It is little wonder the Taiwan Strait has great importance today as a transport route; Chinese military literature proposes a scenario where an enemy (presumably the United States) operates from Taiwan to cut China off from its oil imports. If protecting Chinese oil access is more than military necessity, but instead a national strategy issue for the PRC, then for Japan it is a true matter of life and death. Japan currently receives 90 percent of its oil transported through the Taiwan Strait, 100 percent of its nuclear fuel needs, and 99 percent of its mineral needs; in addition, 80 percent of all container ships travel through the Taiwan Strait, the equivalent of one Japanese ship every ten minutes.[512] The significance of destroying Japan by taking Taiwan is far from the consideration from many American planners. Too many Americans fail to see the inherent danger in a renewed Japanese and Chinese competition. It is as if the ghosts of centuries past are returning at a time of potential American weakness and are more threatening than ever.[513]

Map of the Taiwan Strait.

A further invitation to Chinese aggression comes with apparent Japanese vulnerabilities. An emerging Chinese strategy aimed at Japan's destruction is described in Chinese military literature, noting how a 50 percent loss of imports will break any Japanese resistance. Taiwan is the cornerstone of the offshore island chain known as "First Chain" in the Chinese military literature of today.[514] The opportunity for revenge against Japan after a century of humiliation in the Taiwan Strait could prove to be irresistible.[515]

---

509. Easton, *The Chinese Invasion Threat*, 9.
510. Easton, *The Chinese Invasion Threat*, 15.
511. Easton, *The Chinese Invasion Threat*, 11.
512. Easton, *The Chinese Invasion Threat*, 13.
513. Easton, *The Chinese Invasion Threat*, 12.
514. Easton, *The Chinese Invasion Threat*, 13.
515. Easton, *The Chinese Invasion Threat*, 13.

The Battle: China's War Plan

In this theoretical warfare, the Chinese would begin with surveillance radars eliminated with jamming devices. Intelligence-gathering platforms would then collect information from signals received and targeted for target jamming. American strategic warning satellites could be jammed and degraded, which would enable ballistic missile launches. Electronic feints from artificial radio chatter would be sent from various vehicles and platforms to fool Taiwanese forces and confuse the defense. Initial blows to Taiwan would come from missile attacks prioritized to target and hit runways. This would be followed by air defenses, which would be hit before electronic pathways would be secured by fighter aircraft as special ops forces could be introduced by airborne or vertical assault means. Aerial dogfights would ensue for mastery of the air.

According to Ian Easton, sources available do not indicate the depth of consideration of naval engagements. The potential high losses to either side simply do not matter, or they are not considered due to a lack of recent naval combat experience. Blockading Taiwan with mines and closing down harbors via submarines releasing drifting contact mines at the openings of major ports and the use of bombers to sow belts of mines in waves of varying depth and capacity would quarantine the island. The longer the blockade, the more effective certainly, but also the more time that would be allowed for Taiwanese allies to respond to the attacks.[516] The extent of American or allied support to Taiwan would come from spy satellites and SATCOM (satellite communications), and would allow coordination by command of various task force commanders in varying domains simultaneously.[517]

As targeting zeroes in on coastal defenses in preparation of the attack day, a bombing campaign placing a premium on prioritized targets such as fuel and power grids would follow. A campaign of psychological intimidation to persuade the Taiwanese to abandon the upcoming battle would launch while transportation targets, including bridges, tunnels, infrastructure, and industries, would be threatened.[518] With the head decapitated from the body of war, so to speak, the land operations would begin and in the balance would be who will surrender first.

Amphibious landing operations would require an initial neutralization of Taiwan's outer islands. The Kinmen Islands include the granite island of Greater Kinmen, also known as Quemoy, located 141 miles west of Taiwan, within the Kinmen Island group.[519] Another major thorn in the Chinese side is the Matsu or Matzu group, located 175 miles northeast of Kinmen, which consists of twenty-eight islands and represent another key position off of the Chinese mainland. Like Kinmen, these are granite islands filled with tunnels and fortifications.

In an amphibious assault on Taiwan, the PLA would need to secure these various offshore islands since they represent a security threat by virtue of alerting Taipei to Chinese movements. According to Ian Easton, Chinese military literature places a premium on securing and blockading these islands to offset a threat to the transports ferrying toward the landing beaches on Taiwan.[520]

Sunrise at Yushan Mountain, Taiwan.

---

516. Easton, *The Chinese Invasion Threat*, 86.
517. Easton, *The Chinese Invasion Threat*, 90.
518. Easton, *The Chinese Invasion Threat*, 96.
519. Easton, *The Chinese Invasion Threat*, 97.
520. Easton, *The Chinese Invasion Threat*, 98.

Because the islands surrounding China are so numerous, precious time would be wasted attacking Taiwan, whereas failure to secure each island represents potential disaster.[521] Perhaps this realization persuaded the commandant of the Marine Corps, General David Berger, to envision the boldest change in recent Marine Corps history in 2019. Berger advanced the idea that expensive ships and weapons platforms, including tanks, would be unnecessary. Instead, the Marine Corps embarked on a type of coastal defense force capable of thwarting an enemy's ability to project force; they relied on smaller, lower-cost, and more expendable systems dependent on individual judgment and autonomy.[522]

Nanhu Mountain, Mount Chung Yang, Taroko National Park, Heping District, Taichung, Taiwan.

Per internal Chinese literature, the actual assault on Taiwan would be an air assault in conjunction with paratroopers and remaining special operations troops inserted. The marines would land on assigned beaches behind reconnaissance and demolition teams, who would previously have cleared pathways through obstacles and mine fields. Attack helicopters would continue to take out local radar and listening posts as amphibious troops attempted to link up with the air assault and airborne troops previously dropped inland. A cruel process of cleaning out the enemy would engulf the mountainous terrain of Taiwan.[523]

The problems of planning would include the limited availability of potential landing beaches, of which two figure highest in planning. Jialutang to the south would reflect a pattern seen in 1944 with *Operation Causeway*, whereas to the north, Jinshan South Beach offers the best beach potential, with its distance from the ubiquitous high ground over the beaches standing similar to the Anzio landings.[524]

Apparently, the Chinese military is most comfortable with making Taoyuan Beach the prime landing zone due to its proximity to Taipei, the capital, which is about thirty miles away. As airfields continue to see air assault teams landing and though enemy positions will seek to be bypassed, the other challenge besides the numerous island chains around China and the need to conclude a campaign rapidly is the need for confronting Taiwanese forces on the beaches since the beaches have been prepared defensively ahead of time.[525] Due to the conditions of weather in the Taiwan Strait, geography will also dictate the timing of any assault. The high mountains in Taiwan affect the weather in the Taiwan Strait, which represents a treacherous undertaking on the surface and below.

Taipei, the capital city of Taiwan.

Littered with shipwrecks over the centuries, the ocean bottom will threaten submarine attempts to quarantine the island, while the wind and current conditions make an amphibious assault very

---

521. Easton, *The Chinese Invasion Threat*, 99.
522. Christian Brose, *The Kill Chain: Defending America in the Future of High-Tech Warfare* (New York: Hachette Books, 2020), 229.
523. Easton, *The Chinese Invasion Threat*, 119.
524. Easton, *The Chinese Invasion Threat*, 135.
525. Easton, *The Chinese Invasion Threat*, 139.

unlikely except during certain time periods—late March to the end of April and from late September to the end of October, when winds are light and the waves are lower in height.[526]

Taiwanese mobilization plans assume that two hundred to three hundred thousand men would form up for duty within twenty-four hours.[527] The navy has trained to have over 3,500 sea mines placed in dense underwater patterns around the potential invasion beaches within fourteen hours with an equal amount held in reserve. The lessons of Quemoy (Jinmen) in 1949 are revealed with the R.O.C. forces placing underwater obstacle systems 300 to 600 feet offshore designed to entangle, rip apart, and incinerate small landing boats full of troops. It is believed a stockpile of fifty-three-gallon oil drums for wartime beach defenses would reportedly be filled with 220 pounds of TNT, mixed with gasoline, and chained below the surface waiting for Chinese landing craft to touch and ignite them.[528]

Once ashore, the seemingly endless job of fighting through prepared defense networks, while R.O.C. Air Force jets fly out of hardened bunkers during the initial missile attacks by China, would in turn initiate attacks. The overall Taiwanese battle plan would be to survive the initial engagement then fight through endless interlocking kill zones with close air support. Taiwanese naval forces that are effectively at sea during the initial attack would return to coordinate the fight and counterassaults.[529]

Taiwanese counterstrikes would include home-grown missiles such as the Wan Chine (Ten Thousand Swords) joint standoff weapon launched from fighters dropping submunitions, and the navy would fire Hsiung Feng anti-ship missiles, allowing recognition of Chinese targets from over the horizon. Hardened anti-ship missile bases would join the cacophony of violence causing huge numbers of casualties.[530]

American involvement in war game scenarios, while mercurial at best and weak at worst, is bound to involve some action. With foreign debt held by the Japanese, it is hard to imagine the United States reversing its foreign policy, which has been intact since MacArthur's day. The sobering realization is that in 2007 China shot a ballistic missile into a target satellite in low earth orbit, and in 2010 deployed the world's first anti-ship ballistic missile. In 2018, China even demonstrated its use against carriers. Other decisions by the Chinese include creating artificial islands in 2015 after Chinese intelligence agents had penetrated computer systems in the United States and taken the information of over twenty million Americans who either worked for the federal government or had family employed. Chairman Xi with pride displayed ballistic missiles capable of attacking Guam.[531] The 2016 Taiwanese election of Dr. Tsai Ing-wen, viewed as friendly to the United States, was equally opposed in China, where they saw the friendship between the two nations as a threat. In addition to the independent spirit flowing through Taiwan's political system, it also is obvious the Taiwanese are following policy platform calls for a more robust and home-grown defense industry, probably as an insurance policy against perceived American dysfunction. According to Ian Easton, the resolve of the Taiwanese people likely means that the island, largely ignored for the past couple of decades, will soon return to the forefront of American strategic thinking. Taiwan is the spot most likely to be at the center of any future American action.[532]

Conclusion

The Chinese see the world and geography today differently than the United States and the West. Khan's conclusion is the arc of instability that Peng had remarked upon exists now more than ever. What seems benign to the United States, such as a "pivot to Asia," is seen as a threat, especially while the

---

526. Easton, *The Chinese Invasion Threat*, 150.
527. Easton, *The Chinese Invasion Threat*, 183.
528. Easton, *The Chinese Invasion Threat*, 185.
529. Easton, *The Chinese Invasion Threat*, 191.
530. Easton, *The Chinese Invasion Threat*, 201.
531. Easton, *The Chinese Invasion Threat*, 222.
532. Easton, *The Chinese Invasion Threat*, 225.

United States simultaneously speaks of preparing for war. Beijing views the map of the world and sees itself locked in as a controlled area; therefore, corruption creeps in and a paranoid fear of losing power occurs. Acting emotionally, such as attempting to manipulate Taiwanese elections in 2015, reinforce the anxiety.[533] Perhaps the real issue is the ghost of the past, and the source of that shadow is Japan.

Food and minerals must be obtained from the sea, and the choking sensation of the barrier islands and a cursed coastline combine to create the frightening potential of a blockade for both China and Japan. Chinese fears of the return of the Samurai spirit in Japan as America seems to decline makes the One China principle more powerful than ever as a focus for East Asian insecurity![534]

"Life is hard, but it's harder when you are stupid."—anonymous marine

---

Is today's U.S. military up to the job in facing a hostile Russia and China? Doctrine today would say otherwise. Readiness and investments would probably need to change and a different approach to warfare adopted. The doctrine of America is strong on organization and definitions, but therein may lay the challenge as training is a function of doctrine.

Nineteenth-century thinkers followed Enlightenment views of a universe featuring natural laws and a closed system, such as is demonstrated in the operational model today. A view of the inevitable decline of the West is as old as Gibbon's *Decline and Fall of the Roman Empire*. This view can be traced through geographic minds mentioned previously such as Halford MacKinder, who proved so influential to generations of the early twentieth century. German philosopher of history Oswald Spengler, whose book *The Decline of the West* was published in 1918 and 1923, further reflects this influence. According to Kilcullen, "His ideas reflect, in part, the collapse of civilizational confidence on all sides at the end of the Great War."[535] The degree of expression in literature today noting the end run or the expression of an inevitable end of what can be called the "Pax Americana" is ubiquitous. The solutions to extending an empire's life span can do well to draw from the lessons of the Byzantines.

Another issue is American military expenditures. An eye toward efficiency in expenditures, particularly during frugal financial times, is prudent. A reliance on overly complex and expensive platforms follows a German model similar to the Tiger tank in World War II. The F-35 fighter has parts made in every state of the union for a reason.[536] The needs for platforms to speak to each other in tandem, known within the military as kill chains, are ignored. Within a tank, for example, the commander lays the gun, and the gunner then takes control and fires while the driver halts or pivots as the terrain requires. Now, with networks the tank must be in real-time coordination with the attack helicopters and artillery firing in tandem or speaking to the assaulting infantry. In an opening battle for the Taiwan Strait, it is estimated a kill chain requirement immediately would require launching precise fires against 350 Chinese ships during the first three

U.S. Air Force F-35 Joint Strike Fighter (Lightning II) jet flying.

© Michael Fitzsimmons/Shutterstock.com

---

533. Khan, *Haunted by Chaos,* 224.
534. Khan, *Haunted by Chaos,* 227.
535. Kilcullen, *The Dragons and the Snakes,* 227.
536. Brose, *The Kill Chain,* 244.

days of contact, which would require intelligence of where they are at any given moment.[537] Short-range, traditionally manned jets may prove unnecessary in the Taiwan Strait or be outmoded by an inability to refuel and may therefore be more necessary in a role closer to home.[538] Lighter forces such as Littoral Combat Ships (LCS) rather than the deployment of huge targets such as expensive carriers may also make loss of life less of a vulnerability. Drone waves contending with each other will be inevitable, each necessarily coordinated and linked via kill chains.

In essence, what is needed are jointly integrated and more nimble services. Studying the Byzantine Defense Strategy as well as reviewing the mistakes made by the Roman Empire are instructive in suggesting a way forward. Edward Luttwak may offer a solution. Adored in conservative circles, Luttwak is a nontraditional thinker who proved influential in the expansion of the roles of the American military in the 1970s. However, he is held in great disdain by academics for his systems analysis approach and for his conservative credentials, displayed in two major works: *The Grand Strategy of the Roman Empire* and the *Grand Strategy of the Byzantine Empire*. In the *Grand Strategy of the Roman Empire*, he noted the dangers of deploying reserves to the periphery of the empire and establishing bases abroad. The risk is a result of the opposition knowing that all elements have been deployed and little combat power remains in reserve in either quantity or volume to deploy to make the risk of war preventative. Since the United States has followed a grand strategy of containment in the Cold War, the number of overseas bases has grown tremendously. There are nearly 800 bases in over seventy nations abroad.[539] It would appear the United States is well on its way to creating a war machine capable of self-perpetuation and full of institutional bloat to the extent that there are more admirals currently serving in the navy than there served in both World Wars and even more than there are ships in the U.S. Navy today! In addition to the risk of cost and imperial overstretch as represented by the numbers of bases abroad, Luttwak suggests a way forward.

Littoral Combat Ship *U.S.S. Montgomery* maneuvers through San Diego Bay.

"Work smarter, not harder."—anonymous army sergeant

The Byzantine Empire existed for centuries after the fall of Rome due to the use of the Emperor Maurice's doctrinal manual called the **Strategikon,** probably written in the late sixth century. Considering the Muslim armies were nearly obsessed with the conquering of the citadel capital of Constantinople, the ability of the Byzantine Empire to persevere long after the Roman is noteworthy in itself. In the *Strategikon*, an attempt was made to coordinate various aspects of the army or what today would be called combined arms, focused on understanding the nature of opponents by studying their cultures and ways. Edward Luttwak, in his 2009 book *The Grand Strategy of the Byzantine Empire,* boils down the *Strategikon* into seven points.

1. The first is to avoid war through all possible means, but always be prepared for one to start at any time.

---

537. Brose, *The Kill Chain,* 233.
538. Brose, *The Kill Chain,* 238.
539. Vine (https://www.politico.com/magazine/story/2015/06/us-military-bases-around-the-world-119321/)

2. Gather intelligence on the enemy and his mentality and monitor his movements continuously.
3. Campaign vigorously, both offensively and defensively, but attack mostly with small units; emphasize patrolling, raiding, and skirmishing rather than all-out attacks.
4. Replace the battle of attrition with the nonbattle of maneuver.
5. Strive to end wars successfully by recruiting allies to change the overall balance of power.
6. Subversion is the best path to victory.
7. When diplomacy and subversion are not enough and there must be fighting, it should be done with "relational" operational methods and tactics that circumvent the most pronounced enemy strengths and exploit weaknesses.[540]

There is no substitute for experience. The commonsense approach to using diplomacy and gifts to purchase peace and an emphasis on relying on allies and using force when it can be used to best advantage are timeless pieces of advice for today. In an age when the military commander as an artist must be called upon to conduct violence, the most irrational of acts, the way going forward, will belong to those who have the courage to think "outside the box" and can fly "beneath the radar" by exploiting an enemy's weakness and strength, not broadcasting intentions with clearly defined and self-imposed rules. Perhaps it is time to put the defense back into the Department of Defense and return to a Constitutional Republic of self-governing free peoples living within their means again. Why not employ the adversaries' effectiveness against them in like manner as saw the creation of Cyber Command in 2009? If hybrid warfare can work for the Russians and Chinese, why then cannot America's interests be exercised with imagination using the best aspects of the enemy's approaches against them? As Sun Tzu said, thinking like an opponent can be effective!

> "Know yourself and your opponent."—Sun Tzu

Regarding the use of allies, particularly in the case of the Japanese, one must consider the past and attempt to not repeat the lessons learned, as well as avoid high-profile associations that appeal to the trauma of the Chinese past. Arming allies to fight their own fights would certainly be in accord with the *Strategikon*. For example, Japanese forces in north China, particularly after 1943, failed to conduct stability operations successfully. The idea of providing local security to allow employment to occupy people's time failed because most military leaders failed to control the occupied territory, specific points, or the psychological aspects—to use Vietnam-era language, the "hearts and minds"—of

Japanese ground self-defense force.

the population, seeing only Japanese interests. By 2004 to 2006, Japanese self-defense forces in Iraq that were restricted from using force and only allowed reconstruction missions found themselves forced to create jobs through various projects adjacent to the Japanese camp and made such communities support the presence of the troops there.[541] Attention to the PMESII-PT side of the American doctrinal approach toward the operational environment would also require demanding allies make diplomatic concessions as terms for support.

---

540. Luttwak, *The Grand Strategy of the Byzantine Empire*, 418.
541. Williamson Murray and Peter R. Mansoor, *Hybrid Warfare* (New York: Cambridge Univ. Press, 2012), 253.

In April of 2001, President George W. Bush on the *Good Morning America* show demonstrated American strength and resolve when asked about how far America would be willing to go in protecting Taiwan. He answered with three words, "Whatever it takes."[542] Moving on to other topics such as terrorism, tracking Al-Qaeda, and other issues, what seemed like a typically American expression of harmless bravado no doubt resonated with the Chinese, whose worldview sees a threat on the contiguous border. The country's citizens remain traumatized by the last century of invasions, particularly from the Japanese. To fail to see from a Chinese perspective that Taiwan and Korea are the same dangerous arc bordering the Chinese is to play into the hands of disaster. There is little room for bravado in the exercise of power anymore. The Chinese mind simply cannot forget the past nor can their souls tolerate the loss of face.

Geographic realities remain generally constant, but the Russians and Chinese have changed along with their worldviews in the last three decades, while following broader patterns of expansion and development with new hybrid warfare strategies. The United States must change its approach to the education and use of the military accordingly. There is a need to develop a current operational doctrine that emphasizes shaping the operational environment through special concepts as well as the culture, a product of the histories of Russia and China. Dr. Sean McFate argues we need to develop war artists. It is the contention of this author that the means to future victory in the United States is to understand the strengths and limitations of military force and to develop patterns consistent with success in the past.[543]

Key Terms:

Historical memory
Two-headed eagle
Hybrid warfare
A2/AD
Highway of Death
North Atlantic Treaty Organization (NATO)
Chinese Embassy
Sir Halford J. Mackinder

Aleksander Dugin
Chechnya
Chechen operations
Georgia
New Look
Gerasimov Doctrine
Green men
Intermarium

Finnmark
Syrian refugees
***Unrestricted Warfare* (URW)**
Three Wars Strategy
Lawfare
Amphibious landing operations
Strategikon

---

542. Geoffrey Perret, *Commander in Chief* (Pub City: Random House, 2007), 333.
543. McFate, *The New Rules of War*, 239.

Glossary

Air Battle over Taiwan—Fought in October 1944 to prevent Japanese Air from participating in the Battle of Leyte Gulf, this overwhelming victory by U.S. forces would establish air superiority for the upcoming landings on Okinawa and would prove instrumental in the Japanese decision to use the kamikazes out of desperation.

Air Land Battle (ALB)—Doctrine utilized by the American military relying upon maneuver forces using retrograde positions in a series of defensive battles designed to compensate for anticipated enemy superiority in numbers with technological advances and air power to isolate and interdict enemy supplies and support from reaching the battle field. ALB represented a transition between an active defense role and full spectrum operations.

American Ways of Fighting (AWoF)—The AWoF used in this book demonstrates the operational strengths of the American military and conversely the weaknesses. As a microcosm of the American culture, the military tends to reflect a culture that is demonstrably successful and sometimes weak. It is both fast moving, but rapidly impatient; heavily dependent upon the use of firepower; use of indigenous peoples as scouts for intelligence purposes; and is a highly innovative and learning military force.

Amphibious Warfare—The art of attacking land from sea. Amphibious operations require the elements of surprise and precise timing to compensate for the inherent difficulties in the transfer of command from ship to shore with the simultaneous need for coordination of supporting arms. Much of the world's coastline, harbors, and littoral are vulnerable to amphibious attack. Amphibious Warfare represents an example of American innovation and is still, in large measure, a uniquely American military capability.

Anaconda Strategy—The 2010 strategy employed in Afghanistan by Gen. David Petreaus named after the famous American Civil War strategy proposed by General Winfield Scott, whereby the Union would use geography to "constrict" or deprive the Confederacy of needed supplies. The analogy with Afghanistan possibly referred to the circle of population centers located in the interior of Afghanistan and historically quickly pacified by the British, Soviets, and later the Americans. Petreaus seemed to feel a counterinsurgency could be launched into the southern rural countryside and hit Pakistani sanctuaries. The Anaconda Strategy is not to be confused with Operation Anaconda that was fought in eastern Afghanistan in March 2002.

Armored Division—A between the world wars organizational innovation whereby the traditional infantry division (a unit of about ten to twenty thousand soldiers capable of supporting itself in independent operations) moved on troop carriers and tanks. The American armored division by 1944 represented the first mostly "on wheels" division in world history, unlike the German blitzkrieg of 1940 that saw only the advanced assault elements utilize mechanization, with the main and supporting elements dependent upon foot or horseback.

ASW—Anti-submarine Warfare. The use of destroyers and other naval platforms to sink submarines. Particularly neglected by the Japanese during World War II at great cost to their largely naval empire.

Attleboro—The largest battle fought in the Vietnam War up until the end of 1966 where American firepower brought to bear against the enemy simply resulted in a Viet Cong/NVA retreat into the jungle. A demonstration of how the strategic initiative had passed to the enemy occurred at Attleboro. The decision as to when and where to fight would now in large measure belong to the North Vietnamese.

B-17—A heavy, four-engine bomber developed before World War II by the U.S. Army. Represented a strategic platform designed to cross the Pacific to Hawaii and Alaska. Later used in the strategic daylight bombing of Germany, reflecting the belief it filled a more effective role in Europe while the B-24 would eventually be developed for the Pacific Theater.

B-29—Extreme long-range bomber marked the culmination of aircraft planning during World War II and the Korean War. The B-29 saw service exclusively in the Pacific Theater and is the aircraft primarily responsible for the firebombing campaign against Japan as well as the atomic bombs.

Battles—(see proper name, i.e.) Battle of Leyte: see Leyte.

Biak—Long battle fought from May to August 1944 off New Guinea during Operation Cartwheel (see below) where the Japanese began to allow Allied forces to come ashore (see below) before forcing them to fight yard for yard in slow and costly assaults through terrain marked with prepared obstacles and preplanned fires essentially using enfilade (see below) and covered positions to create a killing field for the purpose of delaying and diminishing the will to fight.

Bloody Ridge—A series of fights from July to September of 1951 against the Chinese by U.S. forces and representing a new type of battle in Korea where territory would be fought in bloody seesaw fighting through difficult terrain. America's enemies continued to develop strategies throughout the modern American military history experience by playing on an American propensity to become frustrated at what appeared to be needless casualties when ground is neither taken nor held.

Bonus Army—Refers to the protestors during the Great Depression in 1932 who had camped out near Washington, D.C., attempting to persuade political opinion to receive financial subsidies on the basis of service in the First World War. Forces of the U.S. Army led by Douglas MacArthur and George Patton broke up the protests with two veterans killed. Marked a controversial use of force by the military against its own citizens.

Breakout—The advance by the 8th Army out of the Pusan Perimeter (see below) on September 15, 1950 in pursuit of North Korean forces fleeing north in an attempt to avoid threatened U.S. encirclement as the marines amphibiously assaulted Incheon.

Cambodian Excursion—A military invasion into Cambodia launched in 1970 for the purposes of supporting a friendly coup and to close down transport trails from North Vietnam. This test of Vietnamization proved generally militarily successful and gave the South Vietnamese a reprieve through 1971 from North Vietnamese aggression. Domestic response to the widening of the war in particular by the anti-war protestors resulted in Congressional repeal of the Gulf of Tonkin Resolution.

Camelot—Term used to describe the telegenic and idealistic excitement surrounding the White House during the presidency of John F. Kennedy.

Carrot and Stick—The concept of using force to either intimidate or coerce an opponent into submission while simultaneously offering tangible benefits for the purpose of establishing an alliance.

Cavalry—The combat arm consisting historically of horses to provide speed. Responsible for screening and observation of the enemy, modern-day Cavalry can utilize helioborne platforms or armor.

CCC—A New Deal depression-era work program in the 1930s that served as a proving ground for future military leaders in World War II.

Cedar Falls—A major operation, the first corps-sized operation in Vietnam during January 1967 that uncovered extensive tunnel systems within close proximity to Saigon. Another large battle that only resulted in a minor setback to the North Vietnamese and Viet Cong further demonstrating the ability of the Communists to fight a protracted war strategy while General Westmoreland continued to try to win the war through US-led conventional hammer and anvil tactics.

Chain of Command—Essentially a pecking order that determines authority and responsibility within a military organization.

Chairman of the Joint Chiefs of Staff (CJCS)—The Chairman is responsible to the President for advisement on military matters and serves as the head of the JCS (see below).

Circular Formation—A naval innovation between the World Wars whereby the inherent weakness of the aircraft carrier is overcome by a protective encirclement of ships. The aircraft carrier acted as the pivot platform for maneuver with all other ships in the group following its movements and lead.

CNN—Cable News Network. Around the clock news coverage 24/7 began in 1980 utilizing satellites for broadcasting. The First Gulf War saw the rise of CNN at a time when satellites provided unprecedented speed and fire control in the First Iraq War. A mutual interest between the military and cable news outlets emerged as domestic public consumption of the news producing enhanced ratings and profits while increasing public support and interest in the war.

Cobra II—The military operation for the seizure of Iraq launched March 2003. Named after Operation Cobra, the breakout of Normandy in World War II.

Combined Action Platoons—Counterinsurgency approach used by the USMC in Vietnam. Involved a platoon of marines and South Vietnamese soldiers residing in a village or hamlet. Designed to demonstrate permanency of RVN government and to use a "carrot" (see Carrot and Stick) approach to providing security and meeting certain basic needs of the civilian population. Importantly, principles of the CAP would be employed by the U.S. Army CORDS program in 1967 using similar principles within the context of the controversial Phoenix program; a key aspect of Vietnamization.

Concealment—The use of smoke or camouflage for the purpose of remaining unseen.

Concentric Rings—The theoretical use of precision guided munitions to destroy the Iraq forces during the First Iraq War using a model of rings as in a target to indicate the levels of priority from the inside ring out. Initial priority targets included leadership followed by economic and population centers in descending priorities with military targets constituting the lowest level of priority. In many ways, the use of Concentric Rings represented a return to the bomber theories remarkable in an age dominated by Air Force fighter pilots.

Converging Columns—Term used as an AWoF (see above) in this text to describe a uniquely American mode of strategy and operations whereby disparate units converge upon an objective from differing directions. The degree of coordination necessary for these difficult maneuvers require dependability, initiative, and resourcefulness in organization. A legacy of the Indian wars where small numbers of frontier soldiers often had to pursue an enemy across vast distances.

Coral Sea—The first naval battle in history employing aircraft carriers where the two opposing navies' vessels did not have line of sight or fire upon each other. The Japanese loss in May 1944 prevented the Japanese from occupying Port Moresby in New Guinea and lessened the threat to Australian and American supply lines.

Cordon—A military formation used to cover and to protect a vital position. Usually used in a large area when a restricted amount of manpower or force is available. Essentially a square shape.

Corkscrew Tactics—Term used by General Simon B. Buckner, the commander of the 10th Army on Okinawa in World War II to describe a single axis of advance technique used to defeat entrenched Japanese with "corkscrew"—use of demolition charges and "blowtorches"—flame tanks and infantry borne flamethrowers.

Counterinsurgency or COIN—Defined by the U.S. Army/USMC FM 3-24 as the military, paramilitary, political, economic, psychological, and civic actions taken by a government to defeat insurgency.

Cover—The use of physical protection from enemy fire. A foxhole for example can provide cover.

Dak To—The last and biggest of the conventional battles in Vietnam during 1967 where the NVA chose the ground to fight and, according to Spencer Tucker, appeared willing to continue to sustain overwhelming 4:1 losses relative to those of the United States in its efforts to defeat US-led forces. Westmoreland's preoccupation with body count increasingly seemed irrelevant.

Daylight Bombing—Refers to the Air War against Germany whereby Americans desired to use the Norden bombsight and the B-17 as an instrument of position, believing airpower could surgically defeat German industry and civilian lives could be spared. The American method stood at odds with the British method of safer attack by bombing at night and somewhat more indiscriminately over a larger area.

Declaration of War—A Congressional power granted in Article 1, Section 8, Clause 11 of the U.S. Constitution. It is the contention of this text that military victory has eluded the United States since World War II in large measure because of the failure to use clearly defined war-making authority granted within the Constitution. Without a declaration of war, a lack of unclear objectives have prevented the development of workable strategies. Dissipating support from a largely uninformed public have contributed to make victory elusive.

Defense Battalion—A euphemistic term used to designate marines stationed in the Pacific in the years leading up to the Second World War. Many defense battalions fought with distinction in subsequent campaigns after the war started.

Defilade—The use of cover (see above) in a tactical position to ensure protection from fires and to enhance the advantage of the defense.

Dick Act—Legislation properly known as the Militia Act of 1903. The Dick Act enumerated the power of the U.S. government to federalize the National Guard during times of emergency as well as established summer annual training and standards of proficiency.

Diverging Columns—A play on words used to describe the dispersal of X Corps from 8th Army during the drive north in the Korean War during the autumn of 1950 after the breakout from the Pusan perimeter and the landing at Incheon. A subtle shift in the war's aims began to materialize from one of liberating the south to freeing the entire peninsula.

Doctrine—The stated intention of the army on how it will fight and standardize equipment, and training to this end.

Doolittle Raid—An innovative air raid launched by the United States against Japan shortly after Pearl Harbor in April 1942 using B-17s propelled from aircraft carriers. Though perhaps inconsequential in overall strategic terms, this raid is illustrative of the irrational nature of warfare and served to bolster morale on the home front at a critical period in the war.

Drop Tank—An additional disposable fuel tank attached to the bottom of fighter aircraft in World War II. Proved instrumental in extending the range of bomber escorts enabling the bombing campaigns and by spring and summer of 1944, in Europe and the Pacific respectively.

EFPs—Explosive force projectiles represented a newer, more potent form of IED (improvised explosive device) probably built in Iran and used by Iranian proxies in the Shiite areas of southern Iraq. After the Samarra Mosque bombing on February 22, 2006 the numbers of U.S. casualties resulting from EFPs increased leading to upgrades to the MRAP II (mine resistant ambush protected) series of vehicles.

Emerging Autocracies—Refers to the increased rise of totalitarianism and bilateral agreements between Russia and China within a decade of the ending of the Cold War. The changes within and between Russia and China may be connected to the heavy reliance upon airpower in the US/NATO intervention into Serbia and Kosovo in 1999 with Operation Allied Force (NATO) and Operation Noble Anvil (US) threatening the Serbs, a historic Russian ally (where World War I began), and the public loss of face to the Chinese due to the destruction of the Chinese Embassy through accidental bombing.

Enfilade—The ultimate aim of any military movement is to achieve a superior tactical position. Due to the nature of modern firepower, projectiles tend to hit in a long beaten zone pattern. Crossing these patterns creates a "crossfire" and ensures a higher probability of hits. Maneuvering into a position to maximize these fires along the enemy's long axis is referred to as flanking.

Eniewetok—A deep-sea anchorage located in the northern Marshall Islands in the Pacific seized February 1944 during World War II. Located about 1500 miles west of Hawaii, Eniwetok's potential as an amphibious and naval staging area by Admiral Chester Nimitz largely determined the course of the island-hopping campaign in 1943 and the need to seize Tarawa and Kwajalein atolls.

"Entirely New War"—Refers to Gen. MacArthur's reaction to the unexpected arrival of Chinese forces into the Korean War and the retreat of the 8th Army on November 26, 1950.

F-86 Saber—First swept wing jet fighter aircraft used with remarkable success in the Korean War. A serendipitous design initially for the pursuit role against Soviet aircraft served to increase its turning ability. The F-86 possibly represented a clear superiority over contemporary contenders such as the MIG-15 at a level not seen since.

Fedayeen—Loyal volunteer paramilitary cadres created in Iraq by Uday Hussein (Saddam's son) in 1994. Designed to prevent uprisings such as had occurred at the end of the First Gulf War by Shiites and other disgruntled minorities, these armed units would increasingly prevent U.S. efforts in Iraq, particularly after de-Baathization.

First and Second Battles of Fallujah—Operation Vigilant Resolve launched April 5, 2004 in Iraq in response to the killing of Blackwater contractors; halted prior to conclusion in negative media publicity. Followed the next year (2005) by Operation Phantom Fury—the Second Battle of Fallujah where massive firepower served to assist marines engaged in the largest urban combat seen since Hue in Vietnam. The military significance of Fallujah probably is somewhat significant, but eventual tactical developments may have proven important in the later "Sunni Awakening" leading up to the surge of U.S. forces in Iraq.

Fraggings—A term from the Vietnam War referring to the unlawful use of violence by one individual against another of the same force, usually a commander or leader. Fraggings are an extreme example of the loss of discipline and morale within a military force and often characterizes a losing effort.

Freeway War—Refers to the campaign against Iraq in the 2003 Second Iraq War assault (see Cobra II); largely dependent upon generally parallel southeast to northwest freeways for an incredibly rapid movement requiring tactical considerations of security at on and off ramps and overhead cover provided to the enemy by overpasses.

Frogmen—The term used for combat divers and underwater demolitions teams in World War II. These highly respected missions would become the basis for Navy SEAL teams in later decades.

Frontal Assault—A direct method for attacking an objective. Frontal assaults are inherently costly and are generally avoided in combat though they offer the benefit of being easily planned and conducted.

General Staff—A formal body of military leaders created by the Root Reforms responsible for advising political leadership on military matters. A modern approach to warfare allowing centralized control over administrative and logistical concerns as well as war planning. This post Spanish-American War innovation would be instrumental in enabling the army to mobilize during World War I.

GI Bill—A law created in 1944 that was instrumental in changing American society by providing benefits to millions of veterans in the form of home loans, educational assistance, and avoiding the issues of bonus payments such as occurred at the end of World War I.

Goldwater-Nichols Act of 1986—The largest military reform effort since the National Security Act of 1947. An increased attempt to create a jointness in military operations after the creation of Air Land Battle doctrine necessitated interservice cooperation. The failures of Desert One in 1980 (Operation Eagle Claw) and problems in Grenada in 1983 saw the role of the Chairman of the Joint Chiefs of Staff increased in power and created a system where theater commanders using a reorganized world map of six major geographic commands answered directly to the Secretary of Defense. Initially tested in Panama in 1989, the reorganization unfortunately led to a degree of micromanagement in the Second Gulf War.

GPS—Global Positioning System is a method of using satellite technology to locate positons on the Earth's surface. Use of GPS in the First Iraq War would prove instrumental in movement of units at unprecedented speed and accuracy of airpower that devastated Iraqi forces with the use of so-called smart bombs such as JDAM (Joint Direct Attack Munition). A dependence upon cruise missiles as a military expedient throughout the 1990s resulted in part due to the amazing precision fire capability offered by GPS.

Graduated Escalation—A historical term used to describe the 1964 decision by President Johnson to gradually increase bombing in Vietnam over the objections of the Air Force Chief of Staff who advocated a more intense approach. It appeared Johnson wanted to send a signal to persuade the North Vietnamese of the futility of aggression. An American reliance upon air power for military and political expediency emerged with the end of the Vietnam Syndrome in the 1980s and appears to have extended into the 2016 war against ISIS.

Greek Civil War—A communist insurgency in Greece, defeated in large measure by the introduction of "American Advisors in 1947." The American grand strategy of providing American support for the purpose of the containment of communism would emerge from the Greek Civil War.

Guadalcanal—The first major land and sea campaign that saw Americans on the offensive in the Southwest Pacific during World War II form 1942 to 1943. U.S. forces secured airfields for the purpose of protecting communication and transportation routes between the United States and Australia. Initially designed to isolate the major Japanese garrison at Rabaul on New Britain Island, a fierce funneling of troops and vicious sea battles would see Americans victorious and advancing toward the Philippines.

Guam Doctrine—Also known as the Nixon Doctrine. Designed to reduce American commitments beginning in 1969 with Vietnamization, the United States attempted to articulate a commitment to its Allies while recognizing the limits of domestic support. Essentially a 1 ½-war strategy resulted whereby the United States would maintain its commitments to Thailand in SE Asia and Japan in East Asia while attempting to contain Soviet/Chinese expansion.

Gunfire Gap—Refers to the interval in an amphibious operation whereby the responsibility for supporting fires to an assaulting force shifts from primarily naval gunfire to shore based artillery. An inherent vulnerability exists during the transfer of responsibility stage of a landing (see Amphibious Operations).

Hamburger Hill—Known as Operation Apache Snow, represented the culmination of U.S. forces using search-and-destroy on a large scale in attempts to prevent Vietnamese supplies from crossing into Vietnam from Laos. The May 11-20, 1969 series of battles in Vietnam for Ap Bia Hill (Hill 927) where a seesaw series of bloody fights eventually saw American forces prevail in large measure due to the quantities of firepower and supporting arms employed. Though an operational success, Hamburger Hill would represent the last costly battle of attrition the United States would wage in Vietnam due to lack of public support at home. President Nixon would announce Vietnamization after the battle in an attempt to distract public attention.

Heartbreak Ridge—One of a series of major hill battles fought in Korea between September and October 1951 north of the DMZ in Korea. Bloody battles of attrition, initially the Americans took Bloody Ridge only to see the enemy falling back on Heartbreak Ridge. These costly, static, seesaw type battles revealed the advantages of Korean terrain to the defense in a static war of attrition. The conclusion of these expensive battles would usher in a new phase of the war utilizing small unit combat patrols; little understood but with far-reaching implications in Vietnam.

Hedgerows—Refers to earthen embankments on the edges of fields offering an advantage to the defense against attackers in terms of cover and concealment. First described by Julius Caesar referring to Gaul (France), and later confronted by Americans in 1944. The breakout at Normandy necessitated traversing these man-made obstacles as did the Arghandab River Valley in Afghanistan outside of Kandahar confronted by U.S. troops in 2010.

"He Kept Us Out of the War"—Presidential campaign slogan used in the election of 1916 by Woodrow Wilson to persuade voters he represented the safe choice regarding U.S. neutrality and the First World War, implying the Republican candidate would take us into war. By April, Wilson had asked for and received a Declaration of War initiating a progressive attempt to bring democracy to the world, an element of American foreign policy since.

Hellcat—The F6F Grumman fighter used by the navy in World War II. Replacing the Wildcat, the Hellcat matched the Japanese Mitsubishi A6M Zero and served as the preeminent carrier fighter during the last half of the war securing air superiority throughout the Pacific theater.

Higgins Boat—A flat bottom boat originally developed by Andrew Higgins and used in southern swamps and marshes. The Higgins boat adapted to provide amphibious lift for assault troops and supplies in World War II.

Highway of Death—Refers to the February 25, 1991 destruction of Iraqi forces withdrawing from Kuwait in the First Iraq War. Graphic press coverage of the carnage in large measure influenced American leadership to end the war with the liberation of Kuwait, not the pursuit and total destruction of Iraqi forces.

Hiroshima—The site of the first use of an atomic bomb on August 6, 1945. Three days later Nagasaki would be bombed also and by August 15, 1945 the Second World War would end.

Ho Chi Minh trail—A major supply route used by peoples of Southeast Asia since ancient times. Traveling mostly through Laos, the trail dictated French Strategy during the first Indochina War and would later result in increasingly successful attempts by the United States to interdict traffic by the use of Special Forces troops and Allies using airpower. After the TET offensive, the United States generally managed to control the flow of North Vietnamese traffic with the use of AC-130 gunships, and with increased use of surveillance sensors by 1971 would reduce the amount of traffic by about half. A war-weary public and declining domestic support for the war prevented the United States from completely closing the trail.

Holding Attack—The name for the tactical maneuver of attack developed before World War II under the guidance of George C. Marshall. The holding attack centered on a base of fire from an automatic weapon shifting or ceasing fires on a prearranged signal, thereby facilitating maneuver forces to strike an opponent from the flanks or rear. The elegance of this tactical concept lay in its application for any level; from the fire team up to an army.

Ia Drang—The first major action between U.S. troops and the North Vietnamese Army (NVA) during November 1965. The battle began when 1st Cavalry Division (air mobile) followed retreating NVA raiding parties into the Ia Drang valley. There American forces decisively defeated elements of three NVA regiments. The overwhelming military victory may have resulted in overconfidence and persuaded American leadership to fight an Americanized conventional fight against the North.

IED—Improvised explosive device. Can be vehicular borne (VBIED) or used as a static weapon activated by a cell phone; used in Iraq and Afghanistan beginning in 2003 and by 2007 constituting the majority of combat deaths.

Incendiaries—Refers to the use of firebombs in World War II against both industrial and civilian population centers.

Infantry-foot soldiers—Historically slower than cavalry and lacking the firepower of artillery, but better suited for holding ground and seizing rough terrain.

Influenza—A pandemic from 1918 to 1919, which largely resulted in the end of World War I and killed more people globally than the War did.

Insurgency—As defined by the U.S. Army/USMC FM 3-24--an organized movement aimed at the overthrow of a constituted government through the use of subversion and armed conflict.

Interdiction—Refers to the attempt to isolate the battlefield from industry or sources of supply usually through the use of air power. Throughout the modern American military period, aviation theorists have debated whether interdiction represented the most efficient use of airpower.

Iraqi Surge—Refers to the January 2007 change of strategy announced by President George Bush whereby the commander of multi-national forces, Iraq (MNF-I) General George Casey, would be replaced by General David Petraeus (author of FM 3-24 counterinsurgency) with a subsequent increase of U.S. forces deployed to Iraq and the use of indigenous peoples (Iraqi Security Forces) to contain an Al-Qaeda insurgency that had developed within Arab communities in a post-Saddam Hussein Shiite controlled Iraq.

ISAF-International Security Assistance Force—The name for U.S. and Allied troops serving in Afghanistan under NATO authority and established by the UN Security council. Initially protecting the capital city, after 2006 the mission for ISAF in Afghanistan began to increase combat operations to the southern and eastern provinces.

ISIS—The Islamic State of Iraq and Syria often referred to by the Obama administration as ISIL-the Islamic State of Iraq and the Levant. This organization claimed to be a caliphate with the authority to wage war against the infidels led by the United States. A Sunni Arab organization in some ways competing with Iranian influence in Syria and Iraq.

Island Hopping—Term used to describe the U.S. strategy during the Second World War by leap-frogging over islands in the Pacific with the objective of reaching Japan. An important element of the island hopping campaign included the use of air cover from seized airfields and bypassing islands of enemy resistance.

Iwo Jima—An island in the Pacific secured during February to March of 1945 for the purpose of obtaining airfields to provide fighter support for bombers flying from the Marianas to Japan during World War II.

JCS—Joint Chiefs of Staff, created by the National Security Act of 1947; consists of the chiefs of each military service primarily responsible for the administration, planning, and readiness of each service. The chiefs are led by a chairman (see CJCS).

Junction City—A major battle in Vietnam with the United States during February 1967 where the Westmoreland strategy of attempting to defeat the enemy in piecemeal battle and through attrition instead met a determined enemy prepared to fight to the death. The numbers of Viet Cong killed led Westmoreland to lead the LBJ administration and the American people to believe the rational approach to warfare had met success and led to a fulfilled request for additional troops and funding.

Kent State University—The 1970 scene of student protests over the U.S. incursions into Cambodia. The Ohio National Guard opened fire, killing four students; served to anger the American anti-war movement and shock a war-weary American public. Successful American intelligence breakthroughs of North Vietnamese radio transmissions beginning in 1968 had resulted in the systematic destruction of North Vietnamese assets utilizing the Ho Chi Minh trail in efforts to resupply their southern forces. The American incursion into Cambodia achieved military success and further resulted in decimating the North's ability to engage in war against the south. The anti-war protests resulting from the Kent State shootings would result in the shutdown of over 500 schools and students who went on "strike" at 350 colleges and universities.

Kim-Il Sung—The dictator of North Korea who had fought with the Soviet Army against the Japanese in World War II. Emerging to power in the north at the end of World War II, Kim represented an antagonist of Syngman Rhee to the south; both men represented totalitarian, and alternative visions to achieve unification of the Korean peninsula.

Krag-Jorgenson—A repeating bolt-action rifle firing a .30 caliber round used primarily by the American military during the Spanish-American and Philippines War. A noteworthy aspect of the rifle lay in its use of smokeless powder, thereby enabling the shooter to remain in contact with the enemy, utilizing continuous fires without risk of losing sight of the enemy.

Kurils—An archipelago of islands to the north of Japan bombed by U.S. forces in mid-1943. The maintenance of a northern front against Japan served to soften air defense assets, thereby spreading defenses thin from converging American attacks from the central Pacific. The Kurils would be seized by the Soviets at the end of World War II and remained in Russian possession after the fall of the Soviet Union.

Land based airpower—Generally considered to have the advantage over carrier-borne airpower due to the increased weight or firepower the aircraft can carry due to increased lift, a function of a longer airfield.

Lawton, Henry W. Major General—An army officer who proved instrumental in the defeat of the insurgency in the Philippines War. In tandem with Arthur MacArthur, he achieved a surge of troops by going to Congress disputing rosy reports from the chain of command regarding the conduct of the war. Lawton pressed for the creation of a battalion of Macabebe scouts. The surge and use of indigenous people contributed to eventual U.S. success in the Philippines.

Learning/Adaptable Military—Described in this text as one of the American Ways of Fighting that represents a historical operational strength. Despite a chain of command, the American military member at each level has traditionally been a resourceful individual capable of exercising initiative and imagination. Institutionally, the American military has been an effective educational instrument, in many ways positively influencing American culture.

Leyte—The Battle of Leyte Gulf In October 1944 may be the greatest naval battle ever fought and certainly represented the largest in World War II. Leyte Gulf saw the Japanese fleet destroyed as a fighting force. Naval actions from the Battle would enable American forces to land in Leyte, beginning a battle of attrition against the Japanese. Future naval operations by the Japanese would be individualistic in terms of ship actions and increasingly suicidal.

Logistics—The procurement, maintenance, and transportation of supplies; maintenance, and taking care of personnel.

Ludendorff Offensive—The 1918 spring and summer German offensives during World War I whereby newly-developed tactics (see Storm Troopers) threatened Allied lines forcing the deployment of Americans into the fighting in Western Europe.

Luzon—The largest island in the Philippine archipelago. Seized from the United States by Japan early in World War II, but by January 1945, the Americans would return and reseize the island with a series of amphibious assaults after an extraordinarily long, expensive campaign ended in August of 1945. Luzon represented the fruition of a U.S. Army led advance towards Japan from the Southwest Pacific fought simultaneously with a naval/marine advance from the central Pacific.

Macabebe Scouts—Served American forces in the Philippine War with reconnaissance and intelligence procurement as well as hunting down guerillas. The Macabebes represented the first of the native Filipinos to serve the American armed forces beginning in the fall of 1899. The Macabebes came from the town of the same name and had a tradition of Spanish military service and a hatred towards the Tagalogs who constituted the opposition to American pacification. See AWoF for the American tradition of using indigenous peoples in warfare.

Maneuver—The use of movement to bypass and envelop enemy forces. American military forces have traditionally relied upon movement and mobility to defeat enemies and to minimize casualties when securing objectives.

Marianas—Island chain or archipelago in the northwest Pacific Ocean used in World War II as a position for launching bombing raids on the Japanese home islands. While Saipan proved to be a challenging operation due to a lack of coordination with supporting arms, in 1944 Guam and Tinian represented classic textbook amphibious operations.

Marjah—The elegant night attack on February 13, 2010 by the 6th Marines in Helmand Province of Afghanistan as part of General Stanley McChrystal's 2009 strategy of securing population centers from Kandahar to Kabaul in Afghanistan using the 2010 "surge" eventually ordered by President Obama.

Market Garden—The largest airborne assault in history occurred in September 1944 with a British led Allied assault of seven bridges in the Netherlands. It eventually failed when mobile units from the 2nd British Army were unable to relieve the airborne troops. Earlier intelligence failures did not record the presence of large German armored units, which proceeded to systematically reseize the bridges from the light infantry airborne troops and eventually wiped out the remnants of the Allied effort at great cost. The result of Market Garden's failure would be increased fuel shortages grounding Allied mechanized forces and enabling German counterattacks that would culminate in the Battle of the Bulge by winter. See Miracle in the West.

Meat Grinder—Tactics used in Korea referring to the brilliant use of American operational military strengths during the various Chinese offenses from the winter of 1950 through the spring of 1951. Americans led by General Matthew Ridgway overextended their lines allowing aerial interdiction, combined with American firepower and mobility to destroy the Chinese attacks. Trading space for time, the meat grinder wore the Chinese down while minimizing American casualties. When the Chinese halted, Americans would begin pushing back, thereby gaining valuable intelligence, and keeping their adversaries from being able to resupply.

Midway—A major aircraft carrier naval battle in June 1942; it was the "turning point" in the Pacific theater of World War II. Midway occurred a month after the Battle of the Coral Sea and with established naval parity, America would be able to go on the offensive against Japan shortly after the landings on Guadalcanal.

Miracle in the West—The expression used by the Germans to describe the relative immobility of Allied forces in Europe by autumn 1944 after the failure of Operation Market Garden. The halt of the Allied advance occurred due to the peaking of German industrial production and seemed to offer the German high command an opportunity to attack the Allies in great force, pushing them back and securing the much needed port city of Antwerp. Operating under intense cloud cover that neutralized the advantage of Allied airpower, by December 1944 the Germans attacked in what is now known as the Ardennes Offensive culminating in the Battle of the Bulge.

MQ-1 Predator Drone—An unmanned aerial vehicle (see UAV below) and weapons platform of increasing importance under the Obama Administration.

Mulberry—Refers to the two floating man-made harbors used at Normandy after the D-Day invasions of June 1944. The one at Omaha beach became inoperational after a storm, forcing the Allies to use the mulberry located at Gold Beach. Allied plans had placed a premium on obtaining the port of Antwerp within three months, but desperate military countermeasures required the Allies to wait six months, contributing to fuel and supply shortages and desperate measures to logistical access points. (See Market Garden.)

Napalm—A petroleum based substance developed during World War II and first utilized in July 1944 as an aerial-dropped flame weapon. Napalm proved invaluable in assisting the Allied breakout from Normandy as close air support compensated for the shortage of artillery rounds due to logistical difficulties (see Mulberry).

NATO—North Atlantic Treaty Organization. The treaty binding many nations of Europe and the Americas into a defense treaty whereby member nations would agree to mutual defense of any member state that might be attacked. The only time this has occurred is after 9/11 when European forces were deployed to Afghanistan.

Neo Cons—Term referring to those advocates of using American military force and capabilities to usher in a time of unprecedented global peace. The neo-cons tended to believe that American democracy combined with unprecedented military capabilities after the collapse of the Soviet Union and the perceived incredible victory in the First Gulf War in 1991 demonstrated the potential to prevent future holocausts. The neo-cons influence generally peaked within the Republican Party and tended to have the most influence in the Bush administrations.

New Look—Refers to the defense policies of the Eisenhower administration whereby spending could be minimized despite the Cold War through an increased reliance on nuclear weapons and technology. Although unable to maintain tradition by demobilizing the American military establishment after World War II, the New Look did attempt to limit military spending and Ike would count this as one of his greatest accomplishments. The aspiring presidential candidate, John F. Kennedy, would be persuaded by Maxwell Taylor in the book *Uncertain Trumpet* of the need for a more flexible military response and a critical redress of a perceived inflexibility or "nukes or nothing" approach whereby American military power had been limited to only a nuclear response in time of war.

"No Land Wars in Asia"—An expression often used in American military circles after the Korean War demonstrating the perceived futility of attempting to use military force upon the Asian continent. Most of the No More Ground wars in Asia believers felt American operational strengths of air and naval power culminated in the offshore defensive strategy adhered to by the Joint Chiefs of Staff after World War II, but abandoned by President Truman with the support of General Douglas MacArthur with the decision to commit U.S. forces for the defense of the island of Formosa (Taiwan). Eventually, the legal precedent of deploying American forces into an undeclared war under the guise of supranationalism would undermine the offshore defensive strategy and initiate the wars in Korea and later Vietnam with dubious results.

NVGs—Night Vision Goggles, in large measure responsible for the unprecedented speed demonstrated during the First Gulf War of 1991. NVGs allowed American military forces to maintain fast-moving formations and operations essentially limited only by the human need for sleep.

Off shore defensive strategy—The belief that American national security in the Western Pacific after World War II could best be served through the use of air and naval power. See "No Land Wars in Asia."

Okinawa—The largest island in the Ryuku island chain to the south of the major Japanese home islands. The scene of brutal fighting in World War II as American forces prepared a launching pad for the invasion of Japan proper. The fighting during April of 1945 further demonstrated Japanese desperation through the use of kamikaze attacks.

Operation Cartwheel—The need to isolate the major Japanese garrison at Rabaul in New Britain during 1942–43 for the protection of Australia initiated several military plans collectively called Operation Cartwheel. The Cartwheel plans would eventually neutralize Rabaul through success in the Solomon, Admiralty, and Russell Islands. The Quebec Conference in 1943 led General Douglas MacArthur to utilize a brilliant series of maneuvers to effectively bypass, cut off, and sever Japanese transportation and communication routes in the Southwest Area of Operations. Cartwheel's conclusion would lead to MacArthur's plan Reno whereby American forces would attempt to move towards Japan from northern New Guinea via Mindanao in the Philippines.

Operation Chromite—The September 1950 invasion of Incheon harbor in Korea by UN forces led by General Douglas MacArthur for the purpose of liberating Seoul and cutting off North Korean troops besieging U.S. forces in Pusan to the south. The invasion of Incheon would occur simultaneously with the breakout of American troops from the Pusan perimeter and would eventually result in a change of mission in Korea from one of simply securing South Korea to liberating the entire peninsula.

Operation Just Cause—The American invasion of Panama in 1989 launched for the purpose of effecting regime change in Panama.

Operation Odyssey Dawn—Bombing operation over Libya under the authority of United States Africa Command (AFRICOM) subsequently transferred to NATO in 2011. Odyssey Dawn apparently represented an attempt to harness the "Arab Spring" with the hope democracy would spread from North Africa into the Middle East.

Operation Restore Hope—One of the many operations ordered by American presidents upon conclusion of the Cold War. Initially an attempt to provide food for famine-torn Somalia, by October 1993 the operation failed with the ambush and loss of 18 servicemen. Media coverage of brutal treatment of Americans and subsequent dealings with a warlord responsible in large measure for the violence confused the American public and discredited the use of U.S. troops for UN "peace keeping" missions. Disdain for non-combat deployments explained the derisive view of "meals on wheels operations" often decried by critics, created political aversion to non-combat roles, which perhaps explained subsequent confusion during the aftermath of the military victory in the Second Iraq War of 2003 with shortfalls in civil affairs planning.

Operation Strangle—The massive use of airpower to interdict Chinese resupply efforts in North Korea. In some ways similar to the Transportation plan in World War II, it attempted to sever transportation routes. Nevertheless, constituted another failure of aerial interdiction since the Chinese only required relatively small amounts of resupply.

Operation Urgent Fury—A 1983 U.S. intervention to overthrow leadership overly friendly to Soviet and Cuban military interests in the Caribbean. The rapid success of the military operations contributed by all services served to boost confidence in the American military and in large measure erased the doldrums from the Vietnam War period. Difficulties of interservice coordination revealed in Grenada would lead in large measure to the Goldwater-Nichols legislation.

Organismic Approach—An analogy or comparison used for the purpose of teaching. A correlation is drawn between a living being and the military. The command section could be seen as a brain center with communications akin to the nervous system. The eyes could be intelligence and movement corresponding to cavalry, etc.

Osama bin Laden—The leader of the terrorist network al-Qaeda responsible for a series of attacks on Americans culminating in the September 11, 2001 attack on the World Trade Center in New York. Bin Laden sought to engage America into a Holy War with Islam in large measure due to American intervention in the First Iraq War.

Overseas Contingency Operation—The renaming of the Global War on Terror used during the Obama Administration beginning in 2009 largely reflective of the drawdown in American conventional operations and commitments in Iraq and Afghanistan. The war would continue relying more on "advisors," special operations forces and UAVs.

Pax Americana—The term used to describe the worldview held after the Cold War that saw American military force and contingency planning as the best opportunity for ensuring a type of global tranquility.

Pentagon Papers—A series of leaks to the New York Times published in 1971 by Daniel Ellsberg revealed the extent of American involvement in Vietnam not previously reported. Eventually the Supreme Court would block the government's efforts to control the publication of the Pentagon Papers. The Papers revealed the extent of President Lyndon Johnson's deceptions of the American efforts in Vietnam and may have in turn feed into President Nixon's sense of being besieged, and possible later paranoia towards political opponents. The Pentagon Papers revealed the nature of the grand strategic objective in Vietnam as a means to limit the growth of Communist China, and since the Pentagon Papers covered the U.S. war from 1945 to 1967, may partially explain the paucity of literature on the Vietnam War after the Tet Offensive in existence today.

Pershing, J.J. "Black Jack"—General of the Armies, General Pershing exercised imaginative leadership thereby influencing enemy actions in Mindanao and Jolo Islands during the Philippine War. Shortly after the tragic loss of his family, Marshall led the Mexican punitive expedition in 1916 and would be chosen upon the death of Frederick Funston to lead the American Expeditionary Force in World War I. Pershing's initiative and professionalism led to the career development of George C. Marshall; perpetuating the American military tradition of grooming effective future leadership.

Phase Lines—Command and control measures graphically portrayed as lines on a map used by tactical planners for the purpose of task organizing operational areas of responsibilities and to ensure safety and efficiency in the utilization of supporting arms.

Philippine Sea—A June 1944 naval battle in World War II whereby an American victory ended large-scale Japanese aircraft carrier operations in World War II.

Port Moresby—A key port in Southern New Guinea ideally positioned for advances upon Australia in World War II. In May 1942, the over-confident Japanese Navy advanced without the protection of land-based airpower and was defeated in the Battle of the Coral Sea in an advance towards Port Moresby by U.S. naval forces. The subsequent Japanese defeat at the Battle of Midway would further slow Japanese attempts upon Port Moresby, thereby allowing Australian and eventually MacArthur's forces to counterattack and advance across New Guinea (see Operation Cartwheel).

Powell Doctrine—A philosophical approach to doctrine reflective of the bitterness in the American military after the Vietnam and Korean Wars. This informal doctrine is attributed to General Colin Powell in the build-up to the first Iraq War and is demonstrative of a post-World War II continuum with its emphasis on quantities of forces and a determination to require firm political support for military endeavors. The Powell Doctrine essentially required both a careful definition of military objectives and national security interests, an exit plan and the use of overwhelming force, along with risk assessments and the utilization of force only after all other means have been exhausted.

Preponderance of Firepower—A historical pattern or American Way of Fighting (AWoF) described in this book demonstrating an operational strength of the American military in the excellence in directing, coordinating, and projecting accurate and overwhelming firepower. As with all of the AWoF, a converse weakness would be the detrimental effects on pacification or winning population support within areas of contention due to high likelihood of accidents and damage.

Progressivism—The idealistic world view that basically held that a democratically elected government responsive to the people's needs represented a positive force for good and one ultimately able to militarily defeat evil. A possible explanation for the rapid growth of what some would characterize as an American century or even an empire after the War in the Philippines would put the United States into a collision course with Japan, thereby leading to World War II. Allied victory in World War II would in turn result in a relatively more powerful United States that, under President John F. Kennedy, would maintain a permanent large-scale peacetime military force during the Cold War. Eventually the lone superpower left after the conclusion of the Cold War, due in part to the Soviet activities in Afghanistan. A shifting of attention towards the Greater Middle East would reinforce what some thinkers would claim as the responsibility of the United States to preemptively use force to protect itself and to eliminate evil which in turn would create conditions for the longest continual U.S. war in history.

Proximity Fuse—A sophisticated use of applied radio technology developed by the British and used by the U.S. fleet in the Pacific in 1944, this secret weapon used an emitted radio signal located within the shell itself that acted as an antenna thus being able to pick up the signal with a preset proximity value allowing the shell to be more accurately detonated. Increased sophistication in the lethality of artillery thanks to the proximity fuse would prove instrumental in blunting the German winter offensive of 1944-45.

PRTs—Provincial Reconstruction Teams represented a joint military and U.S. embassy initiative in Afghanistan beginning in 2002 that recognized the need to approach the war in Afghanistan with a civic action program to improve the lives of individual Afghans. The funneled U.S. funds which utilized the Afghan government as a means to a centralized approach to developing Afghanistan stood at odds with the fiercely autonomous village-run nature of the varied Afghan provinces often far removed from the capital at Kabul.

Pusan Perimeter—Constituted the last stand of American forces in the Korean War. The army and marines held tenaciously to the southern portion of the Korean peninsula generally south of the Naktong River against forces of North Korea during August of 1950. Recent scholarship indicates crypto analysis had broken the North Korean radio traffic and aided by piecemeal communist attacks, the U.S. forces would deflect attacks in a series of desperate battles. The U.S. forces would remain in Korea until the invasion of Incheon (see Operation Chromite).

Rapidly Impatient—An AWoF generally reflective of the fast-pace of American culture. As a microcosm of the culture, the American military tends to do well in a "fast-break" type of combat but conversely tends to do less well in static or stationary fighting. During the last century, time has tended to work against the American public's ability to remain focused or supportive of military operations abroad.

Red Ball Express—A truck convoy system developed by the U.S. Army in Europe during World War II. The Red Ball Express represented an attempt to alleviate supply shortages that had resulted after port facilities at Normandy proved insufficient to support U.S. forces.

Rhee, Syngman—The first president of the Republic of Korea. Led Korea during the Korean War and through much of the Cold War.

RMA—An acronym for "revolution in military affairs." This periodically used term denoted technological changes in the military. The term RMA is associated with overconfidence most recently in Afghanistan thereby rendering irrelevant the requirements for large numbers of troops necessary in the 2003 invasion of Iraq.

Root Reforms—In 1903 provided for the institution of professional development for the U.S. military through various schools ranging from strategy to skill specializations within the specific service branches such as artillery or engineering.

Schweinfurt—The German city and scene of two massive air raids by Allied forces during World War II beginning in August 1943. Attempts to destroy industrial areas identified as essential to the German war effort generally are considered unsuccessful due to devastatingly high casualty rates of 20 to 25 percent. Conclusions drawn from the raids included demonstrable weaknesses inherent in daylight bombing, the limitations of the Norden gunsight particularly in cloudy Northern European climates, and continued arguments against the idea that air power alone could win war.

Selective Service—The government agency responsible for maintaining draft boards and the registration of American citizens eligible for conscription into military service. Created in 1917 in an attempt to ensure a fair and large-scale ability to induct millions the draft has generally only been used in American military history during a time of war.

Shia—Division in Islam generally Persian or Iranian in terms of influence and numbers of followers. Shia is the predominant form of Islam found among Arabs in South East Iraq below Baghdad.

Shock Troop Tactics—Fast moving fighting technique designed to introduce highly-trained soldiers using stealth and short supporting-arms fires of gas and barbed wire blasting high explosives. The light infantry columns and sappers had trained to bypass strongholds and where penetrations succeeded were to be followed by larger units. Developed by Erich Ludendorff, these series of offensives forced the deployments of American troops into the battle line during the spring of 1918.

Sigma II-65—The second in a series of war games used by senior American military leadership during the fall of 1965. The key takeaway here is the burgeoning realization by strategists that limited bombing campaigns in Vietnam being launched may instead result in a prolonged war of attrition that could lead to defeat of the Allied and American effort in Vietnam.

Sky Cavalry—The term used to describe the development of helioborne combat operations. Developing from command and control/observation and medical evacuation during the first year of the Korean War; the ability to mobilize and supply combat troops proved essential to U.S. counterattacks during early 1951 against the Chinese. By the end of 1951, delivery of a combat company and experimentation with assault troops would slow during the frugal Eisenhower defense budget years of the 1950s but came to fruition by the early 1960s with the delivery of the 1958 HU-1B "Huey" helicopter. Hueys soon served as armed and armored weapons platforms called gunships along with the Chinook series of helicopters able to provide true air mobility operations for the movement, supply, and defense of large combat units.

Small Wars Manual—A compilation of the experiences gained by the army and marines in the Philippines and the decades following World War I in the Caribbean. This would become the basis for American theories of counterinsurgey or "pacification" as it was called in Vietnam. The SWM placed a particular emphasis on the need for small unit leadership and patrols to gain intelligence and secure loyalties of indigenous peoples. The SWM perspective would later serve the marines well early into the Second World War at Guadalcanal; ignored by President Johnson in Vietnam and foundational for subsequent American successes in pacifying Iraq.

Sputnik—The dramatic dawning of the Space Age occurred when the Soviets secured a propaganda triumph with the launch of the first satellite, Sputnik. The immediate result of Sputnik's launching would be a strategic investment in submarines and surface-launched ballistic missiles as a means of avoiding potential enemy surveillance from space. The ability to launch a satellite encouraged the space race with the realization that an ability to place an object in space also created the potential for missiles capable of enormous ranges and payloads of nuclear weapons. Long-term technological changes in warfare resulting from entering space are abounding from navigation with GPS to "smart bombs."

Strategic Framework Agreement—An agreement between the United States of America and the Republic of Iraq concerned with the withdrawal of American forces from Iraq signed by President Bush in 2008. It established that U.S. combat forces would withdraw from Iraqi cities by 2009, and all U.S. combat forces will be completely out of Iraq by December 31, 2011.

Sunni—Division in Islam represented mostly in areas to the West of Baghdad in Iraq. These areas are more likely to be influenced by cultures in areas not associated with Iran such as the Gulf States or Saudi Arabia.

Tab System—Indicative of the non-linear nature of the modern battlefield. With precision-guided munitions, the increased accuracy of supporting arms enables an unprecedented degree of mobility and control with a command decision to open or close small areas on the map referred to as tabs. The result of this system of control is an ability to employ smaller units with unprecedented maneuver capability and an ability to destroy larger units.

Tarawa—The series of islands that made up the atoll of Tarawa in the Pacific during World War II contained the island of Betio, the scene of fierce combat and horrific losses in large part due to tidal anomalies. Tarawa persuaded war planners of the need for increased accuracy in hydrographic surveys, the use of frogmen (SEALs), and the need for deployment of rocket propelled munitions to bust reinforced concrete bunkers for future operations.

Terror Bombings—The use by the Allies of incendiary or fire bombs during World War II in an attempt to bring psychological pressures from the people to bear on Axis political authorities to surrender. It is generally believed that the actions of the terror bombings only made the people more determined to fight harder. The failure of interdiction to decisively cripple industrial production may have led the Allies to attempt to wage war directly against civilian populations.

Tet Offensive—A January 1968 bold series of attacks upon the Republic of Vietnam by the North Vietnamese, designed to provide an opportunity for the "oppressed" South Vietnamese to rise up and overthrow the imperialists. The decision by the North to openly attack the South reflected changes in North Vietnamese leadership and strategy. The death of "Smash and Grab" Thanh, the architect of the disastrous 1965 attempt to attack the growing U.S. military presence in Vietnam, and the later ascension to power of Communist Party First Secretary Le Duan, an advocate of aggressive execution of war presented President of the People's Republic of Vietnam (PRVN) Ho Chi Minh with a decision. Ho chose Le Duan's strategy, trumping the "protracted war" strategy of Vo Nguyen Giap in place since 1965. Initial North Vietnamese attacks on Khe Sanh seemed to be made for the purpose of a diversion to draw American attention from the cities of the south, the true objectives. The American public was shocked by the Tet Offensive occurring as it did on the heels of a high profile publicity campaign by the LBJ administration throughout the summer of 1967 to persuade the American people the enemy had been nearly defeated. Media coverage of attacks particularly in Saigon and the long fight to retake Hue would reinforce growing war weariness in the United States. A mini-offensive in May and August and a follow up Tet Offensive in 1969 would result in decisive military defeats for North Vietnamese forces apparently lacking the requisite ability to alter a disastrous series of plans. Nevertheless, most historians feel the United States despite virtual continuous military victories from 1968 would, nevertheless, succumb to despair and eventually leave Vietnam due to the psychological impact of the Tet Offensive.

Thunder Runs—The final advance by Coalition troops in Iraq began on April 5, 2003 with a bold entrance into Baghdad. Designed to be a show of force into Baghdad for the psychological effect of hastening Iraqi surrenders and for launched with the objective of securing the airport. A minimum of available fresh troops made this movement a risky endeavor.

TPFDL—Time-Phased Force and Deployment List. This printout determines priorities and timelines for various units being sent into war. An important document designed to ensure appropriate units are utilized most efficiently to accomplish the mission.

Triangular Division—General George C. Marshall oversaw the transition of the army from using a big "square division" into a triangular division based on three regiments. Each regiment in turn contained three battalions. The formation of the triangular division simultaneously met the needs for the 3:1 time-proven advantage necessary for the offensive against the defense, accepted as historically military necessary. The simplicity of the organizational formula of the triangular division presented an easily learned, flexible system just in time for the U.S. Army in World War II.

UAV—Unmanned aerial vehicle. Developed with the use of GPS and the NAVSTAR system, these advanced "smart" aerial platforms increasingly replaced cruise missiles as the weapons of choice by the United States from the administrations of George W. Bush to Barack Obama.

Unrestricted Submarine Warfare—The German decision to engage in sinking neutral or enemy shipping in neutral waters was instrumental in bringing the United States into World War I. The decision to follow this policy in part resulted from the vulnerability of German submarines (Q ships) to Allied cruisers upon surfacing.

Use of Indigenous Peoples—An American characteristic largely a function of employing native guides or scouts in the Indian Wars against the Native-Americans by the American military.

USS Cole—on October 12, 2000 the U.S. guided-missile destroyer exploded off the coast of Yemen, probably the result of planning by al-Qaeda in an attempt to persuade the United States to enter into war in the Middle East where it was thought the Americans could be defeated by faithful followers of jihad as had the USSR in Afghanistan. One of many attempts to lure the United States into war by radical Muslims since the 1980s.

USS Maine—An American battleship mysteriously damaged by an explosion in the harbor in Havana, Cuba on February 15, 1898. The belief in Spanish complicity would lead to the Spanish-American War and the eventual American responsibility and possession for overseas possessions in the Caribbean and western Pacific Ocean.

USS Missouri—An American battleship and the scene of the unconditional Japanese surrender to American forces represented by General Douglas MacArthur in Tokyo Bay on September 2, 1945 formally bringing the Second World War to an end.

V-1 Rockets—German-made flying bombs used to bombard England from June until October 1944 until Allied forces were able to overrun the launch sites. At this point, the Germans used these prototypes of cruise missiles to hit the vital port of Antwerp, limiting Allied supply efforts in the European campaign against the Germans during World War II.

V-2 Rockets—The beginning of the Space Age started when these German rockets flying at supersonic speeds and silent signatures killed large numbers of civilians in British cities and Antwerp in retaliation for the Allied bombings of Germany. September 1944 marked the beginning of the large-scale attacks. Allied raids later captured German engineers; later the key to Cold War developments in the United States with the Saturn rocket series while other captured Germans served to develop the Soviet missile forces.

Victory Disease—The term used to describe the state of overconfidence that may have contributed to a lack of long-term planning by the Japanese military after 1940. Such failures included adequate anti-submarine warfare (ASW) to defend a vast empire over the seas or the continual funneling of troops into Manchuria and China at the expense of maintaining island outposts in the Pacific.

Volunteers—A classification used for American soldiers during the Spanish-American War. The term U.S. Volunteers served to allow reserve/guard forces to avoid legal restrictions on the use of the militia outside of the United States. U.S. volunteers (USV) replaced the state volunteers after the creation of the USV during March 1899.

Washington Naval Conference—An attempt at arms limitation after World War I by the major world powers using varying ratios of battleship tonnages to limit what each nation could possess in an attempt to prevent another world war. A key and unintended result would be the development of carrier aviation through the use of cruiser hulls, thereby circumventing the limits earlier established at the conference. Changing world conditions in the 1930s would prohibit future successes of arms limitation with the failures of the London treaties.

Whiz kids—A somewhat derogatory term used by senior military officers during the Vietnam War to describe a new generation of analysts and young defense department analysts led by Robert C. McNamara. The Whiz kids generally felt communism could be defeated in Vietnam through a systematic, rational, and logical approach in the development of strategy.

Wonson—The October 1950 landing of U.S. troops into the North Korean port city located to the northeast of the peninsula used during the Korean War; a landing site to launch MacArthur's drive north in an attempt to defeat communist forces and to unify Korea. Wonson had been selected as a landing site in order to head off North Korean troops fleeing north after the successes of Incheon in September had threatened to cut them off. The delayed landing on 26 October 1950 essentially fed 1st Marine Division troops into an established line running from Pyongyang to Wonson held by the UN Command about the same time as the first Chinese offensive would be initiated.

WMDs—Weapons of mass destruction are generally considered to be weapons capable of widespread destruction or able to kill large numbers of people; generally WMDs are considered to be nuclear, chemical, or biological weapons.

Yellow Press—A term used to describe the newspaper and magazine media of the late 19th century blamed in large measure for inciting "War Fever" and anti-Spanish sentiments within the American people particularly after the explosion aboard the *USS Maine*.

Bibliography

Addington, Larry H. *America's War in Vietnam*. Indiana University Press: Bloomington, IN. 2000.

Alexander, Bevin. *The First War We Lost*. Hippocrene Books: New York. 1986.

Alison, Wm. T, Grey, Jeffery, & Valentine, Janet G. *American Military History 2nd Ed.* Pearson: Upper Saddle River, NJ, 2013.

Ambrose, Stephen E. *D-Day: The Climactic Battle of World War II*. Simon & Schuster: New York, 1994.

Atkinson, Rick. *An Army at Dawn: The War in North Africa, 1942–1943*. Holt: New York, 2002.

Atkinson, Rick. *The Day of Battle: The War in Sicily and Italy, 1943–1944*. Holt New York, 2007.

Atkinson, Rick. *The Guns at Last Light: The War in Western Europe. 1944–1945*. Holt: New York, 2013.

Bacevich, Andrew J. *America's War for the Greater Middle East*. Random House: New York, NY. 2016.

Bauer, K. Jack. *The Mexican War 1846–1848*. MacMillan: New York, 1974.

Bolger, Daniel P. *Why We Lost*. New York: Harcourt Mifflin Houghton. 2014.

Boot, Max. *Invisible Armies*. WW. Norton: NY, 2003.

Borneman, Walter R. *1812*. Harper Collins: NY, 2004.

Bowden, Mark. *Worm: The First Digital World War*. Atlantic Monthly Press: New York, 2011.

Brose, Christian. *The Kill Chain: Defending America in the Future of High-Tech Warfare*. New York: Hachette Books, 2020.

Bush, Richard C., and Michael E. O'Hanlon. *A War Like No Other*. Hoboken, NJ: Wiley & Sons, 2007.

Clark, J.P. *Preparing for War*. Harvard University Press: Cambridge, MA, 2017.

Clarke, Richard, & Knake, Robert K. *Cyber Warfare*. Harper Collins: New York, 2010, 132.

Coram, Robert. *Brute*. Little, Brown and Co.: New York. 2010.

Crocker III, H.W. *Don't Tread on Me*. Crown: New York, 2006.

Cumings, Bruce. *The Korean War*. Modern: New York. 2011.

Davidson, Phillip B. *Vietnam at War*. Oxford: New York. 1991.

DeWeerd, Harvey A. *President Wilson Fights His War*. Macmillan: New York. 1968.

Dorr, Robert F. *US Marines Pioneer Air Support in Nicaragua*. Defense Media Network. April 20, 2010. http://www.defensemedianetwork.com/stories/naval-aviation-centennial-the-marines-pioneer-air-support-in-central-america/

Dougherty, R.A. & Gruber, I.D. *Warfare in the Western World Vol II: Military Operations since 1871*. D.C. Heath: Lexington, MA. 1996.

Dreyer, June. *Middle Kingdom & Empire of the Rising Sun.* Oxford University Press: UK, 2016.

Dupuy, R. Ernest & Dupuy, Trevor N. *The Encyclopedia of Military History.* Harper & Row: New York, 1977.

Durschmied, Erik. *The Military History of China.* London: Carlton Pub. Group, 2018.

Easton, Ian. *The Chinese Invasion Threat: Taiwan's Defense and American Strategy in Asia.* Manchester, UK: Eastbridge Books, 2019.

Eisenhower, John S.D. *So Far from God.* Doubleday: New York, 1989.

Elleman, Bruce A. *Modern Chinese Warfare, 1795–1989.* New York: Routledge, 2001.

Fehrenbach, J.S. *This Kind of War.* Potomac Books: Herndon, VA, 2001.

Ferling, John. *Struggle for a Continent.* Harlan Davidson: Arlington Heights, IL, 1993.

Frank, Richard B. *Downfall: The End of the Imperial Japanese Empire.* New York: Penguin Books, 2001.

Frank, Richard B. *Guadalcanal.* Random House: New York, 1990.

Frank, Richard B. *Tower of Skulls: A History of the Asia-Pacific War July 1937–May 1942.* New York: WW Norton, 2020.

Giangreco, D.M. *Hell to Pay.* Annapolis, MD: Naval Institute Press, 2009.

Gordon, Michael R. & Trainor, Bernard E. *Cobra II.* Pantheon: New York. 2006.

Gordon, Michael R. & Trainor, Bernard E. *The Endgame.* Pantheon: New York. 2012.

Halberstam, David. *The Coldest Winter.* Hachette: New York. 2008.

Hansen, Randall. *Fire and Fury: The Allied Bombing of Germany, 1942–1945.* NAL Caliber: New York, 2008.

Hastings, Max. *Armageddon: The Battle for Germany, 1944–1945.* Knopf: New York. 2004.

Hastings, Max. *Korea.* Simon & Schuster: New York. 1998.

Hastings, Max. *Retribution: The Battle for Japan, 1944–1945.* Knopf: New York. 2007.

Henry, Robert Self. *The Story of the Mexican War.* Da Capo: New York, 1989.

Hienl, Robert. D. *Victory at High Tide.* Lippincott: New York, 1968.

Higginbotham, Don. *The War of American Independence.* Northeastern Univ. Press: Boston, 1983.

Hoffman, Frank G. *Conflict in the 21st Century: The Rise of Hybrid Wars.* Arlington, VA: Potomac Institute for Policy Studies, 2007.

Holzimmer, Kevin C. *General Walter Krueger: Unsung Hero of the Pacific War.* University Press of Kansas: Lawrence, KS. 2007.

Horowitz, David. *The First Frontier.* Simon and Schuster: New York, 1978.

Jian, Chen. *China's Road to the Korean War: The Making of the Sino-American Confrontation.* Colombia Univ. Press: Ithaca, NY. 1998.

Kaldellis, Anthony. *Streams of Gold, Rivers of Blood.* London: Oxford, 2019.

Kaplan, Robert D. *Asia's Cauldron.* New York: Random House, 2014.

Kaplan, Robert D. *Imperial Grunts.* Random House: New York. 2005.

Khan, Salaam. *Haunted by Chaos.* Cambridge, MA: Harvard, 2020.

Kilcullen, David. *The Dragons and the Snakes: How the Rest of Learned to Fight the West.* Oxford, UK: Oxford University Press, 2020.

Kretchik, Walter E. *U.S. Army Doctrine.* University Press of Kansas: Lawrence, KS. 2011.

Leach, Douglas E. *Arms for Empire.* Macmillan: New York, 1973.

Li, Xiaobing. *A History of the Modern Chinese Army.* Lexington, KY: Univ. Press of Kentucky, 2009.

Linn, Brian McAllister. *The Philippine War 1899–1902.* University Press of Kansas: Lawrence, KS, 2000.

Luttwak, Edward N. *The Grand Strategy of the Byzantine Empire.* Cambridge, MA: Belknap Press of Harvard Univ. Press, 2009.

Martin, James K., & Lender, Mark E. A Respectable Army: *The Military Origins of the Republic, 1763–1789.* Harlan Davidson: Arlington Heights, IL, 1982.

McCafferty, James M. *Army of Manifest Destiny.* New York University Press: NY, 1992.

McCullough, David. 1776. Simon & Schuster: New York, 2005.

McFate, Sean. *The New Rules of War: How America Can Win-Against Russia, China, and Other Threats.* New York: Harper-Collins, 2019.

McGinnis, Anthony R. "When Courage was not enough: Plains Indians at war with the U.S. Army," *The Journal of Military History.* 76, no. 2 (Apr 2012).

McMaster, H.R. *Dereliction of Duty.* Harper Collins: New York. 1998.

Metcalf, Clyde H. *A History of the United States Marine Corps.* Putnam: New York, 1939.

Middlekauff, Robert. *The Glorious Cause.* Oxford: London, 1982.

Miller, Paul D. *Just War and Ordered Liberty.* Cambridge: Cambridge University Press, 2021.

Millet, Allan R. *Semper Fidelis.* Macmillan: New York, 1980.

Millet, Allan R., and Maslowski, Peter. *For the Common Defense.* Free Press: NY, 1994.

Mingo, Mate. The Navy Is Prepared for Inspections, Not War (2021, March). Available at: https://www.usni.org/magazines/proceedings/2021/march/navy-prepared-inspections-not-war

Montross, Lynn. *War through the Ages.* Harper & Row: NY, 1960.

Murray, Williamson, and Peter R. Mansoor. *Hybrid Warfare.* New York: Cambridge Univ. Press, 2012.

Musicant, Ivan. *The Banana Wars.* New York: Macmillan. 1990.

Overy, Richard. *The Times Complete History of the World.* Times Books: London, 2004.

Pash, Melinda. L. *In the Shadow of the Greatest Generation.* New York University Press: New York. 2014.

Patterson, Eric D. *Ending Wars Well: Order, Justice, and Conciliation in Contemporary Post-Conflict.* New Haven: Yale University Press, 2012.

Peckham, Howard H. *Colonial Wars 1689–1762*. Univ. of Chicago Press: Chicago, IL, 1964.

Perret, Geoffrey. *A Country Made By War*. Random House: New York, 1989.

Perret, Geoffrey. *Commander-In-Chief*. Farrar, Straus and Giroux: New York, 2008.

Perret, Geoffrey. *Commander in Chief*. Random House: New York City, 2007.

Petriello, David R. *A Military History of China*. Yardley, PA: Westholme, 2018.

Pfarrer, Chuck. Seal Target Geronimo. New York: St. Martin's Press. 2011.

Plato. *The Republic*. Translated by Benjamin Jowett. Internet Classics Archive, 2009. Accessed March 20, 2021. http://classics.mit.edu/Plato/republic.html

Prados, John. *Islands of Destiny*. NAL Caliber: New York, 2012.

Prados, John. *Vietnam: The History of an Unwinnable War, 1945–1975*. University Press of Kansas: Lawrence, KS. 2009.

Ricks, Thomas E. *The Generals*. Penguin: New York, 2012.

Rigg, Robert B. *Red China's Fighting Hordes*. Harrisburg, PA: Telegraph Press, 1951.

Rose, Alexander. *American Rifle*. Random House: New York, 2008.

Sandler, Stanley. *The Korean War: No Victors, No Vanquished*. University Press of Kentucky: Lexington, KY: 1999.

Schweikart, Larry, & Allen, Michael. *A Patriot's History of the United States*. Penguin: New York, 2004.

Seth, Michael J. *A History of Korea: From Antiquity to the Present*. Rowan: UK. 2011.

Simcoe, John. *A History of the Operations of a Partisan Corps Called the Queen's Rangers*. Bartlett & Welford: New York, 1844.

Singer, P.W. *Wired for War: The Robotics Revolution and Conflict in the 21st Century*. Penguin: New York, 2009.

Singer, P.W., & Friedman, Allan. *Cybersecurity and Cyberwar*. Oxford, NY, 2014.

Snow, Donald M. and Drew, Dennis M. *From Lexington to Baghdad and Beyond: War and Politics in the American Experience*, 3rd ed. 2010.

Sorley, Lewis. *A Better War: The unexamined victories and final tragedy of America's last years in Vietnam*. Harcourt Brace: New York. 1999.

Sorely, Lewis. *Westmoreland*. Houghton Mifflin Harcourt: Boston. 2011.

Spector, Ronald. *Eagle against the Sun*. Free Press: New York, 1985.

Stewart, Richard W. *American Military History Vol. II: The United States Army in a Global Era, 1917–2003*. Center of Military History: Washington D.C. 2009.

Stokesbury, James L. *A Short History of World War I*. Morrow: New York, 1981.

Tierney, John J. *Chasing Ghosts: Unconventional Warfare in American History*. Potomac: Wash. D.C. 2007.

Tillman, Barret. *Whirlwind: The Air War Against Japan 1942–1945*. Simon & Schuster: New York, 2010.

Toland, John. *In Mortal Combat.* Morrow: New York. 1991.

Trask, David F. *The War with Spain in 1898.* Macmillan: New York, 1981.

Tucker, Spencer C. *The Vietnam War.* The University Press of Kentucky: Lexington, KY. 1999.

Utley, Robert M. *Frontiersmen in Blue.* Macmillan: New York, 1967.

Utley, Robert M., & Washburn, Wilcomb E. *Indian Wars.* American Heritage: New York, 1977.

Vine, David. *Base Nation.* New York: Macmillan, 2015.

Weeks, Philip. *Farewell, My Nation.* Harlan Davidson: Arlington Hts., IL, 1990.

West, Francis J. "Bing". *The Wrong War.* Random House: New York, 2011.

Weinberg, Gerhard L. *A World at Arms.* Cambridge: New York, 2008.

Willmott, H.P. *Empires in the Balance.* Annapolis, MD: Naval Institute Press, 1982.

Woodward, Bob. *Obama's Wars.* Simon & Schuster: New York, 2010.

Woodworth, David R. *The American Army and the First World War.* Cambridge: London. 2014. Pg. 214.

Yoshihara, Toshi. *China's Vision of Its Seascape: The First Island Chain and Chinese Seapower.* Asian Politics & Policy. https://onlinelibrary.wiley.com/doi/epdf/10.1111/j.1943-0787.2012.01349.x

Yu, Maochun Miles. "The Battle of Quemoy: The Amphibious Assault That Held the Postwar Military Balance in the Taiwan Strait," *Naval War College Review 69,* no. 2 (2016) , article 8. Available at: https://digital-commons.usnwc.edu/nwc-review/vol69/iss2/8

http://www.understandingwar.org/sites/default/files/Russian%20Hybrid%20Warfare%20ISW%20Report%202020.pdfhttps://www.cnn.com/2016/06/30/health/americans-screen-time-nielsen/index.html

https://adst.org/2016/08/chinas-fight-for-tiny-islands-quemoy-matsu-taiwan-straits-crises-1954-58/

https://news.usni.org/2020/03/23/new-marine-corps-cuts-will-slash-all-tanks-many-heavy-weapons-as-focus-shifts-to-lighter-littoral-forces

https://www.usni.org/magazines/proceedings/2020/october/marine-corps-infantry-dilemma?fbclid=IwAR1bfgE8M3Jd4_eqQxu2xvO5CJaYzVI3dMsSjVgnVOp1nBQrU5mQ4BlnlwA

https://www.csmonitor.com/USA/Foreign-Policy/2020/0922/Strategic-empathy-H.R.-McMaster-on-foreign-policy-and-China?utm_source=Hoover+Daily+Report&utm_campaign=df398e0d3d-EMAIL_CAMPAIGN_2020_09_23_05_59&utm_medium=email&utm_term=0_21b1edff3c-df398e0d3d-72843637

About the Authors

Robert F. Ritchie IV

Rob Ritchie served in the Active and Reserve Components of the U.S. Marine Corps, enlisted and as an officer, from 1974 until 1998. He served in the Army (VaARNG AGR) as an intelligence analyst and finished military service as a US Air Force Reserve historian, retiring in 2007 after 33 years of total service. Rob currently is an Associate Professor and Director of Military Studies (undergraduate) at Liberty University.

Herbert S. Pieper

Herbert Sterling Pieper, a Tampa, Florida native, now resides in Lynchburg, Virginia. He holds two bachelor's degrees from the University of South Florida in Political Science and History with a focus on American political and military history. Herbert also holds a master's degree in History with a historical documentary film making focus from Liberty University and is currently completing his second master's degree in Intelligence Analysis from American Military University. Herbert is currently a Faculty Support Coordinator and instructor at Liberty University.

Contributor

Stephanie M. Wright

Originally from Northwest Indiana from a family with a long military tradition, Stephanie Wright has had a passion for history from an early age. Stephanie's primary research has been on the Medal of Honor, World War II on the Eastern Front, Finland and World War II, and many other various military history topics. In addition, she has presented her research at the National Phi Alpha Theta Conference and National Conference of Undergraduate Research. While attending Liberty University, Stephanie was employed as a teacher's assistant in the History Department. Having earned her bachelor's degree from Liberty, Stephanie will begin earning her master's degree in history starting in fall 2021.

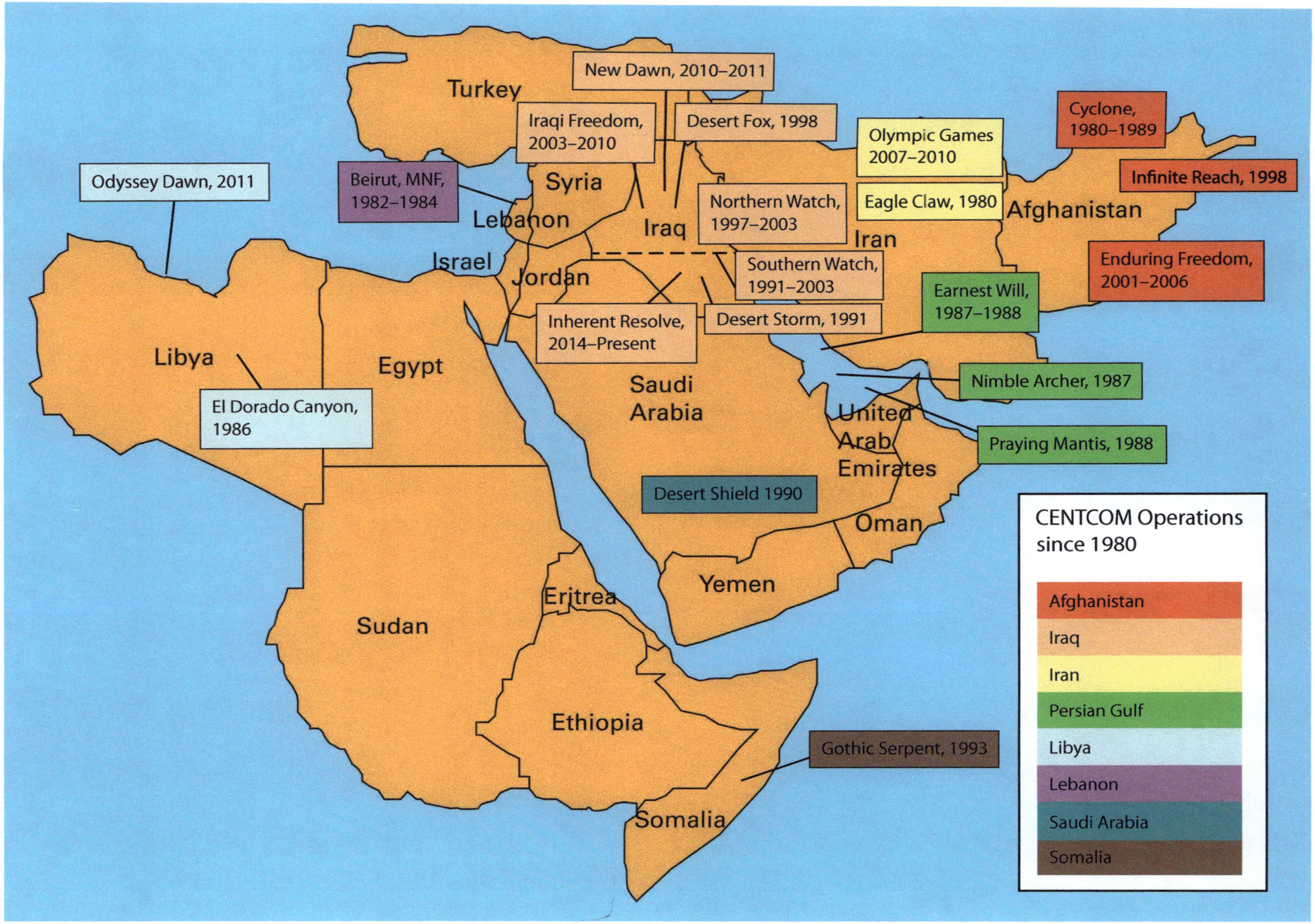

Modification of © Radar_Mark/Shutterstock.com, courtesy of Caitlin Curtis